The British Industrial Revolution

The British Industrial Revolution

An Economic Perspective

EDITED BY

Joel Mokyr
Northwestern University

WESTVIEW PRESS

Boulder • San Francisco • Oxford

Copyright © 1993 by Westview Press, Inc.

Published in 1993 in the United States of America by Westview Press, Inc., 5500 Central Avenue, Boulder, Colorado 80301-2877, and in the United Kingdom by Westview Press, 36 Lonsdale Road, Summertown, Oxford OX2 7EW

Library of Congress Cataloging-in-Publication Data
The British industrial revolution : an economic perspective / edited by Joel Mokyr.
     p.   cm.
   Includes bibliographical references and index.
   ISBN 0-8133-8509-1. — ISBN 0-8133-8510-5 (pbk.)
   1. Great Britain—Industries—History—18th century.   2. Great Britain—Industries—History—19th century.   3. Great Britain—Economic conditions—18th century.   4. Great Britain—Economic conditions—19th century.   I. Mokyr, Joel.
HC254.5.B88   1993
338.0941—dc20   92-21167
                                                                                                 CIP

Printed and bound in the United States of America

The paper used in this publication meets the requirements of the American National Standard for Permanence of Paper for Printed Library Materials Z39.48-1984.

10   9   8   7   6   5   4   3   2   1

Dedicated to
the memory of
JONATHAN R.T. HUGHES

Contents

Tables and Figures

Figures

Acknowledgments

I should like to express my deep gratitude to Ms. Joyce Burnette, upon whose dedication and ingenuity I have relied throughout the editing and typesetting of this book. At Westview, Michelle Asakawa maintained high editorial standards and helped us in innumerable ways. Many thanks also go to Spencer Carr, whose support for this project from the beginning was indispensable.

Joel Mokyr

1

Editor's Introduction:
The New Economic History
and the Industrial Revolution[1]

Joel Mokyr

1. The Industrial Revolution -- A Useful Abstraction

In the past few years, there have been more and more voices that claim, to rephrase Coleman (1983), that the Industrial Revolution is "a concept too many."[2] The feeling is that the term is either too vague to be of any use at all or that it produces false connotations of abrupt change comparable in its suddenness to the French Revolution. The main intellectual motive for this revision has been the growing (though not universal) consensus that economic growth in the early stages of the Industrial Revolution was slower than had hitherto been supposed. The idea of the Industrial Revolution, however, predates its identification with economic growth by many decades. The revision of national income statistics should therefore not, in itself, be enough to abandon the concept. Yet revisionist social historians have found in those revisions the support to state categorically that "English society before 1832 did not experience an industrial revolution let alone an Industrial Revolution. . . . [Its] causes have been so difficult to agree on because there was no 'Industrial Revolution,' historians have been chasing a shadow" (Jonathan Clark, 1986, pp. 39, 66). Wallerstein (1989, p. 30)

---

[1] This essay is a completely revised and largely rewritten version of my introduction to an earlier collection (Mokyr, 1985a). I am indebted to Gregory Clark, Stanley Engerman, C. Knick Harley, David Landes, and Rick Szostak for comments on an earlier version.

[2] Among those, see especially E. L. Jones (1988, pp. 13-27); Clive Lee (1986, pp. 21-22).

suggests amazingly that "technological revolutions occurred in the period 1550-1750, and after 1850, but precisely *not* in the period 1750-1850." Cameron (1990, p. 563) phrases it even more vituperatively: "Was there an industrial revolution? The absurdity of the question is not that it is taken seriously but that the term is taken seriously . . . by scholars who should know better."

The important point to keep in mind is, of course, that from a purely ontological point of view, the British Industrial Revolution did not "happen." What took place was a series of events, in a certain span of time, in known localities, which subsequent historians found convenient to bless with a name. The argument whether the Industrial Revolution is a useful concept is therefore merely one about the efficiency of discourse: Does the term communicate? Do most people with whom we want to converse (colleagues, students, book purchasers) know by approximation what we mean when we use the term? And can we suggest a better term to replace it in our conversations? T. S. Ashton wrote in 1948 that the term was so widely used that it would be pedantic to offer a substitute (1948, p. 4; see also Crafts, 1985a, p. 68). Nothing has been learned since then to warrant changing that conclusion. Continuity or discontinuity, as McCloskey (1987) notes, are rhetorical devices. There is no "test" that we can apply: National income and aggregate consumption grew gradually; patents and cotton output grew much faster. Which one "measures" the Industrial Revolution?

Given this background, the sometimes strident voices calling for the banning of the word from our textbooks and journals seem off the mark. Economic historians, like all scholars, need certain terms and concepts with which they can conduct their discourse, even if arguments about the *precise* definitions of these concepts continue. But it is hard to argue that the concept should be abandoned, for the simple reason that scholars feel that it communicates and insist on using it. In the past six years a number of important books and articles whose titles include the term *Industrial Revolution* have appeared, which demonstrates that their authors believe that the Industrial Revolution means something to their readers.[3]

---

[3] See, for instance, Berg and Hudson (1992); Fine and Leopold (1990); O'Brien, Griffiths, and Hunt (1991); Hoppit (1987, 1990); Hudson (1989, 1992); Hunt and Botham (1987); Komlos (1989a); Lines (1990); MacLeod (1988); Mathias and Davis (1989); Nicholas and Nicholas (1992); O'Brien, Griffiths,

To be sure, arguments about what exactly changed, when it started, when it ended, and where to place the emphasis keep raging. Such scholarly debate about the exact content of a central concept is common -- think of the arguments among biologists about the concept of species. Yet this is insufficient cause to abandon the term altogether: One might as well abandon such concepts as the Reformation or imperialism.

How revolutionary was the Industrial Revolution? Compared to political revolutions, like the American and French revolutions that were contemporaneous with it, it was rather drawn-out, its dates usually set between 1760 and 1830 following Ashton (1948). To be sure, it was punctuated by some periods of feverish activity such as the year 1769, the *annus mirabilis* as Donald Cardwell (1972) called it, in which both James Watt's separate condenser and Richard Arkwright's water frame were patented. But, on the whole, economic changes, even economic revolutions, do not have their Bastille Days or their Lenins. Economics is rarely dramatic, sudden, or heroic. Consequently, some scholars have found the revolutionary aspects difficult to stomach. John Clapham and Herbert Heaton, the doyens of economic history in the 1930s and 1940s, shunned the term *Industrial Revolution* altogether. In contrast, historians in the 1960s wrote of "Great Discontinuities" (Hartwell, 1971b) and "take-offs" (Rostow, 1960). Yet gradualism remained strong. Hughes (1970, p. 45) said it well when he wrote that anything that lasts so long is hard to think of as abrupt, and added that "we cannot think of the events of the past seventy years as sudden. Seventy British years [in the period 1760-1830] passed no more rapidly."

There is merit to this argument, but not enough to abandon the terminology. Revolutions do suppose an acceleration of the rate of change, but how much does the rate have to change in order for it to qualify? Seventy years is a long period, but the changes that occurred in Britain between 1760 and 1830 dwarfed in virtually every respect the changes that had occurred in the previous seventy years.[4] The annual

---

and Hunt (1991); Richardson (1989); Sullivan (1989, 1990); Swain (1986); Szostak (1991); Ville (1987); Wijnberg (1992); Williamson (1987a, 1990a); Wrigley (1988).

[4] As Ashton (1948, p. 41) writes, "In the period 1700-1760 Britain experienced no revolution, either in the techniques of production, the structure of industry, or the economic and social life of the people."

rate of change of practically any economic variable one chooses is far higher between 1760 and 1830 than in any period since the Black Death. The key concept is an increase in the rate of change, not the occurrence of change itself. The cartoon story of a preindustrial static society with fixed technology, no capital accumulation, little or no labor mobility, and a population hemmed in by Malthusian boundaries is no longer taken seriously. Eric L. Jones (1988) has stressed this point more than anyone else. At the same time Jones points out that before 1750 periods of growth were followed by retrenchment and stagnation. The Industrial Revolution was "revolutionary" because technological progress and the transformation of the economy were not ephemeral events. Moreover, it seems too much to demand that an event qualify as a revolution only if it follows a period of total stasis -- most political revolutions cannot meet this standard either. Furthermore, revolutions are measured by the profundity and longevity of their effects. In this regard, what happened in Britain after 1760 is beyond serious doubt. The effects of the Industrial Revolution were so profound that, as Paul Mantoux (1928, p. 25) notes, few political revolutions had such far-reaching consequences. In sum, in considering whether there "was an Industrial Revolution" I cannot do better than cite Max Hartwell, summarizing a career of study and reflection on the topic "Was there an Industrial Revolution?" succinctly: "There was an Industrial Revolution and it was British" (Hartwell, 1990, p. 575). Despite the announcements of opponents of the concept that modern research has demonstrated its vacuity, much recent work that looks beyond the aggregate statistics into the regional and microeconomic aspects of the Industrial Revolution emphasizes the acceleration and irreversibility of economic change in the regions associated with the Revolution.[5]

------

[5] For example, Marie Rowlands (1989, p. 124), who tries hard to find continuity in the economic changes in the West Midlands, is still describing it in dramatic terms: "There can be no question of the revolutionary impact of the introduction of the coal-fired blast furnace into the area from 1766. Within a single generation the furnaces . . . revolutionised not only the south Staffordshire economy but also its settlement pattern and landscape. . . . Agriculture became progressively more difficult, the night sky was illumined with flames and the day darkened with smoke, and the district began to be called the Black Country." Similarly, John Walton, writing of Lancashire, has no doubt that "there is something cumulatively impressive to explain. Nothing

The origin of the term *Industrial Revolution* was long attributed to two French-speaking observers writing in the 1830s, the Frenchman Jerome-Adolphe Blanqui and the Belgian Natalis de Briavoinne.[6] As David Landes shows elsewhere in this book, its origins can be traced back even further. All the same, there is little dispute that the term became popular following the publication of Arnold Toynbee's famous *Lectures on the Industrial Revolution* in 1884. The term is taken to mean a set of changes that occurred in Britain between about 1760 and 1830 that irreversibly altered Britain's economy and society. Of the many attempts to sum up what the Industrial Revolution really meant, the most eloquent remains Harold Perkin's: "A revolution in men's access to the means of life, in control of their ecological environment, in their capacity to escape from the tyranny and niggardliness of nature . . . it opened the road for men to complete mastery of their physical environment, without the inescapable need to exploit each other" (Perkin, 1969, pp. 3-5).

Although economic historians tend naturally to emphasize its economic aspects, the Industrial Revolution illustrates the limitations of the compartmentalization of historical sciences. More changed in Britain in those years than just the way goods and services were produced. The role of the family and the household, the nature of work, the status of women and children, the social role of the church, the ways in which people chose their rulers and supported their poor, what people wanted to know and what they knew about the world -- all these were altered more radically and faster than ever before. It is an ongoing project to disentangle how economic, technological, and social elements affected each other. The event itself transcended any definable part of British society or economic life; it was, in Perkin's phrase, a "more than Industrial Revolution."

What, then, was it that changed in the years that we refer to as the Industrial Revolution? We shall have to leave out of the discussion many of the aspects that made it a "more than Industrial Revolution" -- attitudes, class consciousness, family life, demographic behavior, political power, though all of these were transformed during the same

---

like it had been seen before. . . . The chain of events began in the 1770s and gathered . . . overwhelming momentum in the nineteenth century" (Walton, 1989, p. 64).

[6] Blanqui (1837, p. 389); Briavoinne (1839, vol. 1, pp. 185ff.).

period -- and concentrate on economic variables. Four different schools of thought about "what really mattered" during the Industrial Revolution can be distinguished.[7] The four schools differ in matters of emphasis and weight, yet they overlap to such an extent that many writers cannot be readily classified.

1. **The Social Change School.** The Industrial Revolution is regarded by the Social Change School to have been first and foremost a change in the way economic transactions between people took place. The emergence of formal, competitive, and impersonal markets in goods and factors of production is the basis of this view. Toynbee ([1884] 1969, p. 58) writes that "the essence of the Industrial Revolution is the substitution of competition for the medieval regulations which had previously controlled the production and distribution of wealth." Karl Polanyi ([1944] 1985, p. 40) judges the emergence of the market economy as the truly fundamental event, to which everything else was incidental. A recent contribution in this spirit, which emphasizes the emergence of competitive markets in manufacturing is Wijnberg (1992). Most modern social historians probably would view the central social changes as having to do with labor and the relation of workers with their work environment, other laborers, employers, and capitalists. An enormously influential work in this regard is E. P. Thompson (1963). Some recent contributions influenced by this work are Berg and Hudson (1992) and Randall (1991).

2. **The Industrial Organization School.** Here the emphasis is on the structure and scale of the firm -- in other words, on the rise of capitalist employment and eventually the factory system. The focal point is the emergence of large firms, such as industrial mills, mines, railroads, and even large retail stores, in which production was managed and supervised and where workers were usually concentrated under one roof, subject to discipline and quality control. The work of Mantoux (1928) is a classic example of this school, but Karl Marx's interpretation of the rise of "Machinofactures" also belongs here as do some modern writers in the radical tradition (Marglin, 1974-1975). A classic work discussing the Industrial Revolution from this point of view is Pollard ([1965] 1968). In the same tradition is Berg (1985). More recently,

---

[7] What follows is inspired by Hartwell (1971b, pp. 143-154), although the classification here differs to some extent.

Szostak (1991) has argued that changes in the organization of the firm were the causal factor in technological change and thus primary to it.

A somewhat different microeconomic approach to the Industrial Revolution emphasizes the distinction between circulating capital and fixed capital, a distinction that goes back to the classical political economy of David Ricardo and Marx. Some modern economists have defined the Industrial Revolution as a shift from an economy in which capital was primarily of the circulating kind (e.g., seed in agriculture and raw materials in domestic industry) to one in which the main form that capital took was fixed capital (e.g. machines, mines, and structures) (Hicks, 1969, pp. 142-143; Ranis and Fei, 1969).

3. **The Macroeconomic School.** The Macroeconomic School is heavily influenced by the writings of Walther Hoffmann and Simon Kuznets. Here the emphasis is on aggregate variables, such as the growth of national income, the rate of capital formation or the aggregate investment ratio, or the growth and composition of the labor force. Rostow (1960) and Deane and Cole (1969) are important proponents of this school, and their influence has extended to noneconomists (e.g., Perkin, 1969, pp. 1-2). A recent statement by E. A. Wrigley that baldly defines the Industrial Revolution as economic growth (Wrigley, 1987, p. 3) shows that this approach still enjoys support. Some writers, such as Gerschenkron (1962), prefer to aggregate on a sectoral level, dealing with the rate of growth of the manufacturing sector rather than the growth of the entire economy. Most practitioners of the New Economic History tend to belong to this school, because by its very nature it tends to ask questions about large collections of individuals rather than about single persons (Fogel, 1983, p. 29) and because of its natural interest in quantitative analysis.

4. **The Technological School.** The Technological School considers changes in technology to be primary to all other changes and thus focuses on invention and the diffusion of new technical knowledge. Technology is more than just "gadgets," of course: It encompasses techniques used for the organization of labor, consumer manipulation, marketing and distribution techniques, and so forth. The most influential book in this school is Landes (1969).

The attitudes of many writers regarding the revolutionary nature of the period is to some extent determined by the school to which they adhere. The most confirmed advocates of discontinuity have typically been *technological* historians. Quantitative analysis of patent statistics reveals a sharp kink upward in the late 1750s (Sullivan, 1989). Insofar as the level of technical innovation can be approximated by patenting, this finding lends support to the discontinuity hypothesis. Non-quantitative economic historians with a strong interest in technology have had little difficulty with the discontinuity implied by the use of the concept of the Industrial Revolution. David Landes's chapter in this book represents a summary of this view, which goes back at least to the writings of A. P. Usher and before.[8] Another leading technological historian, D.S.L. Cardwell, uses the term *revolutionary epoch* (which he reserves for the years 1790-1825), whereas Arnold Pacey (1975, p. 216) prefers to apply the term *revolutionary* to the last third of the eighteenth century. In a more recent work, however, he has no qualms about using the term *Industrial Revolution* (Pacey, 1990, chap. 7). H. I. Dutton (1984), Richard Hills (1979, p. 126), and Bertrand Gille (1978, p. 677) stress the technological discontinuities of this period. Maurice Daumas, despite reservations, accepts the concept for the case of Great Britain between 1775 and 1825 (1979, p. 8). Akos Paulinyi expresses the sentiments of many when he writes that "the perception [that denies the revolutionary character of the innovations during the Industrial Revolution] bewildered me because in no book on the history or philosophy of technology is it doubted that the technological changes which took place between 1760 and 1860 introduced a new era" (1986, p. 261). In his recent book on science and technology, Ian Inkster supports this view and adds that "removing the Industrial Revolution may simply lead to boredom" (1991, p. 61). Without necessarily accepting this view, it seems fair to object to a de-dramatization of the events purely because of some preconception that "nature does not make leaps."

On the other hand, historians interested in macroeconomics and emphasizing economic growth have in recent years found little support for discontinuities. In this they differ from earlier aggregative approaches such as Rostow (1960) and Deane and Cole (1969), which

---

[8] Usher (1920, p. 247), in a chapter entitled "The Industrial Revolution," cites with approval J. A. Blanqui for stressing the profound changes occurring in his own lifetime (the 1830s) and adds that the two revolutions, the industrial in England and the political in France, each in their own way contributed to a break with the past "so complete that it is difficult for us to reconstruct the social life of the old régime."

seemed to find sudden leaps in the macroeconomy. As Harley's essay in this book makes clear in more detail, modern research has established that economic growth before 1830 was slower than was previously thought. This could lead to the conclusion that the acceleration, if there was one at all, does not merit the adjective *revolutionary*. Table 1.1 presents average annual compound rates of growth of the economy before and during the Industrial Revolution, contrasting earlier and more recent efforts.

TABLE 1.1 Estimated Annual Rates of Growth, 1700-1870 (in percentages)

Period	National Income per cap. (Deane & Cole)	National Income per cap. (Crafts)	Indust. Product (Hoffmann)	Indust. Product (Deane & Cole)	Indust. Product (Harley)	Indust. Product (Crafts)
1700-1760	0.44	0.3	0.67	0.74	n.a.	0.62
1760-1800	0.52	0.17	2.45	1.24	1.6ᵃ	1.96
1800-1830	1.61	0.52	2.70	4.4	3.2ᵇ	3.0
1830-1870	1.98	1.98	3.1	2.9	n.a.	n.a.

a - 1770-1815
b - 1815-1841
Source: Computed from Harley (chap. 3); Hoffmann (1965)

Compared to Deane and Cole's national income statistics, Crafts's figures reveal an aggregate growth that was much slower during the Industrial Revolution. Industrial production is more ambiguous: Hoffmann's data, computed in the 1930s, clearly show a rapid acceleration during the period of the Industrial Revolution, but Deane and Cole's series is much more erratic and, like the revisionist data of Harley and Crafts, show that most of the quantitative expansion occurred *after* 1800. All the same, Crafts and Harley explicitly deny adhering to a school that would negate the profound changes that occurred in Britain during the Industrial Revolution (1992) and restate that "industrial innovations . . . did create a genuine Industrial Revolution reflected in changes in Britain's economic and social structure," even if their impact on economic growth was more modest than previously believed (p. 3). The point stressed by Crafts and Harley, as well as by students of other episodes of rapid technological change, is worth repeating: There is typically a long lag between the occurrence of changes in technology, even those of fundamental importance, and the time they start affecting aggregate statistics such as industrial production and national income per capita.

Nonquantitative analysts also disagree on the issue. The Social Change School tends to be divided: Toynbee and his contemporary H. Gibbins (1895) thought that the changes that mattered most were rapid. Modern social historians such as Jonathan Clark would clearly disagree. More recent work (e.g., Berg and Hudson, 1992) asserts that the pendulum has swung too far in the direction of gradualism and points to a number of radical and discontinuous social changes. The same holds for the Industrial Organization School; whereas Mantoux clearly believed in sudden and rapid change, modern scholars in this tradition (e.g., Berg, 1985) are more gradualist in their views and stress the dynamic elements in the pre-1760 economy. In any event, there is no justification for extreme statements such as that of Musson (1978, p. 149), who flatly declares that by 1850 Britain was not a very different economy than it had been in 1750. After all, the population of Britain had tripled by that period, and at least in some regions everything, from the landscape to the occupational structure, had been turned upside down. The statement is, perhaps, closer to the truth for southern and eastern England and the Scottish Highlands, but even there it is debatable.

Debates on gradualism vs. sudden change are not specific to the literature on the Industrial Revolution or even economic history. There has always been an intellectual current that believed with Charles Darwin and Alfred Marshall that Nature makes no leaps. Within evolutionary biology, a debate between gradualists and saltationists has been conducted with equal intensity and perhaps similarly inconclusive results (Mokyr, 1990b, 1991a). After many years of undisputed reign by gradualists, a new compromise is emerging that allows for sudden outbursts of accelerated change although not insisting that *all* historical change is necessarily of that kind. It seems that economic historians and evolutionary biologists have been walking on parallel paths.

A moment of reflection and a few simple computations indicate that for a country that undergoes structural change while it grows, very sudden accelerations in the growth rate of the kind that Rostow envisaged are simply impossible. Thus the finding that the aggregate effects of the Industrial Revolution are not overwhelming before 1820 is not surprising. It is useful for this purpose to regard Britain during the period of the Industrial Revolution as a dual economy in which two economies coexisted.   One was the traditional economy, which, although not stagnant, developed gradually along conventional lines, with slow productivity and slowly rising capital-labor ratios.   This sector contained agriculture, construction, domestic industry, and many traditional "trades" that we would now classify as industrial but which in the eighteenth century and before were partially commercial: bakers, millers, tailors, shoemakers, hatters, blacksmiths, tanners, and other craftsmen. The modern sector consisted of cotton, iron smelting and refining, engineering, heavy chemicals, mining, some parts of transportation, and some consumer goods such as pottery and paper. At first, however, only segments of these industries underwent modernization, so that dualism existed *within* as well as *between* various products, which makes calculations about the performance of the modern sector rather tricky.[9] According to McCloskey's (1985) computations, the traditional economy was large, if relatively shrinking. The average size of agriculture and "all others" between 1780 and 1860 was 79 percent of the British economy, meaning that in 1760 it was likely to have composed close to 90 percent of the British economy. Productivity growth in this sector is estimated by McCloskey at about 0.6 percent per annum. During the same period productivity in the modern economy grew at a rate of 1.8 percent per annum.

Two-sector growth models imply that abrupt changes in the economy as a whole are a mathematical impossibility because the aggregate rate of growth of any composite is a weighted average of the growth rates of its components, the weights being the respective shares in output. Even if changes in the modern sector itself were discontinuous and its growth rate very high, its small initial size would limit its impact on the economy-wide growth rate, and its share in the economy would

---

[9] Some approximate idea of the differences between the two sectors can be obtained from comparing pre-1760 rates of output growth to those between 1760 and 1800. Real output in cotton, for example, grew at 1.37 percent per annum in 1700-1760 and 7.57 percent in 1760-1800. In iron output, the growth rates were, respectively, 0.60 percent and 4.10 percent. In two traditional industries the acceleration is less marked: In linen the growth rates were 1.25 percent and 1.44 percent, and in leather 0.25 percent and 0.57 percent, respectively (all data from Crafts, 1985a, p. 23).

increase gradually. In the long run the force of compound growth rates was such that the modern sector swallowed the entire economy. How long was the long run? A numerical example is illuminating here. Assume two sectors in a hypothetical economy, one of which (the modern sector) is growing at the rate of 4 percent per annum while the other (the traditional sector) is growing at the rate of 1 percent per annum.[10] Suppose that initially the modern sector produces 10 percent of total output. Then the aggregate growth rate is at first 1.3 (=.9x1 + .1x4) percent. After ten years the aggregate rate of growth will have increased to 1.39 percent per year. After thirty years of "dual growth" the share of the modern sector will have increased to 21 percent of the economy and after fifty years to one-third. Only after seventy-four years will the two sectors be of equal size (at which point aggregate growth equals 2.5 percent per year), and a full century after the starting point the traditional sector will have shrunk to about 31 percent of the economy. The British economy as a whole was changing much more slowly than its most dynamic parts, because growth was diluted by slow-growing sectors (Pollard, 1981, p. 39). These hypothetical numbers fit the actual record rather well, and they indicate that it is hardly surprising that it took until 1830 or 1840 for the economy-wide effects of the Industrial Revolution to be felt.

In reality the "modernity" of industries and enterprises was a continuum rather than a dichotomy, and the example is thus highly simplified. The distinction between the modern and traditional sectors

------

[10] Note that these rates differ from the ones McCloskey presents, since what is relevant here is *total* output growth, not productivity growth. The average rate of growth of "manufactures, mining, and building" in 1801/11-1851/61 was 3.57 percent, whereas that of "agriculture, forestry, and fishing" was 1.5 percent per annum (Deane and Cole, 1969, p. 170). For the closing decades of the eighteenth century, industrial output grew according to Crafts's calculations at a rate of 2.11 percent per annum and agricultural output at 0.75 percent. Crafts has also revised Deane and Cole's figures for the nineteenth century, but the differences are not large enough to affect the point made here. As was noted above, the rate of growth of the "modern sector" must have been faster than that of "industry." For instance, the consumption of cotton--the raw material of the modern industry par excellence--increased at the annual rate of 10.8 percent between 1780 and 1800 and at the rate of 5.4 percent between 1800 and 1840.

leaves an inevitable gray area, and it has been criticized effectively in recent work as a simplification (Berg and Hudson, 1992). Not all industries that mechanized were growing quickly (e.g., paper), and not all industries in which output was growing rapidly were subject to rapid technological change.[11] In some industries, such as instrument and clock making, important technological changes were occurring in traditionally organized industry. The distinction also abstracts from what actually happened in that it does not take into account that the modern and the traditional sectors affected each other. Although technological change in the traditional sector was slow by comparison, its productivity was affected by what happened in the modern sector. For instance, construction technology may have changed slowly, but improvement in transportation technology allowed the shipment of bricks throughout Britain, which made cheaper and better buildings possible. Agriculture benefited in some ways from technological developments in manufacturing, including the production of clay and, metal drainage pipes and various agricultural machines and implements. The development of coke ovens allowed the extraction of iron from coal. Gaslighting, one of the most neglected of the "great inventions," allowed many artisans and craftsmen in the traditional sector to work longer hours and reduced the cost of night work (Falkus, 1982). These intersectoral spillover effects imply that the distinction between the traditional and modern sectors is to some extent arbitrary. The coexistence of the old and the new is important, and the interaction of the two sectors greatly affected the growth of the aggregate. These interactions do not, however, change the principle of gradual change of the aggregate economy.

Despite the abstraction involved in distinguishing between a modern and a traditional sector, many economic historians still think that two-sector models are useful (Crafts, 1985a; McCloskey, 1985). The modern sector was more than industry but not all of industry. Its production was carried out in workshops or factories where workers were concentrated in workplaces away from their homes, many of which

---

[11] There is no a priori economic reason that suggests that industries in which technological change was rapid would also necessarily experience rapid output growth. If technological progress was especially important in industries for which demand was inelastic, these industries would possibly grow slower than industries for which demand was highly priced and income elastic.

were located in urban or suburban areas. The traditional sector, roughly speaking, covered industries that remained little affected by the new technology. Much of the production was still carried out in the household or small workshop (though some larger establishments employed nonmechanized techniques), where the worker had few personal interactions with other workers or supervisory personnel. The interaction of the two sectors was, of course, reciprocal. From the point of view of the modern sector, the traditional sector was important because it determined the sociopolitical environment in which the new industries operated. And, although the modern sector was largely self-sufficient in capital and partially so in raw materials, it depended on the traditional sector for its labor supply and skills.

Utilizing the distinction between a modern and a traditional sector allows us to summarize what happened to the British economy during the Industrial Revolution as a three-pronged economic change. First, a small sector of the economy underwent quite rapid and dramatic technological change. Second, as a consequence, this sector grew at a rate much faster than the traditional sector so that its share in the overall economy continued to increase. Third, the technological changes in the modern sector gradually penetrated the membrane of the traditional sector so that parts of the *traditional* sector eventually became modernized. The economy grew, but because its sectoral composition changed, it did more than just increase in size, it was "growing-up" (Mokyr, 1976b).

The Industrial Revolution was not a story of rapid economic growth largely because of the composition effects just described. Moreover, in addition to the stormy developments in production technology, the British economy in the eighteenth century was subject to other, more gradual forces that affected the long-term growth of income. The most prominent of these forces were the growth of trade and the division of labor it brought with it. For Adam Smith, not surprisingly, the gains from trade and specialization were the main sources of economic growth. As Table 1.1 indicates, economic growth preceded the Industrial Revolution and thus can hardly have depended on it. E.L. Jones (1988) emphasizes that the technological changes of the last four decades were superimposed on an economy that was already growing. Had there been no Industrial Revolution, growth would have continued in the long run, though at a much slower (and decelerating) rate. The Smithian and the technological elements of economic change, though interrelated at many nodes, could operate independently of each other. The Industrial Revolution was neither a necessary nor a sufficient condition of economic growth. In the very long run, however, without continuous technological change, growth would slowly grind to a halt. The gains from trade and specialization, which in Smith's vision were the key to wealth, would have run into diminishing returns, as further declines in transportation or transactions costs would have yielded smaller and smaller marginal gains.

Despite the disagreements in interpreting the Industrial Revolution, it is appropriate to note that there are many areas of broad agreement. The consensus is that within the relatively narrow confines of production technology in a number of industries, more numerous and more radical inventions occurred during the Industrial Revolution than ever before in so short a period. It is equally uncontroversial that these changes had a far-reaching effect on the lives of only a minority of Britons throughout our period. The Industrial Revolution was, above all, a regional affair, affecting Lancashire and parts of the adjoining counties and the Scottish Lowlands but leaving most of the country without visible marks. As late as 1851, only about 27 percent of the British labor force worked in the industries that were *directly* affected by the Industrial Revolution, although almost everyone had been touched by it indirectly as consumer, user, or spectator.

Furthermore, it is beyond dispute that one of the problems with assessing the macroeconomic and social impact of the Industrial Revolution in its early stages is that it occurred simultaneously with other events whose effects are impossible to disentangle from those of the Industrial Revolution proper. Unlike a chemical experiment, history does not provide us with the circumstances to test the effects of one element by holding the others unchanged. First, for most of the period under discussion here, Britain was at war. Wars disrupted commerce and finance, increased taxation, and siphoned off labor to unproductive uses. Second, the Industrial Revolution coincided with the resumption of population growth in Britain, which until the middle of the eighteenth century had slackened off. There were ever more people who needed to be fed and clothed, threatening to materialize the dire predictions of the Reverend Malthus. The economic impact of population change was further complicated by the fact that it was in large part due to an increase in the birthrate. Like many under-developed countries today, this left Britain with an ever-younger population in which the proportion of small children who did not yet work was increasing.[12]   Third, the Industrial Revolution happened to occur during a period of worsening weather conditions, leading to a string of poor harvests, high food prices, and scarcity. Some of the worst harvests, as fate would have it, coincided with the war years, as they did in 1800/1801 and 1812/1813, compounding the misery.

These three extraneous factors -- wars, population growth, and poor harvests -- were not caused by the Industrial Revolution nor did they affect it directly. From the point of view of the economic historian looking for causes and effects, they are contaminations in an economic experiment that could be carried out only once. Economic history does not lend itself to neat and clean analysis: Even if we had far more data than we do, contaminating events and feedback loops make it exceedingly difficult to reach definite conclusions about causality. Yet the importance of the Industrial Revolution in British and indeed world history is such that we cannot afford not to try.

2. What Was the Industrial Revolution?

Technological determinism does not enjoy a great reputation among scholars, and in many accounts it is usually preceded by the telling adjective "crude." In the metaphor coined by a famous if anonymous schoolboy cited by T. S. Ashton, the Industrial Revolution is defined as "a wave of gadgets that swept Britain." In this view, invention becomes an exogenous variable that then affects the endogenous variables: factories, urbanization, social change, and, with a long lag, economic growth. This is an unsatisfactory cartoon of history. Inventions do not rain down upon an economy like manna from heaven. They emerge in the minds of some people, are communicated, adapted, refined, implemented, and imitated. An innovation may succeed or it may be resisted so fiercely that it never has a chance to compete. Some societies exhibit a quality that, lacking a better term, we will call "technological creativity." Technological creativity is not the same as inventiveness; it also includes the willingness and ability to recognize and then adopt inventions made elsewhere. We have barely begun to understand why some societies are technologically creative and

---

[12] The dependency ratio (defined as those aged 0-14 and those aged 60 and over, divided by those aged 15-59) thus increased from 815 in 1751 to 942 in 1801 (1826 = 1,000) (Wrigley and Schofield, 1981, p. 447).

others are not, and why some societies that are technologically creative at some time cease to be so later on. I will argue below that Britain, indeed, was a technologically creative society, and that we can make some reasonable hypotheses as to why and how she became so. Regardless of its source, the Industrial Revolution was above all an age of rapidly changing production technology propelled by technological creativity.[13]

The story of the most important innovations of the Industrial Revolution has been told elsewhere many times.[14] Without repeating all the details here, it may be useful to make a few distinctions that help to make sense of the story. Technological change consists of the creation of new knowledge and its diffusion and implementation, sometimes referred to as innovation. As always there is a gray area between the two, and here it is rather large. On many occasions when a known technology is introduced in a new place, it has to be modified and adapted to suit a different environment and sometimes a different product, and thus it acquires some of the characteristics of invention. Inventions and innovations are very much complementary processes, and asking whether technological change proceeds more by one or the other is like asking whether a pianist makes music with the left or the right hand. An invention that is not adopted remains a dead letter and at best ends up in a footnote in a text on the history of technology. On the other hand, without new inventions the process of innovation will lose steam and eventually reach a dead end.

We can envisage the relation by using the economist's terms of average- and best-practice technique. At any given point of time an industry uses a variety of techniques. Some producers use the most recent and most up-to-date (best-practice) technique, but because of a variety of diffusion lags, not all firms use state-of-the-art technology all the time. As best-practice techniques are diffused, the average-practice technique pursues and eventually catches up with the state-of-the-art

---

[13] To some students, the definition of the Industrial Revolution in technological terms may seem commonplace, even banal. Yet in some corners there are serious reservations about this view. Braudel (1984, p. 566) states categorically that "if there is one factor which has lost ground as a key explanation of the Industrial Revolution, it is technology."

[14] See, for instance, Ashton (1948); Cardwell (1972); Landes (1969); Mantoux (1928); Mokyr (1990a, chap. 5); Mokyr (1992a).

technique. If, however, the technical frontier advances continually through invention, average-practice never catches up with best-practice. Invention keeps throwing new fuel on the fires of innovation and progress. The rate of progress of an industry is thus a function of both the rate of advance of the best-practice techniques and the mean diffusion lag.

Many of the inventions that made the British Industrial Revolution were, in fact, adaptations of inventions made overseas. Thus the Fourdrinier paper machine, introduced by Bryan Donkin in London in 1807, was originally invented by the Frenchman N. L. Robert in 1798. Gaslighting, the Leblanc soda process, chlorine bleaching, and the wet-spinning process for flax were Continental inventions imported into and perfected in Britain. By being receptive to these foreign technologies, as much as through their own inventions, Britain's industries displayed an unprecedented technological creativity that lay at the foundation of the British Industrial Revolution.

Inventions, too, come in different sizes and packages. If we counted successful inventions mechanically as if they represented one unit each, we would find that the vast bulk of inventions made during the Industrial Revolution -- or in our own time -- were small, incremental improvements to known technologies. Such "gap-filling" inventions are often the result of on-the-job learning-by-doing or of a development by a firm's engineers who see opportunities to produce a good cheaper or better. Over time, a long sequence of such *micro*inventions may lead to major gains in productivity, impressive advances in quality, fuel and material saving, longevity, and so on. At times the accumulated effect of incremental inventions changed the nature of the product. Consider one example: the sailing ship. Since the emergence of the fully rigged, three-masted ship in the fifteenth century, the art of shipbuilding had not been stagnant: Ships were cheaper to build and to maintain, more seaworthy, and more durable in 1800 than in 1450. Yet there had been no radical changes in either planking or rigging, no discontinuous leaps in ship design (Gilfillan, 1935) since 1500. The same is true for technologies as diverse as the cultivation of grains, the smelting of iron ore, the printing of books, and the making of guns.

Far rarer, but equally important, were dramatic new departures that opened entirely new technological avenues by hitting on something that was entirely novel and represented a discontinuous leap with the past. Such *macro*inventions created what Dosi (1988) has called technological paradigms, entirely new ways of thinking about and carrying out production. Within the new paradigm, once it is created, incremental *micro*inventive activity takes over: radically novel techniques need to be adjusted, extended, refined, and debugged.[15] It is rare that a totally new invention is fully ready to go into production from the start. But it is equally clear that without occasional leaps of this kind, the process of continual incremental improvement within an exising technological paradigm would run into diminishing returns and eventually give out.

An exact criterion to distinguish macro- from microinventions is not easy to define. On the whole, a successful macroinvention meets three criteria: novelty, workability, and potential for further improvement. It involves a new technique to carry out production or consumption in a way that was radically different from anything before. Yet a radical idea, even a blueprint, that could not actually be materialized in practice was useless. Without the workmanship, the materials, and the supporting maintenance technology, the new idea would not survive. Macroinventions typically open new avenues to further improvements in production, reducing cost and enhancing product quality, finding new applications and new permutations, so that eventually it also acquired economic significance. However, it need not be a single event. Many macroinventions consisted of a number of steps that together were necessary for the new paradigm to emerge. The number of steps has to be small enough, however, to preserve some sense of discontinuous change.

The steam engine is a case in point.[16] It was conceptually one of the most radical inventions ever made. Energy, as used by people, comes in two forms: kinetic energy (work or motion) and thermal energy (heat). The equivalence of the two forms was not suspected by people in the eighteenth century; the notion that a horse pulling a treadmill and a

---

[15] As one of the great engineers of the Industrial Revolution, John Farey, told a Parliamentary committee in 1828, "The inventions which ultimately come to be of great public value were scarcely worth anything in the crude state, but by the subsequent application of skill, capital and the well-directed exertions of the labour of a number of inferior artizans . . . brought to bear to the benefit of the community . . . such improvements are made progressively, and are brought into use one after another, almost imperceptibly" (cited by Inkster, 1991, pp. 84-86).

[16] For a similar argument, see Cipolla (1965).

coal fire heating a lime kiln were in some sense doing the same thing would have appeared absurd to them. Yet converting heat into work must be regarded as one of the most crucial advances ever made; energy was exploited through controlled fire, the domestication of animals, and the use of watermills and windmills. However, heat and work were not yet convertible into each other, so that wood and fossil fuels could not be used to produce motion and watermills could not produce heat.[17]

By breaking through this separation, then, the steam engine was truly radical. Its invention stemmed from the realization that the earth was surrounded by an atmosphere and that differences in atmospheric pressure could be utilized to harness energy. Suggestions of this kind had been made throughout the second half of the seventeenth century, but the half-baked sketches and flights of the imagination did not add up to much until 1690 when Denis Papin produced a prototype of a piston that moved up and down in a cylinder due to alternative heating and cooling. Thomas Savery's vacuum pump notwithstanding, the first truly successful steam engine was not produced until 1712 when an English engineer named Thomas Newcomen produced the first working steam engine. Large, cumbersome, noisy, and voracious in its appetite for fuel, the Newcomen engine must have appeared fierce and somewhat awesome to contemporaries. It was a prime example of what some have called "a hopeful monstrosity."[18] Newcomen engines were, however, viable and were used widely as pumps in mines where fuel was plentiful and flooding a threat. It was not until 1765, however, that the steam engine could be turned into an economic revolution, when James Watt introduced the separate condenser, as well as a number of other important microinventions.

A second macroinvention of enormous economic importance was the invention of mechanical spinning. Since time immemorial, spinning had been carried out by a distaff-and-spindle method in which the spindle

---

[17] There was one exception to the rule. Gunpowder as used in the West was a method to convert heat into kinetic energy. But it was an uncontrolled conversion, and the uses of gunpowder for civilian purposes prior to the invention of dynamite were limited. It is telling that Christiaan Huygens, a Dutch scientist, proposed in 1673 to build a combustion engine prototype using gunpowder.

[18] The term was actually coined by biologist Richard Goldschmidt to denote mutations that create new species.

was dropped while the worker twisted the rovings of raw material and turned it into yarn. The index finger and thumb of the spinner, or (usually) spinster, were essential to this process, because it was their motion that drew out the fibers and carried out the true "spinning." The addition of the spinning wheel in the Middle Ages did not change that principle; the wheel just helped wind the finished yarn on a rapidly turning spindle. Replacing the human finger by a machine turned out to be a difficult problem, and it took until the last third of the eighteenth century to finally find a solution. When it happened, not one but two inventions emerged, which together changed spinning forever. One was the throstle, or water frame, invented by Richard Arkwright in 1769, which used two pairs of rapidly turning rollers to mimic the human fingers. The other was the Hargreaves spinning jenny (1765), based on the insight that it was possible to impart the twist by the correct turning of the wheel itself, with metal bars guiding the spun yarn onto the spindle. These two were then combined in 1779 by a third inventor, Samuel Crompton, into a hybrid of the two, appropriately called the mule. For more than a century, the mule remained the backbone of the British cotton industry.

The inventions in spinning led to a technology that was radically different from what came before. Economically, its importance was that it delivered a yarn that cost a small fraction compared to the previous technique and yet was of far higher quality than anything that could have been produced in Britain before. The new spinning technology practically created an industry *de novo* (prior to 1770 cotton had been a small industry, in the shadow of its cousins, the woolen and linen industries). Above all, the spinning machines were truly a novel concept, one that could subsequently be further improved. The novelty was in the substitution of a machine for the fine movements of the human fingers, one of the most delicate and flexible mechanisms designed by nature. Although cotton spinning was concentrated in a small part of Britain (Lancashire), its ramifications were truly global. It led to the destruction of the Indian cotton-spinning industry, which previously had supplied the high-quality yarns needed to make calicoes. Across the Atlantic, the growth of the British cotton industry led to the emergence of the cotton economy and the survival of slavery in the United States.

The *economically* most important inventions were not necessarily the most spectacular macroinventions, though that was the case with the steam engine and cotton-spinning machinery.[19] Consider, for instance, the invention of the puddling-and-rolling technique by Henry Cort in 1784, which solved the problem of efficiently converting the output of blast furnaces, pig iron, into what industry needed, wrought iron. Arguably, it was the most indispensable invention of the era because unlike steam power and cotton there was no substitute for iron. Yet Cort's invention was hardly a radical departure; rolling had been practiced for centuries, and the conceptual novelty of the process was modest. On the other hand, consider the Jacquard loom, invented in France in 1804. This loom wove complicated patterns into fabric using instructions that were embedded in an endless chain of cards, which had holes that were prodded by special rods. What these cards contained was a revolutionary new insight: the binary coding of information, a system that was conceptually novel and a harbinger of things to come. The importance of the insight was fully recognized by Charles Babbage, the inventor of the "analytical engine," which was the precursor of the modern computer. Yet the Jacquard loom produced largely an up-market, expensive product (silk and high quality worsteds) and did not produce a very different product than the old draw loom. Its economic significance, compared with Cort's invention, was relatively small.

The most radical of macroinventions of the time had even less of an economic impact: hot air ballooning (invented in France in 1783). It never had much commercial use, and even its military use, though attempted, was less than decisive. Yet it was one of the most radical technological events of all time: the first manned flight, defeating the tyranny of gravity. It was typical of the period, the last third of the eighteenth century, in which traditions, conventions, and old boundaries were recklessly cast aside and new ideas tried everywhere. In the realm of technology, other examples abound: the use of gas for lighting, the bleaching of fabrics with chlorine, new designs in waterwheels, the preservation of food through canning, and the idea of interchangeable parts in clocks and firearms all date from this period.

A technological definition of the Industrial Revolution is a clustering of macroinventions leading to an acceleration in microinventions. The macroinventions not only increased productivity at the time but opened

---

[19] The "social savings" of an invention is defined as the addition to total consumer surplus generated by it. It thus depends on the difference in costs between using the technique in question and the next best alternative.

enough new technological vistas to assure that further change was forthcoming. Such a definition does not pretend to exhaust what happened in Britain in those years. The macroinventions were significant in large part because they created the germs of what came later: a gradual diffusion, adaptation, improvement, and extension of the techniques developed during the Industrial Revolution. The high-pressure steam engine led to the railroad and steamship. Improvements in cotton-spinning were reinforced by innovations in the preparatory stages in yarn-making, such as carding and slubbing. The inventions in cotton manufacturing spread to wool and linen. The cheap wrought iron found many new uses for iron, including construction, water mills, ships, machines, and specialty tools. The Leblanc soda-making process (1787) and bleaching powder (1798) laid the foundation for a chemical industry. In the absence of subsequent microinventions, some macro-inventions remained little more than curiosa. Thus Faraday's invention of the electrical motor in 1821 remained of purely scientific interest until the principle of self-excitation was developed in the late 1860s. Ballooning, too, could not be exploited commercially until small, lightweight engines could be mounted on the balloons for steering.

Despite the obvious importance of changes in technology in the British economy, their analysis and measurement have been slippery, and economists have found it exceedingly difficult to quantify them. Innovations and inventions are difficult to count and they do not follow the laws of arithmetic. An invention may supersede a previous invention, it may be independent of it, or it may in fact supplement it and improve it. The combined effects of two inventions could thus be equivalent to one, two, or a larger number of improvements. Yet economic historians have felt intuitively that if technological change is to be analyzed, it has to be quantified in some way. There are two alternative ways of measuring the level of technological change. One is the counting of patents or related statistics, which is a microeconomic approach. The other is estimating total factor productivity, which is mostly a macroeconomic approach.

Patent statistics have always tempted economists. Jacob Schmookler (1966), whose work is often cited in this respect, was preceded in his interest in patents by economic historians such as Ashton (1948, p. 63) who pointed to the sharp rise in patents as a symptom of the Industrial Revolution. Recently, the patent statistics have been subjected to quantitative analysis (Sullivan, 1989; for the United States, see Sokoloff,

1988, and also Griliches, 1990). Yet the counting of patents has always been subject to sharp criticism. First, it is a measure of *invention*, not of *innovation*. The statistics reveal nothing about the subsequent usefulness of the invention: Arkwright's and Watt's patents would be counted together with that of the inventor who took out a patent on nightcaps specially designed for sufferers from gout and rheumatism. Weighting the patents by their "importance" is of course far from easy. Second, not all important inventions were patented. The reasons for this range from the inability of the inventor to pay the required fee (£100 for England, £350 for Great Britain as a whole) to the inventor's preference for secrecy. This objection would perhaps not be so damaging if the inventions that were patented were in some sense a representative sample of the larger population of inventive activity. But recent research strongly suggests that that was not the case (Griffiths, Hunt, and O'Brien, 1992; MacLeod, 1988). Patenting statistics thus measure the propensity of inventors to patent as well as the distribution of inventive activity over high- and low-patent industries. As such, its usefulness as an index for the level of inventive activity is limited.

Total factor productivity measurements take a completely different road: they are, if anything, measures of innovation, not of invention. The economic logic behind total factor productivity estimates is that output grows due to either increases in inputs or shifts *of* the production function (such as technological change). If the weighted contributions of the inputs are subtracted from the growth rates, the "residual" measures the rate of productivity growth, which is associated with innovation.[20] The two best-known attempts to compute total factor productivity for Britain during the Industrial Revolution were made by McCloskey and Crafts, and they are discussed in detail in the chapter by Harley below. Between 1760 and 1800, Crafts and Harley estimate, total factor productivity "explained" about 10 percent of total output growth; in the period 1801-1831 this went up to about 18 percent. This seems rather unimpressive, but it should be kept in mind that growth is concerned with output per worker (or per capita). If we look at output per worker, we observe that for the period 1760-1830

---

[20] The actual estimation (e.g., McCloskey, 1985) often uses the "dual" approach, which consists of looking at input and output prices. This approach is formally equivalent to the production function approach but utilizes different information.

practically the entire growth of per capita income is explained by technological change.[21] Economic growth was slow, as Harley and Crafts have shown, but what little there was is explained by the residual. As Williamson (1987a, pp. 272-73) notes, this is strikingly different from the contemporary third world experience, where total factor productivity explains relatively little, and much more in line with twentieth century experience in the industrialized world. Differences in the exact procedure are still not entirely resolved.[22] Still, the apparent dominance of invention over abstention suggested by total factor productivity analysis stands out as one of the most striking findings of the New Economic History.

Identifying the residual with technological change is, however, far from warranted. The residual is a measure of our ignorance rather than of our knowledge. Any errors, omissions, mismeasurements, and aggregation biases that occur on the output and the input sides would, by construction, be contained in the residual. Moreover, changes in the quality of inputs would also be captured in the residual. If labor becomes more productive because workers are healthier or better disciplined, total factor productivity will increase though technology has remained unchanged. Furthermore, the residual is affected by

---

[21] The contribution of total productivity toward per capita output can be computed from data provided by Crafts (1985a, p. 81) and Crafts and Harley (1992, table 5):

	Per Capita Growth	Contribution of Capital/ Labor Ratio	Contribution of Resources per Capita Ratio	Total Contribution of Nonlabor Inputs	Total Factor Productivity Growth	Productivity as a % of Total per Capita Growth
1760-1800	0.2	0.2*0.35 = 0.07	-0.065*0.15 = -0.01	0.06	0.14	70
1800-1830	0.5	0.3*0.35 = 0.105	-0.1*0.15 = -0.015	0.09	0.41	82

[22] Crafts and Harley themselves find somewhat larger contributions of capital and correspondingly lower contributions of productivity, which results from their procedures lumping capital together with land and thus overstating total input growth somewhat.

market imperfections and external economies, economies or diseconomies of scale, changes in factor mobility, and so on. The residual is more than productivity change, and productivity change is more than technological change. At the same time, not all technological progress necessarily shows up in the residual.

Technological change was only one event in the series of events that transformed Britain in this period. To what extent it caused the other changes or were caused by them remains a matter of interpretation. Whatever its exact role, it is impossible to provide any definition of the Industrial Revolution without it. Thus, if one insists on economic growth, capital accumulation, or changes in the organization of production as integral parts of the Industrial Revolution, it is difficult to separate them from the changes in technology. Even the most convinced detractors of the concept of the Industrial Revolution will concede two things. One is that although income per capita did not rise much between 1760 and 1830, it is hard to see how Britain could have sustained a more than doubling of its population while fighting a number of major wars had not its economic potential increased.[23] Moreover, the undeniable growth that occurred in the British economy after 1830 would not and could not have occurred without the changes in technology in the previous seventy years.[24]

Secondly, most scholars agree that simple causal mechanisms will not explain something like the Industrial Revolution and that positive feedback and interactive path-dependent models will be needed if the phenomenon is to make sense. One example will suffice to convey this point: Many scholars emphasize commercial changes in this period and regard the rise of a national market and improvement in transport as causes of the changes in technology (Szostak, 1991). Adam Smith, writing before the Industrial Revolution or in its very early stages, had a view of economic development in which specialization and "the gains from trade" were at center stage. Yet improvements in technology

---

[23] The population of England in 1760 was 6.1 million; in 1830, 13.1 million (Wrigley and Schofield, 1981, p. 534). The populations of Wales and Scotland grew at comparable rates.

[24] Gross domestic product per person-hour, which grew at 0.5 percent in the United Kingdom in the period 1785-1820, accelerated to 1.4 percent in the period 1820-1890. Real income per capita between 1820 and 1870 is estimated to have grown at 1.5 percent per annum (Maddison, 1982, pp. 31, 44).

subsequently fed back into improved transport, allowing even greater specialization and internal trade. Due to the inventions of John Loudon McAdam and Thomas Telford, improved roads and canals were constructed. Ships were built with planks cut by steam- or water-driven mills. Eventually, the high-pressure steam engine and the precision-tool industry, developed during the Industrial Revolution, were applied to land and sea transport, leading to changes in commerce that would have been unimaginable even to that inveterate optimist, Adam Smith. Thus gains from trade and specialization interacted with gains from technological progress, and such interactions led to a long and sustained path of economic development. Monocausal, linear models based on concepts of equilibrium or steady states will have difficulty doing justice to the historical reality.

To understand the phenomenon of the British Industrial Revolution, we have to ask two related questions: What were the causes of technological progress in Britain? What other elements permitted its society to adapt and transform itself to absorb the innovations and become the "workshop of the world."

3. The Causes of the Industrial Revolution

Why was there an Industrial Revolution? In this crude form the question is unanswerable. In more focused versions of the question some answers have been provided, and although full agreement is still remote, the discussion is one of the more lively in the historical literature. Examples of more focused formulations are: Why did the Industrial Revolution occur in Britain and not in France (or in the Netherlands, Germany, Spain)? Why did it start in the last third of the eighteenth century rather than, say, a century earlier? Can we find factors that should be regarded as "necessary preconditions" for the Industrial Revolution to have taken place?

To start with the last question, the notion that certain changes were a sine qua non for the Industrial Revolution has become increasingly difficult to maintain (Gerschenkron, 1962, pp. 31-51). Some factors present in Britain facilitated the Industrial Revolution and in this sense can be said to be causal. Others impeded its progress, and the Industrial Revolution proceeded in spite of them. The term *facilitated* does not mean, however, that there were any elements that were indispensable. After all, factors that were neither necessary nor sufficient for the outcome can still be thought of as causal. For instance, heart attacks cause deaths, though not all deaths are caused by them and not all heart attacks are fatal. Moreover, insofar as heart attacks are themselves caused by other factors, it is debatable to what extent they are ultimate causes or just "transmission mechanisms." The causal explanation of the Industrial Revolution runs into similar quandaries. Economic historians have increasingly come to concede that the positive effect that factor X had on the Industrial Revolution does not entitle factor X to the status of "necessary factor." Counterfactual analysis has to be resorted to, at least implicitly, to assess the indispensability of the various elements.[25]

It is not even certain that the question Why did the Industrial Revolution occur in Britain rather than in some other country? is necessarily the best way to approach the material. For one thing, as we have already indicated, the Industrial Revolution was not so much a national as a regional affair. This has been stressed again recently in a collection devoted to this issue (Hudson, 1989). The regional argument was presented most cogently by Sidney Pollard (1981, 1985). Instead of dividing the European continent into "economies," Pollard prefers to look at regions that transcended national boundaries and shared a common economic fate. Thus one ought to prefer a comparison of, say, a region consisting of Lancashire and the West Riding of Yorkshire with a region consisting of southern Belgium and the northern *départements* of France.

Pollard's criticism of the national economy as the unit of analysis is not likely to remain unchallenged itself. The best arguments for the choice of nation-state as the appropriate unit of analysis are still in Kuznets (1966, pp. 16-19), who pointed out that nations share common heritages and histories, and thus people tend to be more interested in

---

[25] Counterfactual analysis involves constructing a hypothetical world that never was. It is helpful in testing the hypothesis that factor X was a necessary condition in bringing about outcome Y; i.e., that in the absence of X, Y would not have taken place. Although the New Economic History is often credited with, or blamed for, introducing this mode of analysis, it has always been a staple tool of traditional historians. Thus Craig (1980, p. 1) begins his magisterial survey of German modern history: "It is certainly unnecessary to apologize for introducing Bismarck's name at the outset. If he had never risen to the top of Prussian politics, the unification of Germany would probably have taken place anyway but . . . surely not in quite the same way."

their national history than in regional histories. Moreover, a nation-state has a common government that is the major legislative and policy-making body, and insofar as it affects economic development, the unit under its jurisdiction should be the unit of analysis. The state was also, in most instances, the agency that collected economic statistics. Consequently, for better or worse, most of our data (e.g., foreign trade statistics, fiscal returns, price and wage figures) come on the national level.

It might be debated whether Britain was a unified economy or not on the eve of the Industrial Revolution (compare Crafts, 1985a, p. 3, and Szostak, 1991, p. 79, with Berg and Hudson, 1992). Yet it was certainly becoming more of one after 1760, and with the possible exception of the United Provinces, it was the most unified economy in Europe. Above all, it is hazardous to disavow comparisons of national units on account of *intra*national variances because the regional differences were themselves a *consequence* of the process of national development. As Rick Szostak (1991) has recently emphasized, no nation can devote itself entirely to one industry. With the improvements in transportation, interregional specialization became an inevitable part of the phenomenon that we are trying to analyze, namely the concentration of some industries in the northwest of the country. The rise of the Yorkshire woolen industry was the mirror image and the "cause" of the demise of its counterpart in the West Country. The south of England remained largely unaffected by the Industrial Revolution because it specialized in agriculture.

A second criticism of the question Why was England first? has been raised in a pioneering paper by N.F.R. Crafts (1985b; see also Rostow, 1985). Quite simply put, Crafts's argument is that much of the Industrial Revolution was self-sustaining. Once the process had started, it fed on itself due to increasing returns to scale and external economies among firms, demonstration effects, self-fulfilling expectations, and other "positive feedback" loops. Just as we have vicious circles in which backwardness breeds poverty and poverty breeds more backwardness, we have virtuous circles in which the reverse is true. More recent work in the theory of economic development has formalized much of this thinking (e.g., Matsuyama, 1991, and the literature cited there). If so, the role of contingency and accident in economic history is far larger than people have supposed. In the extreme view, there is no point in asking why some nations underwent economic development and became rich while others remained poor and backward; it was all a matter of pure luck, a roll of the dice (Crafts, 1985b). In this approach, economic theory has to be complemented by insights from chaos theory: Comparatively minor differences in initial conditions can lead to major differences in historical outcomes. The Industrial Revolution was a "bifurcation point," and in the limiting case causal analysis is useless.

Much of the persuasiveness of this view depends on the accuracy of its premises. If we think of the Industrial Revolution as a sequence of strongly interrelated phenomena, it becomes indeed something close to a single event whose explanation may be beyond us. In reality, however, the set of facts we are trying to explain are to some extent independent events; by 1830 Britain was a leader in a variety of industries, from papermaking to engineering to chemicals. If a coin is tossed once and heads comes up, there may be nothing to explain. However, if the coin is tossed dozens of times and heads comes up in every one of them, a closer look at the fairness of the coin would be called for. Much depends on how independent the events were; if they were strongly correlated, the "chance" explanation may hold true. If the correlation is weak, the plausibility of the "random-event" explanation is weakened. An analogy from genetics is instructive here: We know that mutations are chance events, copying-errors in the DNA. Yet the number of mutations can be affected by radiation or mutagenic chemicals, and a sharp rise in the number of mutations would itself not be a chance event because mutations are unlikely to lead to further mutations. Can we, in economic history, define something equivalent to mutagens, environmental agents stimulating invention and innovation?

a. Geography

Britain's geographical advantages over other economies have often seemed to be good explanations for its economic success after 1750. In a recent book, one social historian states it as self-evident that "England is built [sic] upon an underground mountain of coal. Its exploitation was the motor-force in the revolution in production that created modern industrial society" (Levine, 1987, p. 97).[26] Some major objections can be raised againt the view that places a heavy emphasis on accidents of nature as causal factors. In part, the impact of such accidents is ambiguous. Resource availability plays a somewhat bizarre role in the historiography of technological progress. On the one hand, resource abundance is considered a blessing because it cheapens production and encourages the development of complementary techniques. On the other hand, many authors maintain that the challenge imposed by resource *scarcities* stimulates invention. Thus the deforestation of Britain is alleged to have led to a rise in timber prices, thus triggering Britain into adopting a novel and ultimately far more efficient set of techniques using fossil fuels. The evidence for this oft-repeated tale is far from convincing.[27] As a general statement, however, it suffers from the logical difficulty that the scarcity of natural resources and their abundance cannot *both* be regarded as stimulating factors for technological progress. At most, one can say that nature worked as a "focusing device," to use Nathan Rosenberg's felicitous term. Given a certain level of technological creativity, nature would direct this creativity in a certain direction. Thus coal-rich Britain would focus on Newcomen engines, while coal-poor Switzerland would witness the rise of watchmaking precision and engineering. Many other economies, rich or poor in resources, lacked the technological creativity and achieved little progress in this period. For a focusing device to work, there has to be a source of light.

Geography and physical endowment, like most other factors, are rarely either sufficient or necessary. Britain's geographic good luck was that it was an island and thus had not been successfully invaded since 1066. Being an island also provided it with access to a cheap form of transportation (coastal shipping). Yet being an island does not seem to have done much for Ireland, and good internal transportation was not

---

[26] See also, for example, Parker (1979, p. 61). Coleman (1983, p. 443) even goes so far as to conclude that coal and iron were of greater consequence in determining the pattern of British industrialization than the existence of domestic industry. In making this statement he fails to apply to his own hypotheses the strict empirical standards he demands from others. E. A. Wrigley (1987; 1988, essay 4) has emphasized the importance of coal in the British Industrial Revolution, although his treatment is far more judicious.

[27] For an effective refutation of this argument, see Flinn (1959, 1978).

very helpful to the Dutch economy in generating a phenomenon similar
to the Industrial Revolution. Mineral wealth is equally problematic.
Britain had coal and iron, but coal and iron were traded commodities;
in 1794-1796 it imported £852,000 worth of iron and iron ore, mostly
from Sweden. In the second half of the nineteenth century, it imported
high-quality hematite ores from Spain. Coal, too, was traded, though its
volume expanded only after 1830. Above all, it should be recalled that
much of the Industrial Revolution depended on cotton and that raw
cotton was entirely imported. Trade, it should always be remembered,
liberates nations from the arbitrary tyranny of resource location. On
the Continent, too, the evidence is mixed: Belgium, the first nation to
adopt Britain's techniques, shared with her a wealth of iron and coal;
Switzerland, a close second, had neither. Buying coal and iron from
other economies added to industrial costs, but such additions were, on
the whole, sufficiently small to be dwarfed by other cost differences. In
other words, it is possible to accept Wrigley's (1987) view that
substituting coal for wood was an important part of the economic
transformation of Britain, without attributing undue significance to the
geographical accident of the presence of coal in Britain. Coal had
substitutes; as a fuel, coal-poor nations like the Netherlands and Ireland
relied on peat, while the mountainous areas of Europe relied on water
power. Such substitutions involved costs, of course, but the examples
of Switzerland and New England prove that water power could provide
an adequate energy base for a mechanized industry.

It could be maintained, however, that there were more subtle links
between location and technological change. Small differences in resource
endowment could set into motion chain reactions and steer a nation
along a technological trajectory quite different from one that would
have been followed in the absence of those resources. Britain's use of
coal did not only help by providing cheap fuel; it focused Britain's
attention on the solution to certain technological problems: pumping,
hoisting, and mineral-exploration, which then spilled over to other
industries (Cardwell, 1972, p. 73). Shipping, too, generated externalities
in sawmills, carpentry, instrumentmaking, sailweaving, and so on. Yet
in a deeper sense such mechanical descriptions are unsatisfactory since
they describe opportunities; but clearly these opportunities were neither
necessary nor sufficient conditions for success. Maritime Holland was
not able to use its shipbuilding sector as a gateway into the Industrial
Revolution.

b. Technological Creativity[28]

If it is agreed that at the base of the Industrial Revolution lay something we call technological creativity, some speculation about the factors responsible for it is in place here. To start with, Britain seems to have no particular advantage in generating macroinventions; a large number of them were generated overseas, especially in France. Steampower and cotton technology were British inventions, but many of the other examples cited previously were imported: Jacquard looms, chlorine bleaching, the Leblanc soda-making process, food canning, the Robert continuous paper-making process, gaslighting, mechanical flaxspinning.

Any period of successful technological creativity requires both fundamental breakthroughs and small, incremental, often anonymous improvements that take place *within* known techniques. The key to British technological success was that it had a *comparative* advantage in *micro*inventions. This may seem unorthodox to those who think of the milestones set by Richard Trevithick, Richard Arkwright, and Henry Cort, but it should be recalled that it is possible to have an absolute advantage in both areas yet a comparative advantage in one, although it is not altogether clear whether Britain had an *absolute* advantage in macroinventions.

Evidence for the statement that the British comparative advantage was in improvement and not in originality comes in part from contemporary sources. In a widely cited comment, a Swiss calico printer remarked in 1766 that for a thing to be perfect it has to be invented in France and worked out in England (Wadsworth and Mann, 1931, p. 413). In 1829 the engineer John Farey stated that the prevailing talent of English and Scotch people is to apply new ideas to use and to bring such applications to perfection, but they do not "imagine" as much as foreigners (Musson, 1975, p. 81). Continental Europeans felt frustrated, reflecting Leibniz's prophetic words, written in 1670: "It is not laudable that we Germans were the first in the invention of mechanical, natural, and other arts and sciences, but are the last in their expansion and betterment" (cited in William Clark, 1991). A test of the hypothesis that Britain had a comparative advantage in microinventions is in the establishment of net trade directions. Economies tend to specialize in

---

[28] The following paragraphs draw on Mokyr (1990a, 1992a).

the areas in which they have a comparative advantage. The British economy, roughly speaking, was a net importer of macroinventions and exporter of microinventions and minor improvements. We should of course look at this specialization as a broad central tendency, but in rough lines the distinction stands up. Britain took its major inventions where it could find them, but whatever it borrowed it improved and refined.[29]

On the eve of the Industrial Revolution, Britain was neither a scientific leader nor could it boast of a particularly effective education system. As David Mitch explains in more detail in a later chapter, British education was at its best outside the schools, and Britain trained most of its mechanics and engineers by its age-old apprenticeship system without introducing much formal schooling. In a sample of 498 applied scientists and engineers born between 1700 and 1850, 91 were educated in Scotland, 50 at Oxbridge, and 329 (about two-thirds) had no university education at all (Birse, 1983, p. 16). Yet these people thirsted for technical, applied, pragmatic knowledge, the knowledge of how to make things and how to make them cheap and durable. A few of them were educated at Scottish universities or dissenting academies, but many were self-taught or had acquired their knowledge through personal relations with masters, libraries, itinerant lecturers, and mechanics institutes. By the middle of the nineteenth century, there were 1,020 associations for technical and scientific knowledge in Britain with a membership that Inkster estimated conservatively at 200,000 (Inkster, 1991, pp. 73, 78-79).

For Britain in this period, this system clearly delivered. It produced some of the finest applied engineers in history. As long as technological advances did not require a fundamental understanding of the laws of

---

[29] The case of chlorine bleaching is revealing here. The Swede Karl Wilhelm Scheele and the Frenchman Claude Berthollet clearly produced the original breakthrough, but the commercial value of the idea was recognized by James Watt (whose father-in-law, James McGrigor, was a Glasgow bleacher), and a series of British chemists and entrepreneurs set out to improve on the original invention (Musson and Robinson, 1969, pp. 251-337). The definitive improvement came when a Scottish bleacher Charles Tennant replaced potash with slaked lime as the solution in which chlorine was absorbed. Chemical bleaching, a Continental macroinvention, was made into bleaching powder, a British improvement.

physics or chemistry on which they were based and as long as advances could be achieved by brilliant but intuitive tinkerers and persistent experimenters, Britain's ability to create or adapt new production technologies was supreme. Most inventors and engineers were dexterous merchants or enterprising craftsmen whose technical ideas were often the result of luck, serendipity, or inspiration even if the successful completion of the innovative process required patience, determination, and confidence.

Moreover, some of the industries in which Britain had specialized before 1760 required skilled mechanics. Clock and instrument making, shipbuilding, iron making, printing, wool finishing, and mining required a level of technical skill that came in handy when new ideas had to be translated from blueprints to models and from models to real commodities. John Wilkinson, it is often remarked, was indispensable for the success of James Watt, because his Bradley works had the skilled workers and equipment to bore the cylinders exactly according to specification. Mechanics and instrument makers such as Jesse Ramsden, Edward Nairn, Joseph Bramah, and Henry Maudslay; clock makers such as Henry Hindley, Benjamin Huntsman, and John Kay of Warrington (not to be confused with his namesake, the inventor of the flying shuttle, who was trained as a reed and comb maker), engineers such as John Smeaton, Richard Roberts, and Marc I. Brunel; ironmasters such as the Darbys, the Crowleys, and the Crawshays; chemists such as John Roebuck, Alexander Chisholm, and James Keir were as much part of the story as the "superstars" Arkwright, Cort, Crompton, Hargreaves, Cartwright, Trevithick, and Watt. Below the great engineers came a much larger contingent of skilled artisans and mechanics, upon whose dexterity and adroitness the top inventors and thus Britain's technological success relied. These unknown but capable workers produced a cumulative stream of anonymous and small but indispensable microinventions without which Britain would not have become the "workshop of the world." It is perhaps premature to speak of an "invention industry" by this period, but clearly mechanical knowledge at a level beyond the reach of the run-of-the-mill artisan became increasingly essential to create the inventions associated with the Industrial Revolution. Dozens of scientific journals and the published transactions of scientific societies had appeared by 1800, most of them after 1760 (Kronick, 1962, p. 73). A widespread thirst for knowledge penetrated Britain down to the small towns of the kingdom where itinerant lecturers were in much demand. Much of this "provincial scientific culture," as Inkster (1991, p. 43) has called it, was private, meritocratic, nonelitist and thus in some ways in conflict with the social establishment. The people who worked in applying the principles of physics, chemistry, and biology in their daily work were thirsty for innovations. In this milieu *micro*inventions, the gradual improvement of pathbreaking ideas, will prosper. In the early stages of the Industrial Revolution this ability was the key to Britain's technological success.

It is of course a truism that advantages in skilled labor were a matter of degree, not an absolute. France, Germany, and the Low Countries had their share of able and innovative engineers. But degree is everything, and in the early nineteenth century Britain tried, in vain, to keep the secret of its success by prohibiting the exportation of machines and the emigration of skilled mechanics. Yet as it had imported macroinventions, it exported microinventions and the people who implemented them. The engineers who spread the new technologies to the Continent after 1800 had names like Cockerill, Hodson, Ainsworth, Douglas, and Holden. Insofar as trade patterns reveal comparative advantage, these patterns reveal Britain's technological superiority. Explaining this superiority is a different matter: Landes (1969, pp. 61-64), who was one of the first to call attention to Britain's advantage in mechanics and technicians, spoke of the question of British mechanical skills as "mysterious." Clearly, any explanation will have to take us beyond the narrow boundaries prescribed by economic science.

c. Social and Institutional Factors

It is easier said than demonstrated that Britain had the "right kind of society" to have an Industrial Revolution. After all, what exactly do we mean by social preconditions to industrialization and how do we demonstrate the proposition that they were important? One way to approach the subject is through the concept of a "hierarchy of values." Each society defines in some way the criteria of success. Success means access to certain nonmarket goods such as political offices, membership of social clubs, being plugged into information networks, and in general earning respect from people whose opinions matter. Social status and prestige are always and everywhere *correlated with* economic success but are almost never *identical* with it. In many societies the causation ran from non-economic success to enrichment; victorious Roman generals were rewarded by remunerative governorships. One key to the economic success of a society is essentially the degree to which social respect not only correlates with economic success but is caused by it.[30] The most complete and persuasive attempt to provide a social explanation of the Industrial Revolution based on this idea has been provided by Perkin (1969). Perkin dates the creation of the type of society that was most amenable to an Industrial Revolution to the Restoration of 1660 and the social and political changes accompanying it.[31] He points out that the principle upon which society was established following the Civil War was the link between wealth and status. Status means here not only political influence and indirect control over the lives of one's neighbors but also the houses to which one was invited, the partners that were eligible for one's children to marry, the rank one could attain (that is, purchase) in the army, where one lived, and how one's children were educated. In Perkin's view, the quality of life was determined not just by "consumption," as usually defined by economists, but by the relative standing of the individual in the social hierarchy. Whether this social relativity hypothesis is still a good description of society is an open question, but a case can be made, as Perkin does, that it is an apt description of Britain in the eighteenth century. Perkin cites a paragraph from Adam Smith's *Theory of Moral Sentiments*, which economists -- always a bit selective in what they learned from the Master -- have been ignoring at their risk:

> To what purpose is all the toil and bustle of the world . . . the pursuit of wealth, of power, and preeminence? Is it to supply the necessities of nature? The wages of the meanest labourer can supply them. . . . What then is the cause of our aversion to his situation? . . . Do the rich imagine that their stomach is better, or their sleep sounder in a palace than in a cottage? The contrary has so often been observed. . . . What are the advantages [then] by that great purpose of human life which we call bettering our condition? . . . It is the vanity, not the ease of the pleasure, which interests us. But vanity is always founded upon our belief of our being the object of attention and approbation. The rich man glories in his riches, because he feels that they naturally

---

[30] Economic theorists have belatedly rediscovered this rather obvious fact and have tried to formalize it. See Cole, Mailath, and Postlewaite (1991).

[31] Some social historians argue that the changes started much earlier. Alan MacFarlane (1978, pp. 199-201) explicitly dates the beginning of English "modern society" to some point before the Black Death.

draw upon him the attention of the world. . . . Everybody is eager to look at him. .
. . His actions are the objects of the public care. Scarce a word, scarce a gesture can fall
from him that is altogether neglected. In a great assembly he is the person upon whom
all direct their eyes. . . . It is this, which . . . renders greatness the object of envy and
compensates . . . all that toil, all that anxiety, all those mortifications which must be
undergone in the pursuit of it (Smith, 1759, pp. 50-51).

In Perkin's own words, "To the perennial desire for wealth, the old
society, [i.e., Britain after 1600] added more motivation which gave
point and purpose to the pursuit of riches. Compared with neigh-
bouring and more traditional societies it offered both a greater challenge
and a greater reward to successful enterprise. . . . the pursuit of wealth
was the pursuit of social status, not merely for oneself but for one's
family" (Perkin, 1969, p.85).[32] Examples are not hard to find: The
riches accumulated by Richard Arkwright in cotton spinning bought
him not only all the comforts that money could buy but also a
knighthood and the office of sheriff of the county of Derby. Other
cotton manufacturers who rose to high office included Robert Peel, Sr.,
who became an MP and whose son became prime minister. Brewers,
paper makers, potters, and iron masters became barons, earls, and castle
dwellers. Men of business could, through money, "advance in rank and
contend with the landlords in the enjoyments of leisure, as well as
luxuries," as Malthus (1820, p. 470) put it.[33]

---

[32] Perkin anticipated here the interesting work of Fred Hirsch (1976), who,
although not concerned with history, sets up a framework that complements
Perkin's. Hirsch distinguishes between material goods -- i.e., ordinary
commodities -- and positional goods of which there are by definition a constant
amount. Examples of the latter are social prestige, political power, and
symbols indicating one's relative position. Markets for material goods tend to
be well developed, so material wealth provides easy access to them. Markets
for positional goods are less well developed. The more efficient the markets for
positional goods, the easier it is to acquire them by the means of acquiring
wealth or to lose them by the lack thereof. Therefore, relatively efficient
markets for positional goods should strengthen the incentive to get rich
(increase the marginal utility of income) and make the toil and risks of
entrepreneurship more worthwhile.
[33] Local studies confirm the importance of wealth as a determinant of
status. Urdank, in his study of Gloucestershire, found that "between 1780 and
1850 wealth had become a more obvious criterion for defining status than in
the past, so much so that men with the humblest occupations might call

Perkin's insight is important because it underlines a basic point often overlooked by economists trying to understand entrepreneurial behavior. It is almost always true that an easy opportunity to earn money will not be passed over by a rational individual. Moreover, if there is a divergence of opinion about the expected profitability of an opportunity, one should expect the optimists to replace the pessimists. Unexploited opportunities to quick gains will rapidly disappear. There were opportunities to make money during the Industrial Revolution, but few were quick and easy. Almost all major entrepreneurial figures took enormous risks, worked long and hard hours, and rarely enjoyed the fruits of their efforts until late in life or enjoyed them vicariously through their descendants. Entrepreneurship will be more forthcoming if the rewards of money exceed the costs of risk bearing, hard work, and postponed gratification. Perkin's thesis stresses the benefit side in this equation; in Britain money bought more than just comfort. Money acquired in commerce or industry was less tainted by the stigma of being "nouveau riche." The example set by the elite (the landowning gentry and aristocracy) profoundly influenced the values and attitudes of those who aspired to be like them. In Britain, far more than on the Continent, a materialist element had come to dominate these values. As Landes (1969, p. 70) put it, "The British nobility and gentry chose to meet the newcomers on middle ground: they affirmed their distinction of blood and breeding; but they buttressed it with an active and productive cultivation of gain."

Still, some empirical questions have to be answered before the connection between wealth and status can be accepted as one explanation of England's success.[34] Was the correlation between wealth and social status stronger in Britain than elsewhere? Holland was an urban, capitalist, bourgeois society, indicating that having the "right kind of society" is not a sufficient condition for a successful Industrial Revolution.[35] But what about France? In the eighteenth century

---

themselves 'gentlemen' if the size of their personal estates seemed to warrant the title" (Urdank, 1990, p. 52).

[34] Perkin's further attempts to explain the timing of the Industrial Revolution in terms of population growth and demand are far less successful. Some of these issues will be dealt with later in this chapter.

[35] For economic explanations of the Netherlands' failure to industrialize, see Mokyr (1976a) and Griffiths (1979).

aristocratic titles could be bought, and much of the nobility was a *noblesse de robe*, i.e., of bourgeois origins. Was the aversion to parvenus among the upper class stronger in France than in England? Although the latter question cannot readily be answered, there were two important differences between the two countries in this respect. First, in France, too, money could enhance social status, but the respectable local country gentleman who ran the affairs of the parish was a wholly British institution. Second, in France social status was often literally bought. The price of a noble title reflected a tax exemption, so that the sale of titles was not a one-way street by which the crown soaked up wealth. But nobility implied high standards of consumption in the noblesse oblige tradition. In England, by contrast, wealth was correlated with influence and respect, but one did not necessarily have to part with the former to attain the latter.

Furthermore, Perkin's logic implies an almost dialectical dynamism of the supply of entrepreneurship. If merchants and manufacturers made money in order to buy themselves or their descendants the good life of the country squire, the ranks of the entrepreneurial class would be constantly depleted. Upward mobility by means of wealth thus also led to the eventual destruction of the entrepreneurial class. Having attained their new status, the new elite tended to slam the door shut to further entrants. This "gentrification" of the commercial and industrial class, which has been blamed for the decline of Britain's leadership in the Victorian age (Wiener, 1981), seems a logical extension of Perkin's thesis. Because the debate on the "failure" of Victorian Britain lies outside the scope of this volume, this implication cannot be pursued here.

Society is, of course, more than attitudes and mind-sets. Its importance lies above all in the institutions within which economic activity takes place. Some institutional setups are more suitable for technological change than others, and although institutions eventually may respond to economic and political needs and pressures, these responses are sufficiently sluggish to allow us to point to institutions as a "causal" factor in economic development. Institutions defined property rights and thus the rate of return on inventive and entrepreneurial activity. This has been stressed by North (1981, 1990). In North's interpretation, property rights and incentives are the crucial elements in the story. He stresses (North, 1990, p. 75) that patent laws and other institutions raised the rate of return on innovation and thus stimulated the process of technological progress. Britain's patent law dates back to 1624, whereas France and most of the rest of the Continent did not have such laws on the books until after 1791.

The exact role of the patent system in Britain's Industrial Revolution is hard to determine. A patent is only one way of encouraging a potential inventor to spend time and money on the uncertain road to success. The French government, for instance, awarded pensions through the Royal Academy and through so-called *privilèges* (administered by the king), which were also intended to encourage invention (MacLeod, 1991). North overrates the effective protection that the British patent system provided to inventors; court decisions in infringement cases tended to be unsympathetic to inventors, and patents were overthrown on minor technical points such as scribes omitting one line. In some cases, financial success came without patent protection, as in the case of Richard Arkwright. The court's invalidation of his patent did not stop him from becoming extremely rich. In other cases, when inventions failed to be patented or when patents were lost because of technicalities, inventors were rewarded by Parliament in recognition of their social value. The mule's inventor, Samuel Crompton, and the power loom's inventor, Edmund Cartwright, were both the beneficiaries of Parliament's gratefulness. Moreover, patents and infringements of them led to endless court battles that sapped the energy and resources of technologically creative people. Arkwright and his sometime partner, Jedediah Strutt, spent much time in courts defending their patents. Some innovators, such as John Kay, the inventor of the flying shuttle, and the Fourdrinier brothers, who pioneered the paper-making machine, were ruined by litigation. In many cases, inventors decided to protect their monopoly rents by keeping their inventions secret. If "reverse engineering" was not likely or if the inventor could make his money by employing his machines to produce a final output rather than by selling capital goods, this was often tried. Yet secrecy had its risks: Industrial espionage was an ever-present danger.[36]

The effects of patents on the rate of innovative activity is further clouded by the fact that the patentability of innovations differed a great

---

[36] Richard Roberts, one of the leading engineers of his time, felt that "no trade secret can be kept very long; a quart of ale will do wonders in that way" (cited by Dutton, 1984, pp. 108-111).

deal from industry to industry. Christine MacLeod has estimated that nine out of ten patents arose in industries that saw little innovation and concludes that patents were related to technological change in an erratic and tangential manner and were more closely associated with "emergent capitalism" than with inventiveness (1988, pp. 145, 156-157). Moreover, patent protection, as is well known, is a double-edged sword. If a patentee is a monopolist, the invention's diffusion will be retarded and the industry will grow at a slower pace, unless the inventor's firm can expand as fast as the industry as a whole. The fundamental dilemma in the economics of technological change is that there is a trade-off between generating an invention and its diffusion.[37] The more monopoly protection is used to encourage invention, the slower its adoption and thus its social benefits. Patents imply the choice of a particular point on this trade-off; so do alternative arrangements. Moreover, patents may have had a mixed effect on invention itself; in some cases owners of wide-ranging and vague patents used their power to close avenues they deemed undesirable or potentially competitive. The best-known example of that in the period of the Industrial Revolution is Watt's use of his patent to resist the development of high-pressure steam engines.

All the same, the importance of the patent system for Britain's technological success cannot be wholly dismissed by these objections. As Adam Smith was the first to point out in his *Lectures on Jurisprudence*, patents alone preserved some automatic correlation between the value of an invention and the return received by the inventor. The French system of rewards administered by a governmental committee made the return on invention dependent on political clout more than on the test of the market (Gillispie, 1980, pp. 459-478). Moreover, incentives refer to potential inventors' *ex ante* expectations of being financially rewarded if they were successful. Disappointments and lawsuits were relevant to further technological progress only to the extent that they discouraged others. By definition, each patent is

---

[37] The efficient solution maximizing the social savings could be attained if the patentee could license his patent out and earn royalties equivalent to the monopoly rent. Yet setting the correct prices and monitoring the arrangements were a major difficulty. MacLeod (1991) concludes that only after 1800 did British patentees learn to exploit licenses more profitably, and even then only a tiny minority mastered the art at the cost of extensive litigation.

inherently different from every other one, and so the failure of an inventor to secure a return on his efforts may not have necessarily indicated to others that their fate would be the same. The desire to patent new inventions did not weaken during the Industrial Revolution. Goethe may have been somewhat naive when he wrote that the British patent system's great merit was that it turned invention into a "real possession, and thereby avoids all annoying disputes concerning the honor due," Yet in 1845 the Swiss industrialist Johann C. Fischer concluded that "the system of patents so early introduced there may well have . . . been responsible for manufactured goods possessing so high a degree of perfection" (cited in Klemm, 1964, pp. 173, 296). Britain's greatest post-1830 inventor, Henry Bessemer, believed that "the security offered by patent law to persons who expend large amounts of money in pursuing novel inventions, results in many new and important improvements in our manufactures" (Bessemer, [1905] 1989, p. 82). Not all inventors concurred with this view, but if enough of them saw it this way, the British patent system deserves some credit. H. I. Dutton (1984, p. 203) has argued that for many inventors patents were the only means by which they could appropriate a sufficient return for their effort and that patents thus provided security in an exceptionally risky activity. The patent law was often poorly defined and the courts unfriendly to inventors, but it remained in most cases the best incentive for inventive activity. Dutton argues that the patent laws were a "slightly imperfect" system that created an ideal system in which there was enough protection for inventors to maintain an incentive for inventions, yet was not so watertight as to make it overly expensive for users. If inventors systematically overestimated the rate of return on inventions by not fully recognizing the weaknesses of the patent system, they would have produced more innovations than in a world of perfect information.

d. Government and Politics

British political institutions differed greatly from those of most European countries, and recent thinking by economists has tended to place considerable emphasis on political elements. Some of the differences are obvious: Despite the fact that the Industrial Revolution coincided with two major wars, there was no fighting on British soil, and except for a few serious but localized riots and an abortive uprising in Ireland, Britain was spared the turmoil and turbulence of the

Continent after 1789. The need to allocate resources to the war effort involved a substantial effort on the part of Britain, and the disruptions of trade and the disequilibria caused by the wars and blockades clearly slowed down the development of the British economy (Crouzet, 1987; Mokyr and Savin, 1976). Yet these disruptions were far more deeply felt on the Continent, and the wars widened the gap between Britain and its main competitors in Europe.

Douglass C. North (1981, pp. 147, 158-170) has argued that the British Industrial Revolution was facilitated by better-specified property rights, which led to more efficient economic organization in Britain. The link between property rights and economic growth consists of the greater efficiency in the allocation of resources resulting from the equalization of private and social rates of return and costs. Property rights in innovation (patents and trademarks), better courts and police protection, and the absence of confiscatory taxation are examples of how the same phenomenon could raise the rate of innovative activity and capital accumulation.[38] North points out that well-specified property rights are not the same as laissez-faire. The former were by far more important because they reduced transaction costs and thereby allowed more integrated markets, higher levels of specialization, and the realization of economies of scale. Britain on the eve of the Industrial Revolution was far from a laissez-faire economy, but the net effects of the policies and regulations on the Industrial Revolution remain a matter of dispute. What is clear is that by the time of the Industrial Revolution Britain's government was one of, by, and for private

---

[38] Confiscatory taxation during the French Revolution took three main forms in Europe. First, there was outright confiscation of property, such as the Church lands and the assets of *emigrés* expropriated during the French Revolution. Second, raising armies by conscription, as practiced by France, constitutes a de facto confiscation of labor. Third, the French government (and subsequently the Dutch) defaulted on their debts by reducing interest payments on debts by two-thirds. Moreover, many innovators who had been voted pensions by the *ancien régime* were denied their payments, and some of them, like Nicholas Cugnot, the inventor of a steam-powered wagon, died in poverty. Nicholas Leblanc, the inventor of the soda-making process, tried in vain to make the revolutionary regime recognize his rights on his invention and in the end committed suicide.

property. Yet as the case of Holland demonstrates, that, too, was not sufficient cause for an Industrial Revolution.

More recently, North and Weingast (1989) survey the institutional changes that occurred in Britain in the wake of the Revolution of 1688, in which wealth holders increased their grip on power, and the government was put on a sound fiscal footing and committed itself to respect the existing distribution of property rights. They pose their question starkly: Had there been no Glorious Revolution in 1688, or had the Stuarts won, would there have been an Industrial Revolution? (p. 831). Although they wisely confess ignorance as to how to set up the counterfactual, they point to secure contracting and property rights as a precondition for specialization and impersonal exchange. Without denying the importance of secure contracts as a precondition for allocative efficiency, one could object that the Industrial Revolution was not first and foremost an example thereof. It was an example of Schumpeterian disequilibrium, in which the main dynamic elements came from innovation and rebellion against the status quo. Invention and change may well have come at the expense of an efficient allocation of resources and more static equilibrium conditions. Moreover, the impact of financial markets, the development of which is emphasized by North and Weingast, on the Industrial Revolution is still very much the subject of debate. Finally, it seems unwarranted to imply that before the Glorious Revolution contracts and property rights in Britain were insecure. By taxing according to prespecified and well-understood rules, and by gradually abandoning the Tudors' and Stuarts' reliance on monopoly rights as a source of crown revenues, the post-1689 regime continued a trend that had begun long before and was certainly well established by the Restoration of 1660.

The success of Britain in the late eighteenth century is perhaps surprising to those who firmly believe that taxes and government debts are a guarantee of economic disaster. In 1788, British GNP per capita is estimated to have been about 30 percent higher than that of the French, though such comparisons are inherently hazardous. What is perhaps more surprising is that the tax burden in Britain was almost twice what it was in France: 12.4 percent of GNP as opposed to 6.8 percent. Moreover, the British national debt as a proportion of GNP exceeded that of the French by more than threefold; yet because French finances were much less sound than the British, the annual debt service ratio was comparable (all figures from Weir, 1989, p. 98). These figures do not explain the Industrial Revolution in Britain, but they should serve as a warning for simple-minded explanations that view high taxes and government debts as a prescription for economic disaster. Despite its high taxes, Britain had a viable and strong economy, strong enough to withstand another quarter century of stress following the year to which these figures pertain.

Different in emphasis but equally unequivocal in its certainty about the role of politics in Britain's Industrial Revolution is the view advanced by Mancur Olson (1982). Olson's theory of economic growth is based on the idea that political bodies are subject to pressure groups pursuing the economic interests of their members, even if they come at the expense of society as a whole. Olson is thus led to associate periods of economic success, such as the Industrial Revolution, with the comparative weakness of such pressure groups. Britain during the Industrial Revolution, maintains Olson, was relatively free of class differences and by comparison a socially mobile society so that loyalty to a particular pressure group was not yet very strong. The Civil Wars of the seventeenth century, moreover, had created a stable nationwide government, which made Britain into a larger jurisdictional unit in which it was more difficult to organize pernicious pressure groups (Olson, 1982, pp. 78-83, 128).

Despite a number of inaccuracies, Olson's insight that technological progress depended to a great extent on the political environment is valuable.[39] As I have pointed out elsewhere (Mokyr, 1992b), technological progress almost inevitably runs into resistance by vested interests who stand to lose some of their rents as a result of the revaluation of physical and human capital. It is natural and rational for these groups to organize and try to resist the changes. Because that resistance by definition has to use nonmarket mechanisms, the government plays a pivotal role here. First, the technologically conservative forces might try to use existing organizations, such as guilds or even the government

---

[39] Olson writes (1982, p. 128) that the English Civil Wars "discouraged long-run investment" (a possible but wholly undocumented inference) but that "within a few decades after [the Civil War] it became clear that stable and nationwide government had been re-established in Britain [and] the Industrial Revolution was under way." "Under way" is, of course, an ambiguous phrase, but between the Restoration and the beginning of the Industrial Revolution, as commonly defined, a century or more (and not "a few decades") had passed.

itself, to pass and enforce regulations and legislation inimical to technological change. Second, they may try to use extralegal methods, such as violence, to try to suppress innovation. The attitude of the authorities is thus crucial in determining the outcomes of these struggles. On the whole, the British government during the Industrial Revolution consistently and vigorously supported innovation. Many of the obsolete laws and regulations that encumbered progress (for example by mandating precise technological practices in detail) were revoked. Labor organizations ("combinations," in the language of the day) that were seen as threatening the advance of technology were made illegal and had little effect. In 1809 Parliament revoked a sixteenth-century law prohibiting the use of gig mills in the wool-finishing trade, and five years later it did away with one of the pillars of regulation, the Statutes of Artificers and Apprentices. Violent protests, such as the Luddite riots, were forcefully suppressed by soldiers. As Paul Mantoux put it well many years ago, "Whether [the] resistance was instinctive or considered, peaceful or violent, it obviously had no chance of success" (Mantoux, 1928, p. 408).

Was Britain a laissez-faire economy, and does the Industrial Revolution therefore stand as a monument to the economic potential of free enterprise? In absolute terms, Britain certainly was not a pure laissez-faire economy. A large number of regulations, restrictions, and duties were on the books. But absolutes are not very useful here. Compared with Prussia, Spain, or the Hapsburg Empire, Britain's government generally left its businessmen in peace to pursue their affairs subject to certain restraints and rarely ventured itself into commercial and industrial enterprises. Seventeenth-century mercantilism had placed obstacles in the path of all enterprising individuals, but British obstacles were less formidable than those in France. More regions were exempt, and enforcement mechanisms were feeble or absent. One such enforcement mechanism, widely used on the Continent, was the craft guild, yet by the time of the Glorious Revolution of 1688, the craft guild in Britain had declined into insignificance (Nef, 1957, pp. 26, 32). Market forces were more powerful than politics, even if they were constrained to operate within a framework of laws and institutions produced by political forces. Mercantilism and regulation in eighteenth-century Britain was alive and well, yet it never took the extreme forms it took in France under Colbert and in Prussia under Frederick the Great. In Britain the public sector eschewed any entrepreneurial activity. During the heyday of the Industrial Revolution, even social-overhead projects that in most other societies were considered to have enough public advantages to warrant direct intervention of the state were in Britain left to private enterprise. Turnpikes, canals, and railroads were built in Britain without direct state support; schools and universities were private. Even the less invasive forms of state support, like the policies of William I of Orange in the Low Countries or the Saint-Simonians in France during the Second Empire, were notably absent in Britain. Until the end of the nineteenth century, the British government clearly was reluctant to invade what it considered to be the realm of free enterprise.

The general consensus among historians today is that the regulations and rules, most of them relics from Tudor and Stuart times, were rarely enforced. As the economy became more sophisticated and markets more complex, the ability of the government to regulate and control such matters as the quality of bread or the length of apprentice contracts without an expanding bureaucracy effectively vanished (Ashton, 1948, p. 95). The central government was left to control foreign trade, but most other internal administration was left to local authorities. Internal trade, the regulation of markets in labor and land, justice, police, county road maintenance, and poor relief were all administered by local magistrates. Although in principle these authorities could exercise considerable power, they usually elected not to. This de facto laissez-faire policy derived not so much from any libertarian principles as from the pure self-interest of people who already had wealth and were making more. By ignoring and evading rather than altogether abolishing regulations, Britain moved slowly, almost imperceptibly toward a free-market society. Except for its strictures against the state's intervention in foreign trade, *The Wealth of Nations* was a century out of date when it was published: What it advocated had already largely been accomplished (Perkin, 1969, p. 65).[40] Some regulations were more difficult to ignore than others.

---

[40] The Statute of Artificers (of 1563), for instance, so detested by Adam Smith, required that workers serve a formal apprenticeship before their employment in a trade. Yet in 1777 the calico printers admitted that fewer than 10 percent of their workers had served because "the trade does not require that the men they employ should be brought up to it; common labourers are sufficient" (Mantoux, 1928, p. 453).

The usury laws, which set a ceiling on all private interest rates, are thought by some historians to have had considerable impact on the allocation of resources (Ashton, [1955] 1972, pp. 27-28; Jeffrey Williamson, 1984). There is, however, evidence indicating that the usury laws were sufficiently evaded to limit their impact on the economy.[41]

Even when mercantilist regulations were enforced, their net effects were ambiguous. The silk and light woolen industries tried to stop the import of cheap Indian cottons. This resulted in the Calico Act, which prohibited the importation and sale of printed white calicoes, passed in 1721 and repealed in 1774, and a host of other measures and counter-measures. The maze of protection and subsidization was the confusing outcome of political pressures and counterpressures by interest groups that tried to keep out competition and keep in complements. Because fustians looked much like calicoes, the prohibition was widely evaded, although it remained a nuisance.[42] It has been argued that the mercantilist laws that prohibited the importation of calicoes stimulated the British cotton-printing industry and that high taxes and tariffs on white calicoes encouraged domestic production (Wadsworth and Mann, 1931, p. 144). More recently it has been argued that by encouraging fustians these regulations constituted a "legislative assistance that was important for the mechanization of Lancashire's growing industry," so that "British pragmatism appears in retrospect more productive than Dutch free trade or French style mercantilism" (O'Brien, Griffiths, and Hunt, 1991, pp. 415, 418). Yet evidence for any direct link between the protectionist measures taken and the technological breakthroughs in

---

[41] Although the usury laws were not capable of holding down private interest rates to 5 percent at all times, they distorted the capital market to a substantial degree. A Parliamentary Select Committee concluded in 1818 that "the laws regulating or restraining the rate of Interest have been extensively evaded and have failed of the effect of imposing a maximum on such rate. . . Of late years, from the constant excess of the market rate of interest above the rate limited by law, they have added to the expense incurred by borrowers on real security" (Great Britain, 1818, vol. VI, p. 141). See also Pressnell (1956, pp. 95, 318, 368, 428) and Cottrell (1980, pp. 7-8, 13).

[42] By 1736 fustians were explicitly exempted from the Calico Act, and by this time they contained two-thirds cotton and one-third linen, so that fustians "replaced Indian calicoes as the prime threat to light woollens and silks" (O'Brien, Griffiths, and Hunt, 1991, pp. 414-415).

cotton is absent. What we know with certainty is that mercantilist bounties and encumbrances to trade distorted the operation of the free market, and as soon as Arkwright's patent was secured and his machines producing, he petitioned for repeal of the Calico Act and was granted it in 1774. Most of the important inventions in cotton, including the mule, cylindrical printing, the power loom, and the carding machine, followed in the decade after the repeal of these acts. Until more evidence is forthcoming, it seems reasonable to conclude that technological progress occurred *in spite of* rather than *thanks to* the meddling of a special-interest-driven Parliament in the price mechanism.

The Bubble Act, passed in 1720, required a private act of Parliament to establish a common-stock corporation. However, modern scholars have increasingly realized that this impediment, too, was more an inconvenience than a real obstacle to business activity (Cottrell, 1980, p. 10).[43] Even after the Bubble Act was repealed in 1825 and all remaining obstacles to joint-stock company formation were removed in the Joint Stock Companies Act of 1856, there was no sudden rush to create joint-stock corporations. The prohibition on incorporation was a less formidable obstacle to technological progress and industrial growth than might appear. The same applies to the restrictions on the export of textile machinery and the emigration of artisans (Jeremy, 1977; 1981, chap. 3).

Not all government intervention was equally ineffective, of course. A few government monopolies, such as the East India Company, survived well into the nineteenth century. Moreover, free trade remained a far cry from reality until well into the nineteenth century. During the Napoleonic Wars, tariffs were raised to unprecedented heights (peaking at 64 percent of the value of imports in 1822). A slow trend toward lower tariffs began in 1825, culminating in the abolition of the Corn Laws in 1846 and the repeal of the Navigation Acts, which had severely limited foreign freighters from carrying British goods, in 1849-1854. Yet in the first half of the nineteenth century, Britain's trade was more

---

[43] The Bubble Acts could be evaded by organizing companies under a trust deed, a legal form widely used in the woolen cloth industry in Yorkshire (Hudson, 1983).

restricted by tariff legislation than France's (Nye, 1991a). To be sure, tariffs and navigational restrictions were widely evaded, too.[44]

Another area in which government intervention was important and the law far from a dead letter was poor relief. Here the difference between Britain and the Continent is striking. Nowhere in the world can one find a well-organized, mandatory poor relief system like the English one. The Old Poor Law, sometimes erroneously referred to as "Speenhamland" (in fact, the Speenhamland system of allowances in aid of wages was used in a minority of counties), has had a notably bad press. Three major criticisms have been raised against it. One was the Malthusian complaint that outdoor relief subsidized childbearing and thus increased the birthrate. A second criticism, already mentioned by Adam Smith ([1776] 1976, p. 157), was that the Old Poor Law (and particularly the Settlement Acts) encumbered the free movement of labor and thus hindered its reallocation in a society in which labor markets played an ever-increasing role (Polanyi, [1944] 1985, pp. 77-102; Ashton, 1948, p. 111). Finally, the standard complaint against the Old Poor Law was that it impaired the incentive to work by distorting the leisure-income trade-off, or, in the language of the time, encouraged indolence and sloth.

These criticisms have not fared well in recent years. Indeed, it seems likely that the effects of the Poor Laws on the Industrial Revolution were not nearly as negative as used to be thought. The demographic argument against them has been criticized by James Huzel (1969, 1980). More recently, however, the important work of Boyer (1990) has vindicated Malthus's approach. The use of multivariable regression shows that the introduction of child allowances after 1795 did have an important effect on birthrates.[45] Whether the Old Poor Law was

---

[44] Smuggling was widespread, as can be verified from the fact that at times, when tariffs were reduced substantially, imports increased by a much larger proportion than the reduction of the tariff and a reasonable guess about the elasticity of demand would imply. For example, when the tariff on coffee was reduced by two-thirds in 1808, imports into Great Britain increased from 1.07 million to 9.3 million lbs. in 1809.

[45] The observed birthrate rose by 14 percent, according to estimates of Wrigley and Schofield (1981), between about 1780 and about 1820. Boyer estimates (1990, p. 170) that in the absence of child allowances, the birthrate would actually have declined by 6.4-9.2 percent. He concludes that allowances

somehow responsible for the creation of an army of able-bodied paupers is still unclear and awaits further research. In the absence of any a priori idea of the effect of the increase in birthrate on the Industrial Revolution, however, it is unclear what the long-term economic implications of this higher birthrate were. Moreover, even in the absence of a poor law, population would have grown, and its demographic effects were the most pronounced in the south of England.

As to the geographical immobility imposed by the Settlement Acts, these were to some extent alleviated by the Poor Law Removal Act of 1795 (35 Geo. III (1795) c. 101), which expressly forbade the ejectment of poor immigrants unless they actually became chargeable to the parish. Even before 1795 the system was "by no means such a check on mobility of labour as some of the older writers . . . supposed," because the option to evict was exercised in a haphazard and casual way (P. Styles, 1963, p. 62). Some contemporary opinion agrees with this finding. Sir F. M. Eden, whose opinion according to Redford was "as weighty as that of Adam Smith," thought that the Settlement Laws were too weakly enforced to constitute the hindrance to mobility alleged by Smith (Redford, [1926] 1964, p. 85). Perhaps the primary mechanism by which the Settlement Acts discouraged migration was their sheer complexity and the uncertainty that irregular enforcement implied for anyone contemplating migration. Since migration was, however, a risky undertaking under any circumstances, it is far from obvious to what extent the Old Poor Law made things worse.[46] More

---

in aid of wages did to some extent "create the poor which they maintain" (p. 142). The numbers he provides imply that in the absence of the poor laws, English population would still have been larger in 1826 than it was in 1781, but it would have grown at a much slower rate after 1795. A rough computation suggests that on Boyer's assumptions the population of England and Wales in 1826 without a poor law would have been 9.78 million instead of the 12.4 million estimated by Wrigley and Schofield. From a different perspective, McCloskey (1973) has also argued that the wage supplements paid under the Old Poor Law were likely to have reduced the supply of labor and thus may have raised wages, though the magnitude of this disincentive-to-work effect is unclear and the evidence for it rather weak.

[46] In 1832 out-migration was more important in Speenhamland parishes, which paid allowances in aid of wages or child allowances, in Kent than in non-Speenhamland parishes (Huzel, 1980, pp. 375-378).

to the point, Boyer's analysis shows that the overall magnitude of the Poor Law's effect on labor mobility bemoaned by Polanyi was negligible.[47]

As to the work-incentive effect stressed by T. R. Malthus and his followers, research carried out by Blaug in the 1960s has recently been reinforced by the work of Pollard (1978, pp. 109-110) and George Boyer (1990). They argue that the causality runs the other way: Wage-support payments were made in areas that suffered from seasonal unemployment and the decline of cottage industry, which explains the association of Speenhamland with the agricultural areas of England. Boyer's regressions provide little support for the hypothesis that outdoor relief caused an increase in voluntary unemployment, although it was not possible to estimate the relation between the two directly (Boyer, 1990, p. 142-143). The effect of poor-law variables on male labor income was statistically insignificant, which it could not have been if poor relief had been treated as a substitute for labor income.

Indeed, it could be maintained that the Poor Laws, despite their obvious flaws (in particular their nonuniformity), may have had some overall positive effects on the Industrial Revolution. A comparison with Ireland, which had no formal system of poor relief prior to 1838, bears this out (Mokyr, 1983; Solar, 1983). The social safety net provided by the Poor Laws allowed English individuals to take risks that would have been imprudent in Ireland, where starvation was still very much a possibility. In societies without such laws, self-insurance in the form of large families and liquid assets was widely held, whereas in England even the worst case rarely implied actual starvation. In a recent paper, Solar (1992) extends this argument to the creation of a wage-labor force. The main obstacle to the creation of a wage-labor force was the attachment of the rural population to land. Land served not only as a source of income but also as a form of insurance -- in times of duress it could be mortgaged or sold. It was also a form of old-age insurance; its inheritability made it a bargaining chip with which parents could persuade their children (or other heirs) to look after them in their old age (see also Guinnane, 1991). The existence of the British Poor Law

---

[47] The fact that the British Poor Law was a *national* system rather than a patchwork of local systems, as on the Continent, may have *increased* geographic mobility by reducing the uncertainty involved in migration (Solar, 1992).

provided a substitute for land for insurance purposes and thus reduced the need to cling to land at all costs, thus contributing to the creation of a proletariat needed for the factories and the railroad. The magnitude of this effect is of course not known, but it makes sense as economic analysis.

The Speenhamland system, by subsidizing workers in the off-season, assured a regular labor force during the busy seasons in agriculture (Boyer, 1990). A similar argument may be made for manufacturing: Workers could be laid off during periods of business slumps without fear of having the labor force emigrate or starve. Irish employers, on the other hand, complained about having to continue to pay their workers during slumps or risk losing them (Mokyr, 1983, p. 227). In addition, the practice of pauper apprenticeships and the recruitment of factory workers from workhouses run by local Poor Law guardians provided an important source of labor for the factories, especially in rural and small-town mills before 1800.[48] All this is not to argue, of course, that the Poor Laws somehow "caused" the Industrial Revolution. But it seems that a case can be made that their net effect was not nearly as negative as has been maintained and that they may have had hitherto unsuspected beneficial effects.

Another political difference between Britain and most other European countries was the lack of centralization of political power. Britain's system of government left most of the day-to-day management of affairs to local magistrates, who were, on the whole, respectable residents for whom administration was a form of leisure activity. Whether this government by amateurs was an effective way of providing government services is another matter, but one effect was the relative unimportance

---

[48] Some of the transactions between Poor Law authorities and mill owners resembled nothing as much as slave trade; e.g., the purchase of seventy children from the parish of Clerkenwell by Samuel Oldknow in 1796 (Mantoux, 1928, p. 411). Pollard ([1965] 1968, pp. 194-195) cites the sanctimonious claim by some notorious users of child labor that these pauper apprentices were "more expensive" than paid labor and that they were employed out of civic duty. For a similar view, see Collier (1964, p. 45). Recruiting agents were often sent to scour the surrounding countryside in search of workhouse labor, and some of these children were brought in from the other end of the country, which indicates that for some industrialists pauper apprentices were indeed a cheap and satisfactory form of labor.

of London as an administrative and cultural center when compared to Madrid, Paris, St. Petersburg, or Vienna. In France, for example, Paris traditionally drained large amounts of talent from the provinces, and provincial centers of learning and technology were of small importance compared to those in the capital. This rural-urban brain drain would not have mattered, of course, if industrialization could have been concentrated near the capital of the country. Interestingly, this did not happen anywhere. Neither Brussels nor Paris, nor Berlin, nor Amsterdam, nor any other major capital city in Europe became a center of modern industry. Although some manufacturing activity developed around the capitals, the main centers of modern industry were usually elsewhere. As a result, a highly centralized state in which the capital city drained the countryside of ambitious and able men, strongly attracted to "where the action is," operated at a disadvantage compared to a decentralized state like Britain.[49] In Britain the situation was radically different; provincial institutions like the Manchester Literary and Philosophical Society or the universities of Glasgow and Edinburgh, located near centers of industry, were of central importance to the technological developments of the eighteenth century. Wrigley (1967) has argued more or less the opposite, ascribing to London a major role in creating the conditions leading to the Industrial Revolution. The size of London relative to England's population and its enormous needs in terms of food, fuel, and other products seem to support his claim. Sheer size, however, is not necessarily an advantage. A top-heavy capital might just as well be viewed as imposing a major cost on the country. Wrigley's argument seems better suited to explain commercial development before 1750 than industrial development thereafter. During the Industrial Revolution, indeed, the demographic predominance of London declined somewhat. Between 1650 and 1750 London's share of English population rose from about 7 percent to 11.8 percent. By 1800 this percentage had declined to 10.5 percent.[50]

---

[49] See Cardwell (1972, p. 126) for a similar argument. Interestingly, Ireland, with its centralized government in Dublin, conforms more to the Continental than the British model.

[50] The London population estimates are from Wrigley (1967, p. 44). English population data (less Monmouth) are from Wrigley and Schofield (1981).

Some historians have argued that the British government stimulated the Industrial Revolution by creating a demand for military products, which led to rapid technological change in some industries (McNeill, 1982, pp. 210-212). It is true that some of these externalities can be identified. Cort's puddling-and-rolling technique was completed when its inventor was working on a contract for the Admiralty. Wilkinson's lathe, which bored the accurate cylinders needed for Watt's steam engines, was originally destined for cannon. The correct test for the net impact of military demand is, however, the question whether in the absence of military demand these innovations would have been substantially slower in coming. On that issue most scholars are wisely cautious. Moreover, what little innovation that can be directly attributable to the war had few civilian spillover effects. A case in point is the well-known Portsmouth manufacture of wooden blocks for pulleys to be used on naval vessels, designed by two of the greatest engineers of the time, Marc Brunel and Henry Maudslay. Despite the precocity of this plant, which pioneered interchangeable parts as well as continuous flow processes, it was too specializd to have spillover effects on the civilian sector. Scholars largely agree that favorable external effects were relatively small and that on balance the economic impact of the wars between 1756 and 1815 were negative (Trebilcock, 1969, pp. 477-478; Hyde, 1977, pp. 112-116). Moreover, any hypothesis of a substantial positive effect of the government's war-related activities on technological progress encounters a difficulty: If military efforts created major technological externalities, why did France and other Continental countries not benefit from them to the same degree that Britain did? The research on the French iron industry, for example, shows that the revolutionary and Napoleonic wars did little to stimulate technological progress (Woronoff, 1984).

To summarize, most economic historians would agree that politics was a positive factor working in Britain's favor, although the magnitude of the effect, as well as its *modus operandi*, are still in dispute. The appropriate standard of judgment should be a comparative one, and it seems hard to disagree with the proposition that the specific form of government that had emerged in Britain created an environment that was more conducive to economic development than elsewhere. Some oppressive mercantilist laws were on the books, but most were successfully evaded. Britons were heavily taxed, but taxation was never allowed to become arbitrary and confiscatory. Most important, the right to own and manage property was truly sacrosanct, contrasting sharply with the confiscations and conscriptions on the Continent during the French Revolution and the Napoleonic era. Personal freedom -- with some exceptions -- was widely accepted in Britain. True, the Acts of Settlement remained on the books until 1834, but they were by no means as restrictive as the harsh requirements on the books in France and in Prussia, where workers were required to have *cahiers* or *Wanderbücher,* in which their employment was recorded, and which required them to ask for passes for journeys within the country. Serfdom was still very much in existence east of the Elbe in 1815. The cathartic revolutionary medicine administered to the Continent between 1789 and 1815 by the French was needed to prepare the rest of Europe for the modern age. But the medicine's immediate side effects were so painful that most of the Continent required many years and even decades to recover from the treatment and start to threaten Britain's lead. Britain did not need this harsh shock treatment, since it alone had learned to adapt its institutions to changing needs by more peaceful means, and the English Channel had sheltered it from undesirable political imports.

Britain's political stability contrasts sharply with the history of France, with its four major revolutions in the eight decades following 1789. But was political stability always an asset on the path toward modernization? If investors are wary of investment in politically unstable environments, political stability was an advantage and its absence had a negative effect on industrialization. But how important was that effect? The economic performance of powerful autocratic and "stable" regimes in Russia and Turkey was disappointing to say the least. Moreover, Olson (1982) has insisted that political stability is in fact a rather mixed blessing, because it permits the crystallization of pressure groups whose activities are, in Olson's view, the archenemy of economic development. It is thus unclear how much of the difference in economic development can be attributed to this factor.[51] Still, it is

---

[51] The revolutions in France may have increased the perceived insecurity of property and inhibited capital formation. Similarly, the continuous struggle between landlord and peasant in Ireland before the famine reduced the attractiveness of Ireland as a site for industrial capital (as is the case today in Ulster). The Civil War in Spain (1832-1839) and the Miguelite Wars in Portugal (1828-1834) had similar effects in the Iberian Peninsula.

no exaggeration to say that nowhere in the world was property perceived to be more secure than in Britain. Such security is important in part because it included intellectual property rights, such as patents and pensions awarded in recognition of breakthroughs. Moreover, much technological progress required capital goods in which they were "embodied," from the machinery itself to buildings and sites. Clearly, security of these assets from confiscation or private tresspass was necessary if such investments were to be sustained.

Finally, British society exhibited a degree of tolerance for deviant and heterodox ideas that was unusual, though not unique. Although tolerance was quite different from equal rights, Britain developed in the seventeenth century the ability to accommodate a high level of acceptance of different modes of thinking. The intolerance on the Continent toward dissidents led to the hemorrhage of technical talents from the southern Netherlands and France to countries where they were more welcome. As Landes (1983, p. 219) recounts it, after 1685 (when the Edict of Nantes was revoked) French industry was "crippled by the exodus of some of its best practitioners fleeing a wave of anti-Protestant bigotry and persecution." In many industries, France's loss was England's gain. The Belfast linen industry was, if not founded, certainly enhanced and developed by the technical know-how of Huguenot refugees, especially Louis Crommelin. Nicholas Dupin was an active promoter of companies and operated a number of paper mills in England. The great hydraulic engineer and lecturer John (Jean) Desaguliers, too, came from a Huguenot family as did Denis Papin, who had as much ground for claiming to be "the" inventor of the atmospheric engine as anyone. Crouzet, who has studied the financial activities of these refugees, states that the "persecution of the Huguenots [was] not only a crime, [it] was also a blunder, as France was impoverished by a brain drain which brought wealth to her rivals and enemies" (Crouzet, 1991, p. 224). The direct impact of these individuals on the aggregate economy may not have been vast, but that is less important than their significance as a symptom of the open-minded attitude of agreeing to disagree that flavors the British enlightenment. Such open-mindedness is essential if new technological ideas are to compete in the marketplace on their economic merits. The differences between Britain and the Continent were not absolute here either. At times Britain turned on its most innovative spirits, as it did to the inventor of the fly shuttle, John Kay, who ended up having to flee to

France, and as it did to the great chemist Joseph Priestley, whose unpopular political views caused a mob to burn down his house and forced him to flee to the United States. On the whole, however, the atmosphere in Britain was comparably comfortable for rebels and deviants, of which inventors in some sense are a subspecies.

e. Demand vs. Supply

A large and venerable literature links, in one form or another, the British Industrial Revolution to the growth of the home market, the expansion of consumer demand, and the growth of a "consumer revolution." From the point of view of economic analysis, technological change, capital accumulation, and the rise of the factory are primarily supply-side phenomena. Demand-side factors are more difficult to integrate into the story. Yet economic historians, beginning with a famous paper by Gilboy (1932), have always felt intuitively that demand should be given a parallel role. In price theory it is typically assumed that demand and supply move independently of each other, so that an increase in demand means a movement *along* the supply curve. Any argument that links the Industrial Revolution with changes in demand relies on models that postulate a shift of the supply curve as a response to an increase in demand. North, relying on the work of Kenneth Sokoloff, has recently concluded that innovation and technological change are primarily determined by the "size of the market" (1990, p. 75; cf. Sokoloff, 1988). Less cautious writers have gone further and simply asserted that a "consumer revolution" was a necessary condition for the Industrial Revolution to occur. Thus in an influential paper stating the most extreme position on this question, Neil McKendrick (1982) writes that "the Consumer Revolution was the necessary analogue to the Industrial Revolution, the necessary convulsion on the demand side of the equation to match the convulsion on the supply side."[52]

As I argued in a paper first published in 1977 (Mokyr, 1985b), supply and demand are not symmetrical in long-term economic change. In a historical event like the Industrial Revolution, demand factors can only play a role under certain assumptions that have to be examined carefully. To start with, if production increased and technology changed

---

[52] For a critique of McKendrick's view, see for example Fine and Leopold (1990) and John Styles (1992).

because of a rise in demand for industrial goods, it has to be made clear why demand increased in the first place. Changes in demand are not exogenous to an economic system -- they occur for well-understood reasons. Population, of course, began to increase rapidly after 1750, but this was a worldwide phenomenon and it seems far-fetched to link it directly to the Industrial Revolution. Moreover, population growth in and of itself would increase the demand for food products more than the demand for manufactured goods, and the combination of growing population, bad harvests, and disruption of foreign supplies led to sharply higher agricultural prices, hardly a stimulus for industrial demand.[53] Export demand, too, although of some importance in some industries, does not seem to have been the crucial element in the Industrial Revolution that some scholars have claimed. The role of foreign trade in the Industrial Revolution, however, is sufficiently interesting and controversial to merit a separate discussion.

Secondly, the *modus operandi* of demand-side factors has to be specified and documented. For instance, an increase in aggregate demand due to, say, a rise in the propensity to consume or an autonomous growth in investment will only have an effect if the economy has large underutilized resources that can be brought into production. Such a Keynesian scenario may indeed have been of some importance. Evidence for large amounts of underutilized resources that were brought into production as aggregate demand expanded in the second half of the eighteenth century is, however, lacking. Or, if there were strong positive external economies between firms so that a sharp increase in demand led to an industry-wide decline in costs, demand would be directly linked to higher productivity. Yet the existence of such externalities is notoriously hard to demonstrate.

Thirdly, McKendrick's observations that the Consumer Revolution was somehow correlated with the Industrial Revolution seems open to a level of historical criticism from which it will not easily recover. Work by Lorna Weatherill (1988) suggests that if there was a Consumer Revolution at all, it peaked in the period 1680-1720. The long lag between that event and the Industrial Revolution makes any causal connection between the demand and changes in industrial technology

---

[53] The demand for agricultural goods was inelastic, so that increases in agricultural prices meant that a larger amount of income was spent on agricultural goods, reducing the amount left for manufactured goods.

difficult to support.[54] Equally damaging is the fact that consumer revolutions were taking place elsewhere in Europe. Seventeenth century Holland was, of course, the most obvious example thereof, but recently Cissie Fairchilds (1992) has employed probate records to show that France, like England, experienced a consumer revolution albeit fifty years later. The goods that the French bought were different, but on the whole the absence of an Industrial Revolution following the French increase in mass consumption leads Fairchilds to conclude that the two revolutions were largely independent of each other and that the changes in technology were shaped by supply, not demand-side elements.

The notion that somehow technological change takes place when the demand for it "arises" is thus clearly fallacious. Some scholars refuse to abandon the concept.[55] As T. S. Ashton argued long ago, invention was the mother of necessity, not the other way around (1948, p. 62).[56] All the same, it seems natural to pose the question whether technological change will occur without some prior knowledge that the goods produced will sell. Will it be possible to "find people with income and demand schedules capable of absorbing the increased output?" (Eversley, 1967, p. 211). It should be noted that unless the good produced is totally new and has no suitable substitutes (for example, aspirin), invention usually occurs in markets that already exist. When he improves an existing good or produces it at a lower price, the innovator taps into a market he already knows. By innovating, he undercuts his competitors or those selling close substitutes. The invention of the puddling-and-rolling technique or the continuous paper-making machines, for instance, can be represented as supply curves shifting to the right, with the market sliding down existing

---

[54]Among the goods, the consumption of which increased according to the probate records, were knitted goods, pottery, pipes, clocks, mirrors, and fancy textiles.

[55] Braudel (1984, p. 566) writes flatly that "the efficient application of technology lags, by definition, behind the general movement of the economy; it has to be called on, sometimes several times, to meet a precise and persistent demand."

[56] Economists and historians alike have treated the common wisdom that necessity is the mother of invention with contempt. For some examples of this literature, see Mokyr (1990a, p. 151, n. 1).

demand curves. A prior shift of the industry demand curve is not an essential part of the story.

Still, this does not mean that demand played no role in generating technological change. Adam Smith himself noted that the division of labor was limited by the extent of the market and strongly believed that the division of labor itself was the main agent of technological progress. He thought that highly specialized workmen were more likely to come up with inventions.[57] Innovation usually involved substantial fixed costs, and thus a minimum level of sales was expected by the innovator. In 1769 Matthew Boulton wrote to his partner James Watt, "It is not worth my while to manufacture your engine for three counties only, but I find it very well worth my while to make it for all the world" (cited by Scherer, 1984, p. 13). Some minimum level of demand was thus necessary to cover the fixed costs of research and development. An expansion of demand, through the integration of markets or through a growth in population and income or through an increase in export demand, could thus have stimulated invention.

In fact, however, fixed costs, including those of research and development, remained relatively small in most industries, as the large

---

[57] Smith supports this view by the story of a boy who, while operating one of the first steam engines, tied a string to the handle of a valve, allowing it to open and shut automatically. As Cannan points out in his notes, the story is apocryphal (Smith [1776] 1976, pp. 13-14). On the whole, Smith's ideas of the connection between the division of labor and technological change seem to be lacking in persuasion. He postulates that "the greater the number [of laborers in a workhouse], the more they naturally divide themselves into different classes and subdivisions of employment. More heads are occupied in inventing the most proper machinery for executing the work of each, and it is, therefore, more likely to be invented" (Smith, [1776] 1976, pp. 96-97). In some cases there may be merit to this argument. Some machines were made to mimic the motions of human arms, and the simpler the task, the more such imitation was possible. A division of labor between workers and engineers could create a special class of outsiders who could observe the production process and suggest improvements. Yet how much division of labor was necessary to create the conditions necessary for invention? It could just as well be argued that rigid specialization stifles the cross-fertilization between different activities that is the source of much technological creativity. Adam Smith's own career, incidentally, seems a good counterexample of his belief in the benefits of specialization (Brenner, 1987, pp. 109-110).

number of firms indicates. The costs of invention were small relative to the costs of production. Although men like Crompton and Trevithick worked for many years on their inventions, these costs would still have been covered in a much smaller market. This was true whether industry demand was stationary, expanding, or even contracting. It is, of course, true that in a highly fragmented economy, with high transport costs or internal barriers to trade, the competitive model does not hold. Szostak (1991) maintains that the increase in demand engendered by improved transport led to regional specialization and an accelerated rate of technological progress. Yet, as he realizes, a more integrated economy is not quite the same as an expansion of market demand, even if for the individual producer they may be indistinguishable. In Szostak's model, the *primum mobile* is an improvement in transportation, itself a supply-side phenomenon.

Where changes in demand can and do matter is when demand shifts from an industry that is relatively impervious to technological change to one that is not. It is, for example, quite clear that of the three large textile industries -- wool, cotton, and linen -- cotton fibers lent themselves best to mechanization (although worsted yarns were also well adapted to Arkwright's rollers). A change in demand in favor of cotton would increase output, and insofar as technological change was a function of the quantities produced (as in learning-by-doing phenomena), demand shifts could have affected the rate of technological progress. Demand for cotton, moreover, was price elastic, which means that for any given shift in supply a large increase in sales could be realized leading to further learning. Yet economic analysis sounds a warning bell: The elasticity of demand is important, but a single inventor in an existing competitive industry always faces a very elastic demand curve, much more so than the industry as a whole. All the same, the strong demand for cotton clothes, due in part to fashion, operated as a "focusing device," in Rosenberg's (1976) terminology, with inventors directing their energies to an industry that was expanding.

The same is true for the "leapfrogging" models proposed by Landes (1969), in which a sudden increase in the productivity of one activity (such as weaving) created a demand for improvement in the other, complementary activity (spinning). Sudden demand-induced imbalances may focus the attention of inventors on a profitable avenue, but they do not constitute a complete theory of technological change. Why are some "bottlenecks" solved by technological change while others have

to be accommodated by massive reallocations of resources?[58] Markets
for knowledge existed, to some extent, and a sudden surge in demand
for technical knowledge might well have led to more technical
innovations. Yet as Ian Inkster, in a recent criticism of this hypothesis
points out, if this were the case we should have observed a *higher* price
for this knowledge, which eventually would have choked off the rate
of growth (Inkster, 1991, p. 69). Yet, if anything, the reverse was the
case.

Economists interested in economic growth in the past few years have
come to realize that the standard assumptions of constant returns and
limited externalities do not necessarily hold in historical reality.
Relaxing these assumptions leads to radically different insights into the
dynamics of an economy. Positive feedback can occur, for instance,
when there are learning effects or under increasing returns. In those
cases technological change leads to lower prices, which could lead to
even lower prices. Thus, as historians are gradually learning from
evolutionary biology and chaos theory, accidents and contingency
matter a great deal, and fairly small historical events can set an
economy off into one direction or another.[59] Minor shifts in demand
could trigger the economy to move one way or another and thus could
have been "causal" in the Industrial Revolution (O'Brien and Engerman,
1991). Alfred Marshall, more than any other neoclassical economist,
realized the dangers that such production technologies implied for the
static market equilibrium that is at the heart of standard economics. Yet
it is important to note that although such models are likely to increase

---

[58] Two examples will suffice: In the cotton industry, carding, spinning,
weaving, and bleaching were all complementary, and improvements in one of
these areas stimulated the others. Yet some activities defied mechanization: The
planting and picking of cotton could not be mechanized, which had
momentous consequences for the history of the southern United States. In coal
mining, too, an increase in demand led to relatively few innovations in mining
technology. Here markets replaced the innovation process: The proportion of
workers in the coal and lignite mines in Europe subsequently increased
everywhere, despite the rather obvious shortcomings of this employment.

[59] Paul Mantoux realized this long ago when he pointed out that "only a
negligible quantity of ferment is needed to effect a radical change in a
considerable volume of matter" (1928, p. 103). The best modern papers on this
topic are by Brian Arthur (1988, 1989).

our understanding of historical change, they depend on certain conditions to hold, none of which have ever been satisfactorily demonstrated to have been of great import in Britain during this period: economies of scale, strong externalities, learning effects, and similar sources of positive feedback.[60]

A different approach to the "demand hypothesis" has been proposed recently in a paper by Jan de Vries (1992), in which he argues that changes in preferences could be of importance in explaining some of the economic changes in eighteenth-century Britain. De Vries argues, essentially, that the period was characterized by two separate events: a *supply*-driven *Industrial* Revolution and a *demand*-driven set of changes in household behavior that he calls an "industrious revolution." The idea focuses on the household as a decision-making process: The household can allocate its resources to production for the market or to household production. In premodern Europe, as is still true today, the existence of household work makes the concept of leisure hard to define. De Vries points out that market purchases and household production are imperfect substitutes for each other: Child rearing, food preparation, apparel making, and personal services can be purchased or homemade, but the products are not identical. An increased preference for the consumption of purchased goods requires cash, however, and thus implies greater labor force participation and market orientation. The resources thus reallocated were not idle before, nor were they absorbed by leisure, strictly speaking; they are simply deployed differently. The allocation between household and market depends simultaneously on preferences and on the relative efficiency of the household in producing for its own consumption or for the market.

The industrious revolution, in de Vries's view, was thus a change in allocation from production by, in, and for the household to a more market-oriented behavior. The net result was a vast increase in specialization on a microlevel: Workers came to produce, by and large,

---

[60] One tireless advocate of the role of demand in the Industrial Revolution (McKendrick, 1982) speaks repeatedly of "mass markets," which suggests mass production, an important source of increasing returns. Yet as Styles (1992) has recently warned, applying modern terms of this nature to British manufacturing before 1850 -- manufacturing without interchangeable parts, without continuous flow processes, highly dedicated tools, or uniform standards -- is misleading.

one or two products and buy everything else. Although an exogenous change in preferences cannot be ruled out, such a redeployment could have come as a result of technological changes.[61] First, better technology created and brought close to home some of the market-produced goods that the British consumer wanted to buy: cotton clothes, toys, adornments, tableware, kitchen utensils, clocks, books, and so on. As the array of goods that the consumer could buy increased and their price fell, the consumer would be more inclined to substitute cash income for housework. Second, the technological changes during the Industrial Revolution were biased in favor of production for the market. The factory was of course the obvious locus of the specialization of labor, but even those workers who remained at home found increasingly that they could do better by buying the goods they needed while producing for the market.[62]

The result of the industrious revolution was an alleged increase in the participation of women and children in the labor market, which caused income as traditionally measured to increase (McKendrick, 1974). De Vries (1992, p. 49) notes that the prominent role of woman and child labor during the Industrial Revolution represented a continuation and intensification of an already established trend toward greater paid labor force participation. As he points out, this movement did not start in 1750. It can be traced to the rise of market-oriented cottage industries ("protoindustrialization"), in which women and children played a major role. As the Industrial Revolution progressed, the trend in labor force participation and contribution to household earnings seems to be subject to complex and often contradictory forces (Horrell and Humphries, 1992b). On the whole, the data suggest that the movements over time of non-male earnings declines in the long run after 1815 or

---

[61] De Vries points out that a change in preferences in favor of market-purchased goods would increase the marginal utility of money income. Yet reductions in the prices of these goods would have the same effect, because it is the *ratio* of marginal utility to the price of market goods that is the critical variable here.

[62] Some inventions, particularly those that revolutionized the household in the late nineteenth century, operated in the other direction. Thus the invention of the vacuum cleaner and the washing machine would lead to an increased production of these services by household members rather than buy them at the market.

1820, though the movements differed across regions and occupations. While the wives of elite workers in the formal sector such as factory operators and colliers could retreat to a quasi-middle-class homemaker's existence, those of outworkers and artisans experienced declining household income, forcing them to work harder. Yet at the same time the demand for their services declined. With income and substitution effects thus working in opposite directions, and with the labor force's structure changing, it is not surprising that the actual picture produced by the data is confusing.

All the same, before 1800 or so the trend towards greater market participation accelerated and increased the effective labor input per worker by increasing the length of the labor year and intensifying the pace of work. The labor year could be extended in part by the reduction of seasonal unemployment through technical changes in the transport sector that made it possible to move materials and workers around with greater ease or through improvements in lighting technology that made it cheaper to work at night. Consumption of leisure declined as old and venerable institutions, such as "St. Monday" (the custom of taking Mondays off to recover from the weekend), were abandoned. There is also evidence collected by Clark that indicates that British workers worked at higher intensity than others (Gregory Clark, 1987a). Perhaps the most interesting explanation of this phenomenon is the better level of nutrition that Britons enjoyed by this time, which permitted them to expend more energy in physical labor.[63]

Growing specialization and commercialization, an increasing reliance on the market, and the decline of "autoconsumption" preceded and accompanied the Industrial Revolution. As we have noted, to some extent these trends were themselves caused by the technical changes and to some extent they further stimulated additional technological changes. The idea of the "industrious revolution" is an important one, but it is not tantamount to restoring demand as a central factor in the economic changes that transformed the British economy. Much of the growing reliance on the market was supply-driven, and although changing preferences toward market-produced goods buoyed demand for the products that the new technologies supplied, the contemporaneity of these two trends was only partial and to some extent accidental.

---

[63] This point was first made in a pioneering paper by Freudenberger and Cummins (1976). For more recent work, see Fogel (1989).

f. Foreign Trade

On the eve of the Industrial Revolution, Britain was in many ways an open economy. It exported close to 15 percent of its GNP. Exotic goods, brought in from Asia, South America, and Africa, were widely consumed. Grain moved into the country in years of scarcity and out in years of abundance. People, both emigrants and tourists, came and went. Capital moved in and out of the country with ease. Intellectuals corresponded with their colleagues overseas, and ideas -- technical and philosophical -- moved back and forth over the channel and the Atlantic. It seems natural that this openness would have been an advantage for Britain, setting it apart from such comparatively closed societies as Russia, Spain, or Turkey. Yet the mechanism linking this openness to the Industrial Revolution is far from clear. Part of the difficulty is that during most of the period of the Industrial Revolution political and military conflict disrupted the international economy. Between 1760 and 1815 only two short periods of peace (1763-1776 and 1783-1793) punctuated an otherwise long era of war, blockades, and embargoes. There is also a logical question how trade affected other variables such as industrial technology beyond the obvious consideration of the importation of essential raw materials.

The role of foreign trade in the British Industrial Revolution is hotly contested. Some of the most prestigious scholars in the field have vehemently denied any essential role for exports. Thomas and McCloskey (1981) start their essay by citing Deane and Cole to the effect that overseas trade was of central importance to the expansion of the economy and then add an ominous "we shall see," arriving ultimately at the conclusion that "the strongest effect between commerce abroad and industry at home was from industrialization to commerce, not the reverse. Trade was the child of industry." Trade theorists such as Charles Kindleberger (1964, pp. 264-266) and Ronald Findlay (1982) have come to the same conclusion. Many traditional historians are also of the same opinion, including the leading modern scholar of British overseas trade in this period, who writes:

> I share the view that overseas trade did not have an important *direct* role either in bringing about the Industrial Revolution or in supporting the first stages of its progress. . . . The initiative came from the supply side, from technical change. . . . Though a combination of changes made up the Industrial Revolution, the principal driving forces came from the nature of the inventions in the textile industry . . . and the efficacy of

these inventions, which lifted the market for these inventions, at home and abroad, to an entirely new level. . . . Overseas trade made little contribution to the advent of the Industrial Revolution itself and was not essential in the early stages of its development. Its importance reappeared in the further expansion of the mature industrial economy (Davis, 1979, pp. 62-63).

Yet foreign trade as an essential impetus to the growth of the British economy is a tenacious concept. A recent paper by O'Brien and Engerman (1991) has tried to revive its importance by criticizing the assumptions made by economists who minimize the role of foreign trade. They appear to favor Adam Smith's "vent for surplus" theory of exports and even mercantilist ideas of "employment-creating" exports over the Ricardian notions of comparative advantage. They conclude that "domestic exports may be designated . . . as clearly important and necessary components of industrial growth that occurred in Britain in the eighteenth century" (p. 207).

At least some of the sharp differences of opinion that arise between O'Brien-Engerman and their opponents result from different formulations of the question. Foreign trade's importance can be analyzed in different terms. The *static* question is whether the high level of exports (about 16 percent of national income in 1800) was essential to the high level of income in Britain at that time. The *rate of change* question is whether British income would have grown as fast as it did had it not been for export growth. Finally, a *dynamic* question could be raised as to whether the technological and other supply-side changes we associate with the Industrial Revolution would have occurred equally in a closed economy or one in which exports were stagnant.

Of the three, the answer to the *static* question seems to be the most obvious. Foreign trade was necessary if Britain was to import goods she could not produce for herself or could produce only at enormous cost. Tropical groceries (sugar, tobacco, spices, tea), European foodstuffs (wine, dried fish, corn in years of high prices), and raw materials (timber, hemp, high-quality ores, tar, and of course raw cotton) had to be brought in from overseas. O'Brien and Engerman (1991, pp. 201-202) point out that for this reason, in a closed economy Britain's real income would have been substantially lower, though it is hard to know by how much without specifying what the next best substitutes were. The difference between an open and a hypothetical closed economy was the "gain from trade," and it was of course large because trade occurred in large part with economies whose factor endowments were radically different from Britain's. However, much if not most of this gain was well in place by 1760, when the ratio of exports to GNP was close to its level in 1801 (14.6 percent and 15.7 percent respectively); by the time the first Industrial Revolution came to an end, the ratio had fallen to a level below that of 1760 (Crafts, 1985a, p. 131).

Was the *growth* of exports an "engine of growth" in the period of the Industrial Revolution? The question seems somewhat moot, given that there is a growing consensus that growth itself was comparatively modest before 1831. The intellectual resources that have been dedicated to explain British economic growth before 1830 by growing exports may have been misallocated now that it turns out that this gowth was far less impressive than was hitherto supposed. For what it is worth, however, the evidence suggests that domestic supplies grew faster than foreign demand, so that foreign demand was more a passive than an active factor. After 1800, when more data become available, we can be more certain that British supply increased faster than foreign demand, because Britain's net barter terms of trade worsened continuously (Thomas and McCloskey, 1981, p. 101).[64] At the same time, it seems plausible that Britain's single factoral terms of trade (in which the prices are weighted by the productivity of domestic factors of production) improved, so that the purchasing power of the average Briton to buy imports continued to rise due to growing productivity.

Manufacturing products, of course, were exported in large quantities, and taken together foreign markets would have been difficult to replace. The ratio of exports to gross industrial output increased sharply, from 24.4 percent to 35.2 percent between 1700 and 1760, a period in which output was growing only slowly. Oddly enough, the ratio fell sharply in the subsequent decades, and despite a recovery in the closing years of the century, it never reached that proportion again. The proportions are provided in Table 1.2:

---

[64] The somewhat more uncertain calculations made by Deane and Cole (1969, pp. 319-321) for the eighteenth century show a worsening of the terms of trade for the later 1780s and 1790s as well. This leads them to conclude (p. 83) that the "accelerated growth of foreign trade in the second half of the eighteenth century was associated with an *adverse* movement of the terms of trade."

TABLE 1.2 Export Growth, 1700-1851

Year	Total Exports (£ millions)	Total Exports as a % of Industrial Product	Industrial Exports as a % of Industrial Product
1700	3.8	24.4	n.a.
1760	8.3	35.2	28.9[a]
1780	8.7	21.8	17.9[b]
1801	28.4	34.4	29.9[c]
1831	38.9	21.9	19.7[c]
1851	67.3	24.7	21.0[c]

a - Calculated on the assumption that the proportion of industrial exports to total exports was equal to the value for 1784-1786.
b - Proportion industrial to total exports for 1784-1786 used.
c - Proportion industrial to total exports computed as means of surrounding years.

Sources: Computed from Crafts (1985a, p. 132) and Davis (1979, pp. 88-89).

Table 1.2 suggests that the importance of exports to manufacturing during the Industrial Revolution was most crucial in its "adolescent phase." All the same, if export markets were more than just a trigger, their relative importance should have increased and not declined as the Industrial Revolution progressed. The data clearly do not bear this out. Many scholars have argued, however, that foreign trade did more for growth than the aggregate statistics suggest and that exports were more important in certain key industries. Cotton, above all, depended for more that half of its sales on foreign markets, and insofar as the technology developed for cotton spilled over to domestic industries, the foreign sector's role is understated by the statistics. O'Brien and Engerman also suggest that the wealth accumulated by merchants through foreign trade was invested in British manufacturing and overhead capital, though no evidence is provided to support this point and indicate how large this investment was.[65]

Manufacturing growth benefitted a great deal from exports, but in order to make their point about the economy, O'Brien and Engerman resuscitate the Rostowian notion of a "leading sector" and designate industry in this role. Because exports were so important to manufacturing and because manufacturing dragged the other sectors behind it, they maintain, exports were essential to the entire economy, and "the attention should remain focused upon those forces promoting increases in the production of manufactured goods" (1991, p. 208). Apart from the somewhat poorly defined concept of a "leading sector," the problem with their logic is that it is consistent with any set of facts and thus lacks power as an explanation. When exports stagnate in the 1760s and 1770s, just when a number of key industries were taking off, "domestic demand maintained the growth of industry," which proves that "interactions also flowed the other way" (p. 208). Their statement that the British economy was part of an "interaction of economies that operated within a framework of imperial regulations . . . that created conditions for trade and growth" is basically ambiguous: If they mean the growth that was a direct result of trade, the statement is unassailable if somewhat obvious; if they mean the growth caused by the technological changes in Britain's modern sector, some evidence will be required.[66]

A different way in which exports could have led to growth is if export industries employed labor that would otherwise have been unemployed. Thomas and McCloskey base their thesis on the

---

[65] There is even less evidence for the statement that merchants "created and widened markets for British manufactured goods at home or abroad" (O'Brien and Engerman, 1991, p. 191), nor is there any suggestion as to exactly how merchants *create* markets as opposed to servicing them.

[66] The concept of a leading sector itself may prove to be more lasting than the "take-off hypothesis." Wijnberg (1992, pp. 165-167) defines a leading sector as an industry that is "technologically contagious," that is, in which the conditions for successful innovation such as low barriers to entry and appropriability of inventions spill over onto others. Such explicitly dynamic models are necessary to a consistent "demand-side" interpretation.

"unimportance of exports," on the simple notion that exports used up valuable resources that could have been used for the benefit of domestic consumers but are the inevitable price a country has to pay for the imports it enjoys. This assumes, however, a fully employed economy in which each factor is paid its opportunity cost. Many of the manufactures of Britain during the eighteenth century, however, were produced by rural industry, by men and women whose opportunity cost in the off-season was low. Insofar as export markets provided these workers with employment, an expansion of output can indeed be attributed to exports. In other words, in a closed economy the same employment levels might not be sustainable, so that one of the benefits of trade was an increased demand for labor. It is difficult to prove this point decisively, but O'Brien and Engerman are correct to point out that contemporaries were far from impressed by the likelihood of the domestic economy's maintaining full employment and were obsessed by the specter of unemployment.

Turning to the *dynamic* question, as already noted it is much more difficult to connect the openness of the British economy with technological changes. Export demand may have been a consideration for some innovators, but almost every individual entrepreneur could cover his expenses by the domestic market. The growing dependence of the cotton industry on foreign markets was an ex post phenomenon, not something that *caused* technological change. Ralph Davis argues that cotton expanded overseas after it had earned its spurs in the domestic market and that the export-driven expansion of the industry in the 1790s simply called for a larger number of similar mills (Davis, 1979, p. 67). All the same, the microinventions that kept improving the quality and reducing the prices of the goods produced may have been a function of output and thus of the size of the market. Learning by doing and experience were the sources of productivity increase after the big breakthroughs had been made. Insofar as export markets permitted expanded sales, they led to productivity increases and lower costs. Export-oriented industries in the post World-War II Asian economies have often been "high-tech" and so a large export market may produce a stimulus to the adoption of frontier technologies. The unresolved questions remain, however: Is this connection between exports and technological progress also true for a nation that is generating the new technologies, and not only adopting them? To what extent would the domestic market have been able to replace the foreign markets? What was the elasticity of cost with respect to sales (that is, how strong, really, were the marginal learning effects of overseas sales)?

Even if the nexus between foreign trade and technological progress thus remains something of a mystery, the openness of the British economy was a central feature that determined her economic fate. Openness is not a yes-or-no variable: few economies have ever been hermetically closed and few have been "entirely open" (if that concept could be defined). While openness was thus a matter of degree, this degree was of great importance. One example is the role of agriculture in the industrialization process. In a recent paper, Matsuyama (1992) demonstrates rigorously an intuition long prevalent among economic historians, namely that the relation between agricultural productivity and the rate of industrialization depends on the openness of the economy. In a closed economy, manufacturing depends on productivity growth in agriculture to produce a surplus that will permit the reallocation of resources from farming to industry and to provide a market for manufactured products. It has often been thought that an "agricultural revolution" was a necessary precondition for indus-trialization. Yet in an open economy this is clearly false: food can be imported and paid for by industrial goods. In fact, in an open economy a highly productive agricultural sector signals to the economy that its comparative advantage lies in farming, thus losing the (unforeseen) advantages of industrialization. This is in fact what happened in the Netherlands between 1815 and 1870: an open, free-trade economy with a highly productive agricultural sector, the opportunity costs of labor were just too high to render manufacturing profitable (Mokyr, 1976a). In Britain, despite growing agricultural productivity (the dimensions of which are still heavily disputed) this did not happen. Imports from the Celtic Fringe and the Continent made up the British food deficit (Thomas, 1985). Indeed, Matsuyama's model implies that in an open economy the Industrial Revolution occurred not *because* of but *despite* the growth in agricultural productivity.

The openness of the British economy also meant that technology was continuously stimulated by ideas from the outside. We have already seen the wide influence of French science and inventions on British technology. Throughout the period, close cooperation with French, German, and Swiss manufacturers led to the continuous exchange of technological knowledge. Recently, Arnold Pacey (1990, pp. 117-120) has argued that Asian stimuli were of primary importance to the Industrial Revolution. Indian calicoes and muslins could not be made in Britain using the laborious hand-spinning techniques of India, but they showed the British what could be done, and eventually Crompton's mule was able to produce yarns of Asian fineness. English entrepreneurs sent representatives to Smyrna to study the manufacturing of Turkey-red dye, and plants to produce it were set up in Manchester and Glasgow (Wadsworth and Mann, 1931, pp. 180-181). Technology was enriched by the infusion of foreign elements, and in the long run this exposure effect turned out to be one of the most lasting benefits of the open economy.

A separate issue often raised in this context is the impact of the British Empire. It seems somehow tempting for those who do not have much sympathy for British capitalism to link it with imperialism and slavery.[67] It is hard to see exactly how the imperial policies, which protected British merchants doing business overseas, could have had much impact on the Industrial Revolution beyond, perhaps, assuring favorable treatment in some markets. Empire and foreign policy seem to have conveyed at best a slight advantage. After all, Britain lost one of its richest colonies during the early stages of the Industrial Revolution, and yet after 1783 commercial relations with the young United States were none the worse for wear until complications in Europe drove the two apart again. India was an important market, but it never reached the size that would make it a sine qua non: In 1784-1786 Asia (that is, primarily India) absorbed 13.3 percent of British exports, a share that remained essentially constant until 1854-1856 (Davis, 1979, pp. 96, 100). To be sure, Asia did buy a larger than proportionate share of the output of Britain's most dynamic industry, cotton, but as late as 1854-1856 it bought 22.5 percent of Britain's cotton exports. This is substantial, but Europe, the Near East, the United States, and Latin America, where Britain competed on an equal base, remained equally important markets. Outside Britain, Switzerland and Belgium, two nonimperial nations, were successful industrializers, whereas Holland and Portugal, which controlled a large and rich set of

---

[67] As Engerman (1972, p. 430) put it, in this version history becomes a morality play in which one evil (the Industrial Revolution) arises from another, perhaps even greater evil, slavery and imperialism.

colonies, remained behind. In short, trade with the empire may have been central before the Industrial Revolution, but it lost much of its primacy in the years after 1780, when it might have been needed the most (Cain and Hopkins, 1980, p. 474).

The classic attempt to link imperialism and the slave trade with the Industrial Revolution is the Williams thesis. Eric Williams (1944) argues that profits from the triangular trade (between Western Europe, Africa, and colonial America) helped finance the early stages of industrial capitalism. In particular, Williams argues that the slave and sugar trades encouraged British industrial production and capital accumulation.[68] This thesis, which had long been regarded as discredited, has recently been resurrected, and a special issue of *The Journal of Interdisciplinary History* was dedicated to it (Inikori, 1987; Richardson, 1987; Solow, 1987; see also Inikori, 1989). It can hardly be doubted that the West Indian sugar trade was highly profitable, as Adam Smith ([1776] 1976, p. 412) pointed out. Because the sugar trade depended on slave labor, the slave trade was, not surprisingly, profitable as well. Commercial interests, shipbuilding, and the services and industries catering to the triangular trade prospered, and the towns of Bristol and Liverpool consequently grew (Williams, 1944, p. 36, 62-64). Yet the links between Liverpool and Manchester do not prove Manchester's "tremendous dependence on the triangular trade" (p. 68) and recent work has not been very successful in substantiating Williams's claim that the profits from this trade "provided one of the main streams of that accumulation of capital in England which financed the Industrial Revolution" (p. 52). The intuitive feeling that "the exploitation that really mattered was [that] of African slaves" (Solow, 1987, p. 737) is justifiable in that it surely mattered to the slaves themselves, as it did to Africa and to the areas to which slaves were shipped. Yet that does not necessarily mean that it "mattered" to the same degree to Britain and other European economies that were the main beneficiaries of the triangular trade system. In a classic paper, Engerman (1972) demonstrates that the quantitative effects of the slave trade on the British Industrial

---

[68] As has been often noted, it is not quite clear whether Williams referred to the slave trade alone or to the more extensive triangular trade.

Revolution were negligible.[69] Furthermore, the simple causal links drawn by Williams should be modified. Richardson (1987) points out that the slave trade depended on the demand for sugar, which itself was a function of economic changes in the sugar-consuming economies in Western Europe. Moreover, only 15.2 percent of British industrial exports went to the West Indies between 1784 and 1824, so that only about 5 to 6 percent of British manufactures were shipped to the West Indies. This is not insubstantial, but it does not prove that the West Indies were more than just another market. Above all, however, the West Indies and slavery were important to Britain as a source of products that could not be produced locally. In the absence of West Indian slavery, Britain would have had to drink bitter tea, but it still would have had an Industrial Revolution, if perhaps at a marginally slower pace (Findlay, 1990, p. 40).

If slavery and the Atlantic trade were of essential importance, it was not due to the West Indies but to slavery in the United States. Before 1780 most of the raw cotton came to Britain from the West Indies, but clearly their potential to supply it was limited, and after 1790 the industry depended increasingly on the southern states of the United States. Simply put, without U.S. slave labor it is hard to see how the elastic supply of raw cotton would have been secured. Certain processes in the cotton industry could be mechanized, including some concerned with the production of the raw material (using, for example, the cotton gin). But the planting and picking of cotton in the fields of the southern United States remained a manual process, and as the demand for cotton increased, U.S. slave plantations rapidly switched to cotton. Without U.S. slavery, the British cotton industry would have run into a severe bottleneck. It is here and not in the consequences of eighteenth-century

---

[69] Engerman (1972, p. 440) computes that total profits from the slave trade in 1770 amounted to at most £342,000 (an alternative estimate has the number as low as £44,000). Total GNP in 1770 can be roughly estimated at about £166 million. (computed by applying Crafts's revised growth rates to Dean and Cole's estimate of GNP at £232 million in 1801). Gross capital formation was between 6 and 7 percent of GNP and thus came to about £11 million. Even on the most favorable assumptions, then, the profits of the slave trade, had they all been invested in Britain, would have contributed no more than 3 percent of capital formation in 1770.

triangular trade that slavery truly "mattered" for the Industrial Revolution.

g. Science and Technology

The notion that Britain was the first to undergo an Industrial Revolution because somehow British technological success was due to Britain's having more "advanced" science is unsupportable. The premise itself is in dispute (Kuhn, 1977, p. 43), but even if it were true, the technology developed during the British Industrial Revolution owed little to scientific knowledge, as Mitch's chapter below stresses. The inventions that set the British changes in motion were largely the result of mechanical intuition and dexterity, the product of technically brilliant but basically empirical tinkerers, or "technical designers" (a term suggested by Hall, 1974, p. 148), such as John Wilkinson, Richard Arkwright, John Smeaton, Richard Trevithick, and Robert Stephenson. In a few cases, such as Claude Berthollet's chlorine bleaching and Humphry Davy's safety lamp, inventions were made by scientists of note, but that correlation does not prove that science itself was of great importance. Leading scientists were not wholly specialized at this time and dabbled in technology, just as Galileo, Huygens, Hooke, and Leibniz had a century earlier.[70] Unlike the technologies that developed in Europe and the United States in the second half of the nineteenth century, science had little direct guidance to offer to the Industrial Revolution (Hall, 1974, p. 151).

If science played a role in the Industrial Revolution, it was neither through the "pure" foundation of technology on scientific understanding nor through the role of scientists in invention but rather through the penetration of "scientific method" into technological research: accurate measurement, controlled experiment, insistence on reproducibility, and systematic reporting of methods and materials. Even more important, perhaps, was a scientific mentality, which taught engineers a rational faith in the orderliness and predictability of natural phenomena -- even if the actual laws underlying chemistry and physics were not fully understood (Parker, 1984, pp. 27-28). The scientific

---

[70] The two leading Newtonians of the early eighteenth century, the Dutchman Willem Jacob s'Gravesande and the Englishman (of French descent) Jean Desaguliers, were both active in introducing and improving Newcomen engines in continental Europe (Jacob, 1988, p. 130).

revolution taught engineers the "method of detail," analyzing technical problems by breaking them into components that could be more easily analyzed separately than as part of a whole (Pacey, 1975, p. 137). Engineers such as Thomas Telford, John Smeaton, and John Rennie moved effortlessly between experimental science and practical applications. George Stephenson, a remarkable example of this ability himself, wrote of the great Smeaton as having a "truly Baconian mind" -- a description that fits an entire class of British engineers active between 1760 and 1830.

A further role for science lay in providing implicit theoretical underpinnings to what empirically minded technicians did, even if the complete scientific base had not been fully worked out. Thus the steam engine depended on the understanding of atmospheric pressure, discovered by Continental scientists such as Evangelista Torricelli and Otto von Guericke, which somehow must have filtered down to Newcomen despite the fact that his world was the local blacksmith's rather than the cosmopolitan academic scientist's. Chlorine bleaching depended on the discovery of chlorine by the Swedish chemist Carl Wilhelm Scheele in 1774. Phlogiston theory, the ruling physical paradigm of the eighteenth century, was eventually rejected in favor of the new chemistry of Lavoisier; but some of its insights (e.g., the Swede Tobern Bergman's contributions to metallurgy) were valuable even if their scientific basis was flawed. Cardwell (1972, pp. 41-43) has shown that the idea of a measurable quantity of "work" or "energy" derives directly from Galileo's work on mechanics. The advances in water and steam power in the eighteenth century depended on this scientific base. More often, of course, bogus science produced bogus results, as in Jethro Tull's insistence that air was the best fertilizer. In the "development" stage of the basic inventions, in which revolutionary insights were improved, modified, and debugged to turn them into successful business propositions, pure science played a modest role.

Beyond these direct links, science and the scientific community created the cultural and intellectual background for the tinkerers, the mechanics, and the engineers who made the Industrial Revolution (Jacob, 1988, chap. 5). The scientific revolution of the seventeenth century taught a new approach to the study of nature, a mechanical philosophy in which natural phenomena were studied as independent units, increasingly separated from religious considerations. Without immediately abandoning the belief in a creator, it became increasingly possible to analyze nature without theology or magic. Because technology in its deepest essence involves the manipulation of nature and the physical environment, the metaphysical assumptions under which people operate are ultimately of crucial importance. Science in the seventeenth century became increasingly permeated by the Baconian notion of material progress and constant improvement, attained by the accumulation of knowledge. Jacob (1988, pp. 139-144) maintains that the British enlightenment, more than its counterpart across the channel, regarded science as *useful knowledge*, perceived as "dynamic and progressive in relation to the material order." Although such relations are impossible to quantify, it stands to reason that in that regard science laid the intellectual foundations of the Industrial Revolution by providing the tacit and implicit assumptions on which technological creativity depended.

British science and scientists occupied a different position in society than elsewhere. As Thomas Kuhn states, the old cliché that British science was pragmatic and applied whereas French science was abstract, deductive, and formal seems to have survived the test of time (1977, p. 137; see also Inkster, 1991, p. 42). The origins of this phenomenon may be traced to an intellectual bifurcation of the seventeenth century, when British science came under the influence of Bacon whereas in France more Cartesian ideals triumphed. Bacon advocated that the purpose of science was to raise comforts and living standards, whereas the French traditions followed more lofty objectives. Bacon's science was empirical, experimental, and pragmatic whereas French science was theoretical and abstract. Such generalizations are inevitably hazardous, but water power provides at least one persuasive example. In Britain research on water power was conducted by practical engineers, such as Smeaton, John Banks, John Rennie, and William Fairbairn, in search of a better water mill. On the Continent work on water power was largely theoretical and carried out by mathematicians, such as Antoine Parent, Johann Euler, and Jean Charles Borda (Reynolds, 1983, pp. 196-265).

Yet the roots of the divergence between British and Continental science go beyond that. The Cartesian traditions in eighteenth-century France regarded the function of science to be to support the authoritarian state as the source of all order. In Britain, as Margaret Jacob (1988, p. 93) has argued, the scientists in the 1660s and 1670s forged an alliance with the landed and commercial interests. After these interests triumphed politically in 1688, scientists in eighteenth-century

Britain were on the whole part of the economic establishment, not of the opposition. They regarded it as a natural state of the world to cooperate with engineers and manufacturers to solve pragmatic technical problems. The interactions between them, as we have seen, were institutionalized in the various scientific and philosophical societies that provided the meeting places, and informal contacts further strengthened these ties. Even some members of the landowning elite displayed a strong interest in technology, in part for economic reasons but also out of sheer curiosity. The Earl of Dundonald, the Viscount of Dudley and Ward, the Earl of Balcarres, and others were fascinated by the new technologies. There was a growing communication between scientists, engineers, and businessmen, and they engaged in a common effort to recognize technical problems and solve them. From the early eighteenth century on, scientists in Britain gave popular lectures on mechanical and technical issues, which were widely attended by audiences from the commercial and artisanal classes. The most famous of these lecturers was John T. Desaguliers, a noted physicist who made considerable contributions to the Newcomen steam engine and water power (Musson and Robinson, 1969, pp. 37-45; Reynolds, 1983, pp. 215-217, 280).

The state and official institutions in Britain had relatively little to do with these developments. The generation and diffusion of scientific and technological knowledge in Britain occurred spontaneously, by and for private interests. In France, by contrast, scientists depended on economic and personal relations with the *political* establishment, fostering an elitist and statist approach to science, which was thus particularly concerned with the engineering and technical needs of the state and above all with military needs. The French state subsidized and managed scientific enterprises, whereas in Britain the same role was carried out by the private sector (Gillispie, 1980, chap. 5). The counterparts to the British provincial societies in disseminating technical knowledge were the *grandes écoles*, which trained technicians and engineers. The first of these was the *école des ponts et chaussées*, founded in 1744, followed by the *école de dessin* in 1767 and the *école des mines* in 1783. After the Revolution, these were followed by the *école polytechnique* (1794) and the *école des arts et métiers* (1804) (Artz, 1966). All these institutions were run and funded by the government. In other countries, such as the Austrian Netherlands, the German states, and Russia, the direct intervention of the state was even more noticeable. Science and engineering were creatures of the state, meant first and foremost to serve the military and administrative organs of the government. In Britain, private interests dominated.

The difficulty in linking science and technology in this period is highlighted by one of the few quantitative measures of scientific output --periodicals. Although the value of a periodical is of course proportional to its subject matter, the quality of research, and the scope of its circulation, it is striking that the vast majority of scientific journals published in the eighteenth century appeared not in England or France but in Germany. Kronick shows that over 61 percent of all "substantive serials" appeared in Germany, with France and England accounting for 10.7 percent and 6.9 percent, respectively. The actual gap was smaller, because German scientific journals were comparatively short lived, but correcting for this does not alter the picture (Kronick, 1962, pp. 88-89). Similar gaps, although not as large, hold for the proceedings of scientific societies. The only category in which England led, perhaps significantly, was "translations and abridgements" (pp. 114-115).

On the basis of this background it is easier to understand the dispute between those like Mathias (1979, pp 45-87) and Hall (1974; see also Hall and Hall, [1964] 1988, p. 219), who deny science any serious role in the Industrial Revolution, and those like Musson and Robinson (1969) and more recently Jacob (1988), who try to restore science's role in explaining Britain's uniqueness. David Landes (1969, p. 104) and others have reversed the causal connection and maintain that science owed more to technology that the other way around. The conventional argument that scientific knowledge was unimportant simply because much of what scientists knew was irrelevant to engineers and industrialists can no longer be maintained. Yet Jacob (1988, p. 181) may have gone too far in the other direction when she suggests that the Industrial Revolution occurred in Britain and not in France and the Netherlands because the lack of scientific knowledge on the Continent was such that there "many of the very men who had access to capital, cheap labor, water, and even steam power could not have industrialized had they wanted to: they simply could not have understood the mechanical principles necessary to implement a sophisticated assault on the hand manufacturing process." Certainly there was nothing in the inventions made between 1760 and 1830 that exploited a store of knowledge accessible only to the British. The physics and chemistry of the time were primitive, and the deeper theoretical principles behind such breakthroughs as the steam engine and soda making were not

understood by anyone. France could and did generate highly
sophisticated innovations, including the mechanical toys of Vaucanson,
the Jacquard loom, the continuous paper machine, as well as the
chemistry of Lavoisier and Berthollet. The difference, if there was any,
was of degree, of emphasis, and above all of the depth with which
technologically valuable knowledge had penetrated into the productive
layers of society.

What accounts for the differences in the intensity of interaction
between persons with knowledge and persons of business? Every
civilized society contains individuals who are highly educated and think
for themselves, and individuals who are skilled and produce goods and
services that add up to income and consumption. Technologically
creative societies are those in which these two classes mingle socially,
communicate with each other, and are interested in similar issues. In
Britain the bridge between natural philosophers and engineers was
broader and easier to cross than in other countries, and more than
anywhere else, Britain could count on able people who could
effortlessly move between the world of abstraction, symbol, equation,
blueprint, and diagram and the world of the lever, the pulley, the
cylinder, and the spindle. Information also travelled easier in eighteenth
century Britain than in France, thanks to better passenger travel and
mail services (Szostak, 1991). Yet such bridges existed elsewhere (as one
glance at Diderot's *encyclopédie* will demonstrate), and Britain's
advantage here was as partial as it was temporary.

4. The Inputs: Labor and Capital

Economic growth can be decomposed into increases in the quantities
of inputs and changes in the way inputs are utilized. Increases in output
per worker consist of changes in productivity and the accumulation of
factors other than labor. Separating the two is in practice quite difficult.
A related question, equally controversial and studded with theoretical
pitfalls, is the effect of the initial endowments of factors of production
on the rate at which the modern sector grows. A satisfactory model
would allow us to approach the question, Why was Britain first? from
a different angle. The Industrial Revolution involved massive accumulation of capital and profound reallocation of labor. How did factor
markets carry out these functions? How crucial was the supply of
factors to the Industrial Revolution? Where did the inputs come from,

and how did market mechanisms channel them to where they were needed?

The operations of factor markets in Britain during the Industrial Revolution have been examined recently by Williamson (1987a; 1990a, chap. 7). In this work, Williamson poses the question starkly: How much did the imperfection of labor and capital markets cost the British economy? Questions such as, Were markets perfect? or Did they fail? are somewhat ill posed; factor markets are far from perfect even today, and "failure" is obviously in the eye of the beholder. Williamson's approach is to compare the actual operation of factor markets with an ideal neoclassical world in which competition is perfect, factors flow effortlessly between regions and sectors and the allocation of resources follows the theoretical rules devised by economists. The latter, purely imaginary world is, obviously, more efficient, but theory gives us no guide as to the *size* of the difference. Williamson reasons that if the forgone output due to factor market imperfections was very large, it could conceivably have slowed down industrialization and growth. Working with a multisectoral general equilibrium model, he poses counterfactual questions: How much faster would GNP have grown and industrialization have proceeded if factors had been perfectly mobile? He concludes that these gaps were indeed significant. The labor market imperfection alone was responsible for a 3.3 percent loss of GNP compared with the ideal world, and the capital market for an 8.2 percent loss.[71] More important, manufacturing output would have increased over 60 percent if the capital market imperfection had been eliminated, and manufacturing profits by 114 percent. It should be noted that Williamson's imperfections are intersectoral only; his computations still assume that capital and labor can reallocate themselves effortlessly *within* the sectors. In that sense they represent an understatement of the true values.

Apart from the question of how efficient factor markets were, the roles of labor and capital have been the subject of an interesting and important literature.

---

[71] The combined loss does not equal the sum of these losses because in the model one market can adjust to compensate for imperfections in the other. Indeed, in Williamson's story eliminating both gaps would result in a lower gain in aggregate output than eliminating the capital market gap alone, an anomalous result he ascribes to nonlinearities in the solution of the model.

a. Labor

There are two competing and apparently incompatible views of the role of labor in the Industrial Revolution. One of them sees labor as a scarce resource, in fact as *the* scarce resource, and therefore the Industrial Revolution had a better chance of succeeding in areas in which it was abundant and cheap. The other regards technology as responding to labor scarcity and thus implies that *scarce* labor was an advantage in the industrialization race.

The first model is based on a number of assumptions that should be spelled out.[72] Because the model is not strictly speaking a growth model (it has few implications for the overall growth rate of the economy) and deals more with the composition and technological practices of some sectors, I termed it a "growing-up" model (Mokyr, 1976b). The assumptions are as follows:

1. Capital goods "embodied" the new technology. Then, as now, that assumption seems almost too obvious to justify. Steam engines, mule jennies, blast furnaces, paper mills, chaff cutters, and threshers are all examples of a new technology requiring a large capital expenditure. One cannot have the new technology without making an investment in the equipment that embodied it. Above all, there were factories that had to be built, maintained, heated, lighted, and guarded. The modern sector was physically located, by and large, in large buildings. And in contrast with France and Belgium, in Britain there were no more monasteries to confiscate and convert. This is not to deny the importance of disembodied technological change. It implies, however, that a lack of fixed capital could have retarded the transformation, as I shall argue later. The reverse does not hold: An abundant supply of capital did not guarantee the adoption of technological changes and the emergence of factories, because the owners of the capital could not be relied upon to lend it to aspiring factory owners. What mattered was venture capital, not aggregate savings.

2. The rate of accumulation depended crucially on the rate of profit. In the simplest model, in which factory owners could not borrow and depended on retained profits to finance new investment, this conclusion is trivial. In models with financial institutions, however, this relation is

---

[72] Some of the following material is adapted from Mokyr, 1991b.

not appreciably weakened as long as the past performance of the firm is used as an indicator of its future profitability.

3. Wages were the main cost to the firm. If labor productivity is primarily determined by technological parameters and the prices of output are given, the rate of wages is inversely related to the rate of profit through the factor price frontier. In other words, because the productivity of labor depended on the technology in use, assumed to be accessible to all economies, the main reason why profit rates differed across economies was different wage levels reflecting differences in economic structures or factor endowments on the eve of the Industrial Revolution.

4. Technological change was more or less independent of factor prices. This would be the case if there was little choice in the range of techniques; i.e., the "best practice" techniques at the onset of the Industrial Revolution were the most efficient for any realistic set of factor prices.

5. Goods were internationally mobile, but labor and capital were not. It is assumed that labor was mobile only *within* a region but could not migrate across economies. Neither of these assumptions exactly conforms to the historical experience; they are made only to simplify the story. Hence, if there were no important differences in the propensities of capitalists to reinvest profits in their firms, the model predicts that areas that for some reason started off with low wages would, all other things being equal, undergo an Industrial Revolution at a faster rate.

The growing-up model is different from the standard growth models in that it is a disequilibrium model. Its dynamics depend on the coexistence and interaction of the "old" and the "new" technologies. The traditional sector, which produces the same good (or a close substitute) as the factories, can continue its existence for a long time after the process has started, because the modern sector is still too small to supplant it altogether. As long as the two sectors coexist, the modern sector earns a "quasi-rent," a disequilibrium payment that will eventually disappear when the manual industries have disappeared. Through continuous reinvestment, this rent in its turn provides the fuel for further growth of the modern sector. This model suggests that high-wage economies would have lower profits, lower rates of accumulation, and thus a slower and later Industrial Revolution. The model also predicts that wages in the modern sector would grow slowly if at all as long as the traditional sector remained a large employer. In this sense, the model is comparable to the labor surplus models of Lewis and Fei-Ranis popular in the 1970s. In contrast to those models, however, the "growing-up" model does not have to make any *deus ex machina* assumptions about the wage rate. The modern sector is small enough relative to the rest of the economy to take the wage parametrically (that is, the sector can hire workers at a wage rate that is unaffected by the number of workers it employs) and hence the lower the wage set in the traditional economy, the faster the modern sector could grow.[73]

The second approach to the role of labor in the Industrial Revolution, most closely associated with the work of H. J. Habakkuk (1962), maintains that inventive activity in the nineteenth century was mostly labor saving and that scarce labor thus stimulated waves of technical change. This approach is based on a somewhat peculiar view of technological change, namely, that innovation was a process of choice between more or less equivalent alternatives, similar to the choice made by a firm facing an isoquant. Although Habakkuk was primarily concerned with the period after 1830, his approach extends naturally to the British Industrial Revolution. High wages and labor-supply constraints in Britain, in this view, stimulated the demand for labor-saving technological change (Landes, 1969, pp. 57-60). Yet the application of the model, at second glance, is fraught with difficulties. To start with, it is far from obvious that technological change during the Industrial Revolution was, on balance, more labor saving than capital saving: Von Tunzelmann (1981, p. 165) believes that, on balance, it was about neutral. MacLeod, examining the declared motives of eighteenth-century English patentees, found that only 3.7 percent of them stated that "labor saving" was the main purpose of the invention. Further, it always makes good sense to "search" for labor-saving innovations, even in low-wage economies, because labor always costs something, and thus innovations that reduce labor inputs increase

---

[73] The logic of the model has since been adopted by other writers interested in other regions. In his work on the cotton industry in the South, Gavin Wright (1987) explicitly points to the South's emerging as a "low-wage region in a high-wage economy" as the main reason for the South's success in establishing a successful textile industry after 1880 (pp. 76, 124). Much in Wright's analysis of the postbellum southern industry has analogues in the growing-up model, especially his assumptions about labor and capital markets.

profits. This is especially the case if, as was likely true in low-wage areas, production was highly labor intensive. In addition, as David (1975) has pointed out, the Habakkuk view implies that technological change is "localized" (that is, occurs in close proximity to the techniques actually used rather than over the entire range of feasible techniques). For the Habakkuk view to prevail, such localized technological change has to be stronger in the capital-intensive range of techniques than in the labor-intensive range. In that case a high-wage economy will naturally have chosen a less labor-intensive technique and will experience faster technological progress as the unintended by-product of this choice. Finally, although British wages were higher than on the Continent, some scholars (e.g., Flinn, 1966, p. 31) have insisted that the growth of population met the increased demand for labor and that there is no evidence for any labor scarcity.

Economists have examined the assumptions on which the two alternative theses are based and have made them explicit.[74] The seemingly obvious test of the low-wage hypothesis is that the areas of Britain that industrialized earliest should, at the outset, have had lower wages. The relevant variable here is *nominal* wages, because we are interested in the cost of labor, not in the standard of living. In this regard, at least, the hypothesis seems confirmed. The areas of Britain that industrialized first, the northwest counties of Lancashire and the northern midlands, had lower wages than the south in the middle of the eighteenth century (Hunt, 1986). During the Industrial Revolution this relation was reversed, so that by 1867 the industrial areas had higher wages. Yet although this pattern is repeated in a few other instances, such as the Low Countries (Mokyr, 1976a), it is far from universal. Ireland, by all accounts, had low wages but did not industrialize. Britain itself had higher wages than most of the European continent.

---

[74] The literature stimulated by Habakkuk's pathbreaking book is quite extensive. See, for example, Landes (1965a); Rosenberg (1963, 1967); Saul (1970); Temin (1973). Most of the debate is carried out in the context of Anglo-American differences, with Britain, interestingly enough, considered the *low-wage* economy (though in the period of the Industrial Revolution it would, relative to the rest of Europe, be the high-wage economy). A comparison between Britain and the Continent during the Industrial Revolution would be worthwhile, but so far this has not been attempted seriously.

It must be, then, that the *ceteris paribus* clause in this model did not always hold. For instance, it is important to ask *why* labor was cheaper in one place than in another. If it was purely a matter of opportunity cost, as the growing-up model assumes, the implication that capital accumulation is faster follows. But if labor was cheaper in one place because it was less productive, the model encounters a difficulty. If wages were low because labor quality and thus productivity were low, the advantages of cheap labor vanish. Contemporary authors were aware of this. Arthur Young, writing in the late 1780s, notes that "labour is generally *in reality* the cheapest where it is nominally the dearest" (Young, [1790] 1929, p. 311).[75] In a paper dealing with a somewhat later period, Gregory Clark (1987a) shows the strong correlation of labor productivity with nominal wages, even using the same technology and capital intensity. Clark shows that the high labor cost in the Atlantic economies (always excluding Ireland) was essentially offset by the higher productivity of workers in high-wage countries. Clark concludes that "real labor costs turn out to be as high as those in Britain in most of the other countries except for the very low wage competitors in Asia. The per worker wage rate tells us very little about the true cost of labor" (p. 11).

Labor could vary in its productivity for a variety of reasons. Differences in education seem to have made relatively little difference in productivity, as Mitch's chapter below points out. Another interpretation emphasizes diet: Low-wage workers could not buy enough food, and their malnourishment caused their work to be of low quality. Poorly paid workers could be poorly fed workers. The connection between caloric intake and energy output of workers is well known. Workers on an insufficient diet do not necessarily get sick or die, their entire metabolism simply slows down, to the detriment of their productivity (Scrimshaw, 1983).[76] The dietary model is attractive, because the so-called efficiency-wage model seems quite promising in explaining the failure of premodern, poor societies to develop. Unfortunately, the evidence produced thus far to support this

---

[75] For a survey of contemporary thinking about the "cheap labor is dear labor" issue, see Coats (1958).

[76] For examples, see Allen (1992b); Freudenberger and Cummins (1976); O Gráda (1992); and Scrimshaw (1983).

promising idea is ambiguous.[77] Although recent scholarship has concluded that French workers were, in all likelihood, worse fed than British workers (Fogel, 1989, 1991), the same is not true for the Irish, whose potato diets assured them of a plentiful if somewhat monotonous fare (Mokyr, 1983).

Productivity, however, depended on more than nutrition. Adam Smith thought that "the wages of labour are the encouragement of industry, which like every other quality, improves in proportion to the encouragement it receives. A plentiful subsistence increases the bodily strength of the laborer . . . where wages are high, accordingly, we shall always find the workmen more active, diligent, and expeditious, than where they are low." (Smith, [1776] 1976, p. 91). What Smith seems to be describing, however, is an upward sloping supply curve of labor, which makes people work *more* if the wage is higher. The question is, however, what makes people work *better* or harder per unit of time?

Recent thinking about the efficiency-wage hypothesis has shown that labor productivity can depend on the real wage paid to workers in a variety of ways. A simple model of this type is the shirking model, in which it is expensive to monitor the effort the worker puts in. High wages are a mechanism by which the employer extracts more effort from the worker, because a worker caught shirking risks being fired and losing his or her high-paying job. High wages could also increase productivity through reduced turnover. Another model derives a correlation between productivity and wages through an "adverse selection" mechanism: the worst-quality workers agree to work for less (see Akerlof and Yellen, 1986; Weiss, 1990).[78]

Differences in productivity in the early stages of the Industrial Revolution were also likely to arise from differences in workers' attitudes. Concentrating large numbers of workers (of both sexes) in one room and subjecting them to discipline, regularity, and the increasing monotony of the more advanced technique were some of the

---

[77] The inadequacy of British diets both before and during the Industrial Revolution has been recently documented by Shammas (1990, pp. 134-148). For a dissenting view that maintains that eighteenth-century diets were by and large sufficient, see Riley (1991).

[78] A recent and pioneering attempt to apply this class of models to the Lancashire cotton industry in the first half of the nineteenth century is made by Huberman (1992).

most difficult problems encountered by early factory masters (Thompson, 1967). Cheap labor was no advantage unless it could be effectively transplanted from the traditional to the modern sector. Sidney Pollard (1965, chap. 5) has pointed to the central paradox of the labor-supply question during the Industrial Revolution: "The lack of employment opportunities . . . existing simultaneously with a labor shortage is in part explained by the fact that the worker was averse to taking up the *type* of employment being offered, and the employer was unwilling to tolerate the habits of work which the men seeking work desired" (p. 196).

How a rural, mostly self-employed labor force was enticed to work in mostly urban mills is one of the most interesting questions in the debate on the Industrial Revolution, and yet it has not received much attention in the literature produced by economists. One answer given, ironically, by the social historian Perkin is purely economic: "By and large, it was the prospect of higher wages which was the most effective means of overcoming the natural dislike for the monotony and quasi-imprisonment of the factory" (Perkin, 1969, p. 130). Pollard (1965) and Thompson (1967) suggest a variety of alternative ways in which the factory owners educated their workers in their own image, trying to imbue them with an ethic that made them more docile and diligent. Punctuality, respect for hierarchy, frugality, and temperance were the qualities that the value system tried to convey onto the younger generation. The factory owners used a combination of approaches; they relied first and foremost on semi-compulsory apprenticed child labor from workhouses ("pauper apprentices") and on women driven out of their cottage industries by the rapid mechanization of spinning. Gradually, they created a more balanced labor force by a combination of higher pay and social control. An example is provided by the recent research of Huberman (1986; 1991; 1992). Huberman points out that although in the pre-1800 period the labor market in Lancashire worked in the classical fashion, with flexible wages equating supply and demand, employers soon found that they needed more than a labor force that was available. They needed a labor force that was loyal, reliable, and motivated. To insure this they paid wages that soon became institutionalized as "fair wages" and lost their flexibility. The emergence of such wage rigidity in some industries meant that when demand fluctuated, the adjustments would take place through quantity adjustments: layoffs and short-time became commonplace.

Aside from the question of the productivity of labor, the wages the factory masters had to pay were determined by the other forms of employment open to the workers.[79] The opportunity cost of labor was determined by its productivity in the traditional sector, which still dominated the economy. Before 1850 the modern sector was still relatively small and thus close to a price taker in the labor market. But there was more to the traditional sector than agriculture. At different times the domestic weavers, spinners, nailers, frame knitters, and cutlers, whether they were in the putting-out system or working on their own account, found their economic position threatened as the Industrial Revolution progressed. As the factories gradually expanded, they drove down the price of substitutes and thus the incomes earned by the outworkers and independent artisans in the traditional sector. Slowly at first, but with increasing force, domestic industry was ineluctably transformed by the Industrial Revolution. The modern sector, in a sense, created its own labor force.

Ultimately, then, domestic industry was doomed, but during the long transition its relation with the modern sector was complex. In many industries, mechanized factory production and manual home production were complementary, and although the type of industrial commodities produced in domestic industry changed substantially, the outwork system showed a remarkable tenacity in its struggle with the factory system. The mechanization of spinning led to a short-lived boom in domestic weaving, and some domestic industries, like tailoring, frame knitting, nail making, and boot and shoe production, remained domestic until well into the second half of the nineteenth century (Bythell, 1978). In the woolen industry, Hudson (1983, pp. 135-136) notes a symbiosis between the company mills and the workshops attached to domestic clothiers' homes. Mass production needed special-purpose machinery that could not itself be mass-produced. Rising incomes maintained an upmarket demand for custom-made, high-quality products, such as handmade clocks, fine linen, and custom-made

---

[79] The exact alternative is not clearly defined, which makes the notion of opportunity costs, so beloved by economists, somewhat tricky. By 1815, for instance, emigration has to be considered as a possible factor in setting a floor to the real wage. In Ireland this lower bound was reached by more people than in Britain, and thus Irish migration already became quite substantial before 1850.

furniture (Sabel and Zeitlin, 1985). The wage rate in these "sweated trades" was often very low. Since domestic industry was open to anybody, it set the lower bound on the opportunity cost of labor.

To be sure, the wage rate in the modern sector was higher and rose faster than that in the traditional sector. Still, the wages earned were not entirely independent of each other, unless the labor market was subject to extreme segmentation. Thus the growing modern sector produced its own labor force, and although real wages ultimately could not be kept down, the slowness of their rise in spite of rapidly increasing labor productivity has to be seen as part of the interaction of the modern and the traditional sectors.[80] This sheds an important light on the role of cottage industry prior to the Industrial Revolution. The preexistence of cottage industries was neither a necessary nor a sufficient condition for the modernization of industry (Coleman, 1983). But as Jones (1968) and others note, cottage industries catering to distant markets tended to arise in areas where agriculture paid low wages. These were not necessarily areas in which agriculture was backward and poor. In the English Midlands the heavy soils were not suitable to the new husbandry based on mixed farming and stall-fed livestock. This left these regions at a comparative disadvantage in agricultural production, and they increasingly specialized in manufactured goods. In other areas cottage industries emerged because high population to land ratios reduced average farm size. Much of this specialization crystallized, as was argued in a seminal paper by Jones (1968) and has recently been confirmed by Kussmaul (1990), in the second half of the seventeenth century. This specialization provided the historical background to the supplies of labor that ended up in the factories a century later.

Although the transition from domestic industry to modern industry was at times difficult and varied from region to region, the conclusion that the former was a positive factor in the establishment of the latter has been widely accepted.[81] A number of factors have been proposed as possible explanations of this nexus, including the supply of entrepreneurship by the domestic system, the preexistence of skills, and

---

[80] See Mokyr (1976b) for an algebraic representation of this interaction and some further implications.

[81] For some reflections, see Clarkson (1985, pp. 28-38); Kriedte (1981, especially pp. 152-154); Mokyr (1976b, pp. 377-379).

technological bottlenecks within the domestic sector that led to further innovations. Some of these, like the flying shuttle, increased the productivity of domestic workers. Others, like the power loom, were feasible only in a factory setting. Here, too, more detailed research is needed. Yet it is clear that the role of domestic industry in supplying a more abundant and elastically supplied labor force should become an essential part of this research program.

Above all, it is misleading to view the Industrial Revolution solely as the transition of labor from rural and agricultural occupations to urban and industrial occupations. The critical event was not the creation of an industrial labor force as such but its transformation. In the domestic system workers toiled at their homes, but they were usually only part-time industrial workers, cultivating small plots and hiring themselves out as seasonal wage workers during harvest time. In the modern sector the existence of a large fixed investment implied that part-time operation was uneconomical. The factory worker lost his or her freedom to allocate time between labor and leisure as he or she wished: either the worker wholly submitted to the requirements of the employers and worked the days and hours prescribed by the mill owner or he or she did not work. Although cottage industry in various forms supplied a portion of the labor force needed by the Industrial Revolution (Bythell, 1969, pp. 257-263; Redford, [1926] 1964, p. 41), there were workers, especially in rural areas, who hesitated to make the great leap. Only their sons and daughters realized the hopelessness of the situation and moved (Lyons, 1989; Redford, [1926] 1964, p. 186). Women and children constituted an essential part of the industrial labor force.[82] Berg and Hudson (1992, p. 36) point out that domestic industries released large reserves of cheap and skilled child and female labor leading to high proportions of women and children in the mills. Factories needed dexterity and discipline, and women and children provided these disproportionately before 1850.[83] Children and women's work cushioned the disruptive effects that technological

---

[82] For a recent summary of existing literature on women in the labor force, see Honeyman and Goodman (1991). Recent work on child labor is more exciting. See Nardinelli (1990) and Tuttle (1986).

[83] Berg and Hudson also argue that these age and gender differentials influenced innovation and were influenced by it, but persuasive evidence for this interaction is thus far lacking.

change had on the earnings and employment of married men and allowed the losing economic groups to adjust.

What about immigration? In Ireland, where the collapse of domestic industry in the 1830s was swift and brutal, migration of workers to England and Scotland was widespread (B. Collins, 1981), and these immigrants were an important supplement to the British labor force during the Industrial Revolution (Redford, [1926] 1964, pp. 132-164). As Pollard (1978, p. 113) puts it, "[Irish emigrants] were, in many aspects, the mobile shock troops of the Industrial Revolution, whose role consisted in allowing the key areas to grow without distorting the labor market unduly." Recently, Williamson (1986, 1990a) has questioned the importance of the Irish workers to British industrialization. His calculations assume that the Irish formed an unskilled labor force and that agriculture was more unskilled-labor-intensive than manufacturing. Consequently, he finds that the main impact of Irish immigration was on agricultural output. Although most Irish ended up in rural areas, Williamson points out that their arrival slowed down the migration of British rural workers from the countryside to the cities. It is possible to argue that further disaggregation could overturn this conclusion in some industries. The Irish tended to concentrate in certain sectors and industries, such as mining, construction, and transportation, and in these industries their labor may well have contributed more than Williamson's aggregate computations suggest.[84] On the whole, however, there is little reason to doubt Williamson's conclusion, because the number of Irish in Britain, though considerable, was simply not large enough to make a decisive impact on Britain's economy. It is estimated that in 1841 there were 830,000 "effective Irish" in Britain, of whom 415,000 were Irish born and the rest descendants of Irish emigrants. If we assume that all the emigrants and half of the others were in the labor force, the Irish would have added 620,000 workers, which out of a total occupied labor force of about 6.8 million would have amounted

---

[84] Williamson (1990a, p. 160) points out in a long footnote that if regional and industrial labor markets had been highly segmented, the Irish emigrants might have had a larger impact than his estimates imply, because they entered through urban gates and thus at first, at least, would have depressed industrial wages more, thus raising profits and stimulating capital accumulation. Irish immigrants were highly concentrated in a small number of specific urban occupations (Lees, 1979).

to about 9 percent; not a trivial addition, but not large enough to change the parameters dramatically.

Besides the question of the reallocation of labor from the traditional to the modern sector, there are many other loose ends to consider in the area of labor supply during the Industrial Revolution. One question is what happened to participation rates. We have no clue about these rates for the eighteenth century, and scholars have used population growth rates as a proxy for labor force growth rates. After 1801 the census provides figures for total occupied population that allow us to compute some very approximate participation rates. For what it is worth, the participation rate shows an initial decline from 1801 to 1831 and then rises until 1851 (Deane and Cole, 1969, pp. 8, 143). These changes are small and reflect primarily the changing age structure and measurement error.[85] The concept of a participation rate is perhaps something of an anachronism, because it requires a worker to be able to declare himself or herself as either being in the labor force or not. In a society in which a large if declining percentage of the labor force was economically active in households (farms or workshops), this is not an unequivocal measure even if we had better data. It is thought that the Industrial Revolution mobilized a large part of its labor force by turning part-time workers into full-time workers and transferring workers from "disguised unemployment" to regular work (Pollard, 1978).

On the whole, both cottage industries and factories practiced a division of labor between the genders. In the cottage industries women performed mostly low-skill jobs, left most of the skilled work to men, and were excluded from apprenticeship. Arguments that view the division of labor between genders as the outcome of attempts by men to maintain a social status in the family and the community have frequently been made, but hard evidence that would discriminate between this hypothesis and alternative ways of explaining the data is lacking so far. In a few new occupations, such as mule tending, women were excluded. Some technologies may have been especially designed to use female labor, and the evidence from the Birmingham toy trade

---

[85] Occupied population as a percentage of total population went from 44.86 percent in 1801 to 43.90 percent in 1831 and then rose to 45.28 percent in 1841 and 46.46 percent in 1851.

suggests that women could even operate relatively heavy machinery (Berg, 1985, pp. 221, 311).

Changes in the amount of labor performed per worker were possibly of greater importance to the labor supply than changes in participation rates. It is also a variable for which aggregate information is the hardest to come by. Labor input per worker could increase by lengthening the laboring day and the number of days worked and by reducing involuntary unemployment. Did workers in 1830 work more than in 1760? This view is certainly part of the conventional wisdom. Pollard (1978, p. 162) has no doubt that this is the main explanation for the rise of family income before 1850. Jones (1974, pp. 116-117) and Freudenberger (1974, pp. 307-320) are equally certain that workers toiled longer hours during the Industrial Revolution.

De Vries's idea of an "industrious revolution," presented earlier in this chapter, also implies an increase in labor input per worker and less leisure. This account sounds plausible enough, but can it be sustained by evidence? Unfortunately, we do not know with any precision how many hours were worked in Britain before the Industrial Revolution in either agricultural or nonagricultural occupations. In the cottage industries the distinctions between work, leisure, and social life were not as sharply drawn as in our own time. Most accounts maintain that workers started the week slowly, then picked up steam as the weekend approached, often working very long days toward the end of the week (Hopkins, 1982, p. 61; Thompson, 1967, p. 50). The decline of "St. Monday" (Reid, 1976) could therefore have been less of a net increase in the working week than a rearrangement to distribute the effort more evenly. McKendrick (1974, p. 163) derides the idea that longer hours explain higher incomes, labeling it a "prelapsarian myth of the golden past," and asserts that premodern labor was "grinding toil," as bad as factory labor but less remunerative. It is indeed easy to document many cases of long and hard hours in cottage industries; days of fourteen to sixteen hours were common (Rule, 1983, pp. 57-61). It is not clear, however, how common such long days were and to what extent they did not make up for the customary long weekend or for usually low wage rates. Much of our information here comes from nineteenth-century sources, which may be biased because economic conditions were deteriorating for cottage industry. If labor supply curves were downward sloping or backward bending, as is widely believed, the declining wage rates in domestic industry in the nineteenth century led to longer working days. Still, the idyllic picture drawn by some (Medick, 1981; Thompson, 1967) of working conditions in domestic industry in the eighteenth century is probably unrepresentative of premodern labor conditions. The most recent attempt to answer the question is provided by Gregory Clark (1992b), who concludes from the fact that weekly earnings rose faster than piece rates that workers in factories indeed worked longer.

One reason the comparison of factory and domestic work may yield misleading conclusions is that the representative industry discussed for the nineteenth century is often the textile industry, and especially cotton spinning. The laboring days of workers in the cotton mills before the mid-1840s were long, even by the standards of the time. The labor day was extended by as much as two hours and the number of working days per week was set at six, resulting in working weeks of seventy-six hours, compared to about sixty hours in most other industries. Official holidays were few, and unofficial leaves had to be made up with overtime (Bienefeld, 1972, pp. 30, 49). In mines, too, labor hours were increased during the Industrial Revolution. These extensions were, however, far from universal. A study of Birmingham and the Black Country has found no evidence of longer working hours, and the traditional workday of twelve hours including meals remained the most common practice (Hopkins, 1982). Only a small proportion of the labor force was actually employed in satanic mills or mines by 1840; most British workers were still employed in agriculture, domestic service, construction, and small workshops where work habits changed little.

Another possible source of labor was the reduction of involuntary unemployment. On the one hand, the amplitude of business fluctuations gradually increased after 1760, and as slumps became more severe, short-time and layoffs became more common. On the other hand, improved transportation and communication allowed a more efficient organization of the economy, thus reducing the problem of seasonal unemployment. The notion of large reserves of unemployed workers awaiting a rise in labor demand is much in dispute, although O'Brien and Engerman (1991) and others rely on contemporary opinion that Keynesian unemployment was a serious problem in the eighteenth century.[86] The evidence, however, is not wholly persuasive (Blaug, 1968, p. 15). Of similar interest is the question to what extent modernization reduced the multitudes of unemployables: vagrants, beggars, prostitutes, and other persons on the fringes of society. A glance at Henry Mayhew's description of London in the late 1840s suffices to warn us that the Industrial Revolution did not eliminate these people and possibly caused an increase in their proportion of the British population during the period.

b. Capital

The role of capital is not less controversial than that of labor. Recent work has concentrated on three issues. The first is the question of how capital markets worked during the Industrial Revolution and what effect they had on the process of technological change and accumulation. The other two issues have been raised primarily by economists, namely, the speed at which capital accumulated and the changes in its composition (circulating vs. fixed). On the issue of how capital markets worked, Larry Neal (1990) has recently pointed out that in the eighteenth century there was in fact an international capital market that funneled funds between different countries and that was clearly integrated, except when disrupted by war. There are also signs that British internal markets improved their operations during the Industrial Revolution: Buchinsky and Polak (1993) find that after 1770 there was a growing correlation between London interest rates and Yorkshire property transactions, though they find no sign of integration before that. Hoppit (1986) has reached a similar conclusion based on bankruptcy statistics. Although it would be premature to speak of a well-integrated capital market by 1800, clearly the capital market was becoming larger, more efficient, and more "modern" during the years of the Industrial Revolution.

Whereas the role of capital markets in the British economy as a whole is indisputable, their importance to the Industrial Revolution, properly speaking, is more difficult to assess. The biggest borrowers in Europe

---

[86] Keynes himself, in a famous statement, expressed the view that the writings of the mercantilists suggest that "there has been a chronic tendency throughout human history for the propensity to save to be stronger than the propensity to invest. The weakness for the inducement to invest has been at all times the key to the economic problem" (Keynes, 1936, p. 108).

in this period were governments that needed to finance deficits. The demand for credit also came from merchants with bills to be discounted, entrepreneurs active in canal and road construction, landowners in need of funds for the purpose of enclosure and other improvements, and construction interests. There was some inevitable overlap between these borrowers and what we would consider the "modern sector," but it was relatively small. Moreover, the smallness of the modern sector relative to the entire British economy meant that its demand for loanable funds did not loom large relative to the needs of the economy. Dealing with the supply of savings on an aggregate level, however, is even more misleading than an aggregate analysis of labor markets. Such an analysis assumes the existence of *a* capital market that allocated funds to all competing users, presumably on the basis of an expected rate of return and riskiness. Certain developments, especially the growth of transport networks, would have been slowed down considerably, and possibly aborted, had it not been for capital markets. As far as the manufacturing sector is concerned, however, matters are quite complex.

How did the Financial Revolution, which preceded the Industrial Revolution, affect it? The standard view of the interaction of "the two revolutions" has been that they had very little to do with each other. Postan argued in 1935 that "within industry almost every enterprise was restricted to its own supplies. The Industrial Revolution got under way while capital was not yet capable of moving between 'alternative employments'" (1935, p. 74). This view is now recognized as too simple: Financial markets were far more complex and subtle and their impact more pervasive than the earlier writers assumed. Yet there is little evidence that these financial markets were instrumental in helping modern industry more than vice versa.

Regarding the supply of capital, the most thorough work has been carried out by François Crouzet (1965, 1972, 1985b), complemented for the later period by Cottrell (1980). This work demonstrates that the capital needs of the modern sector during the Industrial Revolution were met from three sources. First were the internal sources in which the investor borrowed, so to speak, from himself using his private wealth (or that of his family) for start-up and plowing his profits back into the firm. Second, there were informal, or "personal," capital markets in which borrowers turned to friends, relatives, or partners for funds. Third, there was the formal capital market in which the borrower and the lender did not meet and in which attorneys, brokers, and eventually financial institutions (banks, insurance companies, stock markets) fulfilled their classic functions of intermediating between lenders and borrowers, concentrating information, and diversifying portfolios. The questions we must ask are, how important were these three forms of finance in the Industrial Revolution? and how can we explain this complex and seemingly inefficient mechanism? Students of the Industrial Revolution agree that most industrial fixed capital originated from internal finance. Crouzet (1965) concludes that "the capital which made possible the creation of large scale 'factory' industries came . . . mainly from industry itself . . . the simple answer to this question how industrial expansion was financed is the overwhelming predominance of self-finance" (pp. 172, 188). In a later paper he qualified this conclusion somewhat but insisted that it remained "broadly valid" (Crouzet, 1972, p. 44; 1985b, pp. 147-148).[87]

In the early stages of the Industrial Revolution, the fixed-cost requirements to set up a minimum-sized firm were modest and could be financed from profits accumulated at the artisan level (Crouzet, 1965, p. 165; Pollard, 1964). Plow-back then provided a regular, almost automatic mechanism by which profits augmented the capital stock. As technology became more sophisticated after 1830, the initial capital outlays increased, and it became increasingly difficult to rely on internal finance to start a business. For railroads this was of course out of the question. For existing industrial firms, retained profits usually remained central to the accumulation of capital. Even in a world in which firms relied exclusively on retained earnings, an intersectoral capital market could function. Individuals who made their fortunes in commerce, real estate, or the slave trade could use these funds to diversify into manufacturing. There were examples of merchant princes entering modern manufacturing, such as the case of Kirkman Finlay, an overseas merchant who entered cotton spinning between 1798 and 1806, and the Wilson brothers who established the Wilsontown ironworks. On the

---

[87] For similar statements, see, for example, Mathias (1969, p. 149) and Cameron (1967, p. 39). Cameron goes so far as to assert that "the rate of growth of capital is therefore a general guide to the rate of profit," though he concedes that alternative investment opportunities for the factory master could upset that correlation.

whole, however, these cases were exceptional (Crouzet, 1985a, pp. 99-100).

The second source of funds, the informal capital market, can easily be illustrated with examples, but it is not known how important this form of finance was relative to other sources. Postan (1935) argues that capital was still a very personal thing, which most people wanted to keep under control. If one lent it out, it was only to an intimate acquaintance or to the government. Even partnerships, which were frequently resorted to in order to raise capital while avoiding the costly process of forming a joint-stock company, were usually closely tied to family firms. The taking in of strangers as sleeping partners merely for the sake of getting access to their wealth was relatively rare at first (Heaton, 1937, p. 89). This caution slowly dissipated during the Industrial Revolution, but active partners often bought out the others, and the advantages of partnership were as much in the division of labor as in the opportunity to raise credit. Many of the most famous characters in the Industrial Revolution had to resort to personal connections to mobilize funds. Richard Arkwright got his first loan from a politician friend, and James Watt borrowed funds from, among others, his friend and mentor, Dr. Joseph Black. Although the phenomenon was thus widespread (Crouzet, 1965, p. 184; Mathias, 1969, pp. 150, 162-163), personal loans are as much of interest as a symptom of how the system operated as for the fact that they were a major channel through which funds were mobilized. Crouzet points out how exclusive and selective these personalized credit markets were: To have access to these informal networks one needed to be a member of them and be "known and well thought of in the local community" (1985a, p. 96). The market for capital can thus be seen once again to have depended on the market for information.

As the modern sector grew, intrasectoral flows of funds between firms became more important, especially flows occurring within the same industry. Insofar as these mechanisms only reallocated funds among different industries in the modern sector, the upper bound that the rate of profit imposed on the rate of growth of that sector did not disappear. Instead of constraining the individual firm, the supply of funds now constrained the modern sector as a whole. Although there were important exceptions, by and large the modern sector pulled itself up by its own bootstraps.

The third mechanism for obtaining capital, the formal credit market, operated primarily through merchants, wholesalers, and country banks.[88] The consensus on the role of the banks is that, with some exceptions, they rarely figured in the financing of long-term investment. Their importance was mainly in satisfying the need for working capital, primarily by discounting short-term bills and providing overdrafts (Flinn, 1966, p. 53; Pressnell, 1956, p. 326). Pollard has made a case for the reexamination of the importance of the banks on these grounds. Given that banks provided much short-term credit, firms short of capital could use all their internal funds on fixed investment (Crouzet, 1965, p. 193; Pollard, 1964, p. 155). Pollard, however, assumes that fixed capital grew at a rate much lower than implied by Feinstein's figures. His own earlier estimates imply a rate of growth of fixed capital of 2.4 percent per annum between 1770 and 1815, whereas Feinstein's fixed capital estimates grew at 4.2 percent per annum in the same period (Feinstein, 1978, p. 74). In manufacturing and trade the discrepancy is larger; according to Feinstein, gross fixed capital formation grew between 1770 and 1815 at 6 percent per annum, as opposed to Pollard's 3.4 percent (Feinstein, 1978, p. 74; see also Feinstein and Pollard, 1988). Thus financial constraints on capital accumulation may have been more stringent than Pollard originally presumed because he underestimated the needs. Recent research on the cotton industry suggests that the ratio of fixed to total capital in the mechanized spinning industry may have exceeded 50 percent (Richardson, 1989). Moreover, substituting fixed capital for circulating capital may have been less simple than he thought, because as industrial output increased, the demand for circulating capital grew as well. Feinstein shows that between 1760 and 1830 fixed capital in industry and commerce increased from 5 percent of domestic reproducible capital to 18 percent, whereas circulating capital in industry and commerce increased from 6 percent to 7 percent in the same period. Was the activity of banks enough to finance an

---

[88] Joint-stock companies were exceedingly rare, in part due to the Bubble Act that mandated they could only be incorporated through Parliament, but also because promoters defrauded their stockholders, and managers usually mismanaged the companies (Pollard, [1965] 1968, p. 25). There were a few exceptions, such as the British Cast Plate Glass Co., established in 1773, which imitated the French Royal St. Gobain manufactory, although it remained a private company.

increase of 164 percent in working capital over seventy years? Cottrell (1980, p. 33) concludes cautiously that there are indications that industrial growth before 1870 may have been blunted by shortages of circulating capital. Honeyman (1983, pp. 167-168) maintains that small businessmen found banks unreliable, and that even for circulating capital, kinship and friendship groups were preferred. The difficulty in obtaining funds led to the selective weeding out of the industry of entrepreneurs of humble origins who did not have access to these informal sources of funding and thus failed to survive crises during which working capital was hard to obtain. From a different point of view, Cottrell speculates that short-lived firms had better access to formal capital markets than firms that survived. The sharp fluctuations in the financial sector dragged into bankruptcy many industrial firms, and this effect may result in an underestimate of the importance of the plow-back of profit as a source of investment, because the firms that left records would tend to be *less* dependent on external finance (Cottrell, 1980, pp. 35, 253-255). Yet it remains to be seen whether enough evidence can be produced to jeopardize the widely held belief in the predominance of internal financing in this period.

Thus capital scarcity and biases in the capital markets slowed down the rate of accumulation and the speed of industrial growth. The reliance on plowed-back profits for investment clearly meant a slower growth rate compared to a world in which borrowers could access savings regardless of its source. In spite of these qualifications, it is still true that if credit markets had not existed at all, the accumulation of fixed capital would have been somewhat slower, though the rehabilitation of the banking system does not go far enough to allot it a truly strategic role in the Industrial Revolution.[89]

To what extent can economic theory explain the picture of the plow-back of retained profits and self-finance? The limited willingness of commercial banks to finance long-run projects is understandable. Banks needed their assets in liquid form to be able to pay depositors on

---

[89] See Cameron (1967) and Crouzet (1972). It is possible that further work on the asset composition of British banks may revise this conclusion for the period after 1844, which might explain Good's (1973) finding that the ratio of banking assets to GNP was relatively high in Britain compared to later industrializers (see also Collins, 1983).

demand since there was no lender of last resort.[90] This constraint was a result of the nature of commercial banks. Investment banks and other forms of financial intermediaries did not have to maintain liquid portfolios. Why such institutions were relatively unimportant in Britain (compared to Continental countries) is still an unanswered question. Yet the reliance on internal finance during the Industrial Revolution is not surprising. Firms tend to prefer internal over external finance, even though economic theory suggests that the reliance on retained profits is inefficient. In the post-World War II United States, too, firms have obtained over 70 percent of their finance from internal funds (MacKie-Mason, 1990).[91] The use of internal funds during the Industrial Revolution is thus not a historical anomaly.

Economic theory has in recent years provided substantial insights into the reason for the persistent "imperfection" of capital markets. In earlier theoretical work such as Hicks (1946) and Scitovsky (1971), firms were perceived to face upward-sloping supply curves of loanable funds, which would be consistent with internal financing. These models were not pursued, however, and their microeconomic foundations were never quite made clear. More recently, though, with developments in the economics of information, our understanding of the economic processes involved has improved.

For instance, Mayshar (1983b) argues that it is not risk per se that causes real-world capital markets to deviate from the theoretical constructs but divergences of opinions among potential lenders with respect to the rate of return. Such divergences would of course gradually disappear in a stationary world in which no new information was created. But in a world of rapid technological change, shifting demand patterns, and a changing political environment, divergences were not only possible but in fact inevitable. Thus rapidly changing

---

[90] The necessity for banks to preserve liquidity was made into a virtue by the so-called real-bills doctrine, which stipulated that if banks confined themselves to short-term, self-liquidating loans (such as discounting commercial bills), the price level would remain stable. Regardless of whether there was any merit in this theory in the short run, in the long run it confined commercial banks to supplying, almost exclusively, circulating capital.

[91] Calomiris and Hubbard (1991), studying the years 1936-1937 found that firms were in fact willing to pay a substantial tax on their invested retained earning rather than go outside for funding.

conditions during the Industrial Revolution effectively precluded the efficient operation of capital markets. Mayshar pictures savers as forming concentric circles around the entrepreneur, with his own funds in the center and next those of the people closest to him (friends and relatives), who were the sources most likely to lend to him. The farther one gets from the center, the more the expectations tend to diverge from the entrepreneur and the higher the rate of interest that he has to pay. Similarly, Stiglitz and Weiss (1981) show how the informational asymmetry between lender and borrower can lead to adverse selection in which a rise in the interest rate causes the borrowers with the safest projects to drop out of the market. This means that interest rates will generally not clear the credit market and credit rationing may be quite general. Under credit rationing, many entrepreneurs found themselves rationed out of the market and hence had no choice but to rely on self-finance. Whether potential borrowers preferred to rely on their own resources or whether they were rationed out of the credit market, the experience of the capital market during the Industrial Revolution clearly shows the applicability of these models.

The assumption of asymmetric information seems especially apposite. Because much of the technology was new, the information gap between entrepreneur and saver or banker was even greater than in our own time. A banker in 1790 would have much less information about the economic potential of a mule or a modern calico printer than he would about the quality of an investment in, say, a flour mill or a fence around enclosed land. Many firms, as well as their technologies, were new and had no reputations of creditworthiness. Young, growing firms tend to be the most severely credit-rationed. Consequently, some of them ended up establishing their own banks (Crouzet, 1985a, p. 19).

On the questions of the size and composition of the capital stock, our knowledge has been increased by Feinstein (1978) and Feinstein and Pollard (1988), who, with their collaborators, have created a data base to investigate the quantitative aspects of capital formation in this period. Feinstein's data permit us to test two hypotheses that have dominated the literature on capital in the Industrial Revolution. One hypothesis is the Lewis-Rostow claim that the investment ratio doubled during the Industrial Revolution. The other is the Hicks-Ranis-Fei view that the truly fundamental change was the shift from predominantly circulating to fixed capital. Both hypotheses have been criticized vigorously, and we are now in a position to assess these criticisms.[92] Feinstein's data imply that the dismissal of Rostow's hypothesis was premature. The ratio of total gross investment as a proportion of GDP rose from 8 percent in 1761-1770 to 14 percent in 1791-1800, and after a temporary setback in 1801-1811 returned to 14 percent for the half-century after 1811 (Feinstein, 1978, p. 91). More recently, Crafts (1983a) has revised Feinstein's estimates, criticizing in particular the price deflators that Feinstein used. Crafts's figures still show a doubling of the investment ratio from 5.7 percent in 1760 to 11.7 percent in 1830; this reproduces the Lewis-Rostow prediction of its doubling with dead accuracy, though somewhat more gradually than Rostow thought, which is hardly surprising in view of the highly aggregative nature of this ratio.

As to the Hicks-Ranis-Fei hypothesis, fixed capital rose from 30 percent of national wealth to 50 percent between 1760 and 1860, while the corresponding ratio of circulating capital declined mildly from 11 percent to below 10 percent. In industry and commerce the ratio of total circulating to total fixed capital fell from 1.2 in 1760 to .39 in 1830 and .30 in 1860 (Feinstein, 1978, p. 88). The absolute amount of circulating capital increased as well during the Industrial Revolution, but its growth was dwarfed by the rise in fixed capital. In this sense, then, the Hicks-Ranis-Fei view is corroborated. The economic reasons for the change in the composition of capital are rather obvious. Improved transportation, communications, and distribution reduced the need to hold large inventories of raw materials, fuel, and finished products. There are well-understood economies of scale in the holding of inventories and cash, so that it is clear that larger firms needed less circulating capital per unit of output than domestic industry. This may have been partially offset by the requirements of new inputs, such as fuel and spare parts. A second factor in the relative decline of circulating capital is the decline of output prices due to productivity growth, which reduced the value of goods in progress and raw materials relative to that of buildings and equipment.

The importance of capital in the Industrial Revolution was not identical to the importance of the Industrial Revolution in capital

---

[92] The Rostow hypothesis was criticized, among others, by Habakkuk and Deane (1962). For a critique of the importance of fixed capital in the Industrial Revolution, see Pollard (1964).

formation. In current prices, in the early days of the Industrial Revolution (1761-1770), manufacturing and mining accounted for only 12.5 percent of gross domestic fixed capital formation. Although the annual investment in industry increased almost 15-fold between 1760 and 1830, the share of mining and manufacturing in 1831-1840 was only 21.1 percent (Feinstein, 1988a, p. 429). Yet without capital the modern sector would not have been able to grow. The unit setup costs of firms was rising steadily, and the number of firms, as the industry expanded, was growing rapidly. Consequently, in iron, cotton, steam, and transport gross capital formation increased by huge factors, and the stock of capital mushroomed to unprecedented levels. In mining, for example, gross capital formation in 1830 was 15.6 times as large as in 1760 (Pollard, 1988, p. 63). In cotton the *stock* of capital in 1788 was only 12 percent of its level in 1833 (Chapman and Butt, 1988, pp. 124-125). All the same, fixed capital in cotton in 1833 was only 1.5 percent of the national stock of reproducible fixed assets. The smallness of the share of the modern industries in the economy is in and of itself not sufficient to show, however, that they were not capital constrained.

Oddly enough, the total factor productivity estimates seemingly imply that capital formation was a comparatively minor factor in the macroeconomics of the Industrial Revolution. The most recent figures produced by Crafts and Harley (1992) suggest that capital accounted for about half of the aggregate growth of the economy between 1760 and 1830. Because capital grew at about the same rate as output and only slightly faster than labor, however, it contributed little to growth proper. In the period 1760-1800 the rise in the capital to labor ratio and in total productivity each accounted for half the rise in per capita income; after 1800 the contributions fall to 30 percent for capital and 70 percent for productivity. Feinstein, who was the first to notice this, rejects this interpretation and points to the importance of capital as the "carrier" of technical progress. Insofar as capital and technological progress were complementary, the arithmetic of total factor productivity estimates are misleading, since these computations assume that the contributions of capital and productivity are additive and independent. A more accurate estimation would try to take into account the interaction between the two.

How important to the course of the Industrial Revolution were the failings of the capital market? Crouzet has concluded that "the eighteenth century capital market seems, to twentieth century eyes, badly organized, but the creators of modern industry do not seem to have suffered too much from its imperfection. . . . English industry, compared with that of the Continent, seems to have overflowed with capital" (Crouzet, 1965, pp. 187-188). This conclusion may be ripe for some reexamination. First, while the comparison with the Continent is probably accurate on the whole, there were important exceptions (Mokyr, 1975). On the Continent, too, self-finance was the norm, and it is not quite clear whether Britain was much better supplied with capital than, say, Belgium. Moreover, it seems inescapable that the Industrial Revolution in Britain would have occurred faster and more efficiently if financial constraints had been less stringent. Given that the modern sector as a whole was at first rather small compared with the rest of the economy, the capital market's imperfection meant that from the outset the rate of profit set a ceiling on the rate of accumulation. The existence of *some* capital markets does not necessarily refute this argument. If these markets channeled savings from one firm to another in the modern sector, the constraint on the sector as a whole remained in force, and fixed capital had to grow by pulling itself up by the bootstraps. Postan put it well in his classic article: "By the beginning of the eighteenth century there were enough rich people in the country to finance an economic effort far in excess of the modest activities of the leaders of the Industrial Revolution. ... What was inadequate was not the quantity of stored-up wealth but its behavior. The reservoirs of savings were full enough, but conduits to connect them to the wheels of industry were few and meager" (Postan, 1935, p.71).[93]

---

[93] Crouzet's statement that the early factory masters "did not suffer" seems oddly incompatible with his own evidence. Two paragraphs below this statement, Crouzet cites the cases of two highly successful firms, the Walker brothers and McConnel and Kennedy, who paid themselves miserably low salaries in order to maximize the income available for plowing back (Crouzet, 1965, pp. 188-189). Some of the most famous inventors and entrepreneurs (Cartwright and John Roebuck immediately come to mind) foundered for lack of working capital, and Richard Arkwright's success is often attributed not to his technical skills but to his virtuoso ability to remain afloat in the treacherous currents of finance during the early stages of the Industrial Revolution.

5. The Factory and the Modern Industrial Firm

The creation of the workplace, in which many workers were assembled together under one roof to jointly produce an output and were subject to discipline and coordination, has become one of the symbols of the Industrial Revolution. To some extent this is a myth: Some large factories did exist before 1750. The great silk mills in Derby and Stockport, the ironworks of Ambrose Crowley in Newcastle, and metalworks of John Taylor and Matthew Boulton employed many hundreds of workers before 1770. Yet such large plants were rare. Large capitalist enterprises were far more common, but they typically left most of the work to be carried out in workers' homes, and only a few stages of the product were completed in centralized sites. In wool, for example, a large employer like Samuel Hill in Yorkshire in the 1740s employed 1,500 workers, mostly in putting-out.

Part of the story of the Industrial Revolution is that these employees were brought to work in centralized plants, thus changing the nature of work and with it the basic functioning of the family and the household. Increasingly, households became specialized units designed for consumption only, whereas production was carried out in a firm, geographically divorced from the home and often subject to different rules and hierarchies. Why did this happen? Some economists, such as Oliver Williamson (1980), declare that by saving on transactions costs, factories were simply more efficient than cottage industries (whether putting-out or independent producers), and thus their rise was inexorable. Such a simplistic approach cannot possibly do justice to the historical reality (S.R.H. Jones, 1982; Szostak, 1989). After all, the domestic system survived for many centuries, and its demise was drawn out over a very long period. Its advantages were many: It kept families geographically intact, it was flexible and more adaptable to fluctuations in demand and supply, and it left the workers free to choose any point on the leisure-income trade-off rather than forcing them into rigid work schedules and the discipline of the factories. Geographical centralization of production under one roof and the imposition of factory discipline did not always go hand in hand and need to be explained separately.

Turning first to the question why the concentration of production in large-scale plants occurred, the most obvious answer is that the new technologies changed the optimal scale of the producing unit and introduced increasing returns where once there were constant returns. Some equipment could not be made in small models that fit into the living rooms of workers' cottages and thus required large plants: iron puddling furnaces and rollers, steam and water engines, silk-throwing mills, chemical and gas works – all required relatively large production units. Heating, lighting, power supply, security, equipment maintenance, storage facilities, finance, and marketing were all activities in which scale economies were obviously the result of technical considerations. Long ago Usher wrote that "machinery made the factory a successful and general form of organization. . . . Its introduction ultimately forced the workman to accept the discipline of the factory" (Usher, 1920, p. 350). Landes (1986, p. 606) has recently restated this argument in unambiguous terms: "What made the factory successful in Britain was not the wish but the muscle: the machine and the engines. We do not have factories until these were available." Both would agree, of course, that factories without machinery were not only possible but actually existed; in the long run, however, their success depended on technology.

Others have rejected this position: Stephen Marglin (1974) set the tone, which was echoed by others as diverse as Berg (1980), Cohen (1981), and Szostak (1989, 1991). Their argument is that technological change was not necessary for the establishment of centralized workshops, which in fact preceded the great inventions of the last third of the eighteenth century. Berg (1985, p. 220) and Szostak (1989, p. 345) point to industry after industry that established centralized workshops employing practically the same techniques as cottage industries: wool, pottery, metal trades, even framework knitting. Marglin's own view is little more than a Marxist tale of woe according to which factories enabled employers to exercise more control over their workers and to squeeze more profits out of them. Technological progress in this interpretation tended to be a by-product of the intensification of social control. The fact that in many industries workshops preceded the emergence of new technologies does not prove, of course, that technological factors were unimportant in the development of the factory, only that they were not the *only* factors. The large workshop's occurrence may have preceded mechanization in many industries, but surely its ultimate triumph was a result of the growing advantage that new technologies bestowed on factories. Marglin's argument is further undermined by the fact that from the point of view of employer control, the distinction between factory and domestic workers is not as sharp as is usually supposed. Many of those workshops were not factories in the traditional sense of the word – they imposed no discipline, observed no tight schedules or regulations, and paid workers by the piece. The employer hardly cared if the worker worked hard or not, if he or she arrived at work on time, took Mondays off, or drank on the job. These workshops were purely "rent and charges" kinds of places and thus were quite different from Marglin's oppressive and tightly controlled mills (Clark, 1992b). On the other side of the equation, social control gradually invaded the domestic economy during the years of the Industrial Revolution. A series of acts passed between 1777 and 1790 permitted employers to enter the workers' premises to inspect their operations, ostensibly to curb embezzlement. Unwin (1924, p. 35) concludes that by this time "there was not much left of the independence of the small master, except the choice of hours."

A more cogent complement to the technological determinism of Landes is provided by economists such as Millward (1981) and Szostak (1991). This reasoning derives from the economics of information. The organization of production by wage labor under any system depends on information that the employer can amass on the effort the worker puts in. Paying workers a piece rate – uniformly practiced in putting-out industries – solves this problem if the employer has no difficulty assessing the quality of the final product and if there are no cross effects between workers' productivities (so that the effort of one worker does not affect the output of another). In the domestic system, employers faced a double problem: Workers could increase their earnings by cutting corners on quality and finish, and the embezzlement of raw materials (which usually belonged to the capitalist) was a widespread complaint (Styles, 1983). The problem of embezzlement, like quality control, was one of information costs; measuring the precise quantities of yarn supplied to a weaver and comparing those with the final output was itself costly, and had to be correlated against normal losses of raw material during the process of production, which the employer did not observe directly. As the division of labor became tighter and the final products more complex, the decentralized division of labor practiced in the putting-out system became increasingly costly. Factories, too, usually paid piece rates, but the monitoring of quality was much easier because the employer could inspect the inputs and the production process as well as the output. Factories also reduced embezzlement and capital costs incurred by workers' negligence. In addition, in factories there was the option of paying workers a time rate, which would be necessary if the marginal product of labor was hard to assess or beyond the worker's control.

Moreover, economists have increasingly realized that all systems in which one individual works for another -- that is, all capitalist systems -- are subject to an agency problem: The employer (or "principal") has to manipulate the incentive system to ensure that his worker ("agent") operates so as to maximize the profits of the enterprise. Factories solved the agency problem by imposing direct monitoring of labor by supervisory personnel overseeing the efforts put in by the workers, their use of raw materials, and the care with which they carried out their tasks. Thus the main advantage of factories in this view was that they permitted the employer to ascertain whether fluctuations in output were due to the worker's effort or to a circumstance beyond his or her control. The incentives set up by the factory system to solve the agency problem were largely negative: A negligent or dishonest worker could be fined, dismissed, or even punished physically (Pollard, [1965] 1968, p. 222).

Some specific examples of this general problem have been proposed as explanations for the rise of the factory system. Szostak (1989, 1991) argues, for example, that the employer used centralized workshops to produce standardized goods of more uniform quality, because more integrated markets and changes in distribution methods in the eighteenth century required these changes (see also Styles, 1992). Standardization and uniformity demanded a special kind of quality control, which required continuous supervision and thus factories. Alternatively, as new technology was embodied in more sophisticated and expensive capital goods, the employers became more concerned with the workers' treatment of these machines, because negligence and sabotage became increasingly costly to the firm. Factories may also have induced innovation directly. Some writers, beginning with Adam Smith, strongly believe that a finer division of labor leads to mechanization because the division of labor splits production up into simpler parts, and simple processes are easier to mechanize. Moreover, in the domestic system the entrepreneur rarely observed actual physical production as it was occurring. Once he actually observed the interaction of his labor, his equipment, and his materials, as happens in centralized workplaces, he was more likely to come up with ideas how to save all three than the absentee putting-out merchant manufacturer.

A third explanation of the rise of the factory has to do with the division of labor and is logically independent of the technological and informational interpretations (though in reality the three were closely intertwined). Dividing labor into small tasks carried out by specialists has two advantages. The first, stressed by Adam Smith, assumes that all workers are the same at first but that the division of labor enhances productivity because specialized workers get better at what they do through learning and experience, because time is saved in moving work between workers rather than workers between different tasks, because of the simplification of tasks allowing more routinization, and because of the putative effect that the division of labor has on invention. Routine and repetitive work tends to be less skill-intensive, cheaper, and possibly more productive. The second advantage, emphasized by Babbage, assumes that workers differ inherently in their abilities and that the division of labor maximizes productive efficiency because workers can specialize in those tasks in which they have a comparative advantage. Specialization assures that workers are not asked to carry out tasks for which they are overqualified (which would be wasteful) or underqualified (leading to costly errors).

The advantages of the division of labor have been challenged by Marglin (1974), but when all is said and done his attack on one of the oldest and most widely believed tenets of economics has been beaten back without causing serious damage. Landes (1986) points out that Marglin fails altogether to deal with the Babbage argument and that his "evidence" for the falseness of Adam Smith's famous pinmaking example is based on a misreading of the literature. Experience and learning by doing are simple facts of life. Perhaps in a pin factory or an automobile assembly plant, the simplest jobs can be learned quickly and little more is learned after a few weeks, but in most skilled jobs, years of apprenticeship are required. Whether the difference between me and my dentist is due to innate abilities or to training, in neither case is it likely that productivity would be enhanced by us swapping jobs.

Yet the division of labor did not require factories. Domestic industries practiced it, and a large part of the function of the merchant entrepreneur was to shuttle goods in process from one cottage to another. In activities where technical factors made domestic production infeasible, such as fulling and calico printing, the manufacturer carried out the work in a "mill." Domestic industry did the rest. Decentralized specialization had advantages, but it also had costs, such as the transport costs of goods in process and the transactions costs of measuring and counting output at each stage.[94] As the division of labor became finer, the final products more complex, and the equipment more expensive, the costs of geographical dispersion rose, and firms switched from decentralized to centralized production.[95] The biggest advantage of rural domestic industries was their ability to switch labor back and forth from industrial to agricultural activities and thus exploit off-season labor. In effect, this means that outwork had access to cheaper labor than factories. It has been argued that the long survival of domestic producers in Britain, as opposed to the swift victory of the factory in the United States, was due to the differences in the seasonality of the demand for labor as British agriculture relied more on grains with its highly seasonal labor demand pattern (Sokoloff and Dollar, 1991). As the short-term mobility of labor increased with transport improvements, this advantage gradually diminished. The long-term decline in transportation costs tipped the balance in favor of the factory in other ways.[96]

All the same, the transition process took a long time and was far from monotonic. For many industries, factories did not mean the instant end of domestic industry but its temporary expansion, because when some activities were moved to mills, there was increased demand for the output of those production stages that remained for the time being in workers' homes. In some industries growth occurred through the

---

[94] S.R.H. Jones (1982, p. 126) minimizes the importance of transportation costs, but he fails to take into account that the geographical dispersion of work involved more costs than just the direct transport costs. Bad weather, for example, could totally disrupt the supply of raw materials and goods in process and thus wreak havoc on production and delivery schedules.

[95] A detailed summary of the advantages of the two systems can be found in Szostak (1989).

[96] Declining transport costs basically led to an increased division of labor, and while a rough division of labor was consistent with putting-out, as the division became finer the advantage moved toward factories. More integrated markets also led to a greater demand for standardized products and for quickly changing national fashions; here, too, factories had an advantage. See Szostak (1989, p. 348).

expansion of the domestic industries.[97] Berg (1985, p. 282) points out that in the Birmingham metal trades, the industry's growth brought about a bifurcation in which large firms, some of which worked through factories, and domestic producers expanded at the expense of "substantial artisans." The final collapse of domestic industry did not come until the middle of the nineteenth century. In the long run, however, the triumph of the factory was as complete as it was inevitable.

The importance of the factory as a social institution can hardly be overestimated. The divorce between household and workplace imposed substantial costs on the industrial worker, from the psychic costs of having to witness family members supervised and monitored by others to the very real costs of the time spent on commuting (Smelser, 1959). The introduction of discipline and order into the lives of workers was another dramatic novelty. Until the Industrial Revolution discipline was largely a family matter. Industrial workers, whether they were independent artisans or part of a putting-out system, rarely encountered the phenomenon. Even on board merchant ships discipline could only be enforced by means of harsh penalties. The transition was not sharp; many factory owners hired whole families and used the family as a tool to enforce discipline.[98] Yet workers detested the mills and resisted discipline, and employers were often desperately looking for solutions to the stubborn problems of absenteeism, drunkenness, sloppiness, and unruliness. "The concept of industrial discipline was new, and called for as much innovation as the technical inventions of the age," writes Pollard ([1965] 1968, p. 217). Firms designed incentives to bring about the discipline, but they also preferred to hire women and children, who were believed to be more docile.

The advantages of introducing worker discipline were not identical to those realized by the factory system as such, as the two were not always coincidental. The gains of discipline have traditionally been regarded as the advantages of coordination. Factories required coordination between different activities of the laborers, as well as

---

[97] An example is the career of Peter Stubs, a Lancashire filemaker, whose business was largely based on a network of outworkers run from the inn he kept in Warrington until he built his first workshops nearby in 1802.

[98] For instance, Robert Peel's factory in Bury employed 136 workers in 1802, of whom 85 belonged to 26 families (Smelser, 1959, p. 185).

between labor and capital. Equipment such as steam engines, overhead costs such as heating, lighting, and fuel, and maintenance and supervisory personnel were fixed costs in the short run, and so if workers were absent or lazy there was costly waste involved. Above all, employers needed workers to be punctual.[99] Discipline was also necessary, however, to maintain quality standards, to avoid embezzlement, to prevent fights between workers, and to deliver goods in time. The equipment handled by workers was expensive, so that errors and negligence could be very costly for the capitalist. Industrial and mining accidents due to workers' mistakes could be expensive and led to strictly enforced rules. Discipline, by regulating the amount of time and effort supplied per worker, saved on hiring costs and reduced the variance of labor input and thus of output. To be sure, it can be argued that some of the costs of the absence of discipline could be overcome by holding larger inventories and by adjusting hiring practices to absenteeism (Clark, 1992b). But apparently such alternatives were expensive and the advantages of discipline were such that most of the famous entrepreneurs of the time, including Josiah Wedgwood, Richard Arkwright, Samuel Oldknow, and Matthew Boulton struggled with the problem. Clark's argument that discipline was a means to extract a greater effort from workers and could be viewed as advantageous to them if it raised their income is interesting but does not contradict the more technical advantages of discipline (Clark, 1992b).

It also seems plausible that the "authority relations," to use Williamson's (1980) term, that came to dominate interactions between capitalists and employees in factories were instrumental in overcoming resistance to technological progress. In the extreme case, the employer not only controlled labor, inventories, and fixed capital but could also choose the technique of production by himself. Outworkers tended to be at the forefront of resistance to new technologies out of fear that laborsaving machinery would reduce the demand for their labor (Calhoun, 1982). Authority and discipline might have reduced, at least for a while, the ability of labor to resist technological progress. The factory, however, did not solve the problem of resistance altogether; unions eventually undermined the ability of the capitalist to exploit the

---

[99] Employers reserved their harshest fines for latecomers, whereas the prize for good (probably docile) workers, not surprisingly, was a clock (Landes, 1983, p. 229).

most advanced techniques. Collective action by workers imposed an
effective limit on the "authority" exercised by capitalists. Workers'
associations tried to ban some new techniques altogether or tried to
appropriate the entire productivity gains in terms of higher piece wages,
thus destroying the incentive to innovate. On the other hand, such
strikes often led to technological advances aimed specifically at crippling
strikes (Bruland, 1982; Rosenberg, 1976, pp. 118-119).[100] On balance,
it is hard to know whether the decentralization of the putting-out
industry, with its obvious potential of "divide and rule," was less
conducive to technological change than factories -- yet this dimension
has been altogether missed by scholars absorbed by static efficiency
gains and transactions costs.

6. The Consequences: The Standard-of-Living Debate

The standard-of-living debate concerns what happened to living
standards during the Industrial Revolution. It is one of the most lively
yet most inconclusive debates in the entire Industrial Revolution
literature. The discussion has been complicated in part because it
became intertwined with political and ideological elements, the
"optimist" school largely finding its supporters among the conservatives,
the "pessimist" school mostly drawing upon socialist and left-leaning
scholars. The philosophical question whether industrial society has been
a positive development in human history reaches far beyond the
relatively modest boundaries of economic history. What should have
been a purely quantitative debate about numbers and deflators has
divided scholars deeply on lines that correlate strongly with ideological
positions. Those like E. P. Thompson and E. J. Hobsbawm, who have
regarded industrial capitalism as enslaving and alienating, have tried to
round off their position by arguing that it was also immiserizing. Those
like T. S. Ashton and R. M. Hartwell, who are sympathetic to bourgeois capitalism and the achievements of free-market societies, have
insisted that industrialism was liberating as well as enriching. Some of
this ideological baggage seems to have been shed in the past decade, but
scholarly opinion has remained divided.

---

[100] The most famous example of an invention triggered by a strike was that
of the self-acting mule, invented in 1825 by Richard Roberts at the prompting
of Manchester manufacturers plagued by a strike of mule operators.

Beyond that, however, there is a certain ambiguity regarding the terms on which the debate is being conducted. This ambiguity has been explained well by Hartwell and Engerman (1975) and further refined by Von Tunzelmann (1985). Three separate debates can be distinguished, which need to be kept logically separate:

1. The factual debate, which is concerned with what actually happened in Britain between 1760 and 1830 or 1850.

2. The counterfactual debate, which tries to identify the *net* effect of the Industrial Revolution on living standards. This question is logically equivalent to asking what would have happened to British living standards if everything had been the same in the period in question except for the technological changes of the Industrial Revolution.

3. The hypercounterfactual question, which asks whether, given everything that happened, it would have been possible to follow a set of economic policies that would have made economic welfare more than it actually was.

The answer to the *second* question, whether without the Industrial Revolution living standards would have held up as much, is eloquently answered in a famous passage by T.S. Ashton in the closing paragraph of his little book (1948, p. 111): "There are to-day in the plains of India and China men and women, plague-ridden and hungry, living lives little better . . . than those of the cattle that toil with them . . . Such Asiatic standards, and such unmechanized horrors, are the lot of those who increase their numbers without passing through an Industrial Revolution." A simple calculation confirms Ashton's eloquence: If we take the weights computed by Crafts for labor, capital, and natural resources, we can compute the change in income per capita that would have occurred due to the growth of population and its pressure on other resources but without any productivity increase.

The counterfactual exercise is set up as follows: Assume that labor and resources changed at their actual historical rates and constrain productivity growth to zero. We have to make some assumptions about the counterfactual rate of capital accumulation. Three alternative assumptions will be employed: (1) the capital/labor ratio would have remained the same (requiring a savings ratio higher than the actual one), (2) the savings ratio would have remained at its historical level (that is, rising gradually), and (3) the savings ratio would have remained fixed because of the lack of suitable investment projects and the changing age structure of the population. Table 1.3 below presents the decline of income per capita implied.

TABLE 1.3 Counterfactual Decline in Income per Capita "Without" an Industrial Revolution (annual changes, in percentages)

Period	Assumption 1	Assumption 2[a]	Assumption 3[b]
1760-1800	0.045%	0.125%	0.185%
1800-1830	0.15%	0.41%	0.46%
Income in 1830 (1760 = 100)	93.9	84.1	80.9

a - Assuming savings rates equal means for period.
b - Assuming savings rates equal actual ones for first decade in the period.
Sources: Rates of change and shares from Crafts (1985a, p. 81). Savings rates from Feinstein (1981, p. 131). Cols. 2 and 3 required the estimation of capital/output ratio, computed from data in Mitchell (1988, p. 864) and Feinstein (1981, p. 136).

The calculations in Table 1.3 actually understate the hypothetical decline in living standards slightly, because they do not take into account the war-related shocks and the string of poor harvests that plagued Great Britain. All the same, they indicate that in the absence of an Industrial Revolution, a rising population -- as Malthus had predicted -- would have encountered declining living standards.

Yet the picture is more complex than that. The closest we can get to a controlled experiment of an economy that had a history similar to Britain's in terms of population growth and supply shocks, but without the Industrial Revolution, is Ireland's. Ashton used the example of Ireland as a warning against what could happen without industrialization, but clearly there are no such simple lessons to be learned from the Irish example. In fact, *average* living standards in prefamine Ireland did not decline much, even if there was a deterioration in the distribution of income (Mokyr and O Gráda, 1988). The Great Famine, of course, was a hugely traumatic event that might well have been, if not averted, much mitigated had Ireland developed more of a modern sector. Had the potato blight not happened, however, our verdict regarding this example of a nonindustrializing country that experienced population growth might have been less harsh. Much of continental Europe also experienced population growth in this age, yet experienced neither an intensive rate of industrialization nor grievous famines. The best we can do is to conclude that Ireland may have been more *vulnerable* to accidental shocks because of the absence of an Industrial Revolution.

Turning to the *third* question, the hypercounterfactual one, modern research has clarified the issues and made an argument regarding the possibility that a more enlightened policy could have smoothened the pains of industrialization. Two of the most prominent cliometricians have made, from quite different points of view, arguments to the effect that "the thesis of the Hammonds that a suitably enlightened government could have brought about higher living standards is vindicated" (Von Tunzelmann, 1985, p. 221). Von Tunzelmann employs dynamic programming to show that it was possible for the British economy to have attained the final values of 1850 and yet have supported a higher consumption level. In the actual experience, in this view, industry tended to be too capital intensive in its early stages. Of course, such an optimal path could only be achieved by the deliberate interference of the government into the price system. Such an interference would, however, have had further ramifications that Von Tunzelmann does not explore. His important insight that things *could* have been better than they were does not necessarily support an argument that government interference would have moved the economy's path from the actual to the optimal. In a slightly different vein, Jeffrey Williamson (1990a) argues that Britain underinvested in its overhead capital, especially in urban areas. The rate of return on social overhead capital was very high, but Williamson argues that an unfair and inefficient tax system led to what he calls "public sector failure." As a consequence, Britain's standard of living was affected by an imbalance between private and public goods. Overhead projects such as sewage, water supply, fire protection, public health, and other "urban amenities" were undersupplied. Williamson's thesis is similar to John Kenneth Galbraith's analysis of the U.S. economy in his famous *The Affluent Society*.

The first of the three debates, the actual standard-of-living debate, is the main battlefield on which scholars have argued for decades. A summary of the debates and some of the best-known papers can be found in Taylor (1975). By the mid-1970s the debate had reached something of an impasse in which neither camp had scored an all-out victory and most other scholars turned elsewhere with their interests. In the 1980s, however, a number of important contributions were made by economists. The debate has bifurcated into one concerning purely economic indicators and a more inclusive set of biological indicators. The most important contributions to the economic evidence were made in the 1980s by Feinstein and Crafts, who examined aggregate consumption, and by Lindert and Williamson's work on real wages.

The message that these economists draw from their evidence is remarkably consistent. Their conclusion is that living standards remained more or less unchanged between 1760 and 1820 and then accelerated rapidly between 1820 and 1850, so that by the middle of the century living standards had improved considerably for a number of decades. Feinstein (1981, p. 136) estimates that consumption per head in 1841-1850 was 72 percent higher than in 1811-1820, and Crafts estimates the rate of growth of per capita consumption between 1821 and 1851 at a lower but still respectable 45 percent (1985a, p. 95). Lindert and Williamson estimate real wage growth between 1819 and 1851 at 80 percent for all "blue collar workers" and 116 percent for "all workers" (1985a, p. 187). Crafts has revised these estimates as well, tempering but not overturning the new optimist message.

Yet these economic indicators have failed to sweep the field. Although it is reasonable to conclude that standards of living did not *decline* for extended periods of time during the Industrial Revolution, declaring an optimist victory seems premature. For one thing, the optimists have essentially conceded the entire period before 1820, thus focusing the debate on the three-and-a-half decades between the Battle of Waterloo and 1850. Yet even for this period, ambiguities remain. The aggregate consumption data produced by Feinstein and refined by Crafts are residuals, the difference between highly speculative data of output and investment. By construction, they cannot account for changes in income distribution, and Feinstein warned that "the basic estimates are far from reliable" and that they should be used with caution. To be sure, they are lent much reinforcement by the Lindert-Williamson wage data, but the feeling is that more confirmation is needed to disperse remaining doubts.

Such confirmation has not been forthcoming. On closer inspection, the real wage data is found to suffer from a number of rather serious defects. One is that they cover only limited data points and that the choice of the end year (1851) by Lindert and Williamson is unfortunate, because that happened to be a year of unusually low prices.[101] The nominal wages changed very little in this period, so that the rise in real wages came almost exclusively from falling prices. Hence, the optimist conclusion is highly sensitive to the correct specification of the price deflator, and its deficiencies weaken the optimist finding even further.[102] When those two biases are corrected together, real wages rise so slowly that Huck (1992, chap. 2, p. 22) concludes that "1850, or some point in the 1840s, should be seen as the key turning point, as opposed to [the] 1820s."[103] Some of the new series produced are illustrated in Table 1.4.

A second defect is that the wage data cover only selected workers. By definition it covers only those employed in the "formal" sector, that is, receiving a wage. Under labor market equilibrium conditions, this objection is unimportant because the wage rate in the formal labor market and the implicit wages earned by the self-employed would move together. But much of the argument for the "modernization" of industry suggests that while factory wages were rising, the real income of most domestic workers and independent artisans were falling (Allen,

---

[101] The only price index covering the entire nineteenth century, the Rousseaux index, points to 1851 as the cheapest year before 1885, and the index is about ˜7 percent lower than the average for 1840-1850. Had Lindert and Williamson chosen 1847--an unusually expensive year--the rise in real wages would have been half of what they report.

[102] This point was made by Crafts (1985d), who points out that Lindert and Williamson use only cotton as their textile price and that cotton prices fell faster than wool. Correcting for these defects, he concludes that the index rose slower before 1820 and fell slower after 1820 than Lindert and Williamson estimate.

[103] Lindert and Williamson's nominal wage series shows virtual stability: In 1819 the wage of all "blue collar workers" was 101.84 (1851 = 100). The revised price index they themselves propose in response to Crafts's critique is 166.6 in 1819 and 141.4 in 1847 (1851 = 100). If we assume that nominal wages in 1847 and 1851 were the same, the implied rise in real wages between 1819 and 1847 is only .52 percent per year. To be sure, 1847 was a year of extreme dearth (although less so than 1839), but the rate of deflation proposed by Lindert and Williamson is sharper than that of Crafts.

124 *Joel Mokyr*

TABLE 1.4 Nominal Wages, Real Wages, and Prices, 1797-1851

1	2	3	4	5	6
Year	Nominal Wages (male adults)	Real Wages (Blue Collar)	Real Wages (all)	Real Wages (Blue Collar, revised)	Cost of Living, Revised
1797	58.97	53.61	42.48	60.6[a]	146.3[b]
1805	75.87	51.73	40.64	–	177.5
1810	84.89	50.04	39.41	–	207.1
1815	85.30	58.15	46.71	–	164.3
1819	84.37	55.68	46.13	69.9	166.6
1827	83.11	69.25	58.99	79.5	131.9
1835	88.77	83.43	78.69	88.0	109.4
1851	100.00	100.00	100.00	100.00	100.0

a - 1781
b - 1795
Sources: Cols. 2-4: Williamson (1985, pp. 14, 17). Col. 5: Huck (1992, p. 48)
Col. 6: Lindert and Williamson (1985b, p. 148).

1992b, pp. 255-256; 296-297; Lyons, 1989). This discrepancy constituted the market "signal" that the death bell was sounding for much of the traditional sector; for our present purpose it means that using formal wages as a proxy for "labor income" may be quite misleading. Furthermore, not all formal market wages are equally useful. The estimates of agricultural wages are especially fragile, and because agricultural workers still constituted over 20 percent of the labor force in 1841, their fate is quite important. The income of farm laborers was determined in part by other factors, such as access to commons and a growing seasonal unemployment, especially of women (Allen, 1992a; Huck, 1992; Snell, 1985). Thus rising *wages* might well have been accompanied by falling *incomes* and *living standards* as growing redundancies in agriculture were not met by a rising demand for labor from nonagriculture, leading, in Allen's words, to "structural unemployment rather than increased manufactured output" (1992a, p.

32). This complication was exacerbated by the decline in the custom of paying workers partly in kind, so that the rise in observed real wages could in part be spurious. Changes in nominal wages in agriculture differed from a 13 percent fall in the east to a 10 percent rise in the southwest between 1824 and 1851.

Most wage data used by Lindert and Williamson pertain to adult male wages. The justification for this is explicitly stated by them (Lindert and Williamson 1985a, p. 194) to be that wage rates of women and children advanced as fast as those of adult male farm laborers (which was considerable slower than that of "all workers"). This conclusion, they feel, will not be overthrown by correcting for changes in employment. Recent research, however, has been divided on this issue. Horrell and Humphries (1992b) confirm Lindert and Williamson's findings about the rise of adult male real wages, though not without some misgivings.[104] Yet their work clearly shows than male and female earnings did not move all the time in the same direction. Robert Allen (1992b, pp. 255-256, 296), who has studied the fate of rural laborers, has emphasized the sharp decline in employment opportunities suggesting that family income fell relative to male earnings. As Allen's males hardly experienced much real income growth, he concludes that before 1850 real family income in rural Britain declined.

Furthermore, rising real wages may have different interpretations. Even a firm believer in the efficiency of labor markets will concede that a rise in real wages may not be an indication of rising living standards if these rising real wages were a compensation for deteriorating labor conditions. If factory work and life in industrial towns and villages became more onerous, dangerous, or unpleasant, rising real wages would have the interpretation of a compensating differential. This effect has been measured in an ingenious paper by Brown (1990), who, like Lindert and Williamson, finds a significant rise in real wages yet concludes (pp. 612-613) that "there was virtually no improvement in

---

[104] Horrell and Humphries add that secular income growth was interrupted by setbacks that tend to be underestimated by trend analysis based on a limited number of observations. They also note, as we have before, that the optimist findings depend crucially on price movements (they deflate their nominal series by Lindert and Williamson's "best guess" cost-of-living index), and insist that questions still hang over the speed by which price falls filtered down to the working class.

living standards until at least the 1840s and perhaps the entire first half of the nineteenth century."

One way to try to circumvent these and similar problems is to look at microeconomic series for the consumption of a popular and income-elastic consumer good. Any such series would have the advantage that it would reflect living standards of both employed and self-employed workers and take into account both the level of income per capita and the inequality of its distribution. Food consumption series are shrouded in rather serious statistical uncertainty. Recent work on the problem, based on fragmentary and indirect data, seems to cast growing doubt that food consumption per capita was rising sharply during the Industrial Revolution.[105] More accurate are the series for domestic consumption of imported consumer goods, such as tobacco and sugar. After correcting for changes in prices and other effects, we can employ these data to infer what kind of income data (given estimated income and price elasticities) would have generated these consumption figures (Mokyr, 1988). The results lend no support to the view that living standards increased before the late 1840s. The dilemma is thus clear: If real incomes of the bulk of British workers increased, and yet they did not eat appreciably more, lived in crowded and unhealthy houses, drank no more sweetened tea, smoked no more pipes -- where did this money go? The consumption of a few small items like hard soap and iron goods may well have increased, but many of the commodities on which we have data, such as bricks, coal, and glass, were as much investment as consumption goods and cannot be used readily for the standard-of-living debate. The only commodity that clearly figures prominently as an item in the improving budgets of workers is cotton textiles.

---

[105] A detailed attempt to patch together existing data is carried out by Helling (1977), whose estimates of per capita grain and meat consumption show no improvement until the mid 1840s. Lindert (1992) seems to believe that workers spent their incomes on rapidly expanding nonfood items. Clark, in his essay later in this book, concludes that given what happened to British agricultural output, sharply rising food consumption is unlikely. Clark, Huberman and Lindert (1993) point to the central dilemma faced by optimist interpretations: the inconsistency between the rise in demand for food implied by optimist estimates of income and the stagnant levels of per capita food consumption suggested by the historical evidence.

An alternative approach to the standard-of-living problem is to look at biological indicators of the standard of living. It has long been recognized that indicators such as life expectancy and physical health are strongly correlated with economic living standards. Indeed, some economists (notably Sen, 1987) maintain that such physical measures *are* the standard of living. Thus in the absence of unambiguous economic measures of living standards, economic historians have increasingly turned to biological measures to try to test the hypothesis of rising economic welfare before 1850. On the whole, these measures have failed to support the optimist case. The broadest measure is the crude mortality rate, which declined more or less in the same period identified by the new optimists as the period of rising living standards: At about 1760, the crude death rate for England was still about 27.5 per 1000, declining steadily (with a few reversals) to about 22.5 per 1000 by 1850. Gross mortality rates, however, are flawed indicators for many reasons, primarily because of their dependence on the age structure of the population. A better measure is the life expectancy at birth. This variable, too, shows some improvement over the entire period, but its rise stops in 1820, and it remains essentially static at about 40 years until 1860 (Wrigley and Schofield, 1981, p. 529). The sharp rise in consumption and real wages claimed by the new optimists should have produced, through improved nutrition and better living conditions, a rise in life expectancy, perhaps lagged by a few years. Nothing of the sort happened. Data on infant mortality, though not available on a national basis, tell very much the same story. In a sample of seven parishes, Huck (1992) finds rising infant mortality rates in the period between 1813 and 1836, with no appreciable decline until 1845, precisely the years identified by Lindert and Williamson as the period of rapid improvement.

A biological indicator that has enjoyed considerable interest in the last few years is human height. It has become widely accepted that height is a function of net nutritional status, that is, the amount of food taken in by children and adolescents net of demands made on their bodies by labor and diseases. All other things equal, a child born in a family that enjoyed a higher standard-of-living would grow up to be taller. The idea that observed height data could therefore be used to approximate the elusive standard of living was proposed by Fogel (1983) and his associates and has since then stimulated a large number of research projects. The research that is most pertinent to the standard of living debate in Britain is Floud, Wachter, and Gregory (1990). Their finding is that net nutritional status, as measured by stature, increased between about 1760 and 1820 and then went into a secular decline for half a century. Indeed, the cohorts born in 1850-1854 are shorter than any cohort born in the nineteenth century, and the levels attained in the first decades of the century are not attained again before the last decade (Floud, Wachter and Gregory, 1990, chap. 4, passim). Based on this evidence, they maintain, the debate on living standards during the second and third quarters of the nineteenth century is still very much open, and (p. 305) "if there were significant gains in real incomes for the working class between the 1820s and the 1850s they were bought at a very high price." In other words, if there were economic gains, they did not lead to *physical* improvements in the lives of English men and women.

The incongruity of the biological indicators, which tend more to support the pessimist case, and the aggregate economic indicators, which on the whole support the optimist case, can be reconciled in three different ways. One is that the biological indicators pertain to the population as a whole, whereas the real wage data pertain largely to the modern and formal sector and thus are not as representative. To put it differently: The Industrial Revolution brought forth losers and gainers. Real wage data alone tend to reflect more the situation of male employed workers, who were predominantly gainers, than upon domestic workers, many of whom were female and self-employed and who, by and large, ended up on the losing side. The failure of microlevel consumption data to reflect the rise in real wages is consistent with this view. A complementary explanation may suggest that while real wages improved, other aspects of living standards deteriorated. These would reflect not only urban living conditions and the harsh conditions of factories but also some less obvious factors, such as the loss of flexible choice between leisure and income brought about by the factory system. Thus rising real wages simply compensated the workers for other losses and there is no obvious case for "improvement." Finally, it can be argued, of course, that biological indicators are difficult to measure and to interpret and that economists should treat them with even more caution than wage or income data. In view of the fragility of much of the statistical material on aggregate income and consumption, however, this view seems difficult to sustain. At this stage, therefore, it has to be inferred that the evidence of a sharp rise in living standards before 1850 is simply too weak to be convincing.

The pessimist case itself, however, should be tempered by acknowledging the well-known pitfalls involved in measuring changes in living standards in an age of rapidly changing technologies. All quantitative studies of living standards measure in the final analysis quantities of goods that incomes can buy. They fail to account for changes in quality. A typical textile product in 1830 was not only cheaper than in 1750 but was also better in terms of the evenness of its fabric, its durability, its ability to absorb and maintain color, its ease of laundering, and so on. The same is true for a wide range of products, from iron pots to glass to steel pens to printed illustrations in books. Moreover, a number of inventions made during this period created completely new products, making welfare comparisons very difficult: Traditional measures of real wages and national income do not adequately capture the economic value (or additional consumer surplus) of the decline of smallpox, the introduction of gaslighting, or the use of anesthesia during surgery.

Part of the standard-of-living controversy is the debate over what happened to the inequality in income distribution. The famous Kuznets curve hypothesis (Kuznets, 1955) suggests that during the first stages of industrialization, income distribution became more unequal, eventually reaching a peak and then improving afterward. A worsening income distribution is one obvious way to reconcile rising per capita income and stagnant living standards for the majority of the population. The argument is discussed by O'Brien and Engerman (1981, p. 174), who maintain that given the rate of growth of income per capita between 1800 and 1850, an unchanging income level of the bottom 80 percent of earners would have meant that their share in income decreased from 75 percent in 1800 to 41 percent in 1850. Such a sharp worsening being unthinkable, they dismiss the argument. The revision of per capita growth rates, however, makes this argument less compelling. At a per capita income growth of perhaps 0.7 percent per year between 1800 and 1850 (instead of the 1.2 percent estimated by Deane and Cole and used by O'Brien and Engerman), a relatively slight sharpening in income distribution might have reduced the growth of income of the bottom of the income distribution to little more than a trickle.[106] The most dedicated proponent of the applicability of the Kuznets curve to Britain during the Industrial Revolution is Jeffrey Williamson (1985), although this belief in part undermines his view that living standards improved rapidly after 1819. There is, however, some doubt about what precisely happened to income equality during the critical years between 1800 and 1867, and until this doubt is cleared up, it is hard to draw any firm conclusions about how changing inequality affected living standards.[107] In a critique of Williamson's work, Feinstein (1988b) denies the applicability of the Kuznets curve to the British experience during the Industrial Revolution and argues that inequality remained more or less unchanged. Some complicating factors, however, still have to be fully accounted for. For instance, there is a difference between the inequality of the distribution of income among households and the distribution among individuals. If poorer families tended to increase family size over time relative to richer families, a constant distribution over household would in fact imply a growing inequality among individuals. A further complication is the decline in poor-relief support prompted by the Poor Law Reform Act of 1834, when spending on poor relief fell from over 2 percent of national income to about 1 percent (Lindert, 1992). Obviously, the reform sharpened the after-tax distribution of income, but it is as yet unclear to what extent changes in the poor law affect the standard-of-living overall.[108]

---

[106] Using the rise in inequality estimated by Lindert and Williamson (1983a) and assuming the share of the poor was little changed between 1850 and 1867 yields a growth of slightly over 0.4 percent in the incomes of the bottom 90 percent of the income distribution between 1800 and 1850. However, the decline of the share of the bottom 90 percent from about 54 percent to about 47 percent is, by Lindert and Williamson's computations, entirely accounted for by the sharp decline in the earnings of the people in the bracket between the bottom 65 percent and the bottom 90 percent, that is, the upper bracket of the bottom 90 percent. Removing these "lower middle class" people and concentrating on the bottom 65 percent reverses the picture, and incomes in this group increased by 0.90 percent per year.

[107] Allen (1992b, p. 285) argues that in agriculture landlords were the only gainers from the agricultural revolution before 1850.

[108] The estimates of the share of the bottom 40 percent in income distribution range between 10 and 14 percent of income (Williamson, 1985, p. 71). A decline in poor-relief transfers from 2 percent to 1 percent would have,

7. An Assessment

The New Economic History has traditionally been iconoclastic, and the Industrial Revolution has not been immune from attacks on the usefulness of the concept. Such attacks are to be welcomed simply because they force a reconsideration and reevaluation of the conventional wisdom. The Industrial Revolution may not, in fact, have been nearly as abrupt and as sudden as some of its historiography suggests. Yet its importance as an event in economic history stands undiminished. Before the Industrial Revolution technological change and economic growth did occur sporadically in the experience of Europe and Asia but were invariably checked by stronger forces. After 1750 the fetters on sustainable economic change were shaken off. There were lags and obstacles to overcome before technological creativity and entrepreneurship could be translated into higher living standards, but the secular trend pointed clearly upward. What ultimately matters is the irreversibility of the events. Even if Britain's relative position in the developed world has declined in recent decades, it has remained an urban, sophisticated society, wealthy beyond the wildest dreams of the Briton of 1750 or the bulk of the inhabitants of Africa or Southern Asia in our own time. Britain taught Europe and Europe taught the world how the miracles of technological progress, free enterprise, and efficient management can break the shackles of poverty and want. Once the world has learned that lesson, it is unlikely to be forgotten.

Regarded with the critical eye of statistical analysis, the events of the Industrial Revolution themselves may seem to us small and even insignificant because they affected only limited areas and products. But historians' judgment is inevitably colored by hindsight and rightly so. Examining British economic history in the period 1760-1830 is a bit like studying the history of Jewish dissenters between 50 B.C. and A.D. 50. At first provincial, localized, even bizarre, it was destined to change the life of every woman and man in the West beyond recognition and to affect deeply the lives of others, even though the phenomenon remained confined primarily to Europe and its offshoots. Although the center of the stage has long been taken over by others, Britain's place of honor in the history books is assured: It will remain the Holy Land of Industrialism.

---

by itself, reduced the incomes of the very poor by something between 7 and 10 percent.

2

The Fable of the Dead Horse; or, The Industrial Revolution Revisited

David S. Landes

Now without intending to depreciate in any manner the heroic efforts of the French Revolution and the immense gratitude the world owes the great men of the Republic, we think that the relative position of France and England with regard to cosmopolitism is not at all justly delineated in the above sketch [by Louis Blanc]. We entirely deny the cosmopolitic character ascribed to France before the Revolution, and the times of Louis XI and Richelieu may serve as proofs. But what is it M. Blanc ascribes to France? That she could never make predominant any idea except it was to benefit the whole world. Well, we should think M. Louis Blanc could not show us any country in the world which could do otherwise than France is said to have done. Take England, for instance, which M. Blanc places in direct opposition to France. England invented the steam engine; England erected the railway--two things which we believe are worth a good many ideas. Well, did England invent them for herself or for the whole world? The French glory in spreading civilization everywhere, principally in Algiers. Well, who has spread civilization in America, in Asia, Africa and Australia, but England?

–Friedrich Engels
The Northern Star, 11, no. 530 (18 December, 1847)

When in teasing mood I sometimes suggest to my students that the beginning of the end of the Ancient World is to be found not in Alaric's capture of old Rome in AD 410, not in the Turkish sack of new Rome in 1453 nor, indeed, at any of the much canvassed dates in between, but in an event which occurred in England in the early eighteenth century, they tend to look blank, baffled or bored according to temperament. Yet the case can be argued that the division between Ancient and Modern was marked in 1709 when at Coalbrookdale in Shropshire, Abraham Darby first successfully smelted iron with coke, for it was this development which launched mankind, slowly at first, but with progressively increasing rapidity, into the totally new world of an expanding and innovatory technology and introduced into the human consciousness the wholly novel concept of self-sustaining growth, both technical and financial.

–Donald C. Earl, *On the Absence of the Railway Engine*, (1980)

The Industrial Revolution once got a student of mine into what might have been serious trouble. It was 1963, the eve of the Berkeley eruption, and this young man had joined with other politically precocious demonstrators in occupying an auto dealership in San Francisco by way of pressing the cause of nondiscriminatory hiring. He was arrested, and a hostile policeman denounced him as a "revolutionary." "Why do you call me a revolutionary?" he asked. "I can see that book you're holding there," said the policeman. The book was T. S. Ashton's little handbook of that name, which the student was reading for my course in economic history. *Revolution* is a potent word.

I

What may well be the first use of the term "industrial revolution" dates from 1799, when a French envoy to Berlin with the German name of Otto wrote that his country had already entered upon the industrial revolution.[1] As the name came into wider use, especially among such political economists as N. Briavoinne, it was intended to convey the sense that a number of European countries had passed, were passing, or were about to pass through a profound and momentous change that would alter them forever.[2] What is more, this was a

---

[1] "*La révolution industrielle est commencée en France.*" Louis-Guillaume Otto (1754-1817) was a career diplomat whose highest post was that of ambassador to Vienna from 1809 to 1813. I owe the Otto reference, which is the earliest use of "industrial revolution" to come to my attention, to François Crouzet, who had it from Annick Pardailhe-Galabrun (1990), member of the Centre de Recherches sur la Civilisation de l'Europe moderne, Université de Paris-Sorbonne (Paris IV). The document in question is from a memoir attached to a letter of 18 messidor An VII (6 July 1799), France, *Archives des Affaires étrangères*, Mémoires et Documents, Angleterre 136, f. 352.

[2] *Revolution*, as used in the text above, has the sense of "an instance of great change or alteration in affairs or some particular thing" (*OED*, s.v., III, 6, b), a sense that well antedated, by a century and a half, the use of *revolution* to denote brusque or abrupt political change. The same anteriority is true in French, where the Littré cites, among other examples, the Abbé Raynal's prescient remark (*Histoire philosophique et politique des établissements et du commerce des Européens dans les Deux-Indes* [1770-1773], XIV, 47) that "a great revolution is under way in the commerce of Europe, and it is already too far advanced not to be consummated." This was as close as pre-Revolutionary France could get to the term "industrial revolution," for the word *industrie* was

change of universal import: no corner of the globe was immune to its effects, which were seen by many, including radical political dissenters, as intrinsically and "objectively" progressive. As the epigraph above shows, this was true even of Friedrich Engels, but also of Karl Marx, for all their denunciation of the abuses and suffering that accompanied the rise of "modern industry" (Engels, 1845; Marx, [1867] 1887).

In those days the Industrial Revolution was not yet a theme of scholarly analysis and debate, although the name itself was soon consecrated by use and the political-social-economic implications of these changes became matter for state policy and political polemic. Thus there is a substantial body of literature, going as far back as the late eighteenth century, dealing with the strategic, national implications of the new industrial technologies and the urgent necessity for other countries to follow Britain (Alexander Hamilton, J. A. Chaptal, Friedrich List, Gustav Mevissen, *et al.*); and there is another literature from about the same period describing and debating the social and moral conditions and consequences of the new industrial system.

It was not until the 1880s, about a century after the introduction of machines and factories into the manufacture of cotton textiles, that people whom we might describe as academic scholars began to look back on this development and assess its implications. One dates the beginning of this new stage with Arnold Toynbee's *Lectures on the Industrial Revolution* (1884), which were intended for night students in Manchester (hence largely working men continuing their education after a day's labor) and took as their theme the unhappy consequences of the new mode of production for the condition of the working class. Toynbee's view of the Industrial Revolution was that it was sudden, rapid, and drastically unfavorable in its reorganization of labor and its larger social effects. This regretful point of view was sustained and continued by the work and writings of other social-activist scholars— Sidney and Beatrice Webb for example, partners in Fabian socialism, and J. L. and Barbara Hammond – and it remained the dominant

---

then used primarily to denote diligence. It was routinized in its modern sense of a sector of the economy, particularly that sector concerned with manufacturing, only in the second quarter of the nineteenth century (Henri Sée, 1925; Hauser, 1931). On the word *commerce* as subsuming industry in the eighteenth century, see Viennet (1947, p. 3, n. 2).

orthodoxy for almost half a century, into the 1920s. (Note that this discussion deals exclusively with the British experience. There were, however, Continental students of economic change who were less negative in their judgment, at least in their comparisons of the European experience with the British [Gustav Schmoller, Max Weber, Paul Mantoux].)

The first major breach in this pessimistic construction came from John H. Clapham, then Fellow of King's College and later professor of economic history at Cambridge University. In a comparative study of France and Germany (1923), to which he gave the still unaccustomed title of *Economic Development*, he contrasted the swiftness of German industrialization to France's "leisurely movement" in that direction. Clapham presented this transformation as a natural and inferentially desirable aspect of modernity: the French, he implied, had paid in wealth and strength for the slowness and incompleteness of their development, retarded in his view by want of coal and the high cost of fuel (1923, pp. 56, 234-235). Not that they had stood still or lacked for "inventiveness, endurance, or organising capacity" (p. 232). They had changed, but it was more evolution than revolution. In the meantime, the people of both countries had benefited from "the solid economic gains" of the nineteenth century. This, he asserted prudently, was "a purely historical conclusion, . . . which involves no blessing and no cursing of the social system of Europe in the first decade of the twentieth century" (1923, p. 407).

Then, beginning in 1926, Clapham brought out a major study in three volumes of the *Economic History of Modern Britain* that made the point that the Industrial Revolution in Britain was less cataclysmic than had been maintained, that rather it was partial and gradual. Basing himself on the census of 1851, he noted that even in the mid-nineteenth century, at the time of Britain's triumphant Great Exhibition, the most numerous occupations were the old ones, agriculture and domestic service, and that even industry was still organized predominantly in small units using older methods and sources of power (1952, chap. 2).

Different but in the same tradition was T. S. Ashton, professor in the London School of Economics, who continued the emphasis on empirical data and argued explicitly that the Industrial Revolution had been a good thing not only in its effects on the standard of living (hence directly contradicting the Hammonds) but even more in terms of what might have been. In a highly influential little handbook of

1948, *The Industrial Revolution, 1760-1830*, much used as a school text, he contrasts the condition of Britain with that of the poor, overpopulated parts of the world and states that there but for the grace of modern industry went we (p. 111): "There are to-day on the plains of India and China men and women, plague-ridden and hungry, living lives little better, to outward appearance, than those of the cattle who toil with them by day and share their places of sleep by night. Such Asiatic standards, and such unmechanized horrors, are the lot of those who increase their numbers without passing through an Industrial Revolution."[3]

The work of Clapham, Ashton, and others really turned the debate on the social consequences of industrialization around. Instead of seeing modern industry through guilt-blurred eyes, people had to face the fact that the empirical data supported the optimists, that is, those who saw the bottom line as positive. The pessimists hung on by shifting ground and arguing on the basis of subjective appreciations: even if real wages rose, they said, the quality and security of life diminished. This was an ironic turn for Marxists and *marxisants*, who had always stressed the primacy of the material. In the long run, however, the judgment had to be favorable if only because there was no denying the evidence: the British working classes did not live well, but they lived better and longer than their ancestors, and as Ashton put it, they certainly lived better than they would have, had their numbers increased without the gains in productivity made possible by mechanization, inanimate power, and factory manufacture.

That still left the question open whether there had not been a transitional phase of deterioration. This was what Eric Hobsbawm argued, for example, saying that things got worse until the 1840s and then improved. The rejoinder came that if things got worse temporarily, this decline was concentrated in the first two decades of the nineteenth century and was the result of war rather than industrialization; or that the picture was mixed, with some (most) sectors or branches improving, while others (handloom weaving, for example) shrank and suffered. Such arguments were a far cry from the unre-

---

[3] This point of view has since been supported by the demographic researches of E. A. Wrigley and R. S. Schofield (1981). See section III, and n.6 below.

lievedly bleak judgment of an earlier generation or, for that matter, from the absolute immiseration thesis (the condition of the working classes getting steadily worse) put forward by some Marxists.

All of this, however, has not put an end to the controversy. The standard-of-living question is the stuff of eternal disagreement, not so much because the facts are or are not ascertainable (although they are complex enough to sustain a variety of interpretations); or because scholars will not rest so long as there is something to argue about (although that is also true). No, what keeps the controversy going in my opinion is that the two adversary opinions are also seen as shibboleths, as clues to and tests of political stance (Landes, 1976).

II

Ashton's ode to industrialization announced a period of positive emphasis on the Industrial Revolution as a major break in the course of history, the opening of an era of sustained technological change and economic growth. It also continued and was reinforced by an older tradition, going back to writers of the nineteenth century and summed up by such students of the history of technology as A. P. Usher and Lewis Mumford, that stressed the material content and definition of the Industrial Revolution.

I count myself in that group. The Industrial Revolution, as I defined it in the *Cambridge Economic History of Europe* (the manuscript went back to the mid-1950s but was not published until 1965 -- see Landes, 1965b), was a complex of technological advances: the substitution of machines for human skills and strength; the development of inanimate sources of power (fossil fuels and the steam engine); the invention, production, and use of new materials (iron for wood, vegetable for animal matter, mineral for vegetable matter); and the introduction and spread of a new mode of production, known by contemporaries as the factory system. The emphasis was on the gains in productivity and quality these changes made possible, their cumulative character, their ramification from a few leading branches into other industries and into transportation, their stimulus to creativity and innovation, and lastly the consequent gains in product and income per head. What is more, the argument went, these changes could not be and were not limited to the British Isles. Rather they changed the relative wealth and power of nations and in so doing compelled those who pretended to commercial and political parity with Britain to follow suit--which they did. The

British example was not the model for the rest of the world: given its originality and particular circumstances, it could not be that. But it was both a challenge and a source of knowledge, ideas, and experience–positive and negative.

In short, by this thesis, the Industrial Revolution was seen as a major break of worldwide impact. In my own work, I described the transition from pre- to post-Industrial Revolution as the puberty of nations. Others argued along similar lines, in particular Walt Rostow, who invented the term *takeoff*, which he defined as simply another way of saying "industrial revolution." This had the merit of being catchy – always an advantage in the contest for attention--and of figuratively emphasizing the notion of sustained growth (flight) as a result of passage from level motion to an upward trajectory. Unfortunately, it also conveyed a sense of rapidity, metaphorically telescoping the work of decades into the image of a fast-climbing aircraft.

For Rostow, the Industrial Revolution was a stage that all countries would pass through on their way to higher levels of development, with Britain and Europe leading the way for the laggards. Along these lines, Rostow described his influential essay on *The Stages of Economic Growth* (1960) as a "non-communist manifesto" -- one that would show the world how the West could bring growth and economic advancement more efficiently than could the Soviet Union. Such a deliberate challenge caught the attention of readers, but it was also a lightning rod that drew strong ideological opposition. One does not attack a religious icon like *The Communist Manifesto* with impunity.

<h2 style="text-align:center">III</h2>

Yet it was not left-wing political adversaries who gave Rostow, and indeed the whole discontinuity school (the Industrial Revolution as a major break or breakthrough), their hardest time. (How could they? The abruptness of the social shock of industrialization had always been a staple of their negative appraisal.) Criticism came from academics even more, and it began and has rested with new techniques of quantitative, macroeconomic analysis. Just as numbers turned the standard-of-living controversy around, so it is numbers that challenged and pretended to overturn the orthodoxy concerning the character and significance of the Industrial Revolution.

The first manifestation of the difficulty came with the perceived incompatibility of one of Rostow's key assertions with the empirical data, and this perception in turn was the result of the application of national income accounting to the distant past. Here the prime mover was Simon Kuznets, who with his colleagues in the National Bureau of Economic Research had shown what could be done by way of reconstructing past national accounts for the United States and who was mobilizing similar research projects in other countries. Among those laboring in this vineyard was Phyllis Deane, then a lecturer in Cambridge University, who brought out in the late 1950s a number of articles estimating British economic growth in the eighteenth century. In 1961 the International Economic Association brought together a group of economic historians, historical economists, and straight economists in Konstanz (Switzerland) to assess and discuss Rostow's *Stages*. Such special attention was no small honor, and Rostow was justifiably delighted. What is more, he managed to maintain this happy, sweet demeanor throughout the meeting in the face of a barrage of heavy and not always sympathetic criticism (I couldn't have done so) and even edited the volume of proceedings, which was published two years later (Rostow, 1963).

Among the papers presented was one by Phyllis Deane and H. J. Habakkuk on the takeoff in Britain that addressed itself to the effect, among other things, of the Industrial Revolution on the accumulation of capital. Their target in this regard was an assertion by Walt Rostow (drawing on an observation [speculation] of Arthur Lewis) that one of the salient characteristics (manifestations) of industrialization is a sharp rise in the rate of saving and investment, a shift from under 5 percent to 10 percent or more of income, and that this was in fact what had happened in Britain. Now this was presumably a verifiable hypothesis, and Deane and Habakkuk questioned it, if they did not disprove it. Using reasoning as much as data, they argued that the accumulation of capital in Britain was slower than the Rostow thesis seemed to require ("the Rostow model of the take-off requires that it should have been largely compressed within the space of two decades"). Their language was cautious: "It does not seem reasonable to suppose. . . . It is difficult to credit that a change of this order of magnitude could have occurred. . . . The contemporary estimates are, of course, highly speculative, and we have little evidence against which to check them" (1963, pp. 74-76). Nevertheless, the sense conveyed was of slow increase over a period of decades. They did not address themselves to the later years (the second and third generations) of the Industrial Revolution, nor did they pretend to contradict the accepted orthodoxy "that the crucial transformation occurred fairly rapidly--certainly within the century between 1750 and 1850, probably in a considerably shorter time" (p. 63). But they did stretch and blur the chronology: "In the end it seems that the most striking characteristic of the first take-off was its gradualness. Professor Nef has traced the process of industrialization back to the sixteenth century. The sustained rise in the rate of growth in total output probably dates back to the 1740s" (p. 82). As for capital formation, the sense that emerged was that it was not until the building of the capital-hungry railways after 1830 that the rate rose close to the level asserted by Rostow.

TABLE 2.1 Great Britain: Growth Rates in Real Output, 1700-1860 (percentage per year)

| | Industrial Output | | GDP | |
	Crafts	Deane & Cole	Crafts	Deane & Cole
1700-1760	0.7	1.0	0.7	0.7
1760-1780	1.5	0.5	0.7	0.6
1780-1801	2.1	3.4	1.3	2.1
1801-1831	3.0	4.4	2.0	3.1
1831-1860	3.3	3.0	2.5	2.2

Note: Figures for 1700-1801 are for England and Wales; thereafter for Great Britain.
Source: Crafts, 1989b, p. 66.

That was then a little cloud, no bigger than a man's hand, but it became a tempest. In subsequent years, further research (Pollard, Feinstein, Crafts, Harley) seemed to show that, just like capital formation, all the macroeconomic variables grew slower than the "revolutionary" character of the Industrial Revolution might have led one to expect and slower even than the Phyllis Deane series.[4] See, for

---

[4] Feinstein's estimates of the investment ratio (domestic investment as a proportion of gross domestic product) and its course also differ considerably from those of Deane (1961, 1965) and Deane and Cole (1962), and by implication Deane and Habakkuk (1963). Deane has capital formation growing at an average of no more than 3 percent per year in the seventeenth and early eighteenth centuries; this rate begins to rise in the middle decades of the eighteenth century, rising in the last quarter to "a sustained average of more

example, the comparison of growth estimates offered by Crafts (shown in Table 2.1).

Note, moreover, that these rates are not of growth per head. Those would show an even slower increase, even a decline for some of these years. Jeffrey Williamson (1990b, p. 1), apparently building on Crafts, Leybourne, and Mills (1989), reminds us that British national income, when deflated for population, grew at about 0.3 percent per year in the last decades of the eighteenth century -- "hardly impressive."[5] To be sure, Great Britain was then experiencing a population miniexplosion (five to ten times the rate of increase of the first half of the century [Komlos, 1989b, p.209; Deane and Cole, 1962, p. 8]), and it could be argued that the very fact of being able to so multiply without incurring a Malthusian rupture--very different from earlier historical experience-- was in itself evidence of the unprecedented power of the new technology (Komlos, 1989b; North, 1981). Wrigley and Schofield, the primary researchers in the field, have put it quite emphatically (1981, p. 412):[6]

---

than 5 percent," maybe a bit over 6 percent; and then the rate goes up again in the 1830s with the coming of the railway, reaching about 10 percent in the late 1850s. Feinstein's timing is the reverse; his is a picture of rapid increase in the last decades of the 18th century, from 8 percent in the 1760s to a peak of 13 percent in the 1790s, followed by a slight reduction and leveling off throughout the first sixty years of the next century (Feinstein, 1978, pp. 30, 91).

[5] Compare Jackson (1992, p. 4, Table 2), growth for the period 1770-1815. This contrasts sharply with Deane and Cole (1962, p. 78), which shows annual growth in "real output" per head of 1 percent from 1770 to 1800 and in "industry and commerce" of 1.4 percent over the same period. But this in turn may well be too high: Deane and Cole have strange and, to me, improbable dips in a number of categories (see figures for 1770 and 1780; also Jackson, 1992, pp. 4-5, Table 2), and these make growth very sensitive to choice of end points. These and other aberrations signal as well as anything the errors built into these macrostatistical manipulations.

[6] See also Wrigley and Schofield's Figures 7.11 and 7.12 (1981) on the combined effect of fertility and mortality in determining intrinsic rates of population growth and especially Figure 10.4, charting the coincidence over time between population growth and real wages. (This is reproduced as my Figure 2.1.) The discontinuity of the late eighteenth century and the exceptional character of the nineteenth are unmistakable. I want to thank

The possibility that the period before 1800 can be subdivided should not be allowed to obscure its general uniformity of experience, nor the decisive nature of the break occurring during the industrial revolution, a change so decisive that it must reflect a dramatic rise in the rate of growth of the economy as a whole. . . . Perhaps for the first time in the history of any country other than a land of recent settlement rapid population growth took place concurrently with rising living standards. A basic feature of the human condition had changed. . . . England crossed a threshold into a new era.

Still, if we focus, as many New Economic Historians do, on the arithmetic of income aggregation, a rate of 0.3 percent is very small. If one took into account margins of error, it could be something; but it also could be nothing.

Along with this diminution of the spurt, this reduction of the mountain to a hillock, has gone a renewed emphasis on the long and impressive preparation that made the Industrial Revolution possible. On the level of technology, this approach went back to J. U. Nef's tale (1933, 1934) of Britain's precocious recourse to fossil fuel, which he called a first industrial revolution. But there was also the early example of mechanized factory production afforded by the Lombe silk-throwing mill in Derbyshire (1719); Thomas Savery's steam pump (late seventeenth century) and Thomas Newcomen's engine (ante-1712); Abraham Darby's successful use of coke to smelt iron (1709) -- these and other inventions and innovations occurring well before the cluster that we commonly denote as the Industrial Revolution (1760s on). And on the level of growth, the argument has been made that preindustrial Britain was not standing still, that growth was an old story. The latest estimates in this area, by Graeme Snooks (1990) in a communication to the Tenth International Congress of Economic Historians at Leuven, build on Domesday Book (1086) and Gregory King's income figures (1688)--so, two end points six hundred years apart and nothing in between--to suggest a rate of growth of national income of 0.49 percent per year; of income per head of 0.29 percent; of productivity per head of 0.23 percent. This is high precision to the fourth decimal place on a tenuous base over a very long period, to the point where Knut Borchardt was moved to remark in discussion that he found the paper "wonderful, in the sense that it is full of wondrous things."

This macroeconomic reconstruction and diminution of the Industrial Revolution has been reinforced by a number of new studies of particu-

---

Claudia Goldin for drawing my attention to this material.

FIGURE 2.1 Great Britain. An End to Malthusian Penalties, 1781 on.

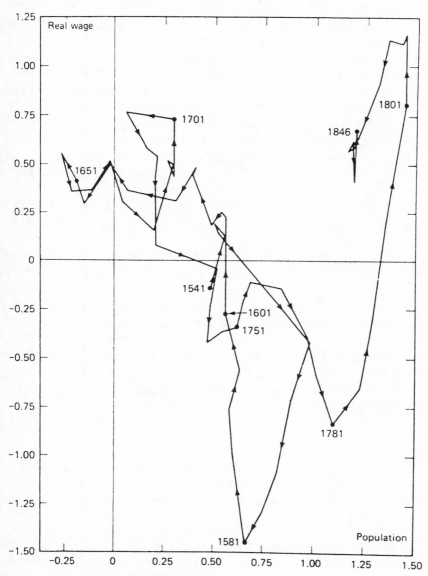

Source: Wrigley and Schofield (1981, p. 410).
Reproduction by courtesy of the Cambridge University Press.

particular sectors. S. D. Chapman (1971), A. E. Musson (1976), G.N. von Tunzelmann (1978), Dolores Greenberg (1982), and others have pointed out that steam power, for example, long seen as the technological heart of modern industry, was adopted slowly and piecemeal; that water power long accounted for the larger share of the inanimate energy employed in manufacture, to be passed by steam only in the second half of the nineteenth century; and that indeed use of animal (including human) power remained important (cf. Samuel, 1977). Along similar lines, G. R. Hawke (1970), following in the footsteps of Robert Fogel (1964), calculated that the railways, for all their importance, "only contributed about 10 per cent of [British] national income in 1865" (Cannadine, 1984, p. 157).[7] And F. T. Evans (1982), denouncing the "iron and steel propaganda of the Industrial Revolution," pointed out that in the mid-nineteenth century timber and wood were not scarce (some prices were even falling) and continued to be used widely for industrial purposes.

The revisionist thesis has been reinforced by comparable quantitative work on the Continental countries, in particular France, the country of choice to cut Britain down to size. Half a century ago, John U. Nef was warning scholars against a sharp contrast between British progress and Continental retardation in the eighteenth century: "The rate of industrial change from about 1735 to 1785 was no more rapid in Great Britain than in France, a far larger country with nearly three times as many people" (1943, p.5; also pp. 14, 19-23). A quarter-century later, François Crouzet (1966) made a similar argument on the basis of a comparison of British and French trade statistics.[8] And more recently,

---

[7] I cite Cannadine because my primary concern here is the impact of this work on the consciousness of the scholarly community. Hawke's estimate of railway social saving in 1865 as a proportion of income in 1865 is 4.1 percent (Hawke, 1970, p. 196).

[8] Nef, citing "for what they are worth" the data of Levasseur (1911, I, 512 n. 2), had already suggested that French trade grew faster than British in the 18th century (1934, p.22). The data in question were the retrospective estimates of French officials assembled toward the end of the Old Regime--principally those of A. M. Arnould, assistant director of the Bureau de la Balance du Commerce from 1785, and a certain Bruyard, head of the Bureau de Commerce from 1756. For the grievous inaccuracies and lacunae of these returns and their pronounced upward bias of growth, see Landes (1972, pp. 62-65).

J. Marczewski, T. J. Markovitch, Maurice Levy-Leboyer, Crouzet and others have produced data showing that French industry, long seen as slow and technologically laggard, grew quite respectably in the nineteenth, and particularly the first half of the nineteenth, century. Meanwhile, taking the opposite tack, that is, arguing from French slowness and reasoning from the Gerschenkron model (the later, the faster), Richard Roehl (1976) suggested that France, rather than Britain, was the first industrial nation; while Nick Crafts (1977, reprinted in Mokyr, 1985c), picking up a hint from E. A. Wrigley (1972), played with the idea that it was only a matter of chance that Britain industrialized first; that France might easily have taken the lead instead.[9]   And Patrick O'Brien and Caĝlar Keyder argued in a particularly provocative monograph (1978) that mass production was not the only way to industrialize; that France, with its small craft shops and manufacturing units, grew more or less as fast as Britain; and that when quality of life is taken into account, France probably did better.

---

[9] The article cites approvingly a critical remark by Everett Hagen (1967, p. 37) concerning "retrospective" analysis: "Explanations of Britain's primacy . . . consist mainly of a not very convincing sort of retrospective inference ('something must have caused Britain's primacy in time, so presumably the earlier conditions overtly observable did')." And Crafts translates: "In other words, the favourability of certain conditions in England has been inferred from the result with the likelihood of *post hoc, ergo propter hoc* fallacies" (Mokyr 1985c, p. 123). But of course such retrospective analysis is intrinsic to historical method, to say nothing of such other fields as medicine where etiology and causation are the heart of the story. That such analysis *may* give rise to *post hoc* and such errors is true; that it *is likely to* do so is a function of the quality of the scholarship.

The Crafts article also makes something of a stochastic model in which a "lucky" gain can translate into a string of further advantages; so that in the eighteenth century, one key innovation might have (could have) developed into an industrial revolution and put the British economy far ahead of the French, whose chances *ex ante* were equally good (Mokyr 1985c, p. 127). This point is further developed in Mokyr's introduction to this volume (Chapter 1).   I find such mathematical modeling surreal if amusing: the *deus ex machina* is a useful tool in fiction, and no one's life is immune to accident, but macrohistory, that is, large and complex institutional change, does not work this way.   In any event, the argument does not hold in the case of British priority in industrialization, as contemporaries well understood.

All of this has given rise to a reassessment of the nature and significance of the Industrial Revolution. Thus A. E. Musson (1978, p. 61): "The older view of the Industrial Revolution--that it was a sudden cataclysmic transformation, starting around 1760--clearly is no longer tenable"; and again (p. 149): "British economic historians have generally tended to place too much emphasis on the Industrial Revolution of 1750-1850 by comparison with developments in the second half of the nineteenth century. . . . Truly, much of the England of 1850 was not very strikingly different from that of 1750."[10] Similarly, N. L. Tranter (1981, p. 226): "The British Industrial Revolution was a very modest affair which emerged slowly from the past as part of a long, evolutionary process, not as a sharp, instantly recognizable break from traditional experience: its technology was small-scale and comparatively primitive; it needed relatively little additional investment capital; its capacity for introducing labour-saving technology was circumscribed; and its pace was gradual and uncoordinated." And Sylla and Toniolo (1991, p. 9): "There was no 'kink,' no take-off in a Rostovian sense. Nor was there a 'discontinuity' around 1780, where a time-honoured tradition places the beginning of the so-called Industrial Revolution. If anything, the start of the Industrial Revolution has to be pushed three decades back, but even then, the acceleration that took place hardly allows one to speak of a sudden substantial change in the growth of

---

[10] My first inclination on reading these lines of Musson was to assume that he was referring to some kind of general state of mind, a sort of popular historical myth; which may be the case. But Crafts, Leybourne, and Mills (1991, p. 125) remind us that Eric Hobsbawm, in his now-classic handbook on *The Age of Revolution* (1962, p. 28), spoke of the 1780s as the point where "all the relevant statistical indices took that sudden, sharp, almost vertical turn upwards which marks the take-off." They focus on the suitability of 1780 as a turning point; I would express surprise that a good Marxist like Hobsbawm would adopt a term from Walt Rostow's "non-communist manifesto." The point is that metaphor can be misleading as well as illuminating. Still, we shall see that Crafts *et al.* (1991, p. 132), using the latest cliometric estimations, offer charts of British trend growth that support Hobsbawm's image. For some citations of other users of a revolutionary vocabulary, including me, see Mokyr (1991a, p. 255).

industrial output."[11] And Knick Harley, dismissing what he feels to be the conventional wisdom (1990, p. 22): "It seems impossible to sustain the view that British growth was revolutionized in a generation by cotton spinning innovation."

IV

Authoritative? The problem is that not everyone is persuaded by the new, would-be orthodoxy; and this obstinacy has sorely tried the patience of some of the more passionate adherents of the new dispensation. Thus Eric Jones, in his latest book *Growth Recurring* (1988), believes every revisionist word and gives the back of his hand to what he calls the "technicist" interpretation.[12] Is this disparaging adjective his invention--a way of deriding all that fuss about new ways of doing things?[13] In any event, Jones clearly has no use for those who do not or will not see the light: he describes the "old interpretation" as "a dead horse that is not altogether willing to lie down" (p. 19).

Even more vexed is Rondo Cameron, once an active contributor to our understanding of the diffusion of the new industrial technology. He is now seized with remorse and has been calling at every opportunity for the abandonment of the term *Industrial Revolution* on the grounds that it is inaccurate, unscholarly, and misleading; and the stiff-necked refusal of some to see the light has only made him shriller. For

---

[11] This statement is part of an introduction to the essays in *Patterns of European Industrialization* and is intended to convey the contribution by Crafts *et al.* in that volume. I do not think it reads that essay correctly, which is much more cautious on the question of discontinuity (see p. 125)--indeed more cautious than its own data would permit (see figs. 7.1 and 7.2, p. 132). See below, Section V and Figure 2.2.

[12] Jones (1988, p. 19). On the tendency to presume that newer is truer, compare Robert Merton's fallacy of the latest word, cited in Gudmund Hernes (1989), which deals with the similar running debate on the merits of the Weber thesis.

[13] He has company. Knick Harley echoes this depreciation of technology in the following terms (1990, p. 40): "The technological breakthrough in industry occurred in Britain in part because of the dynamic character of the economy but Britain probably also benefitted from a lucky draw in the random process of invention." It does seem strange to me that economists (or economic historians trained as economists) should think that major differences in the direction and pattern of invention are or were a random process.

Cameron now, to write Industrial Revolution with capital letters is to "deify" it. And to reject what he calls "recent new knowledge" is to behave like a "fundamentalist ayatollah of economic history" (1991, p. 1165). He is sure to find further grief: the name Industrial Revolution is not only consecrated by clarity and convenience, it accords, as we have seen (note 2), with good, old English usage of the word "revolution." It will not go away.[14]

Meanwhile, what has the dead horse been saying?

One response has been to question the message of the new numbers--to point out that it is in the nature of statistical aggregation to smooth discontinuities and asperities and to drown sectors of innovation and change in a sea of tradition. (In effect, this is a reminder of the limits of aggregation: the national income/product approach, for all its claims to understanding and authority, is not good enough [cf. McCloskey, 1991, p. 99, citing Gerschenkron, 1968, pp. 34-35].) The Industrial Revolution, after all, was an exercise in selective, unbalanced growth, so that changes in a few branches, however spectacular, took some time to work through to the rest of the economy.[15] Note further that some of these changes were destructive as well as constructive, that is, they shriveled some branches while swelling others; and that aggregate gains necessarily reflect this process of compensation. One might even argue that it is precisely this demonic aspect, this drastic contrast

---

[14] But what of the suggestion that we speak of evolution rather than revolution? This is the subject of Joel Mokyr's essay "Was There a British Industrial Evolution?" (1991a); also of the final chapter of his new book *The Lever of Riches* (1990a). To be sure, Mokyr's evolutionist model (Gould, Goldschmidt, *et al.*) has room for macroevolutionary mutations and leaps, hence for evolutionary revolutions or revolutionary evolution. Yet Mokyr points out and criticizes the fact that economic historians, in using the evolutionist model or metaphor, have implicitly adopted the purely gradualist version; and it is not unreasonable to suppose that some readers, like reviewers who know a book by its jacket, may never get past his title. In any case, "industrial evolution," however true, is not a substitute label for industrial revolution.

[15] Mokyr (1985c, p. 5) offers an arithmetical hypothetical on this point: if the modern sector starts with 10 percent of output and grows at 4 percent, while the traditional 90 percent grows at 1 percent, it will take 75 years for the former to account for half of output. McCloskey (1991, p. 100) suggests that we call this the weighting theorem, or maybe the waiting theorem.

between new and old that is the measure of the revolutionary character of the new technology. What matters is not the initially low rate of increase but the fact of a new trend of continuing and accelerating growth. More on this below.

One may make a similar point about regional disparities. Pat Hudson (1989, p. 1) points out that aggregate data and averages conceal significant spatial differences in development and miss the discontinuities and the important foci of innovation and transformation. Recent research into real wages would support this regionalist view. Thus we have significant differences in wage trends and levels between the manufacturing districts of the North and the agricultural South--the former go up, the latter fall (Hunt, 1986; Hunt and Botham, 1987; Schwarz, 1990)--and that is as it should be in a process of uneven growth.

There is also the alleged dampening effect of exogenous influences. Jeffrey Williamson (1984, 1987a), for example, while recognizing the limits of aggregation (1987a, p. 273), finds in addition external reasons for a low rate of growth. In particular, he would draw attention to the fact that British government financing, especially in wartime, crowded out investment in industry, which could not take advantage of its technological opportunities. Not everyone would agree with that, in part because the issue is complicated by earlier movements of capital into Britain and by the debt-melting effects of inflation, and obscured by the incompleteness and artificiality of the statistical data (Mokyr, 1987). Still, one could make the argument that, other things equal, Britain would have grown faster had it been able to put resources into productive rather than destructive activities. A quarter-century of almost continual war during the period of the French Revolution and the reign of Napoleon did not help.

A second approach has been to question the reliability (robustness) of the numbers. For some they have the authority of mystery and apparent precision; but even practitioners of the cliometric art have serious doubts. Joel Mokyr compares some of this quantitative jousting to "a fight between two toddlers blowing soap bubbles at each other. Their weapons are too dull to decide the issues at stake" (1987, p.

308).[16] These macro- and microstatistical calculations are all of them
bold and ingenious constructs. They build on a variety of theoretical
assumptions, often unspecified, that shape (distort) reality to the needs
of calculation; make generous use of proxies, interpolations, and
extrapolations to fill in the spotty data; make drastic assumptions about
the changing composition of the work force and draw inferences
therefrom about the changing composition of product; and combine
data from different sources, assembled at different times for different
purposes.

To be sure, there is what we may call the law of abundant error
(analogous to the law of large numbers), which comforts arithmeticians
in the hope that mistakes will cancel out. In this instance, though, such
hope would seem to be unjustified. There is bias as well as error in
these techniques and numbers: bias toward smoothing and bias
downward in calculation of rates of change. These indexes, for
example, do not incorporate new products and improvements in quality
over the period of comparison and thus necessarily underestimate the
extent and rate of real growth (Mokyr, 1990b). They also aim at
compromise, try to arrive at measures that fall between change *ex ante*
and change *ex post*. Such a compromise makes sense when calculating
price changes; but where quantities are concerned and one is trying to
reckon the impact of technological progress, it necessarily under-
estimates the extent of the achievement.[17]

---

[16] Mokyr's reference is to the statistical measure of agricultural output.
But it is a good image and would apply as well to many of the other statistical
quarrels that fill the literature.

[17] The compromise solutions to the classic index number problem,
designed originally for the construction of price series, are particularly
unsatisfactory in measuring the significance of growth due to technological
change. So far as I can tell, all calculations of British industrial or national
growth thus far bias downward the contribution of such rapidly changing
branches as cotton, iron, and machinery, partly because the indexes employed
do not use prices for the year of origin (which are the only ones that convey
the productivity effect), partly because they underestimate or do not (cannot)
catch the gains in quality and novelty. The usual formulas (A. L. Bowley,
Irving Fisher, François Divisia) aim at producing reasonable composite series
by using one or another compromise mean, not at measuring the impact of
productivity change. I submit that the proper way to gauge productivity gains
is by using a Laspeyres volume index, that is, by using zero-year prices

Worst of all, the "cliometricians" generate their numbers in a static context that does not take into account the interactions of change. Every gain is "cut down to size" -- a fraction (say, the saving of labor produced by an innovation) of a fraction (that part of a given branch affected by the change) of a fraction (the place of that branch in the larger economy). By the time the arithmetic is done, innovations of literally global impact (say, the transformation of cotton spinning) are reduced from earthquake to tremor. Donald McCloskey, in a new introduction to a forthcoming new edition of *The Economic History of Britain* (Floud and McCloskey, 1981), calls this effect Harberger's Law and recognizes that it truncates reality. It makes it impossible, for example, to account for a twelvefold increase in income per head in Britain since 1780 (McCloskey 1992) -- not to mention, I would add, even greater gains in other industrial nations. The fault, he says, lies with the economists: "It is in fact something of a scientific scandal that economists have not explained modern economic growth" (McCloskey, 1992, p.33). Coming from a hitherto true believer like McCloskey, that is a serious indictment. Following up on his charge, I submit that the

---

throughout: in other words, how much would it have taken to produce that amount of goods using the older technology?

Compare McCloskey (1981, p. 108), who implicitly uses a Laspeyres-type comparison to demonstrate the impact of the Industrial Revolution: "What was extraordinary about the industrial revolution is that better land, better machines and better people so decisively overcame diminishing returns. Had the machines and men of 1860 embodied the same knowledge of how to spin cotton or move cargo that they had in 1780 the large number of spindles and ships would have barely offset the fixity of land. Income per head would have remained at its level in 1780, about £11, instead of rising to £28 by 1860."

Note that this approach is in some ways analogous to the concept of social saving, which is the economy yielded by a given innovation (or cluster of innovations) by comparison with the next-best alternatives, on the reasonable assumption that improvement in the older technology would have occured even in the absence of the innovation. Such a fictive comparison demands, of course, much imagination and boldness. (Compare Fogel, 1964, who plays, but only plays, with the question, what if the alternative to the railway were, not canals or not only canals, but precocious automotive transport.)

"new economic historians" have been looking in the wrong direction; they would do better to turn toward history.[18]

V

The long and the short of it is that the quantifiers have built brave structures on shaky foundations (Berg and Hudson, 1992; Jackson, 1992). Perhaps the best of them, Charles Feinstein, warns in a recent essay that his numbers for the key variables of British economic growth can be little more than "insecure guesses," that most estimates of output and income before the late nineteenth century are likewise "guesstimates," and that attempts to measure and date changes in the investment ratio or assess the contribution of capital to the growth of output and productivity will continue to be a hazardous undertaking (cited in Cole, 1989). Hazardous indeed. In its short history, cliometrics has already seen considerable revision and re-revision of findings that once seemed authoritative for their numerical character. Why assume that we have heard the last word?

---

[18] While deploring the limitations of static analysis (it cannot explain what happened), McCloskey (1992) does give it credit for demonstrating the "nots" -- by which he means the things that are not true, the alleged causes that will not explain enough. In this way, he argues, static arithmetic shows us that one cannot explain modern industrial growth by foreign trade or transport improvements or literacy or scientific advance or whatever. The difficulty here is one that seems especially to afflict economists: a passionate seeking after The One Cause, the prime mover, and the consequent serial demolition of one good cause after another. Why? Because as every economist knows (another axiom), one good reason is enough, so one looks for the good reason and the inadequate reasons are bad. Unfortunately, since everything is substitutable and nothing is indispensable (another axiom), good reasons are hard to come by. As McCloskey puts it (1992, p.23), "We have not discovered any single factor essential to British industrialization." Surprise. No wonder some have been tempted to see the whole thing as a stochastic phenomenon.
Note that historians do not have this problem. They do not pursue the will-o'-the-wisp of the single essential factor. On the contrary, they rejoice in and gain honor by multiple causation: one good reason is enough, but two good reasons are even better. Historians know that a given factor may not explain everything, but so what? It combines with other factors to play its role in the actual process. On this level, it is essential. So are others. Change the circumstances, and you change the result.

But let us assume just that and concede that the "guesstimates" of scholars like Feinstein and Crafts are smart, informed, and reasonably close to what actually happened; that as Crafts put it in a confident moment, "The dimensions of economic change in Britain during the Industrial Revolution are now reliably measured" (Crafts, 1989c, p. 416). Some people are better guesstimators than others because they are not merely guessing; they have some data to go on, and they possess superior critical faculties. Indeed, *for the purposes of this essay*, I am prepared to believe them all, even when they differ. That still leaves the question of interpretation. What does all this mean?

The first thing to note in that regard is that this debate over continuity vs. discontinuity is an old business. Historians never tire of it, because it provides matter for endless retort and rejoinder. It is the stuff of controversy and debate, and controversy and debate are the stuff of Ph.D. theses and professional reputations. The Industrial Revolution is only one of a large number of topics that have generated such arguments: think only of Pirenne's *Mahomet et Charlemagne* (was the fall of the Roman empire a major break?); or the still hot issue of the character and consequences of the French Revolution (Tocqueville's continuity vs. Republican and socialist doctrine of the world transformed); or that favorite Japanese *topos*, how much credit to give to Tokugawa antecedents of Meiji growth.

On this level, there is more noise here than light. In the Industrial Revolution debate, as in most of these others, both sides are right: History, of its nature, is a constant interplay of continuity and change. Everything has its antecedents; but nothing remains the same, and some changes are more drastic and rapid than others.

None of this is new, then. It should be recognized that earlier generations of historians of the Industrial Revolution, for all their emphasis on its revolutionary character and consequences, were explicitly aware of its gradual penetration of the larger economy and its protracted character. I have already cited Clapham in that regard. He did not have national income constructs, but he did have the census, and that told him volumes about the tenacity of older branches of economic activity. Nor were they unaware of the long preparation of these developments: history, like nature and vacuums, abhors leaps and random walks, and generations of scholars worked to understand why England, and why England first. Let me recall William Cunningham, author more than a century ago of what we may call the first textbook

in British economic history: "The History of industry does not describe
a series of remodellings made from without, but a slow and continuous
growth that takes place from within" (1885, p. 2); and, then again, on
the importance of preparation (1907 [as reprinted in 1922], p. 610):

> It was not an accident that England took the lead in this matter; the circumstances of
> the day afforded most favourable conditions for the successful introduction of new
> appliances. Inventions and discoveries often seem to be merely fortuitous; men are apt
> to regard the new machinery as the outcome of a special and unaccountable burst of
> inventive genius in the eighteenth century. But we are not forced to be content with
> such a meagre explanation. To point out that Arkwright and Watt were fortunate in
> the fact that the times were ripe for them, is not to detract from their merits.

Or take Abbott Payson Usher, who focused on technological aspects
of the story and might be expected, more than anyone, to stress the
revolutionary character of these innovations:

> The Industrial Revolution was thus a revolution in every sense of the word, except that
> of suddenness of transition. But the extraordinary character of the transformation must
> in itself be sufficient to convince one that such changes in the matters of daily life could
> not take place suddenly. Particular machines can be brought to public attention within
> a brief space of time; the form of industrial organization can be changed, though that
> would inevitably require a longer period. But the Industrial Revolution was more than
> any such formula could possibly imply. The "Great Inventions" were merely a stage
> in a long development of a new mechanical technique, neither the beginning of the new
> order nor its culmination. The rise of the modern factory system was only one of the
> many results of mechanical change, industrial dislocation, and commercial development.
> The abandonment of the idea that the Industrial Revolution was sudden involves a
> considerable readjustment of chronology for the entire movement. The study must be
> carried farther back into the past and continued down nearer to the present time. The
> establishment of even approximate limits is obviously difficult.

This in 1920 (p. 271). (I would note in passing that Usher, the product
of an earlier, more literate era, understood here that the word
"revolution" has more than one meaning.)

Reading this and other warnings of the gradualism *cum* rapidity of
these developments (I would stress, as Ashton did, this paradoxical
combination),[19] one wonders whether the "New Economic Historians"

---

[19] "There is a danger of overlooking the essential fact of continuity"
(Ashton, 1948, p. 2). I would note that Ashton had misgivings about the word
revolution. He, along with J. H. Clapham, Herbert Heaton, and others of his

of today have ever read this literature (it is hard enough to keep up with new material); or if they have read it, whether they remember it. It is as though economic history were like physics: the older works fall into rapid desuetude and well-deserved oblivion because they no longer have the story right.

For surely, if the "New Economic Historians" had been aware of this literature, they would not have been shocked to "rediscover America"—to find overall industrial growth of 3 percent per year; and low rates of capital formation in an industrial revolution of low capital requirements; and water power playing an important role throughout; and small enterprise coexisting with large; and agriculture persisting and improving alongside industry; and railways generating perhaps a tenth of British national income in the mid-nineteenth century.

Instead they would have asked such questions as, what is slow? or what is fast? what is large? what is small? And what matters in assessing significance: level or trend? aggregates? or foci of change?[20] If you

------

generation, made it a point to warn the reader of its nomenclatorial shortcomings, not only because the Industrial Revolution was gradual but because they would have preferred a word without, for them, unhappy political connotations.

[20] I am reminded of a dinner of the Friends of Business History at Harvard back in the 1960s where I had been asked to comment on the contribution and significance of the so-called New Economic History. In those days, this meant above all Robert Fogel, whose work on the contribution of the railroad to U.S. economic growth was the sensation of the day. (It had everything: lots of numbers, a new technique of argument [counterfactuals], and a surprise ending: the railway had marginally contributed less to U.S. economic growth than anyone would have guessed--maybe 4 percent of national income in 1890, at most 6 or 7 percent.) Anyway, I sat down at the head of the table, all prepared to say something measured, safe, and wise, like: The New Economic History is still small and poses serious problems of method and significance, but . . . it does use powerful techniques; it makes more, and more explicit, use of economic theory; and it will become more important with time. But when I looked around, I saw facing me across the way none other than Fogel himself, in Cambridge on a short visit from Chicago. Intimidating. I said my say, but as you can well imagine, my monologue became something of a dialogue with Fogel. And this was the livelier because also in the room was my own teacher, Abbott Payson Usher, long retired and into his 80s but as sharp as ever. And he asked the big question of the evening, namely, how big

were an investor, how would you reason? Where would you place your bets?

And so for the British Industrial Revolution. The rates of change were low by twentieth-century standards, and also clearly lower than these historical income accountants had expected. But were they *low*?

They were certainly not low by comparison with what had gone before. Not that there had not been growth before. There had to be, and that was part of the preparation for industrial revolution. That was one of the reasons Britain came first: thanks to the cost advantages of rural putting-out, its textile manufacture in particular was growing faster than those of other European countries in the centuries preceding the invention of the new carding and spinning machinery and the development of new power sources.

But we also know that, from about the 1760s, growth took an upward turn and proceeded at a higher rate. There was, in other words, a discontinuity, a break in the curve. We know that by extrapolating backward. It takes some ninety-nine years for income decreasing at 0.7 percent per year (Crafts's estimate of the rate of growth in the early eighteenth century) to halve; go back two centuries, and even at this slow pace, one arrives at impossibly low levels of income. Use Crafts's 1.3 percent rate for the end of the century (after the early innovations of the Industrial Revolution), and it takes only thirty-eight years for income to halve.

We also have the estimates of aggregate industrial output, which try to include both modern and traditional sectors.[21] They tell a story of

---

is 5 percent or 6 percent? (Those were the percentages I recall our playing with that evening.) To that question, no one--not even Fogel--had an answer.

[21] The traditional sector poses special problems of measurement in that it is less amenable than the newer branches to estimates of output, whether direct or indirect. Crafts resolves this difficulty by assuming that there were no productivity gains in these branches over the decades in question: "This sector was responsible for perhaps 60 per cent of industrial employment and probably experienced virtually no productivity growth at all during 1780-1860" (Crafts, Leybourne, and Mills, 1991, p. 116). Such a statement unwittingly expresses an ignorance of technological change in branches not yet mechanized but gaining steadily from Smithian innovations in the organization of labor and from improvements in tools and materials. The watch and clock trade is an excellent example (Landes, 1983). Cf. Berg (1985), who does not start her

industrial revolution. The latest series of trend growth for Britain (Crafts, Leybourne, and Mills, 1991, pp. 132-134; see the accompanying Figure 2.2) shows a sharp swing upward beginning shortly after the middle of the eighteenth century and peaking about 1830 -- very close to the dates advanced by such scholars as Usher and Ashton half a century and more ago.[22]   On the basis of this curve, one can argue about the timing -- push the break (kink) up ten years, push back ten years, mark from trough, mark from the point where trend passes the earlier peak -- but there is no mistaking the fact (though the authors and their editors seem to mistake it) that there was a break in trend and that industrial growth was now faster than before and did not recede again to early eighteenth-century levels.

So something had changed. That something was essentially technology -- the way of doing and making things -- with substantial and ramifying effects on productivity, prices, and size of market. In that regard, I am astonished by the assertion of Eric Jones that "the nexus between technology and economic growth is not particularly strong" (1988, p. 54), for such an assertion is simply wrong in fact and in logic. Although it helps to distinguish between growth (or what Jones prefers to call "intensive growth," that is, growth per head) and technical change, if only because one can conceive of gains in income per head that do not derive from gains in real productivity (for example, windfalls

---

story in 1700 by accident and is especially good on the metal trades; also, on the second part of this period (1830-1860), the first volume of Clapham's classic and still useful *Economic History of Modern Britain* (1930). These branches, described imperfectly by Crafts as "traditional, small-scale and catering for local markets without entering into international trade" (Crafts, Leybourne, and Mills, 1991, p. 116), were not standing still.

[22] For the purpose of establishing and dating economic discontinuities, it is interesting to compare the statistical techniques of three-quarters of a century ago with today's. They were, of course, simpler then: Usher (1920, pp. 310-312) took as his measure of gains in productivity the unadjusted selling price over time of single, homogeneous commodities: in the case of the textile manufacture, of No. 40 and No. 100 cotton yarn. The result in both instances, especially in the latter, is a curve exponentially downward from 1770 and pretty much leveling off after 1830--very much like a learning curve. (See Figure 2.3) For this datum (the timing of the Industrial Revolution), I have more confidence in this kind of proxy than in the ingeniously complex aggregations of today's cliometricians.

FIGURE 2.2 Great Britain. Trend Growth of Industrial Output, 1700-1900.

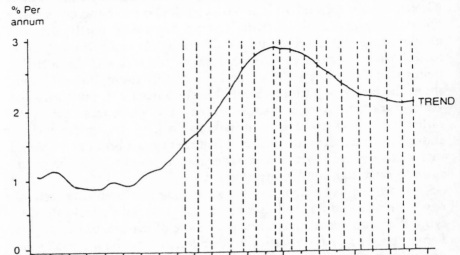

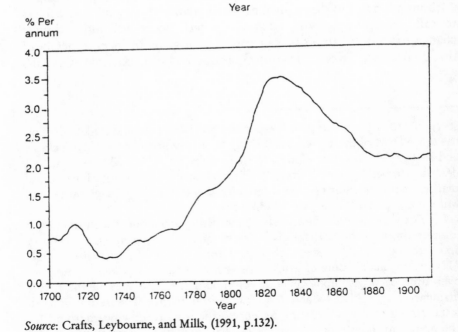

Source: Crafts, Leybourne, and Mills, (1991, p.132).

from newly discovered resources, or favorable changes in relative prices and the terms of trade, or increases in trade and profits therefrom, or rents derived from growth itself), it is a mistake to think that such increase can be sustained if not accompanied and supported by technological advances.[23] These may take the form of hardware or software: of new products or new ways of producing; or even of new and more efficient forms of organizing labor (Adam Smith's progressive division of labor would fall into this last category).[24]

VI

These changes in technology, everyone agrees, did not happen overnight. Old ways and forms persisted alongside the new. But however gradual, these changes were deep and unprecedented, with comparably serious consequences, both positive and negative, for the condition of the population. There is no room here to do justice to the tenacious and probably everlasting debate (which numbers will not settle) between the optimistic and pessimistic views of the social impact of the Industrial Revolution in the late eighteenth and early nineteenth

---

[23] That is the soft form of the proposition. I would argue the hard form: although such technology may be imported, as is often the case with multinationals or joint ventures, unless an economy possesses technological autonomy--that is, the ability to generate its own innovations--technical advances will not ramify and the modern sector will remain encapsulated, a kind of industrial plantation. Landes (1991, 1992); cf. Krikkiat and Yoshihara (1989).

[24] On the implications of division of labor for technological innovation, one has only to consider the history of clock and watchmaking and the invention of special-purpose tools that later found application in the manufacture of machines. Mokyr (1990a, p. 323, nn. 7-8), would cast doubt on this connection and asserts, "Before standardization and interchangeable parts, . . . the simplification of work brought about by the division of labor as such was not significant." But it was precisely this simplification, which grew out of specialization and made possible batch production, that suggested the utility and method of interchangeable parts (cf. Landes, 1983, chaps. 16, 18; also Landes, 1986). Mokyr cites Brenner (1987), who cites Smith's own intellectual versatility as a kind of argument against the alleged advantages of work specialization. *C'est pour rire?*

160

FIGURE 2.3 Great Britain. The Learning Curve in Textile Manufacture: The Selling Price of Cotton Yarn and the Cost of Raw Cotton, 1779-1882.

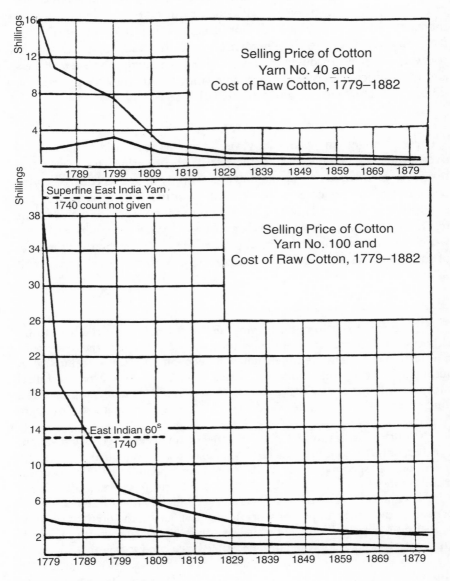

Source: Usher (1921, p.311).

centuries. There is truth on both sides, and the balance depends in part on the dates chosen for comparison.

What needs stressing, however, is the rapidity with which technological change impinged on the livelihood and consciousness of workers and translated into protest, much of it violent. Changes may have been making their way in some regions more than others, in some industrial branches more than others, and slower than some enthusiastic scholars may have thought. But do not tell that to the people affected: the pauper apprentices; the women who were sent to work in the mills where their husbands or fathers would not go; the displaced craftsmen; the residents of once-green valleys, now renamed the Black Country; the Irish immigrants who did the dirty work. Or, for that matter, to the winners of the new, industrializing world: the managers, merchants, and shopkeepers, the newly skilled and the "labor aristocracy," the consumers of the new commodities and of older ones now within reach, the multiplying professionals in growing towns and cities. The machine breakers did not need to wait seventy-five years for the new technology to work through its potential to know they were hurting. The doctors who had to deal with new health problems in mining villages and urban slums and wynds in the 1790s quickly understood that industry was growing and changing and injuring people. Meanwhile, conservative moralists in distant lands were, already in the 1760s and 1770s, lamenting the effects of material seduction and stimulation on once-simple rural populations (cf. Muller, 1990, pp.170-172). For all of their contemporaries and others, personal experience was a good proxy measure of revolution; and for us, with our subtle number play and 20/20 hindsight, it is a fair reminder that there is more to life, work, and death than macrostatistics can tell.[25]

---

[25] I would add to that the silent effects, the ones that contemporaries could not begin to appreciate. My favorite is the consequences for health of the introduction of cheap cotton underclothing, replacing the body linen used by the wealthy and giving something new to the working classes. In a world of primitive and collective toilet and washing facilities, the greatest endemic threat to health was gastrointestinal infection, easily passed by unwashed hands that had come into contact with body wastes. The lack of easily cleaned undergarments was an invitation to skin irritation, scratching, and thus transfer of pathogens from body to hands to food to digestive tract. The new underclothing, in combination with new and cheaper soaps, probably did as

VII

When the British began to move ahead of their neighbors and inaugurated a new, more productive mode of production, they did so because, building on earlier gains, they found technological solutions to the stresses and opportunities of widening and deepening markets. They substituted machines for men; they used more and more inanimate power; they found new materials or made old materials and products better, bigger, and faster; and they organized all of this in larger units that brought labor together under supervision.

This does not mean that they had a monopoly of discovery and invention. On the contrary, their neighbors and rivals on the Continent were as advanced as they were in science and created their own innovations to meet the needs and opportunities of their economies: One thinks, for example, of the French improvements in silk manufacture or their production of sugar from beets once colonial supplies were cut off or their manufacture of alkalis by the Leblanc process in response to a similar problem. But the British innovations had wider economic consequences because the demand for these products was potentially larger and the supply more elastic (compare cotton and silk for cheapness) and because they had wider ramifications within the larger economy (thus multiple uses of iron and the general applicability of advances in power technology). They were the stuff of an industrial revolution. *Pace* Nick Crafts (1977), the French changes were not.[26]

The nations of continental Europe, of course, understood that. They also understood that such innovations enhanced enormously Britain's wealth and political strength while threatening industries and crafts

---

[26] There is also good reason to believe that the level and diffusion of mechanical skills were more favorable in Britain. One may reasonably infer that from the difficulties the Continental countries had copying the British machines. Whence this superiority? I would lay heavy emphasis on the British advance in clock and watch manufacture (clockmakers constituted the preferred pool of skilled workers for the making and maintenance of textile machinery, and the wheelwork was commonly known as clockwork) and on the precocious recourse to water and steam power in mining and industry. (Landes, 1969, pp. 61-63; Landes, 1983, pp. 219-227; also Berg, 1985, pp. 266-268, Mokyr, 1990a, pp. 235-239.)

everywhere else, to say nothing of their deleterious consequences for social stability and for what some would now call "family values" (Muller, 1990). In short, the Industrial Revolution was upsetting the European balance of power; and the other nations understood that if they did not follow Britain's suit, for all the risk and discomfort that that entailed, they were condemned to secondary, dependent status.[27] (This was the same judgment made by Japan almost a century later: modernize or become another China.)

Fortunately for these Continental follower countries, they were not able to read the "New Economic History." So they did not think they were doing just fine, maybe even better than Britain, and that cheap imports, haute cuisine, and picturesque landscapes were an adequate compensation for lower wages and incomes. Nor for that matter did they listen to British injunctions about the advantages of an international division of labor in which Britain would be workshop of the world and they would supply food and raw materials.[28] Instead they read Alexander Hamilton, J. A. Chaptal, Friedrich List, and the other advocates of strong and deliberate measures to promote industrial change. And they caught up with, in the case of Germany even passed, Britain -- much to Britain's surprise.[29]

---

[27] In a strange, even bizarre, excursion, Donald McCloskey has tried to decouple Britain's economic lead and the strategic interests of other countries, and by implication to devalue its significance, by arguing that the nations of continental Europe should not have been concerned about British industrial gains for political reasons, that industrial power was (is?) not a vital ingredient of political and military power: "In economics there are substitutes, even if there are not in chemistry" (1990a, p. 42; also McCloskey, 1988, p. 647; and McCloskey, 1990b, p. 295). That inference from theory strikes me as dead wrong, but even if it were right, it would not be relevant to the decisions of contemporaries of the Industrial Revolution, who thought otherwise. But then they had not had the benefit of courses in neoclassical economics. A little theory is a dangerous thing.

[28] Cf. Kiesewetter (1991). For a similar siren song regarding the consolation for the United States of being able to buy good, cheap foreign goods at the expense of U.S. wages and employment, see Baumol, Blackman, and Wolff (1989) and Williamson (1991).

[29] As in France and Prussia, so in the British colonies of North America. Already in the 1760s, the growing resentment of the colonists against British protectionist trade policies and fiscal initiatives gave rise to an interest in

In sum, the basis of wealth, hence power, had been transformed. Those nations that were able to emulate these new technologies became rich, richer than anyone could have dreamed. By comparison the rest of the world was poor; and with the spread of European dominion, the widening European presence, the ever more visible contrast of the industrial artifacts and material exigencies of the white man and the limited resources of people of color, the poor came to know they were poor. As a result of these gains in productivity, the gap between Europe and its overseas offshoots (the "West") on the one hand, and the preindustrial Rest on the other, already significant in the sixteenth century but still quantitatively modest, now became a gulf. If we accept the bold estimates of Paul Bairoch (1979), income-per-head ratios between Europe and the great Asian empires went from 1:1 or 1.5:1 in the eighteenth century to 20:1 or even 50:1 in the twentieth. For comparison of the growing spread between the developed and the underdeveloped countries, see Table 2.2, which also rests on Bairoch's estimates. These last are composite averages. At the extremes (Switzerland vs. Mozambique), the income gap today (1990) is 300 or 400:1.

Such a chasm is not impassable, but is large and difficult enough to be a source of resentment, discouragement, humiliation, and hostility.

This gap between industrial and nonindustrial, rich and poor, is probably the most serious political, social, and moral challenge of our time. How to close it? By helping poor countries to do what their predecessors have done: they have to effect their own industrial revolution. This will not be the same as the old; it cannot be. Donald McCloskey warns that the Industrial Revolution as accomplished in

---

promoting import substitution. And since the subservient colonial governments could not be expected to pursue their own protectionist policies, the leaders of this movement called for a voluntary boycott of British manufactures. Among the more active of these visionaries was Benjamin Rush, newly graduated in 1768 from Princeton and beginning his medical education at the University of Edinburgh. See his letter of April 1768 to Thomas Bradford, publisher of the *Pennsylvania Journal and the Weekly Advertiser*: "Go on in encouraging American manufactures. I have many schemes in view with regard to these things. I have made those mechanical arts which are connected with chemistry the particular objects of my study. . . . Yes, we will be revenged of the mother country" (quoted in Brown, 1989, p. 557).

Britain is a poor model for would-be industrializers.[30] That it is, for it is an obsolete model. The technological content of modernity keeps changing, and that very change of content is another process that has been accelerated by the Industrial Revolution.

TABLE 2.2 Relative Backwardness of Groups of Countries, 1800-1970 (GDP per capita in 1960 U.S. dollars)

	1800	1860	1913	1950	1970
Developed Countries					
(A) Average	198	324	662	1054	2229
(B) Most Developed	240	580	1350	2420	3600
Underdeveloped Regions					
(C) Average	188	174	192	203	308
(D) Less Developed	130	130	130	135	140
Relative Backwardness					
B/A	1.2	1.8	2.0	2.3	1.6
A/C	1.1	1.9	3.4	5.2	7.2

Source: Hikino and Amsden (1993, p. 6-7).

---

[30] Cf. McCloskey (1981, p. 104): "The fascination in poor countries now with industrialisation on the British pattern, complete with exports of manufactures (in an age of ubiquitous skill in making them), puffing railways (in an age of cheap road transport), and centralised factories (in an age of electric power) would seem odd without the historical example in mind."

My own sense is that the "fascination" sketched out above has been shaped more by mid-nineteenth-century national economics and Marxian doctrine than by recollections of British industrialization. I would also observe that the ambition to export is a useful incentive to come up to standard, that poor countries no longer think much about building railways, and that the scale of factories is in large part a reflection of the production function. Some things call for large scale, while the multiplication of smaller units calls for entrepreneurial initiatives that are often harder to come by than the conventional factors of production.

The details pass, but the substance remains; and this revolution (I use the word advisedly), for all that some historians would depict it as a small, gentle bump on a preexisting trend, was in Britain and has been elsewhere a wrenching, compelling force for change. In all the annals of human history, no innovation has been so universal in its appeal, so ecumenical in its impact.

VIII

But if such is the power of technology, why do we see these major, revolutionary innovations take so long to drive out older methods? Why do we see small units persist and even flourish alongside the factories of the new industrial order? Why do such older techniques as water power persist and even grow in efficiency and application?

These questions are not so difficult as they may seem, especially if one does not subscribe to simplistic views about the nature of technological change. Few innovations ever sweep the field. The electric lamp, for all its intrinsic superiority, did not put an end to gaslighting or, for that matter, to kerosene lamps and candles. And in spite of desktop and laptop computers, there are still people who type their manuscripts or even write them out by hand and then have secretaries, spouses, or friends transcribe.

For one thing, the early versions of innovations are always less than satisfactory, full of problems that have to be worked out, but also full of opportunity. As a result, they may begin only marginally better than the older techniques, and they need a lot of work and attention. This was true, for example, of the new spinning machinery, perhaps the most immediately advantageous of the new equipment of the Industrial Revolution. It worked well at first only on the coarser yarns, for only they had the strength to withstand the still irregular motions of the working parts. It took two generations to devise machines smooth enough in their motions to make the higher counts, higher even than could be made by human hand, and it was not until after 1815, for example, that British yarn was able to penetrate the Indian market and kill off the fine hand-spun yarn of the Indian peasant.

Secondly, older equipment does not ordinarily die and just abandon the field to its newer rivals. On the contrary, the users of old equipment are moved by competition to imagine their own improvements, so that the greatest technological gains often take place in obsolescence. Sailing vessels, for example, reached their peak only after the introduction of steam. Water power was enormously improved in the late eighteenth and nineteenth centuries, the biggest advances perhaps being the adjustable breast wheel (cf. Mokyr, 1990a) and the use of the turbine in place of the wheel. And today mechanical watches are better than they ever were, even though the quartz watch is simply, flat out, a superior timekeeper.

Thirdly, older technologies often have special, local advantages that ensure continued application. Water power, for example, was not available everywhere, but where it was abundant, it offered a cheaper alternative to steam: capital requirements were considerably lower. The same for wood fuel as against coal: in a timber-rich country like the United States, it paid to throw logs into the locomotive firebox. The same for the putting-out system and domestic manufacture, which offered real advantages over the factory in circumstances that made possible dependable performance. In the mid-nineteenth century, for example, a number of the new power-loom enterprises worked along with domestic manufacturers, because this enabled them to handle the variance in demand without sinking unnecessarily large sums into fixed capital. There was, and continues to be, a symbiosis between newer, larger-scale modes of manufacture and older, smaller units. Why should we be surprised that the old did not disappear overnight?

IX

The question has been raised, why, if the written record and (I would say) the numbers are so clearly on the side of a gradual but profound revolution, of a prepared discontinuity, of "a long period of steady acceleration in the trend rate of industrial growth" (Crafts and Harley, 1992, p. 10), is this new orthodoxy so dismissively triumphant? Why are people so ready to argue that the new data constitute a revelation, that the term *Industrial Revolution* is a misnomer, that nothing of the kind happened, or that if it did, it had little effect?

I shall hazard a number of reasons:

1. This is one more example of the kind of cyclical revisionism that characterizes all the social sciences. The best way to attract attention, get a Ph.D., get a good job, get promoted is to stand things on their head. As a cynic once put it, we climb on the backs of our predecessors.

2. David Cannadine, in a provocative historiographical article of 1984, argues on Crocean grounds ("all history is contemporary history")

that this new turn in opinion reflects a larger change in public and political mood; that the slowing of economic growth in the 1970s (oil shock) and the growing doubts about its inevitability and even desirability led to a more negative assessment of the Industrial Revolution and turned the "dissenting views of the 1960s and even some of Clapham's dissenting views of the 1920s" into a new orthodoxy (1984, p. 162). Joel Mokyr strongly disagrees and feels that the moods, modes, and substance of economic history can be explained by endogenous considerations. I agree with Mokyr. Cannadine's Crocean interpretation might apply better to the views of Clapham, Ashton, Heaton, *et al.* in the interwar years.

3. The fallacy of misplaced concreteness. Constructs and figments become reality. This is largely because numbers have power to lull the skeptical and intimidate the uncomprehending mind. They seem somehow more authoritative, and what's more, today's numbers are by definition better than yesterday's.

4. The move toward quantification has resulted in a skewed recruitment into economic history. We do not get many historians any more, and that is a loss--of sense of proportion and of knowledge of context. (We are stronger in some respects, weaker in others. In a way, I am reminded of the Industrial Revolution: some branches grow, others shrink.)

5. The cliometricians, thrilled by technical mastery, are too quick to scorn the quantitatively innocent; and these, *mutatis mutandis*, return the compliment. Here is Roy Porter (1992, p. 35) on E. P. Thompson's sense of intellectual and moral outrage: "How could an industrializing movement that shattered the lives of millions of workers be reduced to percentages and graphs? How dare number-crunching econometricians continue to ignore those workers who once had been exploited by the profit system?" In short, we are talking past one another.

6. Economics, as generally practiced, is incapable of dealing with an industrial revolution; it deals with questions of efficiency and distribution and takes as its fundamental premise a version of the law of conservation of mass and energy: there is no room for transformation. And since most revisionist "New Economic Historians" are by training, temperament, and self-esteem devotees of (neo)classical economics, they are similarly blinkered. Donald McCloskey, a "New Economic Historian" of many parts, pinpoints the trouble in a forthcoming essay: "The kind of growth contemplated in the classical

models, embedded now deep within modern economics as a system of thought, was not the kind of growth that overtook Britain and the world in the late eighteenth and nineteenth centuries" (1992, p.28).

7. Anachronism is the enemy of understanding. The high rates of growth of the latter half of the twentieth century make those of the eighteenth century look trivial. Similarly, the costly technologies and spectacular product innovations of today devalue the primarily process innovations of the Industrial Revolution. Else what meaning to give such statements as that of Tranter (1981): "Its technology was small-scale and comparatively primitive."? Compared to what?

8. Rhetoric and loose imagery are the enemies of understanding. The best of the definers of the traditional position were cautious and moderate in their propositions, as are the best of the cliometricians. Much of this debate, as always, is at second and third hand -- epigoni vs. popularizers.[31]

X

When all is said and done, then, the supposedly new and revisionist picture of industrialization is not that different from the old. It is richer, more detailed, sharper in its analysis of the evidence. But talk of drastic revision strikes me as misleading and contrary to fact. To be sure, it is not easy to find a straightforward statement by the clio-metricians of the new and corrected past. Most revisionist generalizations take the form of broad criticisms of alleged convention, if not easy demolitions of straw men (and straw horses). But I would refer the reader to Knick Harley's reconstruction in the present volume-- what he calls "a coherent new view of British growth" (Chapter 3 in this book). Without repeating his view in all its details, the sense may be inferred from a few main points:

The main growth occurred in cotton textiles. Cheaper cottons displaced competing textiles. . . . Large urban concentrations of industry occurred because the steam engine freed textile mills from water power and because the British economy redistributed labor and capital from rural agriculture to urban industry with considerable facility. . . . By 1840 Britain had achieved a notable economic leadership. Growth was clearly different after 1840 than it had been in previous centuries. . . . The economic change

---

[31] It was Jacob Metzer who first put this suggestion to me, at a seminar in Jerusalem. I agree.

in Britain in the late eighteenth century and early nineteenth century marked the beginnings of modern economic growth.

We also have Crafts and Harley's verbal translation (1992) of the estimates of British industrial trend growth for the eighteenth and early nineteenth centuries (see Figure 2.2): "The distinguishing characteristic of the British case is a long period of steady acceleration of industrial growth from the mid-eighteenth century through to the second quarter of the nineteenth century."

In the context of the technological changes that generated that growth, I would call that tacit (unwitting) recognition of an industrial revolution.

In the end, then, I come down on the side of Friedrich Engels. Steam and even more the clock, used as metaphorical symbols for a much larger complex of technological changes, transformed first Europe and then the world. The Revolution was a revolution. If it was slower than some people would like, it was fast by comparison with the traditional pace of economic change. Different aspects of life operate on different calendars (cf. Fernand Braudel's geological-geographic, socioeconomic, and political times), and one must not expect to change an economy as one would a regime -- as the nations of eastern Europe are finding out. Now as before, no serious history of Europe or the world will be able to make sense of our times without taking the Industrial Revolution and its sequels as the progenitors of a new kind of modernity. We are its children, and children often try to diminish or kill their parents; but that does not change the fact of paternity or its importance.

> *I never saw a dead horse stand,*
> *I never hope to see one;*
> *But I can tell you, out of hand,*
> *I'd rather see than be one.*[32]

---

[32]   With apologies and thanks to Gelett Burgess.

3

Reassessing the Industrial Revolution: A Macro View[1]

C. Knick Harley

Since the mid-nineteenth century, the standard of living in Western Europe and its offshoots has increased steadily. The relationship between the human population and the environment changed, apparently as a result of the Industrial Revolution in Britain between 1750 and 1850. The change was dramatic, perhaps comparable to the neolithic development of settled agriculture, and needs to be explained if we are to understand modern economies. The Industrial Revolution led to factory industry, the modern industrial city, and an urban industrial proletariat, but recent reassessment suggests that the sudden Industrial Revolution was not the only engine of modern growth. The eighteenth and early nineteenth centuries need to be examined anew for other sources of growth.

Recent demographic history provides a long perspective on European growth (Lee, 1973, 1988; Wrigley and Schofield, 1981). Juxtaposing English population and the real wage of workers for the last seven centuries (Figure 3.1) reveals dramatic change about 1800. In earlier

---

[1] An earlier version of this chapter was presented in the C Session, "New Ways to Think About the Industrial Revolution," at the Tenth International Economic History Congress in Leuven, Belgium, August 1990. I have benefited from comments there and from workshop participants at the University of Western Ontario, Indiana University, Universidade Nova de Lisboa, and Universidad Carlos III de Madrid. I have specially benefited from comments by Joel Mokyr and Nathan Sussman.

centuries over long periods, real wages rose and fell in inverse relationship to population, but real wages were without secular trend. The Black Death in the fourteenth century killed about a third of England's population, and population remained low until the early sixteenth century. Workers in the smaller population enjoyed nearly twice the real wages of their preplague ancestors. Population then grew during the sixteenth and first half of the seventeenth century, and wages

FIGURE 3.1 Population and Real Wage. England and Wales, 1250-1980 (Logarithmic Scale)

Sources: Crafts (1989a); Phelps Brown and Hopkins (1956); Wrigley and Schofield (1981, pp. 563-595).

fell to preplague levels. History conformed to economists' theoretical expectations, first developed by David Ricardo about 1800, that wages in an economy constrained by limited resources vary inversely with population.

Since Ricardo's time, population's inverse relationship to wages has disappeared. Between 1820 and 1980 English population grew from 11.5 million to more than 45 million (a rate of 260 percent per century). In the previous five centuries, population grew about 14 percent per century and, roughly, technology and capital stock improved enough to maintain the standard of living. The statistics are imprecise, but the broad picture is clear: The relationship of population to environment changed radically. The transformation of the European economy is indisputable; but its nature remains unclear. Was it sudden or protracted? Was change pervasive or localized? Did new manufacturing technology change the economy? What roles did agriculture and foreign trade play? Recent research has reappraised these persistent questions.

1. Conceptions of the Industrial Revolution

Most observers since the nineteenth century have thought that key industrial innovations in the late eighteenth century transformed the economy and altered society rapidly and fundamentally. Friedrich Engels begins his 1845 *The Condition of the Working Class in England* with the following sentences: "The history of the English working classes begins in the second half of the eighteenth century with the invention of the steam engine and of machines for spinning and weaving cotton. It is well known that these inventions gave the impetus to the genesis of an industrial revolution. This revolution had a social as well as an economic aspect since it changed the entire structure of middle-class society" (Engels, [1845] 1958, p. 9).

In the paragraphs that follow, Engels compares the idyllic life of quasi-artisan prefactory textile workers who controlled their work with the life of proletarian workers in Manchester in the 1840s. This view quickly became a part of the Marxist historical dialectic. Near the other end of the political spectrum, Benjamin Disraeli, in his novel *Sibyl*, similarly describes the displacement of a humane, well-ordered world by a disjointed capitalist society.

Professional historians have expressed similar views. Arnold Toynbee, in his famous 1884 *Lectures on the Industrial Revolution in England*, pictures society "suddenly broken in pieces by the mighty blows of the steam engine and the power loom" ([1884] 1969, p.226). The succeeding generations of historians, particularly those like the Hammonds and the Webbs, associated with the Fabians and concerned with social issues, shared this view. In the interwar years, Sir John Clapham presented a gradualist view in his massive economic history of Britain without displacing the prevailing class-oriented view of the Industrial Revolution.

After World War II, historians shifted their interest to economic development. They shared a prevailing belief, or at least hope, that industrialization would quickly eliminate the poverty prevalent in most of the world and sought a model of growth in European industrialization. Walt Rostow, in his *Stages of Economic Growth* (1960), developed an emphatic and popular model in which a dynamic leading sector and markedly increased investment led to "take-off into self-sustained growth" over a couple of decades. Britain "took-off" between 1783 and 1802. Such precise dating inevitably drew challenge. Nonetheless, much of the historical literature looked for a brief period with lessons for development planning in contemporary low-income countries.[2]

In the last thirty years, economic historians have increasingly relied on quantitative evidence and estimates of key economic aggregates. Pioneering aggregate studies--Walther Hoffmann's (1955) index of industrial production and Phyllis Deane and Arthur Cole's (1962) indices of national income--have had enormous influence. In the 1950s historians trained in formal economics (the New Economic Historians) began to influence the writing of economic history. They attempted to unite formal models of the entire economy with quantification. Their search for data led them to Hoffmann and Deane and Cole.

Hoffmann's index appeared in German in the interwar years and in English in 1955. Although the index received considerable criticism, it became widely quoted. Deane and Cole (after rejecting Hoffmann's index for the eighteenth century as "too narrowly based to be conclusive" (1962, p.41)) produced an independent estimate of industrial growth as part of estimates of national income. Hoffmann's and Deane and Cole's different procedures yielded similar estimates that confirmed

---

[2] David Cannadine (1984) presents an interesting analysis of views of the Industrial Revolution over the last century. He links interpretation to the concerns of the societies in which the historians wrote.

the long-held view of a major structural change in British industry in the fifty years before 1830. Both indices showed that industrial output grew less than 1 percent per year from 1700 to about 1770 and then jumped to a rate of 2.5 percent per year over the next half century and accelerated a bit more in the following decades.

Deane and Cole's national income estimates remained the unquestioned backdrop of research until recently. Quantitative research into individual industries showed that Deane and Cole's aggregate growth could not have resulted only from the famous technological change in textiles, iron, and steam, even with very free assessment of linkages to the rest of economy. A synthesis emerged that married Clapham's appreciation of the economy beyond the famous sectors with Deane and Cole's quantitative estimates.[3] In the 1960s Max Hartwell articulated the view that change occurred in a wide range of sectors (Hartwell, 1971a). A generation later, Donald McCloskey summarizes the view of growth emerging from widespread, but uneven, technological advance with a meteorological metaphor (1981, p. 106): "The gadgets came more like a gentle (though unprecedented) rain, gathering here and there in puddles. By 1860 the ground was wet, but by no means soaked, even at the wetter spots." Research and synthesis in the Hartwell-McCloskey spirit had changed the general impression of the Industrial Revolution by the early 1980s. The study of individual industries had revealed gradual, often incremental change. Innovations in textiles, iron, and power could have had only modest impact on the standard of living. The idea of a heroic industrial revolution caused by the initiative of a few great entrepreneurs had given way to a view in which change was broadly based within the fabric of British society.

In the last decade, reassessment of the aggregate growth has again changed the idea of the Industrial Revolution. The sharp increases of industrial production and income growth during the last quarter of the eighteenth century now appear to have been an artifact of inappropriate index construction by Hoffmann and Deane and Cole. It now appears that in manufacturing change was largely concentrated in the famous industries, that agriculture contributed much, and that growth accelerated gradually over many decades.

---

[3] Deane and Cole undertook the early work (see 1962, chap. 6).

2. New Aggregate Estimates

In order to assess Britain's growth, we need to account for the entire range of economic activities. Particular industries can expand at the expense of other activities, so to understand growth we need estimates of aggregate economic performance. Prior to the mid-nineteenth century, statistical information is extremely spotty. Even in modern industrial societies, construction of national income statistics presents theoretical and data problems; for eighteenth-century Britain the problems are much greater, and national income estimates can only be controlled conjectures. Nonetheless, growth cannot be understood without them. Factors of production moved between alternate uses, and some sectors could grow even in a static economy. Aggregation is necessary to strike the balance between growing and contracting sectors.

Ideally, national income estimates summarize complete enumerations of economic life. Factor incomes, values added in various sectors, and the value of final sales each sum to national income. Modern statistical bureaucracies collect all these data to construct national income statistics. But estimating national income prior to the beginnings of modern national income accounting in the mid-twentieth century requires creative use of population censuses, tax returns, and other available quantitative data. In the early 1960s, Phyllis Deane and W.A. Cole completed a massive research project that provided estimates of historical national income for Britain. These estimates remain the foundation on which all others have built. Over the past decade, though, N.F.R. Crafts (1985a) has effectively criticized Deane and Cole's estimates and provided substantially different national income estimates. Many details of Crafts's work are speculative, and controversy surrounds various of its aspects, but in general outline his conclusions have largely displaced those of Deane and Cole.[4]

Estimates of British national income prior to the mid-nineteenth century involve projection backward into periods of less and less adequate data. Comprehensive enumeration of British life began with the first decennial censuses of population in 1801. The early censuses were pioneering exercises and of poor quality by modern standards, but gradually the enumeration became more reliable. By mid-century the

---

[4] Inevitably, Crafts's new work has attracted criticism. See Berg and Hudson (1992); Hoppit (1990); Jackson (1990, 1992); Mokyr (1987); Williamson (1987a). For a discussion of these criticisms see Crafts and Harley (1992).

census contained useful occupational information. The census of 1841, although judged to be somewhat incomplete, contains the earliest reliable labor force data from which to construct labor income estimates (Deane and Cole, 1962, pp. 139-140). Income tax during the Napoleonic War and after its 1842 reimposition by Sir Robert Peel provide information on property income (Deane and Cole, 1962, p. 164ff.). Deane and Cole use these sources to estimate factor incomes and national income from 1801 on. The evidential basis was weak before 1841 but improved thereafter. Officials began collecting comprehensive agricultural output data in the 1880s, and the first census of industrial production occurred in 1907.

Some political commentators before the nineteenth century attempted to estimate national income from data available to them,[5] but estimates of national income prior to the 1840s consist primarily of projections backward. Population (from censuses and earlier estimates), incomplete output series, and inferences of various sorts have been used in attempting to project from the relative certainty of the mid-nineteenth century to earlier dates.

The best preindustrial estimate of the extent of the British economy was made by Gregory King in the late eighteenth century. King was a member of the inner circle of late-eighteenth-century government and had access to such data as the government had available to calculate aggregate activity. His journals have survived and show his use of tax records. As Peter Lindert (1980) has recently shown, King almost certainly underestimated the extent of nonagricultural activity in the country outside London. Lindert has revised King's estimate using more careful assessments of occupations from local censuses and burial records. The resulting social table provides valuable information on the industrial structure of late-eighteenth-century Britain and can be used to construct an estimate of income that provides an important independent check on estimates based on projections back from more reliable nineteenth-century benchmarks. The revised estimate of national income in 1688 comes to about £55 million at 1688 prices. Inflation after 1750, and particularly in the final years of the eighteenth century, complicates comparison of this estimate with nineteenth-

---

[5] These estimates are discussed in section 6 below. See Deane (1955) and Lindert and Williamson (1982, 1983a) for a discussion and assessment of these estimates.

century calculations but a good guess is that prices doubled[6] between King's day and the first census in 1801. Cole (1981, p. 65) estimates the value of income in England and Wales in 1801 to be £200 million. Over the same period English population increased by three-quarters. In very round numbers, which is the best that can be done with this kind of calculation, these figures suggest only a small increase--less than 5 percent--in real per capita income $(200/(55x2)/1.75=1.04)$. The calculations here are much too speculative to stand alone, but they may offer some rough check on other procedures.

Until recently, even British population prior to 1801--a prime input to any early national income estimate--had been poorly understood. Fortunately, extensive research under the direction of E. A. Wrigley and R. Schofield (1981) over two decades has greatly improved matters in this regard. Even here historians have had to rely on estimates constructed from partial evidence, but most now feel confident that the estimates accurately convey the course of eighteenth-century population.

Industrial Production

Traditional interpretations see a transformation of industrial technology in late eighteenth century initiating modern growth. Cotton and then other textiles were transformed, Watt radically improved the steam engine, and various advances led to the smelting of iron with coke. How much did these improvements lead to growth in industrial output as a whole and in national income?

Data

Underlying data for industrial production come from various sources and suffer various problems of reliability. The British state was remote from most economic activity and lacked the statistical apparatus of a modern state or even, for that matter, of a more centralized and interventionist France. Most of the reasonably comprehensive data that do exist were created by the state in raising revenue. Customs duties on internationally traded goods and excise taxes on domestic consumption provided the bulk of the state's revenue. Records necessitated by the administration of these taxes provide the most reliable data. But large areas of manufacturing avoided the state's fiscal

---

[6] This price change is the average of O'Brien's (1985) agricultural (with rough allowance for the famine prices in 1800) and industrial prices.

attention, and here tax records provide little information. Fortunately, historians have studied the most important of these industries and have provided estimates of growth. Nonetheless, we have little information for a considerable portion of manufacturing.

The underlying data are clearly imperfect and must be used with care. Individuals certainly had good reason to avoid the state's revenue officers and to understate the values on which taxes were collected (Hoppit, 1990). Certainly evasion occurred, but Britain was an island with limited ports, and domestic excises were collected primarily on goods produced in large-scale enterprises that the excise officers could monitor (Mitchell and Deane, 1962, pp. 242-244). Fortunately, the revenue figures will correctly indicate trends in growth even if there was widespread evasion if the extent of evasion was constant over time.[7]

Textiles and clothing together made up nearly half of manufacturing in mid-eighteenth-century Britain. We can trace the growth of the new cotton textile industry with some confidence since all Britain's raw cotton was imported. The customs data, although alternative sources differ slightly and some cotton was used for non-textile purposes, provide good information on the general trend. Unfortunately, we have much less precise records for the initially more important older textiles that used domestic raw materials -- wool and linen. Some records of the sale of woolen cloth in the West Riding of Yorkshire exist. But the West Riding contained only a portion of the industry, and we know that its importance increased from the eighteenth to the nineteenth century, so this data cannot be used as an index of the industry's total output. The best indications come from estimates of the amount of wool produced in Britain -- provided by contemporary estimates and other indicators -- plus imports of wool. Phyllis Deane (1957; Holderness, 1989, pp. 171-174) provides a detailed assessment of these sources and her conclusions have been accepted as providing an indication of the industry's broad trends, although considerable uncertainty exists. The linen data are similar to those for wool (Deane and Cole, 1962, pp. 202-205) in their sources and accuracy. Silk, a relatively small industry in Britain, depended on imported raw materials whose quantities were recorded by customs, but there is only limited

---

[7] Crafts and Harley (1992) considers implications of problems in the data at some length.

information with which to calculate value added (Deane and Cole, 1962, pp. 207-211). Clothing trends can be estimated from the estimates of textiles retained for domestic use.

Metal production and mining have also required careful historical assessment. Fortunately, the scale of mining and smelting operations make them easier to trace in the historical sources than more dispersed smaller-scale activities (such as many parts of textile production and food processing). Estimates of primary iron production and coal output can be made from these sources (Hyde, 1977, pp. 204-206, Pollard, 1980). The estimates of primary iron production plus iron imports can be used to provide an indication of the trend of output in the highly dispersed metalworking industries (Harley, 1982, pp. 273-275).

Excise tax records reveal the histories of some other industries. Leather, a large preindustrial manufacturing sector, was taxed. So too were beer production and paper and printing (Deane and Cole, 1962, pp. 50-62; Hoffmann, 1955, pp. 291-330; Mitchell and Deane, 1962, pp. 247-67). The output of food processing industries can be inferred from agricultural output. Estimates of capital formation have provided the basis for estimating the level of activity in the construction industry (Feinstein, 1978, p. 40; Feinstein, 1988a, p. 446). But for about 10 percent of industrial activity there is almost no indication of trends of growth; here output probably more or less kept pace with population growth.

Table 3.1 presents the rather uncertain indices of output (with 1841 outputs set to 100) for various industries in 1770 and 1815. The very rapid growth of cotton textiles stands out; output in 1770 was just 0.8 percent of its 1841 level. By contrast, other industries grew slowly. Metal production, the second fastest growing industry, stood at nearly 7 percent of its 1841 level in 1770; other large industrial sectors -- the other textiles, leather, and food and drink -- were already nearly half as large in 1770 as they became by 1841. Aggregate industrial output is the sum of the output of all industries aggregated at appropriate prices, and its growth is a weighted average of the very different histories of different activities. In particular, an estimate of aggregate industrial production will grow much faster if fast-growing cotton textiles have a large weight than if they have a small weight.

TABLE 3.1 Indices of Output, Various Industries (1841 = 100)

Industry	1770	1815
Cotton	0.8	19
Wool	46	65
Linen	47	75
Silk	28	40
Clothing	20	43
Leather	41	61
Metal	7	29
Food and drink	47	69
Paper and printing	17	47
Mining	15	46
Building	26	50
Other	15-50	40-60

Source: Harley (1982, p. 273) with building modified to reflect new estimates of "Total buildings and works" (Feinstein, 1988a, p. 446).

Weighting

Because various parts of manufacturing grew at very different rates, indices of aggregate output will vary if different weights are used. Fortunately, there is agreement that appropriate aggregation involves summing the quantities of various commodities valued at their prices at some base date. A key step in constructing the index is the identification of appropriate prices and quantities for various base dates. During the Industrial Revolution, relative prices changed rapidly, particularly as technological advances drove down the prices of cotton textiles. Consequently, different base years will produce different, but equally legitimate, indices.[8]

---

[8] In 1841 cottons were only a third as expensive relative to other manufactured goods as they had been in 1770 and only half as expensive as in 1815. Aggregation using 1770 prices (a Laspeyres index) will value the large 1841 cotton textile sector more than will aggregation using 1841 prices (a

In practice, output indices are usually constructed as a weighted average of industry output relatives. The appropriate weights are the various industries' shares in output, or value added, in the base year. This procedure is equivalent to aggregating with base year prices. Quantifying the base year structure of the industrial sector to provide appropriate weights for aggregation presents the greatest challenge to constructing an index of industrial production for Britain prior to the 1840s. An ideal base would come from a comprehensive enumeration of outputs and inputs of all industries in a census of industrial production. But the first such census occurred only in 1907. Without an industrial census, compromises have to be made.

Occupational classifications in the population census of 1841 provide the earliest reasonably comprehensive substitute for an industrial production census. I chose to use these data as a proxy for ideal but unavailable information on value added by specific industries (Harley, 1982). This procedure resulted in a much lower weight than Walther Hoffmann had used for cotton in his pioneering index. As a result, my index grew much more slowly.

I assigned weights for 1841 in proportion to 1841 labor force by industry (with women, children, and handloom weavers given half the weight of adult males). I estimated value added shares for earlier benchmark dates by projecting the 1841 employment shares backward

---

Paasche index) and will lead to an estimate of more rapid growth. This discrepancy is an unavoidable index number problem. Some compromise between initial and terminal weights, which has intuitive appeal and support in formal consumption theory, leads to Fisher's Ideal and the Divisia indices (presented below). Nonetheless, an inherent problem exists because we are attempting to aggregate when strict conditions allowing aggregation are absent.

Laspeyres and Paasche index numbers are usually calculated by constructing a weighted average of quantity relatives of components. The appropriate weights consist of the shares of each component in the value of total output in the base period (on which the quantity relative are also based). If initial shares are employed, the index is Laspeyres; if terminal shares, Paasche. Fisher Ideal index is the geometric mean of the corresponding Laspeyres and Paasche indices. The Divisia index differs in its construction. For very small changes an aggregate's rate of growth equals the weighted sum of the growth rates of its components, each weighted by its share in the aggregate. For large changes, of the sort we are considering, an appropriate procedure is to use the geometric mean of initial and terminal shares as weights.

using industry output indices and adjusting for the change in relative prices of cotton textiles and iron. This provided logically consistent shares for 1841, 1815, and 1770. Cotton value added was adjusted to reflect relative prices 1.8 times as high in 1815 as in 1841 and 3 times as high in 1770 as in 1841. Adjustments for iron used an 1815 relative price 1.2 times its 1841 level and an 1770 price 1.8 times the 1841 level. The industrial structures implied by these calculations are presented in Table 3.2. Inevitably, my procedures to substitute for nonexistent manufacturing census data introduced possibilities of error. Employment and value added did not correspond exactly. In addition, I made no attempt to adjust for relative price changes except in cotton and iron, primarily because reliable data do not exist. I felt, however, that the gains from using the (fairly) complete enumeration of the census and maintaining clear consistency among bases outweighed shortcomings.

Shortly after my index appeared, N.F.R. Crafts (1985a, pp. 17-34) independently reestimated industrial production. His data on sectoral growth were mostly the same as mine (although there were some minor differences), but he approached the crucial issue of weighting somewhat differently. Whereas I attempted to maintain consistency by projecting back from a comprehensive 1841 labor enumeration, making explicit adjustments for relative price changes, Crafts employed separate estimates of industrial output at current prices for 1770, 1801, and 1831. His shares differ somewhat from those derived from the census employment data. Most importantly, his weight for cotton, although still below Hoffmann's, was nearly twice mine, and so his aggregate growth rate was higher than mine but still much below Hoffmann's.

Recently, Crafts has recognized that he over-weighted cotton, at least in the early nineteenth century, because he failed to account for inputs other than raw cotton that the industry purchased. He has revised his index downward, bringing it much closer to my own (Crafts and Harley, 1992). Crafts's new figures are incorporated in Table 3.3 and Figure 3.2.

Knick Harley

TABLE 3.2 Industrial Structure, 1841, 1815, and 1770

Industry	1841	1815	1770
Textiles			
Cotton	.10	.08	.01
Wool	.08	.11	.15
Linen	.04	.06	.08
Silk	.03	.02	.04
Clothing	.13	.12	.11
Leather	.11	.14	.19
Metal	.11	.08	.05
Food and drink	.04	.06	.08
Paper and printing	.02	.02	.01
Mining	.08	.08	.05
Building	.18	.15	.12
Other	.09	.09	.12

Source: Harley (1982, p. 269).

Comparison of New and Old Estimates

Hoffmann and Deane and Cole overestimated the growth of industrial output and so understate the level of eighteenth-century industrial output. Hoffmann's overstatement arose from the industry weights he used for the late eighteenth century. He constructed a 1783 base to weight sectors for that time period. He estimated that cotton textiles constituted 6.7 percent of industrial output -- just about Crafts's weight but larger than mine. Hoffmann estimated that the industrial output series he had available covered 56.4 percent of total industrial output. To construct an index, he had to estimate the growth of the remaining 43.6 percent, either explicitly or implicitly. He proceeded by raising the weight of each included industry in proportion (by a factor of 1.79 = 1/0.564). This raised the weight of cotton textiles to 12 percent of the index. Hoffmann's procedure implicitly, but incorrectly, assumed that some other industries, 79 percent the size of cotton, grew as fast as cotton.

TABLE 3.3 Indices of Aggregate Industrial Production, 1700-1841

	Harley	Crafts	Hoffmann	Deane & Cole
1770	-	13	8	9
1730	-	-	10	10
1760	-	19	12	14
1770	23	-	14	13
1780	-	25	16	15
1790	-	-	23	18
1801	-	37	32	23
1811	-	-	40	24
1815	46	-	-	-
1821	-	-	51	57
1831	-	85	72	85
1841	100	100	100	100

Source: Crafts and Harley (1992, table 2) (revised from Harley [1982, p. 276], calculated from mean of Divisia range; Crafts [1985a, p. 26], calculated using series with weights based on geometric average of adjacent years [Divisia]). Hoffmann [1955, appendix]. Deane and Cole (1962), calculated from data pp. 78, 166; Deane and Cole's current price data has been deflated by Rousseaux's industrial price index.

Deane and Cole proceeded differently and used distinct procedures for the eighteenth and nineteenth centuries. For the nineteenth century, they constructed estimates of current incomes by sectors. These calculations combined estimates of labor income based on the census and property income estimates from the income tax assessments.[9] They then deflated these current income estimates with Rousseaux's index of industrial product prices to estimate output volumes.

[9] See Deane and Cole (1962, chaps. 4 and 5). They point out that these data were suspect before 1840, since the early censuses did not contain reliable occupational information and the income tax was repealed at the end of the Napoleonic War.

FIGURE 3.2 Estimates of Industrial Production (Logarithmic scale, 1841 = 100)

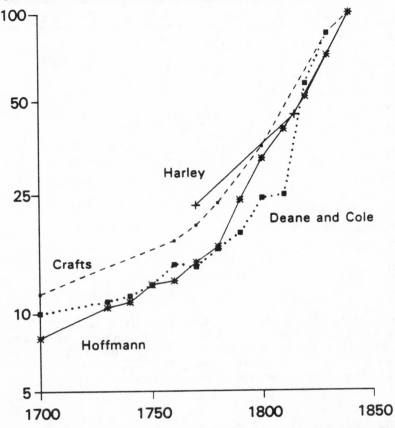

Source: Crafts and Harley (1992, table 2), Hoffmann (1955, appendix), Deane and Cole (1962).

Unfortunately, Rousseaux's index inadequately represented industrial prices and exaggerated industrial price decline in the early nineteenth century (Crafts, 1985a, pp. 30-31). For the eighteenth century, Deane and Cole divided the industrial sector into two parts: a domestic portion and an export portion. The output of domestic industry (one third of the whole in 1700) was estimated from excise series (Deane and Cole, 1962, p. 76). They felt that the direct statistical base for the export industries was inadequate. They decided, after a extensive discussion (pp. 50-61), that "it seems fair to assume that the volume of imports and exports may provide us with a reasonably accurate index of the growth of those industries which entered largely into overseas trade." Eighteenth-century growth of trade provided their estimated growth of export industrial output, but the procedure has no sound theoretical basis. In particular, the procedure is undermined because much of the late-century growth of trade occurred with the Americas where population grew more rapidly than in Britain or elsewhere and where the war temporarily closed markets to non-British exporters.

The data do not permit precise conclusions, but my and Crafts's critical evaluations of industrial production, although differing somewhat, pointed to a common conclusion: Industrial growth, particularly growth per capita, in the decades after 1770 was much slower than had generally been assumed. I estimated industrial growth from 1770 to 1815 at 1.6 percent per year or 0.6 percent per year per capita. Crafts estimated faster growth: about 2 percent per year in aggregate and 1 percent per capita. Both these estimates are well below Hoffmann's 2.6 total and 1.6 per capita. The extent of the differences can best be appreciated by comparing the levels of industrial output per capita in 1770 to levels in 1815. My calculation implies per capita output of 76 percent of the 1815 level, Crafts's of 64 percent, and Hoffmann's 49 percent.

Crafts and I have recently reassessed our industrial production indices in light of a decade's research and criticism (Crafts and Harley, 1992). The estimates, although inevitably imprecise because of problems in the underlying data, seem to have withstood criticism. Industrial growth was much slower than had previously been assumed. With industry's share of national income at just under a third from the 1780s to the 1830s (Crafts, 1985a, p. 45; Deane and Cole, 1962, p. 166), industrial growth generated per capita income growth of 0.2 or 0.3 percent per year. At these rates, income would double only in two hundred to three hundred and fifty years -- not the stuff of sudden transformation.

Incomplete data make it impossible to construct anything more precise than controlled conjectures about industrial growth during the Industrial Revolution. Crafts's and my indices probably define the bounds of the acceptable conjectures. The conclusion that industrial growth was much lower than economic historians had assumed for a generation on the basis of Hoffmann's and Deane and Cole's estimates has been established. Uncertainty, of course, remains; its most important source is the weight of cotton textile production in the aggregation. My weight may be a bit low as a result of failure to account adequately for the value added in chemical and other industries involved in the finishing of cotton cloth and also perhaps from an underestimate of the decline in cotton cloth prices in the industry's early years. Crafts, on the other hand, may overweigh cotton. He has now reduced his 1831 weight for cotton to remove the industry's purchase of inputs other than raw cotton but, because of uncertainty in the underlying estimates of earlier cotton output, has made no such adjustment to earlier weights. Although probably less important than appropriate weighting, many indices of sectoral output growth are crude approximations. The errors in individual series are unlikely to be strongly correlated, so we may hope that the error in the aggregate is less than the error in individual series. Nonetheless, estimates of industrial production are approximate.

Agriculture

Agricultural output must also be estimated from imperfect primary data. B. A. Holderness, in his recent assessment, summarizes the general view of those of us who have bravely or foolishly attempted to estimate aggregate output for periods before official statistics existed (1989, p. 174): "The section on production and productivity is so replete with expressions of doubt, uncertainty, and disbelief that it reads like a litany for skeptics. It is obviously necessary to keep in view the doubtful character of all estimates of production not founded upon the bedrock of agricultural census returns. Nevertheless, precision in detail is not essential to the assessment of probable magnitudes or the direction of trends." Agricultural estimates have various sources of support. Primary among them, roughly in declining order of reliability, are data on prices, estimates of population, and estimates of areas under cultivation, crop yields, animal stocks, and marketed weight.

Deane and Cole estimated eighteenth-century agricultural growth by assuming that per capita consumption remained unchanged (1962, pp. 65, 74). Their index of output was population adjusted for net imports of grain. Crafts points out that this procedure was inadequate because demand for food in low-income societies has considerable price and income elasticity that Deane and Cole ignored (1976; 1985a, pp. 38-44). Since relative agricultural prices were the same in 1760 as in 1700, only income effects needed to be considered in comparing these dates. Crafts allowed an income elasticity of demand from food of 0.7 and estimated agricultural growth of 0.6 percent per year, about 0.2 percent above the growth rate of population. After 1760 agricultural prices rose relative to other prices, complicating analysis. Crafts used two independent procedures for this period. In his first procedure, he deflated estimates of current values of output by an agricultural price index (O'Brien, 1985). For 1760 he used Peter Lindert and Jeffrey Williamson's (1982; 1983a) estimate of the value of agricultural output based on Joseph Massie's contemporary estimate. Deane and Cole provided estimates for nineteenth-century census years. In his second procedure, Crafts assumed a price elasticity of -0.8 and the income elasticity of 0.7 and solved simultaneously for national income and agricultural output. The two procedures generated similar estimates for 1760 to 1800: growth rates of 0.44 and 0.50 percent per year, respectively. A greater discrepancy appeared between 1801 and 1831; deflation yielded 1.18 percent annual growth, while demand estimates produced a 1.88 percent. Crafts has used the lower estimate in subsequent work.

Crafts's estimate of agricultural output and productivity growth has been criticised for both the slimness of its evidential base and the apparent inconsistency with general views of modern growth. As Crafts himself acknowledges and Joel Mokyr (1987, pp. 305-312) has explored in greater detail, the estimates of agricultural growth are undeniably insecure. Jeffrey Williamson, who has put forward a somewhat different overall view of Britain's growth, rejects the view that agricultural advance was of similar magnitude to industrial advance. He draws on analogies to industrialization elsewhere: "Central to all industrialization accounts past and present has been the view that modern sectors exhibit much faster rates of productivity advance while traditional sectors lag behind." He also suggests that Crafts's productivity estimates cannot fit into a consistent macroeconomics of the Industrial Revolution (1987a, p. 273-274).

Historians of British agriculture have recently provided independent estimates of aggregate agricultural output based on the history of production (Allen, 1992a, cf. table 1, p. 35; Chartres, 1985; Holderness, 1989) that generally support Crafts's calculations. The estimates combine acreage and yield estimates for grain, and estimates of herd size and animal size for animal production, at fifty year intervals from 1700 to 1850. Over the century and a half these production estimates grow at about the same rate as Crafts's estimate: Crafts's estimate projected a 1700 output that is about 10 percent lower than the independent output estimates. Put slightly differently, Crafts estimates output growth at 8.7 percent per decade, whereas the Holderness-Allen series estimates 8.1 percent.

The Holderness-Allen estimates do not attempt to estimate short-term movements, but they raise some doubts about the timing of agricultural growth that Crafts proposes. Crafts's inferences from price data and income suggest relatively rapid initial growth, near stagnation for a generation or so after mid-century, and finally very rapid growth in the early nineteenth century (although considerably slower than Deane and Cole propose for this period). The Holderness-Allen series indicates nearly steady growth with only small acceleration (the index grew at 0.77 percent annually from 1700 to 1750, 0.80 percent from 1750 to 1800, and 0.85 percent from 1800 to 1850). Estimates of grain yield vary but suggest a still different pattern: slow yield increases during the eighteenth century and little acceleration in the nineteenth (G. Clark, 1991d). Animal products, however, were about half of final output in agriculture by the mid-eighteenth century.

Greg Clark is currently examining productivity in British agriculture. He has concluded that much of the increased output normally attributed to technological change should properly be considered as the result of costly investment in soil fertility. This is a convincing argument that shows that technological change played a smaller role and capital formation a larger role in British growth than most narratives have allowed, although some will argue that Clark has slighted the interconnection between knowledge and investment (Clark, 1992b). In Chapter 4, Clark presents some new research on technological change based on price data that suggest very slow productivity increase during the eighteenth and nineteenth centuries. As he points out, these results conflict with other evidence. In part a resolution may be reached by recognizing possible shortcomings in the price data. In particular, if Clark had used O'Brien's recent output price data (1985) rather than price data from Phelps Brown and Hopkins (1956), his calculations would have shown considerably greater technological change. His calculations also seem to pay too little attention to the regional nature of British agricultural change. Qualitative studies of the organizational and technological change in British agriculture in the late eighteenth and early nineteenth centuries emphasize differing regional patterns and the introduction of mixed agriculture in which animal husbandry played a key role (Jones, 1981a; Thirsk, 1987). It may be that Clark's data are concentrated in the clay Midlands where change was slow and have failed to capture productivity growth that affected other farming environments.

Clearly, agricultural change will repay more detailed analysis. In assessing the agriculture estimates, however, it is important to remember that we are projecting backward from firm knowledge about the end of the period. In the middle of the nineteenth century, British agriculture had the highest productivity in Europe. Agriculture employed only a small proportion of British resources but still fed most of her people after decades of rapid population growth. Britain's agricultural superiority had emerged in the previous two centuries from myriad improvements in different agricultural regions that occurred at different times. It is unlikely that precise dating of aggregate productivity advance is possible.

Although uncertainty seems inevitable, certain conclusions are inescapable. In particular, if agricultural growth was as slow as some of Crafts's critics suggest, British agriculture was extraordinarily productive in the early eighteenth century, and Britain must have attained agricultural superiority over most of its European neighbors before that. Anthony Wrigley's work on the ratio of urban consumers to agricultural producers indicates this is improbable. The proportion of population in towns in Britain only began to diverge from that of the rest of Western Europe in the eighteenth century (1986, p. 147).

Agriculture made up a large portion of the eighteenth-century British economy. Consequently, estimates of agricultural growth make up an important part of estimates of British aggregate growth prior to the mid-nineteenth century. If agricultural growth was slower in the century before 1850 than Crafts has estimated, then aggregate growth was also slower. Overall, Crafts's reassessment has already led economic historians to conclude that growth was slower than they had previously thought. Slower agricultural growth implies even higher British standards of living in the middle of the eighteenth century and an earlier date for the beginning of Britain's economic lead. If this is the case, historians will have to devote their attention to earlier periods of change.

Services

Measuring the service sector, difficult even in modern economies, cannot be done with any accuracy for the late eighteenth century. Deane and Cole divided eighteenth-century services into "government and defence" and "rents and services," and Crafts has continued to rely on these estimates. Reported government expenditures were deflated by the Schumpeter-Gilboy price index.[10] Rents and services were assumed to grow with population growth. Crafts also considered a trade and commerce sector, which Deane and Cole had subsumed in industry for their eighteenth-century calculations, and assumed that it grew with national income (Crafts, 1985a, p. 28). For the early nineteenth century, Deane and Cole estimated current value of output primarily from census employment. They obtained quantity estimates by deflating current value by Rousseaux's price index. Crafts rejected Deane and Cole's deflation; the deflator was inappropriate, and the results were highly implausible. Instead, he constructed alternate estimates based primarily on employment estimates (1985a, pp. 34-37).

National Income

Recent reevaluation has fundamentally altered the picture of aggregate growth. Crafts's and Deane and Cole's indices of national income are compared in both aggregate and per capita terms in Table 3.4 and Figure 3.3. Deane and Cole show a shift to high growth of per capita income coinciding with the textile innovations of the late eighteenth century. Crafts's data show no such shift. Per capita growth increased slightly about 1780 or 1800, but if there was a break in the trend instead of an acceleration over perhaps as much as two centuries, it occurred after the Napoleonic Wars (Crafts, Leybourne, and Mills, 1989).

The main criticism of Crafts's calculations has been that he exaggerated agricultural growth. However, lower agricultural growth would reinforce his conclusion by implying slower income growth and a still more protracted and gradual acceleration of national income, further reducing the significance of the traditional Industrial Revolution era.

---

[10] Jackson (1990) criticizes some of Crafts's procedures but overstates the significance of his findings. There are no demonstrably "correct" procedures, and the maximum difference he produces is under 0.2 percent per year for the period 1760 to 1800 -- a cumulative difference of 8 percent, which is swamped by the various uncertainties within the calculations.

FIGURE 3.3 British National Income, 1700-1870

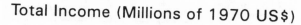

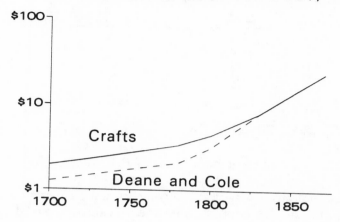

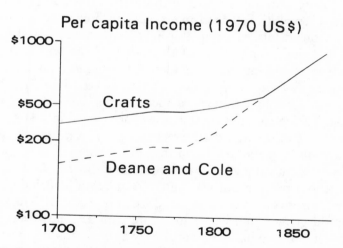

Sources: Crafts and Harley (1992, table 4); Deane and Cole (1962, pp. 78 and 106).

TABLE 3.4 National Income, 1700-1870, Crafts and Deane and Cole
(U.S. 1970 $, after Crafts)

	Crafts		Deane and Cole	
	Total (mn.)	Per capita	Total (mn.)	Per capita
1700	2.0	330	1.3	190
1760	3.0	400	1.9	250
1780	3.4	400	2.1	250
1800	4.5	430	3.2	310
1830	8.1	500	8.1	500
1870	23.6	900	23.6	900

Sources: Crafts and Harley (1992, table 4); Deane and Cole (1962, pp. 78 and 106).

3. A Coherent New View of British Growth

The new indicators of aggregate income suggest a coherent picture of growth in Britain that contrasts with the previously accepted view. Industrial change now appears largely confined to the famous sectors of the Industrial Revolution. The main growth occurred in cotton textiles. Cheaper cottons displaced competing textiles that had not shared its rapid technological change. Part of the industry's growth came from British consumers buying cotton textiles, but even more came from the British industry's capture of foreign textile markets. The British economy became increasingly industrial and urban as the "modern" textile sector grew. The cotton industry became concentrated into large urban areas in response to the new cotton technology. The steam engine allowed textile mills to abandon water power for urban sites, and labor and capital moved from rural agriculture to urban industry. Urbanization was not without friction but was much more rapid in Britain than it has been in most societies that have made such transitions. The income gains from the growth of urban industry were modest, however. Much of the growth of urban industry was simply a concentration of activity. Furthermore, the export of two-thirds of cotton output transferred benefits of British technological change to foreign customers.

Agricultural change appears to have played a large role in British growth, although its exact extent and timing are hidden in the complexity of the rural economy. Agricultural technology advanced much less, to be sure, than technology in the leading industrial sectors but probably more than in other industrial and service sectors. Also, British agriculture, most likely because of its class structure, released labor and capital to growing sectors quickly by comparison to the history of industrialization elsewhere.[11] The labor force in the primary sector of the economy, although it increased from 1801 to 1851, fell dramatically as a proportion of the total labor force. Primary production employed 40 percent in 1801 but only 25 percent in the 1840s (Crafts, 1987, p. 257). Other European economies did not reach this low a share of primary sector employment for another century. During the early stages of industrialization in most countries, labor left the primary sector very slowly, and a large gap opened between labor productivity in agriculture and industry. No such gap appeared in Britain. Deane and Cole's estimate for 1840 (1962, p.152, 166) shows 25 percent of the labor force engaged in the primary sector and an essentially equal share of income produced by the sector (24.9 percent). The average European economy ("European norm") at that level of income had a labor share in the primary sector that exceeded the sector's income share by some 40 percent. Later in the nineteenth century, cheap imported American food became available, and the share of income in the British primary sector fell more rapidly than the share of labor. By the eve of World War I, 15 percent of the labor force remained in the primary sectors, while only 10 percent of the income originated in these activities. Even so, Britain remained unlike the European norm, where at a similar level of income, primary production employed 29 percent of labor and produced 15 percent of income (Crafts, 1985a, chap. 3).

From 1770 to 1830, the years of the classical Industrial Revolution, real income grew only modestly, and the standard of living improved only slowly. Relatively rapid change in the large agricultural sector (which was about half of the labor force, but somewhat less of income, in the mid-eighteenth century but declined rapidly in the early nineteenth) proved about as important to growth as the more famous new industrial technology--which was limited to a relatively small part of the economy (not more than 40 percent of industry, or 12 percent of national income, even in 1841). Not all scholars share this view of agriculture's contribution. The evidence is shaky, and some believe that Crafts has exaggerated agriculture's achievements. But to the extent that agricultural growth has been exaggerated, so too has the growth of

---

[11] This hypothesis and the origins of the class relationship in British agriculture have been explored at some length by Robert Brenner (1976).

196 C. Knick Harley

income, and British income in the early eighteenth century has been underestimated.

Assessment of any general view of early British growth must appreciate that our view is inevitably projected backward from the relatively reliable data that became available in the mid-nineteenth century. Britain's economic position in 1840 is well understood. Britain had achieved a notable economic leadership, and continuing economic growth had become established. From 1840, when per capita income was still low, to 1910 British income per capita grew at 1.2 percent per year. Simple back projection shows that the growth rate must have accelerated in the century before 1840: Income growing at 1.2 percent doubles every 58 years, and eighteenth-century growth at that rate implies impossibly low per capita income in 1700. Contemporary observers and historians broadly agree on Britain's economic lead at the middle of the nineteenth century. During the previous century, British textile firms had achieved international predominance by revolutionizing the technology of production. British iron masters had become low-cost producers by pioneering technological change (Allen, 1979). British agriculture also led the world in productivity.

Measurement of Britain's leadership is difficult. Quantitative estimates of nineteenth-century production elsewhere are even more uncertain than those for Britain. Certainly, Britain had a large lead in the "new" industries. British mills consumed over half of all the world's raw cotton in the 1840s; British furnaces produced about a third more pig iron than all the rest of Europe (Mitchell, 1975, pp. 391-392)--and a much larger proportion of the iron produced using the new coke-smelting technology; and Britain contained the largest modern woolen industry. Paul Bairoch (1982; 1989, p. 37) probably overemphasized these "new industries" when he showed that Britain's industrial sector, in per capita terms, produced some four times as much as its French equivalent and five times as much as Germany and nearly three times as much as Belgium and Switzerland, the most industrialized Continental economies. Calculations from more comprehensive national income figures show that British industrial output per capita was 60 or

70 percent higher than Belgium's and two and a half times Germany's.[12]

Industrialization must not be confused with output per capita, tempting though the equation seems. Britain's per capita output also exceeded that of her neighbors -- a quarter over Belgium and two-thirds over Germany, with France occupying an intermediate position (Crafts, 1983b; Maddison, 1982). The British lead was based only in part on the manufacturing industry, and the British lead should not be overdrawn. In many industries the British possessed little superiority and undoubtedly lagged behind established Continental producers in many areas of production. British agriculture contributed to high incomes. Bairoch's (1989, p. 37) calculation of caloric net output per male worker in European agriculture for 1860 may again have exaggerated Britain's leadership, particularly over the Low Countries where nonfood production was important. His figures show the Danes closest at 87 percent of British productivity. French and German output per worker was about half the British level, with Belgium and the Netherlands slightly farther behind. Recent estimates for 1870 show a more modest British advantage but still reveal a sizable gap. British productivity in these calculations approximately equalled that of Denmark, Holland, and Belgium--which had recently undergone rapid technological change--and exceeded that of France by about 15 percent and that of Germany by nearly 50 percent (Van Zanden, 1991, p, 226).

The economic change in Britain in the late eighteenth and early nineteenth centuries marked the beginnings of modern economic growth. The basic character of the economy changed from one governed by the balance of land and population to one dominated by technological change and capital accumulation. Robert Solow's (1957) procedure of estimating the contributions of factor inputs to output growth and identifying a "residual" growth due to "technological change" constitutes the first step in "explaining growth" within an aggregate neoclassical framework. The procedure assumes that national output can be adequately represented as an aggregate produced by a well-specified production function. Also, competition is assumed to result in factor prices proportional to marginal products. In these circumstances, the growth rate of output due to a factor's growth equals

---

[12] Calculated from national income estimates in Crafts (1985a, chap. 3) and industrial shares in Mitchell (1975, pp. 799-800).

the growth rate of the factor times its share of total income. The "residual," or "total factor productivity growth," is the difference between the measured output growth rate and the growth predicted by the growth of inputs.[13]

Total factor productivity calculations are presented in Table 3.5. Some two-thirds of the acceleration in output growth between the early eighteenth century and the mid-nineteenth century was due to increased rates of factor growth. Historians have long known that population growth accelerated in the final decades of the eighteenth century. Savings and investment maintained the capital stock per capita at approximately the 1760 level. Productivity growth occurred in both industry and agriculture. If Crafts's somewhat speculative calculations can be believed, productivity advanced somewhat faster in agriculture than in the economy as a whole.

TABLE 3.5 Sources of Growth, 1700-1860, Crafts' Estimates (percentage per year)

	Growth Rate				*Contribution to Growth*			
	Income	*K*	*L*	*T*	*K*	*L*	*T*	*"Residual"*
1700-1760	0.7	0.7	0.3	0.05	0.24	0.15	0.01	0.3
1760-1800	1.0	1.0	0.8	0.2	0.35	0.40	0.03	0.2
1801-1831	1.9	1.7	1.4	0.4	0.60	0.70	0.06	0.5
1831-1860	2.5	2.0	1.4	0.6	0.70	0.70	0.09	1.0

Notes: K - capital; L - labor; T - land. Factor shares for the calculation are: capital, 0.35; labor, 0.5; land, 0.15.
Source: Crafts and Harley (1992, Table 5), with allowance for land.

Somewhat earlier, Donald McCloskey brought together information pertaining to various industries and sectors in an interesting attempt to find "the location of ingenuity." The aggregate growth of total factor productivity--calculated by subtracting aggregate input growth from estimated aggregate output growth--conceptually equals a weighted average of the total factor productivity growths of individual industries. McCloskey produced "crude approximations to annual productivity

[13] The restrictions for precise equation of the residual to technological change has led many to question the relevance of the exercise (Berg and Hudson, 1992). Despite the undoubted room for error, these calculations seem quite robust (Crafts and Harley, 1992).

change by sectors" for various modernizing industries and for agriculture (1981, pp. 108-117, 124-127). The estimates for these sectors, appropriately weighted, implied a growth of aggregate total factor productivity only slightly over half of the total factor productivity implied by aggregate calculations using Deane and Cole's national income estimate. McCloskey attributed the remaining unaccounted aggregate total factor productivity to "all other sectors" and concluded that "ordinary inventiveness was widespread in the British economy 1780 to 1860" (1981, p. 117).

Revised national income estimates change the conclusion, however. Deane and Cole's aggregate implied a rate of technological change of 1.19 percent annually, but Crafts's revision implied total factor productivity growth of only 0.55 percent annually. The productivity growth McCloskey estimated for the modern sectors and agriculture completely exhausts Crafts's aggregate productivity growth (Crafts, 1985a, p. 86; 1987, p. 250).

McCloskey's exercise, although a precarious and uncertain process of identifying residuals of residuals, is extremely interesting and warrants reconsideration. Not only did McCloskey's original calculation depend on Deane and Cole's income estimates, his estimates of individual sector contributions to total factor productivity growth contain several errors. He exaggerated productivity change in several sectors (cotton, wool, and shipping).[14] In addition, McCloskey's estimate of agricultural productivity growth lies well below Crafts's. Table 3.6 presents revised sectoral growth rates (with McCloskey's original calculations for compari-

---

[14] McCloskey exaggerated productivity change in cotton textiles by overstating the decline in cotton cloth prices (he compared the price of a fancy muslin--a velveret--in the 1780s with an ordinary printed gray cloth calico in 1860). Gray calico sold in the 1760s and 1770s for about three (not fifteen) times its price in the mid-nineteenth century (Harley, 1982, pp. 271, 286-291). For worsteds and woolens, McCloskey attributed the rate of productivity growth between 1805 and 1860 to the entire period. History of the industry indicates little technological advance before the early nineteenth century, so the appropriate rate of change for the entire period needs to be lowered. Finally, McCloskey used North's (1968) estimate of productivity change in North Atlantic shipping as an estimate of technological change in coastal and ocean shipping. Recent work (Harley, 1988) has shown much slower technological change in shipping.

son). Productivity growth in the modernized sectors was only two-thirds the rate McCloskey calculated. Nonetheless, the contributions of these sectors and a dynamic agriculture practically exhaust estimated aggregate total factor productivity change.

TABLE 3.6 Sectoral Contributions to Productivity: Annual Percentage Growth, 1780 - 1860

	Share	Produc-tivity	Contribu-tion	McCloskey's Estimate Productivity	Contribution
Cotton	0.070	1.9	0.13	2.6	0.18
Worsteds	0.035	1.3	0.05	1.8	0.06
Woolens	0.035	0.6	0.02	0.9	0.03
Iron	0.020	0.9	0.02	0.9	0.02
Canals and Railways	0.070	1.3	0.09	1.3	0.09
Shipping	0.060	0.5	0.03	2.3	0.14
Sum of modernized	0.290	1.2	0.34	1.8	0.52
Agriculture	0.270	0.7	0.19	0.4	0.12
All others	0.850	0.02	0.02	0.6	0.55
Total	1.410		0.55		1.19

Source: McCloskey (1981, p. 114), with revisions discussed in text.

Aggregate calculations reveal only slow per capita growth during the Industrial Revolution. Radical technological change had transformed cotton textiles and iron production, but these sectors were too small to do much to accelerate aggregate growth. Other industries remained largely unchanged. But aggregate growth was only part of the change occurring in Britain. A visitor approaching Manchester in the 1840s might be excused for disagreeing with the view that change had been slow and localized. Before him, beneath the pall of factory smoke, lay a phenomenon -- threatening or promising depending on his beliefs -- that had not existed when he was a boy: the great industrial city, much smaller, to be sure, than London, but quite different. Here was a society dominated not by the traditional elite but by factory owners and threatened by a proletariat. Manchester was home to new industry, created by the technology of Arkwright, Crompton, and Watt and tied to foreign trade for both its raw materials and its sales. This city, created by new industrial technology and trade (and Liverpool, Glasgow, and Birmingham like it), shook the foundations of British aristocratic society. Its factory-owning middle class, with their growing economic power, had already forced reform on Parliament and agitated for free trade. Their employees, the new "proletariat," raised more radical demands for the People's Charter--manhood suffrage, secret ballot, equal electoral districts, abolition of property qualifications of MPs, salaries for MPs, and annual Parliaments. The Industrial Revolution may have increased per capita income only slowly, but it had created cities and classes that challenged the established order.

Cities grew to accommodate newly concentrated industry. Industry, particularly cotton, about two-thirds of whose output went overseas, was greatly enlarged by exports. The cotton industry, freed from dependence on rural water power by the steam engine, created the industrial city. By 1840 the populations of both Manchester and Liverpool approached half a million; about the same number lived in the other Lancashire textile towns. Similar, although somewhat less intense, cotton-based urbanization had occurred in the western Scottish Lowlands. Iron had a lesser effect. Birmingham, the center of metal fabrication, had grown rapidly but was still some 25 percent smaller than Liverpool or Manchester.

During the early years of Victoria's reign, British firms dominated the world's modern industry.[15] Many contemporaries and historians have talked of a British monopoly. But despite British dominance, there was no monopoly; rather this was competitive capitalism. Firms entered the cotton industry easily and sold in competitive markets. They were unable to prevent prices from falling to the cost of production, and the benefits of technological change passed to consumers as lower prices. British customers benefited but so equally did the foreign two-thirds of cotton textile customers. The competitive structure of the cotton

---

[15] Bairoch (1982) estimates that Britain contained more than half of modern industry in 1840. Britain took 55 percent of the world's raw cotton output and accounted for substantially more of value of output because of the higher average count of yarn spun in Britain (Ellison, [1886] 1968, pp. 100, 146).

textile industry meant that although the world gained from the improved technology in British exports, Britain gained little extra from those exports.

Britain exported cottons to obtain raw materials and foodstuffs. In the twenty-five years after the Napoleonic Wars, technological change nearly halved the labor and capital needed to make a piece of cloth in

TABLE 3.7 Cotton Textile Production and Consumption, Effects of Terms of Trade

| | Quantities | | Prices | |
	1815	1841	1815	1841
Output	100	520	1.0	0.5
Raw Cotton	25	160		
Consumption				
Cotton	40	210	1.0	0.5
Imports	35	75	1.0	1.0
Aggregate Consumption				
1815 prices	75	285	100	380
1841 prices	55	180	100	327

Source: Harley (1982); Ellison ([1886] 1968), p.56; Von Tunzelmann (1978), p.229.

Lancashire. The competitive market drove textile prices down, and in 1840 an exported piece of cloth could purchase only half the foreign food it had commanded at war's end. The same technological change that generated industry growth caused the terms of trade to deteriorate.

Because price changes transferred the benefits of technological change to foreign consumers, conventional aggregation overstates the benefits to Britain of the cotton industry's growth. Calculations in Table 3.7 illustrate the orders of magnitude involved. In 1841 Britain produced 5.2 times as much cotton textiles as in 1815. About 60 percent of output was exported in both years. Think of these exports first as paying for the industry's imported raw cotton and the remainder purchasing a representative bundle of other imports for consumption. In 1815 the raw cotton imports cost about a quarter of the total value of output; in 1841 the proportion was somewhat higher at 31 percent. About 35 percent of the output in 1815 was exported for foreign consumption goods. In 1841 about 29 percent of output was exported in exchange for foreign consumption goods -- 4.3 times as many textiles were exported as in 1815. But a given piece of cotton cloth could now purchase only half as many imports. The quantity of cotton produced increased 5.2 times, but the consumption (cotton goods and imports) it provided to British consumers increased less than four times (3.8 times, if the cotton and imports are valued at 1815 prices, or 3.3 times, if they are valued at 1841 prices). Exports thus had only modest direct impact on national income. But, at the same time, exports greatly increased the industry's size and its social impact. It is possible that much of the dynamics of economic change may be found in the implications of these structural changes.

4. A Crafts-Inspired Computational General Equilibrium Model

The view of British growth that has emerged as a result of Crafts's and my reassessment of the aggregate statistics for the British economy has gained wide acceptance, but controversy remains. The evidential basis of the aggregates remains imperfect and can support some variety of interpretations, although probably a narrower range than critics at times imply (Crafts and Harley, 1992). In addition, some have questioned the internal coherence of our view of growth, suggesting that the rapid agricultural growth that Crafts proposes is inconsistent with industrialization in a relatively open economy. Jeffrey Williamson asserts that "Crafts' revisionist view of unbalanced productivity advance favouring agriculture will have a hard time accounting for the relative demise of agriculture and the relative expansion of industry during the industrialization surge after Waterloo" (1987a, p. 274).

One step in testing a general view of growth is to construct an explicit numerical model and explore its properties. Such a model provides numerical indication of general orders of magnitude and highlights key assumptions while insuring that the view is logically consistent. A simple computational general equilibrium model with simple production and utility functions that incorporates Crafts's view does reproduce the general outline of actual historical changes.

The model highlights several features of the Crafts-Harley view of British industrialization. First, it emphasizes growing agricultural productivity. Second, the portion of manufacturing in which technological change occurred very rapidly is distinguished from the rest of manufacturing and services where change was slow. Textiles and iron amounted to only a little over a third of industry, even in 1840 after their rapid growth. Third, growth sharply altered British terms of trade.

The terms of trade must be integral to an assessment of the British Industrial Revolution. In a subsector of British manufacturing, technology changed rapidly and output grew fast as domestic and export sales grew. Cotton textiles was at the forefront of the change. The new technology was British, and British firms became the only exporters of importance. Technology revolutionized the industry, drove down prices, and caused export growth. Deterioration of the terms of trade reflected the driving force of change.

Britain's terms of trade also suffered because imports of foodstuffs and raw materials could only be increased by paying higher prices. Shipping was a large part of the cost of British imports before iron and steam revolutionized transportation during the second half of the nineteenth century, so the mere fact that Britain was small relative to world output did not insure an elastic supply of bulky imports. To increase supplies of grain or timber British importers had to tap more distant regions and incur higher transportation costs. By 1850, even with higher prices supporting wider hinterlands for the Baltic ports, traditional grain sources became insufficient to supply British needs. Still higher prices were needed to obtain imports from the Black Sea and America (Farley, 1965/1966; Harley, 1980).

The explicit computational model contains two trading countries--Britain and "the rest of the world."[16] The modeled British economy and the rest of the world were both made up of four producing sectors: agriculture, "modern" industry, other industry, and services. Each sector produced using capital and labor; agriculture also used land. The basic building blocks of the model were functional representations of production technology and consumer preferences. The specific form of these functions represented reasonable guesses; the

---

[16] The model building has relied on an available computer program (Rutherford, 1988). The modeling follows quite closely similar modeling exercises that have recently been conducted in development economics and in analyzing issues of international trade policy (Robinson, 1989; Shoven and Whalley, 1984).

data did not permit their more formal estimation. The production technology was Cobb-Douglas in all sectors except agriculture, which had a CES function with an elasticity of substitution of 0.5.[17] Factor markets allowed factors to move among sectors and equated factor prices across sectors. A representative, utility maximizing consumer in each country owned all factors (so the model has no class or distribution features). The utility functions incorporated a Cobb-Douglas subaggregate -- manufactured goods -- of "modern" and other industrial goods. The manufactured goods subaggregate and agricultural and service goods entered a CES utility function that had an elasticity of substitution of 0.5. International trade occurred in agriculture and 'modern' industry. Foreigners purchased British "modern" industrial goods at British prices, but British agricultural imports incurred a transportation cost that increased as imports increased.

Values of output in 1841 (see Table 3.8) provided a benchmark to which the model was calibrated. Model solution that incorporated stylized changes in technology and factor supply provided analysis of British growth. In the calculated pre-Industrial Revolution equilibrium, British labor force and capital stock were reduced to 1770 levels. Industrial Revolution technological change was modeled as Hicks-neutral and as occurring in British agriculture and "modern" industry. Pre-Industrial Revolution British agriculture, following Crafts's calculations, used 1.75 times 1841 resources to produce a given output. British "modern" manufacturing used 2.8 times 1841 resources. The rest of the world partially shared technological change in modern industry, at a reasonable guess using 1.5 times the resources in 1770 as were used in 1841.

The model was very simple and the parameterization crude. Calculated results indicate the likely contours of change but share the underlying weaknesses of the model's weak evidential base. The calculated pre-Industrial Revolution equilibrium (summarized in Table 3.8) supports Crafts's general view. Industrialization emerges as consistent with relatively rapid improvement of agricultural technology. Industrialization resulted from the export success of "modern" industry and diminishing returns in agriculture in face of growing population

---

[17] A lower elasticity was chosen to accommodate the observation that the share of agricultural income going to rent increased as settlement became denser in the nineteenth century.

and income. A utility index shows per capita utility 12 percent lower before the Industrial Revolution.

Calculations with the model can help to separate various effects. Starting from the 1770 equilibrium, agricultural technological change alone would have caused Britain to become a substantial exporter of agricultural goods. A similar calculation with 1841 population and capital resources but with 1770 agricultural technology, indicates that such a Britain would have depended heavily on foreign food, producing only half its actual 1841 agricultural output. Other industries would have absorbed resources and been more that twice their actual 1841 size. In the model with unchanged agricultural technology, the pressure of Industrial Revolution population growth on the fixed land stock would have more than offset the benefits from improved industrial technology and observed capital accumulation. In contrast, modeling agricultural improvement, historic population growth, and capital accumulation, but not industrial advance, provides about a third of the welfare improvement that arose from agricultural and industrial technological change combined.

Although this model supports the Crafts-Harley view, it does not provide strong evidence of its absolute correctness. The data are sufficiently weak that other specifications could reasonably be considered and similar models would support other narratives. At the simplest level, it is useful to use the same model and examine the criticism that Crafts exaggerated agricultural productivity growth. If the model is projected back from its 1841 benchmark with only a third of the agricultural productivity growth used above, it calculates an alternative economic structure for 1770. In this case, agriculture is about 50 percent larger than reported in Table 3.8 and per capita utility is just 3 percent below its 1841 level. The per capita growth seems improbably low. More growth, however, can be introduced by allowing productivity growth in services.

5. Summary of the Crafts-Harley View

Revision of the basic aggregate estimates of British growth combined with a neoclassical framework -- presented starkly in the computational general equilibrium model above -- provides a general view of the changes in the British economy during the late eighteenth and early nineteenth centuries. Revolutionary changes in industry were largely

TABLE 3.8 A Computational General Equilibrium Model

	1841 Benchmark	Calculated 1770
Quantities		
British output		
Modern industry	12.4	1.8
Other industry	22.0	9.9
Agriculture	22.1	8.2
Services	43.5	17.6
British factor supplies		
Labor	53.1	22.8
Capital	38.1	16.4
Land	8.8	8.8
Rest of world output		
Modern industry	11.2	11.2
Other industry	126.4	128.3
Agriculture	297.0	293.7
Services	219.2	216.8
Rest of world factor supplies		
Labor	332	332
Capital	205	205
Land	120	120
British trade		
Exports, modern	6.8	0.9
Imports, agriculture	6.8	2.0
Price		
Modern industry	1.00	2.11
Other industry	1.00	0.76
Agriculture	1.00	1.00
Services	1.00	0.76
British labor	1.00	0.76
British capital	1.00	0.75
British land	1.00	0.37
British utility per capita	100	88

Source: Author's calculations.

confined to the famous sectors of textiles, iron, and transportation. Even in combination, the technological change in these sectors contributed only modestly to growth of aggregate output. The famous industrial technology caused national income to grow about a third of a percent annually. This would require two centuries to double income. Equally, however, industrial change helped to change social structure, demographic behavior, and savings habits. It certainly remains possible that these social changes stimulated growth. Nonetheless, it seems impossible to sustain the view that British growth was revolutionized in a generation by cotton-spinning innovations.

The new estimates of national income identify a long period of transition. Growth probably began to accelerate in the last years of the seventeenth or the early years of the eighteenth century. In the late eighteenth century, important innovations occurred in some industries, but per capita national income growth accelerated only modestly. Accelerating agricultural change contributed about as much as industrial innovation. Modern economic growth became fully established in Britain only in the railway age.

Despite the moderate impact of industrial technology on aggregate growth, changes in economic activity greatly altered British social structure. By the 1830s a combination of the rapid growth of the urban-based textile industries, that exported most of their product, and the decline in agriculture's share of the labor force produced the first urban industrial economy. Both industrial technology and mobility out of agriculture were important. The rapid technological change in textiles and iron led to dramatic price declines that gave British producers an advantage they quickly seized--the ability to supply a large portion of world demand in these industries. In the 1840s, British cotton producers exported some sixty percent of their production (Ellison, [1886] 1968, p. 60). The iron industry exported a quarter of its output and the woolen industry about 20 percent (Deane and Cole, 1962, pp. 196, 225).

Britain's transformation required a movement of labor and other factors of production from agriculture to industry as well as improvements in industrial technology. By historical standards, the British adjusted very rapidly. Agriculture's high level of technological accomplishment, the rapid growth of productivity, and the transfer of labor probably arose from the social structure of rural Britain. A large portion of both agricultural entrepreneurship and labor was separated from control of land. This separation of labor from the means of production made labor much more responsive to market signals than it would otherwise have been.

6. The Distribution of Income: An Alternative Focus

The Crafts-Harley view has combined new macroeconomic estimates with economic modeling to study output growth and structural changes in Britain after 1750. We have emphasized the unevenness of technological change, the movement of productive factors from agriculture to industry, and the impact of particular technological change on Britain's exports and terms of trade. The results have helped us to understand British industrialization, but the model, as must any attempt at understanding, has necessarily simplified in order to concentrate on certain features of the historical experience. We have focused on aggregate growth, trade, and structural change and have not addressed all interesting macroeconomic issues. In particular, many contemporaries and historians have seen issues of income distribution, which our approach is poorly equipped to address, at the heart of the British industrial experience.

Contemporaries, from classical economists to radical reformers, paid close attention to distribution. They saw industrialization as a process that primarily enriched the propertied classes while, at best, bypassing the working class and more likely immiserising a proletariat. A generation ago, the extent to which Deane and Cole's estimates of per capita income and per capita consumption grew faster than estimates of real wages indicated a considerable redistribution away from the laboring class. Income per capita in 1851 was estimated to be 2.3 times its 1780 level, and per capita consumption 2.4 times its 1780 level but the Phelps Brown and Hopkins index of real wages increased only by 30 percent (1956). It is now clear that the Phelps Brown and Hopkins data were confined to workers who fared poorly during the period and their price deflator was too narrowly based, but even on Lindert and Williamson's (1983b) high estimate, real wages only doubled.

The new estimates of national income have eliminated the distributional effects implied by the earlier aggregates. Crafts estimated per capita national income growth at 70 percent between 1780 and 1851 and consumption growth at 75 percent (Crafts, 1985a, p. 103). New estimates of real wage growth suggest about the same or slightly more rapid growth. Williamson and Lindert and Crafts have more or less agreed that real wages, on average, grew about 85 percent between 1780 and 1851. Real wage estimation remains bedeviled by the differing experiences of various labor groups, but wages and national income per capita now seem to have grown at about the same rate, removing a presumption for strong shifts in distribution away from labor (Crafts, 1989a, pp. 76-84).

Historians have long known that there was a wide variety of experiences within the working classes. In the north, incomes were initially low but improved much faster than in the south. Industrial opportunities improved more than agricultural opportunities. Regional and occupational income patterns altered: northern wages overtook southern wages, and agricultural workers fell behind. Industrial technology impoverished some, most notably the handloom weavers, while creating a "labor aristocracy" of workers with skills made more valuable by technological change. Economic historians have traced the diversity of the Industrial Revolution's impact and have spent much time identifying and studying both winners and losers--both between the propertied and laboring classes and within the laboring classes.

Recently, some of this investigation has been placed explicitly within a macroeconomic view. Peter Lindert and Jeffrey Williamson have traced the evolution of the income distribution from the late seventeenth century by reworking and improving estimates of earnings of various classes made by various contemporaries (Lindert, 1980, 1986; Lindert and Williamson, 1982, 1983a). The work has generated income-based national income estimates to compare with Crafts's production-based estimates. Williamson has developed a model of British industrialization that directs attention to the income distribution and that contrasts sharply with aspects of the Crafts-Harley view.

Williamson's Model of British Industrialization

In his recent book *Did British Capitalism Breed Inequality?* (1985) Williamson analyzes the British economy using a model focused on distributional issues. He incorporates features that have appeared in narratives of British industrialization but that Crafts and I questioned or rejected. The model deserves consideration both for its distributional focus and because of its disagreements with our views.

Williamson's model had two principal features. First, he followed traditional narratives. He saw rapid technological change in manufacturing industry leading growth, with agriculture lagging, and he contrasted gains for skilled labor with small gains for the lowest classes. In addition, he approached Britain's industrialization using a general interpretation of early industrialization formed by his interpretation of more recent experiences in the Third World since World War II, in Japan, and in the United States (1985, pp. 87-90, 183; 1987a, pp. 269-270, 272-273). To him, economic growth began discontinuously. New industrial technology created a disequilibrium that provided opportunities for an acceleration of investment and growth in manufacturing. "Unbalanced productivity advance has always been viewed as the primary supply-side force driving industrialization and urbanization. Since the rate of technological change has always been viewed as far higher in modern than in traditional sectors, industry 'leads' and agriculture 'lags' in capital formation, output expansion and job creation. So said the qualitative accounts of the British industrial revolution, and now there are some tentative numbers documenting the process" (1985, p. 89).

Williamson's explicit analysis of British industrialization used a multisectoral general equilibrium model. The model possessed four primary inputs -- farmland, capital, unskilled, and skilled labor. Separation of labor into two classes provided the distributional features he wished to emphasize. Primary inputs (in some cases combined into "resources," an intermediate good produced by a mining sector) and imported raw materials produced three final goods: agriculture, manufacturing, and services. Agriculture employed unskilled labor, capital, and land but no skilled labor or intermediate products. Mining used only unskilled labor and capital. Manufacturing used skilled and unskilled labor and capital, as well as resources from mining and imported raw materials. Services were produced with skilled and unskilled labor, capital, and domestic intermediate goods (Williamson, 1985, chap. 8).

Two features of Williamson's analysis contrasted sharply with the Crafts-Harley models. First, we saw changes in Britain's terms of trade as central to the Industrial Revolution. In contrast, Williamson modeled Britain as a small country that facing international prices in traded goods, so that prices of agricultural and manufactured goods and of imported raw materials were exogenously determined. The second important difference occurs in our perceptions of technological change, which we and Williamson all modeled as exogenous. We felt that it was vital to distinguish between the minority of manufacturing industries that were transformed by technology and the rest of manufacturing, and we accepted evidence showing relatively rapid technological change in agriculture. Williamson did not distinguish among industries in manufacturing but assumed rapid technological advance in industry as a whole (just over 1 percent annually) and slow technological change in agriculture as well as in services and intermediate goods (0.3 percent annually).

Williamson analyzed the economy from 1821 to 1861 (and from 1861 to 1911) by examining the equilibrium output quantities and endogenous prices (for factors of production, services, and domestic resources) that his model predicted in response to exogenous changes in technology, factor supplies, and international prices. The skilled and unskilled labor pools grew at essentially the same rate. Capital formation occurred at a considerably higher rate than labor force growth. Both technological change and investment stimulated manufacturing. More rapid technological advance drew mobile capital and unskilled labor to industry, and capital formation stimulated the capital-intensive industrial sector. The stimulus to manufacturing was partially, but only partially, offset by exogenous deterioration of manufactured goods' prices--caused by international factors (1985, appendix E). In response, the industrial sector grew about 3.2 percent per year, while agricultural output grew about 1.4 percent per year, and income inequality increased.

Williamson's narrative of the Industrial Revolution emphasized increasing income inequality. The higher growth of industry differentially increased the demand for skilled labor and widened the wage premium of skilled workers. The model predicted an increase in the premium of skilled over unskilled wages of nearly 40 percent between 1821 and 1861 (1985, pp. 130-131, 151-160, cf. table 10.5). Since Williamson also generated new data that showed a similar increase in the skilled wage premium, he saw this result as justifying the use of the model's logic as an explanation of British historical change. Independent assessors have doubts about this data, however, that question the model's usefulness.

Current Knowledge of Distributional Changes, c. 1700 to c. 1850

Williamson's modeling of the Industrial Revolution was heavily influenced by his and Peter Lindert's investigation of occupational patterns and wages. In *Did British Capitalism Breed Inequality?*

Williamson presented new wage data that showed an increase in the ratio of the wages of skilled workers to the wages of unskilled workers. Earlier work had focused on unskilled workers and the relatively small subset of skilled workers in manufacturing jobs that became unionized during the nineteenth century.[18] Williamson collected wage data for the clerical and middle classes, skilled occupations that employed a large portion of the labor force, primarily using information about civil service pay. His data showed that wages in these occupations increased much faster than either skilled manufacturing wages or unskilled wages. He concluded that the premium of skilled wages over unskilled wages rose by 40 percent between 1815 and 1851, rather than the 10 percent rise older data had shown.

Unfortunately, independent evidence and the behavior of various individual new series suggested that the wage quotations were incompatible over time. Experts rejected Williamson's assertion that "incomes levelled across the late eighteenth century and the French Wars; inequality surged from Waterloo to mid-century; and incomes levelled again during the late nineteenth century" (Feinstein, 1988b; Jackson, 1987). After assessing Williamson's estimates, Charles Feinstein concluded that "the general picture is one of broad stability, most notably in the ratio of skilled to unskilled pay and in the overall distribution of earnings" (1988b, p. 728).

A second strand of Lindert and Williamson's research on income distribution has made an important contribution to our understanding of incomes in the eighteenth and nineteenth centuries. They carefully reexamined and improved income estimates from the "social tables" that were produced between the late seventeenth and the nineteenth centuries by contemporaries Gregory King, William Massie, Patrick Colquhoun, and Dudley Baxter (Lindert and Williamson, 1982, 1983b). These contemporaries attempted to enumerate the various classes in the kingdom along with their incomes. Gregory King produced the first table toward the end of the seventeenth century to demonstrate the folly of William of Orange's war policy. In 1760 William Massie produced a similar table to demonstrate exploitation by the protected West Indian sugar planters. In the nineteenth century, similar tables were compiled with more scientific and less polemical intent and

---

[18] Much of this data had been collected by Arthur Bowley and George Wood in the late nineteenth and early twentieth centuries.

benefited from improving basic statistical information. Patrick Colquhoun drew on the first census and the income tax data to estimate incomes in the first years of the nineteenth century. Dudley Baxter enjoyed improved versions of these and other sources when he made his estimate for 1867 (Phelps Brown, 1988, pp. 305-306). The efforts of King, Massie, and Colquhoun were heroic; as E. H. Phelps Brown (p. 306) remarks they generally "have been regarded as having done no more than what was a notable achievement in its day, but as too slightly based to have much chance of being accurate."

Lindert and Williamson, without fully overcoming the basic problems of limited underlying data, have improved these sources "to arrive," as Phelps Brown remarks, "at reasonably firm conclusions." The income distributions show high levels of inequality by standards of modern Britain and other developed countries and also, although less sharply, by comparison to other late-nineteenth-century societies. Summary measures indicate that inequality increased from the late seventeenth century to the mid-nineteenth century before beginning to fall to twentieth-century levels -- a pattern of rising and then falling inequality as growth proceeded that they call the Kuznets Curve. This represents a modification of the earlier view (O'Brien and Engerman, 1981; Soltow, 1968) that concluded from the same sources that the income distribution did not change significantly before the twentieth century.[19]

Lindert and Williamson's summary measures, however, do not adequately represent the distributions of income they found for eighteenth- and nineteenth-century Britain. E. H. Phelps Brown has recently analyzed their data using the technique of "Pen parades," which provided greater insights into the differing experiences of various income groups.[20] He concludes that the changes in income

---

[19] Lindert and Williamson's estimates show lower inequality in the early years mainly because of revised occupational figures from Lindert's investigation of burial registers (Lindert, 1980). Crafts has suggested that figures based on King are particularly uncertain and may well understate inequality by failing to consider the very low wages then prevailing in the North (Crafts, 1989a, p. 87).

[20] The "Pen parades," named after the Dutch economist Jan Pen, who originated them, are graphs of individual income levels displayed against percentiles of the income distribution. For a discussion of interpretation of

distribution between King's and Massie's estimates can be seen as a continuous process (although Colquhoun's data seem to show some wartime interruption with losses to the very poor and gains to the very rich). Phelps Brown's characterizations of the changes are quite different from those of Williamson and Lindert, and his summary merits quoting at length (pp. 314-315):

> In sum, the structure of incomes had changed between 1688 and 1867 from a stack of three tiers to a smooth gradation. To characterize the structure of 1688 in that way is to simplify it overmuch; but in contrast with the later structure it does appear as formed of three groups – the cottagers and labourers, who made up half the whole number of income recipients; "the aristocracy of labour" – the craftsmen, and with them the farmers and the professional – a middle group with incomes substantially higher than the labourers' and rising fairly steeply within their own bounds; and at the top some very high incomes indeed. By 1867 this arrangement had been changed markedly. The lowest group had risen relatively to the others, and differed less among themselves. The middle group had ceased to differentiate itself so sharply from those below, both in the rate at which incomes rose and as a proportionate part of all income. So far, the movement had been towards greater equality. But the top group had become relatively richer than ever. The Pen parade serves to display and locate these varied changes, in whose presence any one measure of inequality means little.

The current best assessment of the history of British wage structure leaves Williamson's analysis of British industrialization without crucial support. It seems likely that the model failed to approximate the historical record because technology change and the demand for skill did not occur as he modeled them. Rapid advances in industrial technology appear to have been confined to a relatively small portion of the total industrial sector. Textiles did not notably demand skilled labor. Other more skill-intensive industry grew more slowly. After 1830 the major change in the demand for labor came from the railroads, stimulated by technological change and capital accumulation. Railroad construction required mainly unskilled workers. In addition, agriculture probably did better than Williamson assumed.

The British certainly experienced varied changes in their well-being during the Industrial Revolution. Incomes in different regions changed at different rates; workers with certain skills and in particular industries clearly benefited and others lost. Some, like the quarter of a million handloom weavers and their families and agricultural workers in the

---

income distributions, see Phelps Brown (1988, chap. 9).

southern grain areas, obviously suffered; others, like most northern workers in industry and agriculture, gained.[21] The labor market and the capital market were segmented along regional, industrial, and class lines and did not equate returns throughout the economy. More efficient factor markets would have increased output, perhaps considerably (Williamson, 1987b). But the inefficiencies did not originate in the eighteenth century and probably declined despite sharp differences in the regional impact of technological change.

Full understanding of Britain's transition to modern economic growth requires the consideration of market segmentation due to region, class, custom, and other sources of inertia. Rapid change altered the distribution of income. During extended periods of disequilibrium, some growing sectors gained extraordinary benefits and some declining sectors suffered extraordinary hardship. New equilibria were characterized by altered distributions of income. Regional and industrial variety tend to be obscured in aggregate macroeconomic assessments and need continued careful study before we can fully understand either the sources or the consequences of the Industrial Revolution (Berg and Hudson, 1992).

7. Why Was Growth so Slow?: War and the Nature of British Growth

British economic growth accelerated only gradually before the middle of the nineteenth century. In comparison with the early growth of other now-advanced countries, British growth was slow, slower even than previously thought. Jeffrey Williamson has suggested that Britain grew more slowly than more recently industrializing societies primarily because of the twenty years of war with Revolutionary France and Napoleon. In making this suggestion, he raises two important issues: What was the nature of early British growth, particularly in comparison with the emergence of modern growth elsewhere? What was the impact of the Napoleonic Wars, which were an important and expensive part of the history of the period?

------

[21] In various places, Crafts has drawn attention to regional issues (1982; 1985a, pp. 104-107; 1989).

Competing Overviews of British Growth

Crafts and Williamson brought basically different underlying views to a comparison of British growth with growth that began later in other countries. Williamson worked with the hypothesis that modern economic growth began with a generally applicable pattern exemplified by experiences of the contemporary Third World economies, the nineteenth-century United States, and twentieth-century Japan. These examples led him to expect modernization to begin with rapid growth generally and with particular emphasis on manufacturing. In the initial spurt, productivity increased rapidly in the modern sectors and capital formation accelerated, driving growth. He felt that only the stress of war deflected Britain from the general pattern (1985, pp. 87-90, 183; 1987a, pp. 269-270, 272-273).

Crafts worked from a different underlying vision that emphasized the differences between Britain and the later industrializing economies of Europe (1985a, chap. 3). In his framework the United States, Japan, and the contemporary world are unpersuasive analogies. Britain pioneered industrialization over a long period during which appropriate institutions and technologies slowly emerged. In the late eighteenth century, revolutionary changes occurred in a few manufacturing industries -- particularly textiles and primary iron. Most final metal products and most other industrial goods were still produced in old ways. The evidence, imperfect though it is, suggests that agriculture, far from being a lagging sector as in many later industrializations, experienced more rapid technological change than most of the economy outside the new industries.

From Crafts's perspective, the slow emergence of British growth seemed only natural. But from Williamson's perspective, the slow growth during the "'heroic phase' of the First Industrial Revolution" required attention. He commented that "even during productivity slow down, OPEC fuel-crunch, Malthusian burdens, and capital scarcity abroad, the Third World managed per capita income growth rates around 3.2 per cent per annum in the 1970s, ten times that of Britain prior to the 1820s!" In addition, "Britain was a low saver . . . the rate of capital accumulation was so modest that hardly any capital-deepening took place at all" (Williamson, 1985, p. 162).

Williamson suggested possible reasons for this unusual early British growth. He first rejected the possibility "that the conventional dating of the first industrial revolution is just plain wrong." Instead he proposed "that Britain tried to do two things at once--industrialize and fight expensive wars--and she simply did not have the resources to do both effectively" (1985, p.162).   In particular, he saw wartime government borrowing crowding out productive investment.   In the absence of war, he believed that capital formation, structural shift, and growth would have been much more rapid, following a normal pattern of early industrialization.

FIGURE 3.4 Military Expenditure and National Income, 1690-1830 (constant prices, ave. 1720-1744)

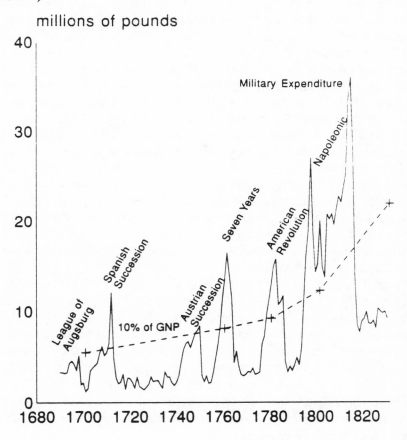

Sources: Table 3.4; Mitchell and Deane, 1962, pp. 389-391, 396; O'Brien, 1985, pp.787-795.

War

The French wars greatly complicate analysis of the British Industrial Revolution and Williamson was certainly right in insisting that they not be ignored. Revolutionary France declared war on Britain in 1793, and intense warfare continued until Napoleon's final defeat in 1815. The conflict was one of history's great wars, the conclusion of the epic conflict between England and France that had begun in 1689. During the 126 years between 1689 and 1815, England was at war for 73 years, and at was against France for but 2 of these. Figure 3.4 summarizes British war expenditure in relation to GNP.[22] These were major wars; the Napoleonic Wars stand out less for their intensity -- the previous struggles had annually taken about the same share of national income-- than for their duration.

Patrick O'Brien (1991) has recently surveyed the impact of the Hanovarian state on the British economy. During the eighteenth century, the modern nation-state evolved from conflicts arising from France's Continental ambitions and Britain's opposition. In the end, with the Treaty of Vienna and the restoration of the French monarchy, the British could take satisfaction: The struggle had been expensive, but British vital interests had been defended and advanced. Although not the dominant power in continental Europe, Britain had emerged as the greatest world power. O'Brien summarizes the economic balance sheet (pp. 30-31):

> By any standards the expenditures on the armed forces required to underpin the kingdom's foreign and strategic policies look massive, and possibly profligate. On the credit side, between 1688 and 1815 no invasions of the homeland wasted the domestic economy. Before 1805 no great power emerged on the mainland of Europe capable of obstructing the kingdom's trade with the continent. Foreign aggression against British commerce and territories overseas declined in significance. After the recognition of its independence in 1783 the United States was "reincorporated" into the Atlantic economy with Britain at its hub. Meanwhile diplomacy backed by military force had compelled the rival Empires of Portugal, Spain and Holland in the South Americas and Asia and the Mughals in India to concede entrées to British trade and ship.

---

[22] The government expenditure figures are the sum of army, navy, and ordnance from Mitchell and Deane (1962, pp. 389-391, 396), deflated by the average of O'Brien's (1985, pp. 787-795) industrial and agricultural price indicies. The income figures are Crafts's (Crafts and Harley, 1992, table 4).

In the nineteenth century, growth undoubtedly benefited from the peaceful, liberal, and competitive world order that followed the Treaty of Vienna. The eighteenth-century wars had used about 10 percent of a modest per capita income. If these resources could have been devoted to investment or even to raising the still-modest margin over subsistence for much of the population, they would, other things being equal, have sped growth, just as a "peace dividend" did after 1815. Other things, of course, were not equal. The stability of the nineteenth century arose from the resolution of the conflicts of the eighteenth and the political stability of the states that had emerged. Such conditions did not prevail earlier and it is unrealistic to imagine such a counterfactual world. Nonetheless, it is useful to consider Williamson's proposition that military spending primarily diverted resources from investment, thereby seriously slowing growth.

War, of course, was expensive. It was fought with men and equipment that could otherwise have produced consumption and investment goods. Furthermore, war disrupted the normal patterns of economic activity. As David Ricardo observed at the time, "The commencement of war after a long peace . . . generally produces considerable distress in trade. It changes in a great degree the nature of the employments to which the respective capitals of the countries were before devoted; and during the interval while they are settling in the situations which new circumstances have made the most beneficial, much fixed capital is unemployed, perhaps wholly lost, and labourers are without full employment" (quoted in Mokyr and Savin, 1976, p. 201).

The costs of war--the men and equipment involved and the maladjustments in the economy -- had to be met in real terms before or as they were incurred, even though governments borrowed to finance most wartime activity.[23] Some costs were met before the conflict--men were trained, and equipment was produced in peacetime and stored. The HMS Victory, Nelson's flagship at Trafalgar, for example, was built in the naval dockyard at Chatham between 1759 and 1778. Figure 3.4 shows, however, that these expenditures covered only a small faction of wartime costs. Government had to obtain large amounts of

---

[23] Mokyr and Savin (1976) provides the best attempt to analyze the impact of the Napoleonic Wars. They pay particular attention to disruption as well as diversion to military uses.

resources for military use after hostilities began. There were four possible sources those resources: (1) from abroad, (2) from previous under-utilized capacity, (3) from investment, or (4) from consumption. Resources from abroad and the mobilization of previously underemployed resources played only minor roles. Increased taxation took resources primarily from consumption. A large part of war expenditure was financed by borrowing; to what extent did this crowd out investment?[24]

In wealth holders' portfolios government debt competed with claims on real private assets. In an extreme, every pound of new government debt might have displaced a pound of potential private investment. Unlike private investment, government wartime expenditure did not increase the capital stock and future productivity, so growth would slow. Williamson argues "that the one-for-one crowding-out assumption may not be such a poor description of behaviour during the British industrial revolution" (1985, p. 117).

Full-employment macroeconomic models (Modigliani, 1961) inspired the crowding-out hypothesis. In such models, current output and individuals' savings -- the willingness to accumulate assets, either real capital or government debt -- are exogenous. Government demand for funds pushes the real rate of interest up until private investment is reduced by the amount of government borrowing.

The view that wartime crowding out greatly slowed investment has been challenged by an examination of details of the war years. Joel Mokyr points out that Williamson exaggerated the resources that the government obtained by debt finance and that wartime dislocation was probably greater than he estimated (1987, pp. 293-305). The history of savings and the interest rate does not correspond well with the predictions from the crowding-out model. Figure 3.5 summarizes investment, government borrowing, and their sum ("total savings") as a proportion of income in the late eighteenth and early nineteenth centuries. Contrary to the model, "total savings" do not appear independent of wartime activity. They increased sharply during the war and then fell back. The volatility of measured "total savings" was

---

[24] Williamson's original statements seemed to imply a one-for-one crowding out. He has made it clear that he had a somewhat more modest intent but still saw crowding out as the major source of government funds (Williamson, 1987a, p. 286).

222

C. Knick Harley

almost entirely caused by the volatility of government borrowing.
Charles Feinstein estimates that gross capital formation increased quite
steadily through the war despite government borrowing (1988a, p. 446).

In his discussion of crowding out, Williamson points to construction--
some two-thirds of investment -- as being particularly hurt. If construction had been crowded out, the postwar stock would have been
below its equilibrium value and would have yielded excess profits to its
owners. Investors would have responded with a postwar construction
boom to compensate for the wartime shortfall. But brick production
showed little variation during the war,[25] and Feinstein's decadal
estimates of construction increase throughout the wars and show no
postwar boom. The postwar increase in construction equals the
increase from the 1790s to the 1800s (1988a, p. 446).

FIGURE 3.5 Investment, Government Debt and "Total Saving" by Decades, 1760s-1840s

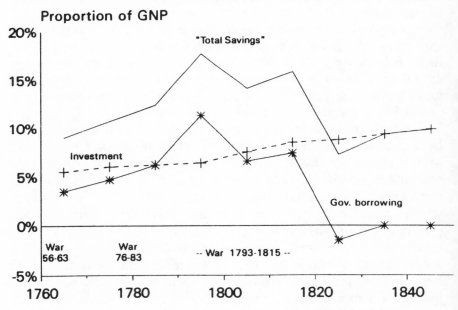

Sources: Table 3.4; Feinstein (1988a), p.427; Williamson (1984), p.697.

---

[25] The rate of growth slowed somewhat during the war, but the slowdown
cannot be statistically distinguished from the random movement of the series
in other years (Mokyr and Savin, 1976, p. 217).

Crowding-out models rely on rising real interest rates to discourage private investment, so examination of interest rate movement also provides insight into the wartime process. The real interest rate is an elusive concept. The market rate of interest represents the exchange of present and future monetary amounts. Nominal interest rates provide evidence of real interest rates only when corrected for expected changes in the value of money. Certainly, the changes in the value of money concerned investors in the inflationary war years, but there was no easy way for contemporaries to predict the future of prices. On one hand, the Bank of England's abandonment of convertibility of its notes into gold in 1797 and wartime inflation made faith in the stability of money untenable. But informed investors probably expected, realistically as it turned out, that the termination of hostilities would bring the restoration of gold convertibility and price deflation. Various procedures to model expectations of price inflation reveal that nominal interest rates rose less than the expected inflation, so real rates fell (Black and Gilmore, 1990; Heim and Mirowski, 1987, 1991; Mokyr, 1987, p. 300; Mokyr and Savin, 1976, p. 209).

The history of investment and interest rates suggests that crowding out of investment was not the principal source of resources for war use. Where, then, did the resources to fight the war come from? An "inflation tax" seems the most likely mechanism (Bordo and White, 1991). By using inflationary finance the government got resources from those -- including particularly wage earners -- who failed to anticipate inflation fully. Inflation probably also benefited well-placed wealthy individuals who purchased government debt with much of their gains. Real wages certainly lagged during the war years. The distribution of income shows a wartime interruption of the leveling process that had begun in the eighteenth century. In particular, the incomes of the very richest increased (Phelps Brown, 1988, fig. 11.2, pp. 311, 313).

War undoubtedly affected the macro performance of the British economy as it entered into modern economic growth. Military campaigns and the associated government finance diverted resources from uses that would have led to more rapid growth. The precise magnitude of that impact is not yet well understood. In a peaceful, liberally organized international economy, Britain would have grown more rapidly, but a liberal economy only emerged from eighteenth-century warfare. Williamson's hypothesis -- that an end to the wars in 1763 would have nearly doubled the rate of capital formation, creating a "heroic phase" of the First Industrial Revolution that would have conformed more closely to the periods of rapid initial growth elsewhere--seems overstated. There is little evidence that government borrowing primarily crowded out private investment. The slow, gradual increase in investment accompanied the long evolution of modern growth.

8. Conclusion

Recent reassessment of Britain's path to mid-nineteenth-century economic predominance emphasizes three important characteristics. First, the beginnings did not occur as a "heroic" breakthrough in the third quarter of the eighteenth century but as a long evolution. Second, British agriculture--probably because of a greater separation of ownership, entrepreneurship, and labor--developed and adopted productivity-enhancing changes on an unusually large scale. Because agriculture was still a large sector, productivity growth there considerably improved the standard of living. Agriculture also released factors of production to other activities, not completely without friction but extremely rapidly by international standards. Third, a few key innovations of exceptional impact established British firms as technological leaders in textiles and iron production. With this technological advantage, British firms came to dominate international trade in those goods, and the growth of these industries converted Britain into an urban industrial economy. The social impact was large, but the technological breakthrough cheapened only a small part of the goods the British consumed and probably contributed less than agricultural change to the growth of per capita income.

Britain's early emergence into modern economic growth occurred as the culmination of long historical processes. Agriculture's growth owed much to the particular class structure of landownership. The British state had provided security in a turbulent international environment successfully, if expensively. Internally, the state had, largely fortuitously, created an institutional framework that supported growth.

The famous technological breakthroughs in industry that we call the "Industrial Revolution" were a part, but probably quite a small part, of the process of growth. Modern industry first emerged in Britain in part because of the dynamic character of the economy. Much of Britain's particularly industrial and urban character in the nineteenth century resulted, however, from an unusual technological history in cotton and iron. British development of dominance in these new urban industries came from exceptional technological breakthroughs, reinforced by the generation of war that delayed foreign competition. The combination of technological breakthrough and the war's enhancement of the comparative advantage was an unusual event – probably in part a "lucky draw" in the random process of invention (Crafts, 1977). In a long perspective, Britain would probably have led in modern growth, but her particular nineteenth-century position as "workshop of the world" depended heavily on particular – fortuitous – breakthroughs in cotton and iron technology.

Comparative advantage in textiles and iron, coupled with rapid movement of resources from agriculture, led to rapid industrialization and urbanization. Since industrial productivity was only modestly above agricultural productivity, industrialization and urbanization, per se, resulted in little increase in aggregate output and real wages. The competitive structure of British industry conferred the benefits of technological change in the new export industries on consumers, many of whom were foreigners. There were some gains from international specialization, but the British gained little from the exports that made their island the "workshop of the world." Growth involved much more than the famous export sectors and the "Industrial Revolution" they brought.

Modern economic growth began in Britain as a particular historical event and followed a different path there than in economies that followed. Recent work on continental European industrialization suggests that Britain is a poor model for initial growth there. These economies, too, accelerated slowly rather than emerging suddenly under the influence of a leading sector. Their structure differed from Britain's. The countries that started to grow later often grew faster than Britain had. Attempts to understand the British Industrial Revolution by suggesting a close correspondence between the experiences of the contemporary Third World, early twentieth-century Japan, and the nineteenth-century United States appear particularly anachronistic. Both the historical circumstances and the particular conditions of the economies were very different from that of eighteenth-century Britain. The United States industrialized as an expanding continental economy, and the others were late followers.

Britain's pattern was closer to that seen elsewhere in Europe than to more remote economies, but even in the European context, Britain was a leader and followed a different path.

4

Agriculture and the Industrial Revolution: 1700–1850

Gregory Clark

1. Introduction

Since at least the time of Toynbee (1884), the historically literate person has known that the modern world began with not one but *two* revolutions in Britain in 1770-1850. One was the Industrial Revolution. The other, which was as important, was the agricultural revolution. For by the mid-nineteenth century British agriculture had achieved levels of output per acre and per worker that apparently far exceeded those of medieval England and of the underdeveloped economies of Eastern Europe. Table 4.1 shows the productivity of British agriculture in 1850 compared to its medieval counterpart, and to the rest of Europe in the mid-nineteenth century. As can be seen, output per acre was triple that of Russia, and output per worker was triple or greater. Output per acre in Britain in 1850 was at least three times as high as in medieval England, and output per worker may have increased by as much. Britain's productivity advantage in the nineteenth century lay particularly in high levels of output per worker. Thus sometime between the late middle ages and the end of the Industrial Revolution Britain seemingly experienced an agricultural revolution, which made it not only the most efficient producer of industrial goods in 1850 but also one of the countries with the highest output per acre and per worker in agriculture. Indeed, as we move from the West to the East of Europe, we seemingly move back in time, with Russian agriculture in the late nineteenth century apparently the equivalent of medieval English agriculture.

227

TABLE 4.1. Agricultural Performance Circa 1850

Location	Output/Acre[a]	Output/Worker[a]	Total Productivity[b]	Share Grain
Method 1				
England, 1851	13.3	249	100	.51
England, 1300	4.1	56	34	.75
Method 2				
Britain 1851	12.6	272	100	.48
England, 1300	6.1	97	50	.49
Netherlands, 1850	11.8	148	76	.32
Belgium, 1850	15.4	100	73	.48
Ireland, 1851	9.8	127	67	.40
France, 1850	10.3	120	66	.48
Germany, 1850	7.1	113	56	.44
Romania, 1870	6.4	109	53	.30
Austria, 1854	6.8	87	50	.36
Sweden, 1850	5.7	100	49	.30
Hungary, 1854	4.5	82	41	.48
Russia, 1870	3.0	80	34	.51

a - bushels wheat equivalent
b - England 1851 = 100
Note: I assume that the shares of capital, labor, and land in costs are .2, .4, and .4 respectively, and that output per unit of capital (which is unobservable) is constant across countries and time.
Sources: Clark (1991a), supplemented by information on the total cultivated acreages of the various countries, sometimes drawn from a later date when such information became available.

The importance of the agricultural revolution in creating the modern world is, indeed, perhaps greater than that of the Industrial Revolution. For suppose that all that had happened to the world was an industrial revolution. In preindustrial societies such as Russia in the nineteenth century, up to 75 percent of the population was engaged in agriculture, and people consumed food at subsistence levels.[1] Industrialization would have created a fall in the prices of industrial products relative to those of agriculture, but the effect on overall income levels would have been very small since most of the resources of the society would still have had to be devoted to obtaining a subsistence supply of food. People would have had an abundance of cheap industrial goods, but they would have spent most of their income getting a basic calory supply. Most of the population would have still labored in the agricultural sector. Consequently, urbanization would not have occurred. Further, the great population growth associated with industrialization would have been impossible if yields per acre did not increase. Thus the agricultural revolution contributed more to the character of the modern world -- urban, industrial, and densely populated -- than did the Industrial Revolution. But because the increases in income created by the agricultural revolution were spent mainly on industrial and urban goods, its contribution to the creation of modern society is unappreciated. It is the shy child obscured by the brash outpourings of its less-subtle cousin.

Although it has been widely accepted that an agricultural revolution, defined in the broad sense of a substantial increase in output per acre and output per worker, did occur in Britain sometime prior to 1850, questions remain regarding *when* this revolution occurred, *what type of revolution it was, what caused it,* and what the *connection* was between agriculture and the Industrial Revolution.

2. Dating the Agricultural Revolution

Although there is little consensus on the exact dating of the agricultural revolution, the bulk of modern writers agree that the Industrial Revolution coincided with a period of great agricultural advance.[2] For most, this belief is produced by a few simple but seemingly ironclad arguments. The population of Britain increased

---

[1] See, for example, Cipolla (1980, p. 75).

[2] See, for example, Beckett (1990, pp. 5-10); Chambers and Mingay (1966); Crafts (1985a, pp. 40-42); Deane and Cole (1967, pp. 62-75); Mingay (1969, p. 479); Mingay (1977, pp. 1-3). Although some writers such as Mingay (1977) and Jones (1965) have argued that the agricultural revolution extended all the way back to 1660, none has agreed with Kerridge (1967), who argues that the agricultural revolution was over by 1767.

from 8.5 million in 1770, which did not much exceed its maximum medieval level, to almost 21 million by 1851.[3] Since even by 1851 only one fifth of British food was imported, the population fed by the agricultural sector nearly doubled in the Industrial Revolution.[4] The upper curve in Figure 4.1 shows a rough estimate of the required food production in Britain from 1770 to 1850 on the assumption that consumption per person was constant.[5] As can be seen, total output doubles, with most of the growth concentrated in the early nineteenth century.

Since both output per person and real wages are widely believed to have increased in Britain after 1800, that should have boosted food consumption even more because at higher incomes people consume more food. In studies of the value of food consumed compared with income for groups of workers at particular times in the late eighteenth and nineteenth centuries it has been found that consumption per capita, c, is well predicted by a function of the form,

$$(1) \qquad\qquad c = a(w/p)^{\epsilon}$$

where w/p is real income and ϵ is the elasticity of demand for food, which seems to be about 0.7.[6] Figure 4.1 also shows the implied food consumption in Britain adjusting crudely for income per person by using either real output per capita or the real wages of "blue collar" workers in England. Crafts (1985a) calculates that real output per capita grew by 65 percent in the Industrial Revolution, implying an

---

[3] The information for England is drawn from Wrigley and Schofield (1981, pp. 534-535). The population of Scotland and Wales is assumed to be in the same proportion to that of England in 1770 as it is in 1850.

[4] This calculation counts as food only those items that contained calories (thus it does not count imports of coffee and tea). Lindert does a similar calculation in which he estimates food imports circa 1850 to be about 20 percent of consumption in England and Wales (Lindert, 1992). Beckett (1990, p. 5) notes that "few historians doubted that the major increase in agricultural output must have coincided with the growth of population."

[5] Required domestic output is calculated as estimated consumption minus net food imports.

[6] See Crafts (1985c, p. 153); Clark, Huberman, and Lindert (1992).

FIGURE 4.1. Predicted Agricultural Output in Britain, 1770-1850

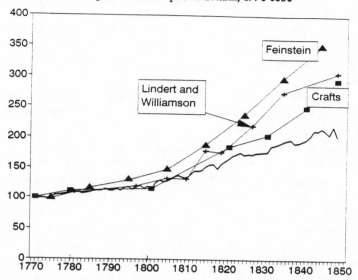

Notes: The solid line shows the food output required in Britain to keep consumption per capita constant. The marks show the output required given evidence on real wages and on output per person.

Sources: Real wages: Lindert and Williamson (1985b). Output per person: Crafts (1985a, p. 95); Feinstein (1981, p. 136); Wrigley and Schofield (1981, pp. 532-534). Food imports: Mitchell (1988, pp. 221-234); John (1989).

increase in British food output of 193 percent.[7] Real wages rose by 79 percent on the basis of the "blue collar" index, so the increase in required overall food output is about 208 percent.[8] Including income per capita measures concentrates the increase in required food output even more in the period 1800-1850. Thus output of food from British agriculture should have tripled in the first half of the nineteenth century. Indeed, the population and wage evidence seems to support

---

[7] Crafts (1985a, p. 95). Feinstein calculates that real output per capita grew by 124 percent, so that domestic food production had to increase by 255 percent (Feinstein, 1981, p. 136).

[8] The real wage index for "blue collar" workers is derived from the wage series of Lindert and Williamson (1983b), deflated with the prices of Lindert and Williamson (1985a). With this real wage series, output in agriculture had to increase by 160 percent between 1810 and 1850.

the claim of F.M.L. Thompson that 1815-1880 witnessed a "Second Agricultural Revolution" (Thompson, 1968).

Unless there were large increases in the cultivated acreage during the Industrial Revolution, yields per acre should have tripled. The available evidence on the total cultivated area is weak but suggests that there was little net gain.[9]

The other elements that seem to indicate profound changes in agriculture in the period 1770 to 1850 are the blossoming of intellectual interest in and writing about agriculture, and the great institutional changes being wrought in the countryside by the Parliamentary Enclosure movement, which was replacing the vestiges of communal cultivation in the remaining open-field villages with a purely private agriculture. New books and periodicals about agriculture were published at an increasing rate up until the 1840s. Thus whereas on average less than one periodical devoted to agriculture was published per year from 1681 to 1760 in England, the rate rose to more than three per year in the late eighteenth century, and twenty per year in the first half of the nineteenth century (Sullivan, 1984, p. 276). Societies devoted to agricultural improvement flourished in the late eighteenth century. By 1800 there were at least thirty-five such societies, and there were over six hundred by 1855 (Wilmot, 1990, p. 9). Among the landed elite, the pursuit of agricultural "improvement" had become a patriotic duty and a mark of enlightenment and sophistication. By a happy coincidence of virtue and profit, it was believed that raising tenants' rents to market levels was one of the ways to promote agricultural progress, through pressing tenants into more profitable cultivation practices (Wilmot, 1990, pp. 36-46). With all this smoke it would seem there would have to be fire in the form of agricultural progress. But most of all, there was after 1770 a general feeling that people were living in an age of improvement--that barbarous practices were being replaced and old evils remedied on all sides--and that a new era of scientific agriculture had dawned.

There has been equivalent optimism about increases in output per worker.[10] The direct evidence on output per worker in agriculture

---

[9] Prince (1989, pp. 30-33). Holderness estimates that from 1750 to 1850 there was a 35 percent increase in arable land, but most of this must have come at the expense of pasture (Holderness, 1989, pp. 126-127).

[10] See, for example, Allen (1992a, pp. 12, 38); Crafts (1985a, pp. 40-42).

before 1850 is even more elusive than direct yield evidence, so again various indirect stratagems have been used to estimate output per worker in agriculture. One method is to try to estimate the percentage of the population employed in agriculture, l_A, and then use the fact that if i is imported food consumption per capita, output per worker in agriculture, q_A, will be

$$(2) \qquad\qquad q_A = (c-i)/l_A.$$

The census of population gives estimates of the share of the work force in agriculture for each decade in the nineteenth century, though the earlier figures are very imprecise. These suggest that the share of the labor force in agriculture was less than 25 percent at mid-century and about 36 percent in 1801. Crafts (1985a) extrapolates the labor force share in agriculture back from 1801 using information on occupations gathered from probate inventories by Lindert (1980). He concludes that the share of the labor force in agriculture in 1760 on the eve of the Industrial Revolution was between 48 and 56 percent. Thus since Crafts estimates that food consumption per capita rose by nearly 50 percent during the Industrial Revolution, from equation (2) the implied output per agricultural worker in 1850 relative to 1770 rose by 150 percent.[11]

Agriculture facilitated the industrial transformation of Britain not only by feeding the expanded population of the urban proletariat but by releasing to the cities about 25 percent of the population who would have been required in the traditional agricultural system to feed the growing population. The gains in output per worker allowed about 5 million people to be engaged in industrial rather than agricultural production in 1850, feeding the urbanization that is characteristic of this period. Therefore, we see again how vital agricultural productivity advance was to the changes characterizing the Industrial Revolution.

Thus on the reckoning of most economic historians the agricultural and industrial revolutions were simultaneous, and the question of the connection between the two is paramount. Why should agricultural productivity boom just in the period when such a boom was needed to

---

[11] Wrigley (1985) uses a similar method to argue for substantial increases in output per person in agriculture in the eighteenth century.

ensure that the growing population could be fed? There is no direct connection between the changes occurring in agriculture and the industrial innovations of the period. The innovations of Hargreaves, Crompton, Arkwright, and Cartwright that revolutionized textile production were largely remote from agricultural technology. The steam engine was used to some extent, mainly in the north of Britain and mainly to thresh grain. But it served principally as a labor saving device. It had no direct effect on output and little indirect effect through saving on horse feed, which was previously grown on the farm. Nor is there any general sign that population growth in and of itself was capable of calling forth proportionately more food production. In previous periods of population growth in England, as in the sixteenth century, the pressure of population produced declining living standards for workers and thus apparent declines in food consumption.[12] So why do the agricultural and industrial revolutions so conveniently dovetail?

3. Direct Evidence of Agricultural Change

Recently the timing of the changes in the agricultural sector has been thrown into doubt, despite the apparently ironclad evidence presented by the population and wage evidence just discussed. The doubts have been created by a number of different sorts of evidence about both yields and output per worker from the agricultural sector itself.

If agricultural output tripled during the Industrial Revolution, it had to be the result of the combination of three mechanisms: yield increases on particular crops, changes in the composition of output in favor of crops that had a higher value, and an increase in the amount of cultivated land. The total output change would be these three effects multiplied. But even in combination, the changes directly observed seem far too modest to have produced the required tripling of output from 1770 to 1850.

The direct evidence on yields for particular crops uniformly shows that yields per acre increased by amounts much smaller than threefold. There is little satisfactory direct evidence on yields in Britain prior to the late nineteenth century, when national censuses were first made. Modern economic historians have attempted to fill the void with

---

[12] Phelps Brown and Hopkins (1956).

various indirect stratagems: partial yield surveys, probate inventories, and labor input information. There are various partial surveys of grain yields before the national census, extending back to 1770. On the basis of these surveys, Holderness concludes that wheat yields in England by the mid-nineteenth century were 28 bushels per acre, at the end of the eighteenth century they were 21.5 bushels per acre, and in the middle of the eighteenth century at least 18 bushels per acre (Holderness, 1989, pp. 138-140). This is an increase of only 56 percent.[13] Also, we see that yields increased by only 30 percent from 1800 to 1850, when the real wage and population evidence demands almost as great an increase as from 1770.[14] Holderness's conclusion that wheat yields in the mid-eighteenth century were 18 bushels per acre requires the assumption that the most extensive yield data collected for this period, that of Arthur Young for 1767-1770 is completely wrong. For Young's data show wheat yields to be nearly 24 bushels per acre.[15] For barley and oats, Holderness finds an increase in yields of only 46 percent and 43 percent in the course of the Industrial Revolution (Holderness, 1989, p. 146).

Mark Overton initiated studies of probate inventories as a way of studying crop yields (Overton, 1979). When someone died there was an official inventory of their possessions drawn up and lodged with the local court. For farmers, part of their possessions were crops growing in the fields. The value of these crops just before harvest compared with the price of grain should indicate the expected crop yield. The problem is discovering the relationship between crop valuations and the yield of the crop, and the researchers using this method have disagreed on this.[16]

---

[13] It also implies that prior to 1750 there were significant yield gains since the medieval period, because medieval yields seem to have been only about 12 bushels per acre.

[14] Allen and O Gráda, and Turner give figures for grain yields for circa 1800 and 1850 that suggest a similar average yield increase of 31 percent between these dates. Allen and O Gráda (1988, p. 102); Turner (1982, pp. 506-510).

[15] Allen and O Gráda (1988, p. 102).

[16] The problems are how to allow for such elements as the tithe and harvesting, carting, threshing, and marketing costs, which reduce the value imputed to the crop, and how to eliminate those inventories that give not the

This makes it hard to have confidence in the absolute levels of yields recorded, though information on the movement of yields over time is probably more reliable. Unfortunately, the probate inventories recording this information extend only from the late sixteenth to the early eighteenth centuries. But these studies generally report significant yield gains for grains from the early seventeenth century to the early eighteenth century. Thus in terms of yields, the agricultural revolution seems a much more drawn out affair, beginning around 1600.

None of the sources just cited gives grass yields, even though animal products were about half of British agricultural output by 1850. Clark (1991b) uses the amount of time required to cut wheat and hay to estimate the movement of yields all the way from the middle ages to the nineteenth century. The reasoning is that heavier yields required more labor per acre to cut, particularly in the case of reaping wheat where much of the labor was in binding the straw. The labor input evidence suggests that for wheat there were steady yield gains from the late sixteenth century to the mid-nineteenth century so that most of the rise of yields had been completed by 1770. The independent labor cost data given by Young turn out to be quite consistent with a yield as high as 24 bushels of wheat per acre. The gain in wheat yields in the Industrial Revolution period is estimated as less than 25 percent. For grass there is no evidence of any yield increase from 1560 to 1890. Since the majority of the cultivable land in England was grassland, this again argues for low overall yield growth during the Industrial Revolution, unless animals became much more efficient at utilizing grass. The net yield gain on all land would be somewhere between 12.5 and 50 percent only, the higher figure resulting from assuming Holderness to be correct about grain yields and assuming equal gains on the pasture side.

The second mechanism that could operate to increase yields is changes in the composition of output in favor of crops that have a higher value. In medieval England, for example, a common arable rotation would be two years of grain crops followed by a bare fallow. By 1850 relatively few farmers would have a bare fallow in their arable rotation, replacing it with such crops as clover, sown grasses, turnips, or potatoes so that the land never lay unproductive. Did these new rotations boost total

---

value of the standing crop but the costs put into the crop. See Allen (1988); Glennie (1993); Overton (1991).

output significantly even though individual crops saw modest yield gains? Or were there switches from pasture to arable that again increased yields? The short answer is no. The total area of bare fallow in the mid-nineteenth century was about 3 percent of agricultural land. In 1770 it would be at most 10 percent.[17] Thus replacing the traditional arable rotations would increase yields by at most 8 percent. Nor would a switch from pasture to arable produce much gain. The value of net output per acre of pasture was not much less than for arable, perhaps about one fifth less, and not much land was switched in this interval.[18] Certainly no more than one fifth of land was switched from arable to pasture in this period, for a net overall yield gain of at most 4 percent. Thus the maximum gains from changes in crop composition would be a puny 12 percent.

The third mechanism that could increase yields is gains in the total area cultivated. As noted previously, there is little evidence for other than minor gains in the total cultivated acreage in the period of the Industrial Revolution. Perhaps 10 percent of the land was converted from use as rough pasture to improved pasture or arable land.

Thus overall output at the end of the Industrial Revolution compared to the beginning is estimated at,

$$(1.125 \text{ to } 1.5) \times (1.12) \times (1.1) = 1.39 \text{ to } 1.85.$$
$$\text{yields} \qquad \text{crop mix} \quad \text{area} \qquad \text{total effect}$$

That is, output increased by between 39 and 85 percent on the basis of the direct evidence from agriculture. This implies that as much as half of the domestic food output in 1850 implied by incomes and population is missing!

Holderness reaches the more optimistic conclusion that "broadly speaking, output from English agriculture rather more than doubled between 1750 and 1850" (Holderness, 1989, p. 174). But this is still a very bleak assessment if we consider the supposed consumption demands. And to get even a doubling of output, Holderness often makes optimistic assumptions where the evidence leaves a range of choices. Holderness concludes, for example, that overall grain

---

[17] Holderness estimates it at even less than this in 1770 (Holderness, 1989, p. 133).

[18] Batchelor (1808) gives detailed figures on which this calculation is based.

production in England roughly doubled during the Industrial Revolution only because the grain area increased by 26 percent (Holderness, 1989, p. 146). But there is little hard evidence on the areas planted in various crops for any of these years. He also finds that meat production roughly doubled from 1750 to 1850. Now the numbers of cattle and sheep, as he notes, probably increased by little in this period, so most of the gains in production had to come from animals being larger.[19] But there is again little evidence on animal sizes. What information there is establishes only that slaughter weights might have stayed the same in the course of the Industrial Revolution, or they might have as much as doubled. Holderness opts for a figure where meat output doubles during the Industrial Revolution. But he could have equally well concluded from the evidence that meat output stayed the same over this period, or that output tripled. For dairy output Holderness again, by various complicated calculations, concludes that output roughly doubled, again falling short of supposed consumption demands.

It is even harder to find direct evidence on output per worker in agriculture than to find evidence on yields per acre. There have been two recent approaches to the issue. Allen uses information from Arthur Young's tours of 1767-1770 to estimate the number of workers per acre in England and Wales in the eighteenth century. He concludes that the number of workers per acre stayed roughly constant from the beginning of the eighteenth century to the mid-nineteenth century (Allen, 1992a, p. 38). Allen believes, partly on the basis of the estimates of Holderness (1989), that output per acre increased by 240 percent from 1700 to 1850 and 125 percent from 1750 to 1850. Thus output per worker must also have more than tripled between 1700 and 1850 and more than doubled between 1750 and 1850. Allen, like Crafts, believes a great increase in labor productivity was a key element of the agricultural revolution. Since the population more than doubled during the Industrial Revolution, the share of the labor force in agriculture in 1770 must have been above 60 percent, and in 1700 was about 80 percent. Allen thus argues for a sustained increase in output per worker in agriculture and a sustained decline in the share of the

---

[19] Holderness concludes that for Britain from 1770 to 1860 the number of sheep increased by 40 percent, the number of cows by 11 percent, and the number of swine by 35 percent (Holderness, 1988, p. 32).

population in agriculture, all the way from the beginning of the eighteenth century to the mid-nineteenth century.

Clark (1991a) tries to estimate output per worker by estimating the man-days required for the various farm tasks over time. There is evidence from piece rate payments in agriculture on output per worker in specific tasks. This shows that it took just as long to thresh a bushel of wheat or mow an acre of meadow in the mid-nineteenth century as in the three hundred years before. And for tasks such as reaping wheat or mowing spring grains, the time taken per acre was longer, though increased yields do imply that output per worker in bushels rose by modest amounts. When we look at the details of British agriculture we find that for many tasks -- including harvesting and threshing grain, manuring, and many of the tasks in animal production -- the labor inputs would be largely independent of the yields, so that the rise in yields would produce much smaller gains in output per worker (Clark, 1987b, 1988, 1991a). Clark concludes that the changes in agriculture in this period, both in terms of yields per acre and in terms of switches to new rotations, would not have had much effect on the output per worker. Clark thus argues that increases in output per worker were modest all the way from 1560 to 1850 and that most of the increase would have occured prior to 1770 since that is when most of the grain yield increases occurred.[20]

It turns out that there is little disagreement about the size of the agricultural labor force over the Industrial Revolution period. We shall see later that I estimate the labor force in 1770 to be about 48 percent of the British population. This is not that much less than Crafts and Allen estimate for England, at 56 and 60 percent respectively. The disagreement centers on the movement of yields per acre, which has implications for output per worker. Notice that the share of labor in agriculture above implies that already on the eve of the Industrial Revolution Britain was a relatively developed country as measured by the proportion of the population engaged in agriculture. India, for example, reported 66 percent of its labor force engaged in agriculture in 1981 (Central Statistical Organization, 1987, p. 28).

---

[20] Note that this conclusion need not necessarily contradict the finding of Allen (1992a) that labor inputs per acre were not much different in 1770 and 1850. For the farms from which the labor input data for 1770 is drawn had reported yields per acre that would be close to those typical of 1850.

Thus the evidence on the timing of the agricultural revolution has produced conflicting visions. There are still old-guard revolutionists, such as Crafts (1985a) and Harley in this book, who stand by the powerful evidence from wages and population and tightly couple the agricultural and industrial revolutions. There are the moderates who, based on information from the agricultural sector itself, posit a more drawn out agricultural revolution beginning in the seventeenth century; these include Allen (1992a); Jones (1965); Mingay (1977); and Overton (1991). And there are dissenters such as Kerridge (1967) and Clark (1991a, 1991b), who (for very different reasons) argue that the first agricultural revolution was largely complete by 1770, so that the agricultural revolution clearly preceded the Industrial Revolution. Below we shall consider ways of deciding between these views.

4. What Kind of Revolution?

We have so far characterized the agricultural revolution simply as an increase in output per acre and output per person. But these events characterizing the agricultural revolution could have two different sources. The first is *intensification*. This occurs when the growth of output per acre and per worker is created by using more intensively some other input to agriculture. Until 1850 the major other input to agriculture was capital, embodied in buildings, fences, land improvements, animals, advance payments to workers, seeds, and tools. Indeed, the amount of organic material maintained in the soil, which determined its fertility, was itself a decision about how much capital to invest in production.[21] Later, much agricultural advance was achieved by importing to the agricultural sector chemical fertilizers containing nitrogen and potassium. The second way output per acre and per worker can grow is through *efficiency gains* (alternatively called *productivity gains*). In this case, improvements in technique or organization increase the output produced by any given bundle of land, labor, and capital inputs. Economists view *efficiency* gains as a "better" source of output increases because they are seemingly costless, whereas gains in output from *intensification* require resources to be committed

---

[21] The organic material in the soil decayed gradually releasing nitrogen. The amount of nitrogen available seems to have been the major constraint on crop growth in preindustrial agriculture. The more organic material in the soil, the greater the release of nitrogen. See Section 8 of this chapter.

that could otherwise be consumed to increase incomes. Also, we would expect that output gains from *intensification* would occur only when the cost of capital or other inputs fell relative to the value of output. By contrast, *efficiency* gains might arise from accidental discoveries or the spread of knowledge from elsewhere or the lifting of restrictions on techniques that could be used or organization that could be employed.

Although there has been a long tradition, starting with Young, which discusses the agricultural revolution mainly in terms of increased use of capital and hence in terms of intensification, modern investigators of the agricultural revolution, such as Crafts or Allen, have concluded that it represented mainly efficiency gains and thus contributed significantly to the overall growth of income per capita in Britain in the period of the Industrial Revolution because it did not draw capital away from other uses. They reach this conclusion by estimating directly the increase in capital inputs to agriculture in this period, which they find to be modest.

Table 4.2 shows the estimates of the level of efficiency in agriculture for years before 1850 derived by comparing outputs and inputs. Crafts, representing the old guard, concentrates the agricultural revolution in the period 1800-1850. Allen puts most of it between 1700 and 1800. Both find that the efficiency of the agricultural sector increased by substantial amounts sometime between 1700 and 1850. Both these estimates of efficiency growth imply that either in the eighteenth or in

TABLE 4.2 Estimated Productivity Levels, 1700-1850

	1700	1760	1800	1850
Crafts	-	58	62	100
Allen	43	-	78	100

Notes: The estimates of Crafts refer to Great Britain, those of Allen to England and Wales only.
Sources: Crafts (1985a, p. 41-42), Allen (1992a, p. 42).

the early nineteenth century agriculture was experiencing faster productivity growth than the rest of the economy.[22]

Crafts and Allen work with a very restricted definition of capital, however. They look at buildings, fences, machinery, and animals. But a major element of the capital in agriculture is in the soil itself. The fertility of soil depends on, among other things, the amount of nitrogen and other compounds it contains. Maintaining these stocks requires investment in the form of manures and nitrogen-fixing crops. As we shall see below, the most plausible theory explaining why yields increased in the agricultural revolution is that farmers discovered the importance of nitrogen fixing-crops. But if they used these on a large scale, they would have been investing vast amounts in increasing the soil capital, which would not be captured by the accounting of capital done by Crafts and Allen.

Output gains from *intensification* of production in agriculture could link the agricultural to the Industrial Revolution if the Industrial Revolution created changes in relative prices that spurred the intensification. We shall consider next how relative prices changed in this period.

5. Searching for the Agricultural Revolution Using Prices

The difficulties involved in fixing the timing of the agricultural revolution and determining what kind of revolution it was, should be resolvable by considering the movement of input and output prices in agriculture over the years before 1850. If, as Crafts and Allen believe, there was an agricultural revolution based on efficiency advances, then we should be able to detect this by looking at these prices. The reasoning is as follows. The total value of agricultural output necessarily

---

[22] Crafts's finding of greater productivity growth in agriculture than in the general economy during the period of the Industrial Revolution has been criticized by Williamson (1987a), who argues that if agriculture was experiencing such rapid productivity growth it should not have been a declining sector of the economy. This criticism is misguided, I think, since it neglects the fact that agriculture employed a fixed input--land. Harley shows in this book in a computable general equilibrium model that rapid agricultural productivity growth is quite consistent with a declining agricultural sector and is required by the assumed overall income growth.

equals the total amounts paid to the inputs in agriculture. The revenue received by the farmer has to be paid to someone. There are three main inputs: land, labor (including the farmer's labor), and capital. We can represent this identity formally as,

(3) $$p \cdot Q = r \cdot K + w \cdot L + s \cdot T$$

where Q, K, L, and T are the quantities of output, capital, labor, and land, and p, r, w, s are the prices of each of these. Dividing both sides of the identity by revenue $p.Q$, we get,

(4) $$1 = \frac{r}{p} \cdot \frac{K}{Q} + \frac{w}{p} \cdot \frac{L}{Q} + \frac{s}{p} \cdot \frac{T}{Q}$$

We expect that in the period of the agricultural revolution there was a substantial increase in both output per acre, Q/T, and output per worker, Q/L, whereas output per unit of capital, Q/K, probably changed little. In that case, for the identity above to still hold true, at least one of the real prices of the factors of production, r/p, w/p, and s/p, must rise. And the amount by which these real prices rise indicates how big the productivity gains are. But note that a gain in land yields, Q/T, need not show up as an increase in real rents, s/p, but depending on market conditions might instead show up as a rise in real wages or an increase in returns to capital.

Even if the agricultural revolution occurred as a result of *intensification* in the form of capital embodied in land, price information should reveal at least the dating of the agricultural revolution. For we would expect that if extra investment created the agricultural revolution, it would mainly be in the form of investments in soil capital, land improvements, and buildings. Agricultural land is typically rented as a bundle that includes the soil capital, the improvements, and the buildings. Thus if output was increasing because of such investments, it should still show up as an increased payment to the owner of the combined land and capital bundle. Thus an examination of prices should reveal when the agricultural revolution occurred, but will not tell us what type of revolution it was. But if output was to grow through intensification, then we should be able to observe a decline in the relative price of capital in this period that induced farmers to invest more in soil productivity.

There have been a number of attempts to calculate productivity increases in agriculture during the Industrial Revolution, beginning with McCloskey (1981), who first proposed the calculation.[23] The most complete though still rudimentary attempt is Clark (1991b), where the productivity of English agriculture in 1770 compared with 1850 is measured. This calculation suggests that the level of productivity in agriculture in 1770 was 86 percent of that in 1850. This is a surprising result for both the old guard and those with moderate views on the agricultural revolution. As we see in Table 4.2 Crafts estimates that productivity in 1760 was only 58 percent of that in 1850, whereas Allen estimates that as late as 1800 productivity was only 78˙ percent of the 1850 level.

The Clark (1991b) test depends on Young's and Caird's estimates of rents circa 1770 and 1850, looks at only these benchmark dates, and does not incorporate such factors as land taxes. Clark (1991c) estimates the productivity of the agricultural sector going back to 1611 using new information on land rents, wages, and the rate of return to capital, and incorporating taxes on land.

Figure 4.2 shows some preliminary estimates of the movement of land rents, wages, and capital costs in the period 1700 to 1850 for England and Wales south of Lancashire and Yorkshire (the northern fifth of the country was excluded because of the problems of getting enough price information for these areas). The series here are all deflated by the price of agricultural output, as equation (4) requires.

The rent series includes the poor rate, taxes paid for support of the local poor by the land occupier, as part of land rent. The poor rate was typically modest in the early eighteenth century, but in the years after 1780 it reached very high levels, amounting to about one-fifth of the owner's market land rent by the beginning of the nineteenth century and staying at nearly that level until after 1850.

---

[23] Others include Hueckel (1981) and Mokyr (1987).

FIGURE 4.2 Real Rents, Wages, and Capital Costs, Southern England, 1700-1850

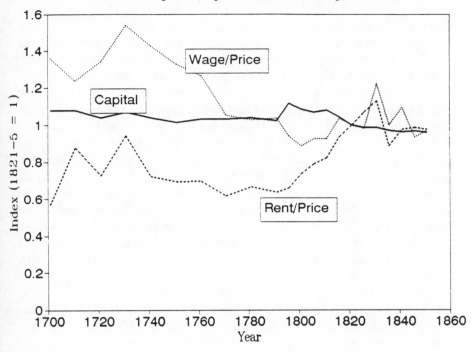

Note: The real price of land, labor, and capital are set equal to 1.00 in 1821-1825.
Source: Clark (1991c).

The rent series is composed mainly of observations of the sale of land or a new contract to lease land, so that it measures peoples' best estimations of the market value of land at various dates. As can be seen, real land rents in most of the country were 70 percent of their value in 1701-1730 as in 1850. Real wages, measured in terms of the prices of agricultural output, were again almost as high in the early eighteenth century as in the mid-nineteenth century. Agricultural workers in the south of England did not fare particularly well in the Industrial Revolution. Finally, farmers' capital costs were flat in this period, because rates of interest changed little.

If we consider relative prices of land, labor, and capital, we see that in the period of the Industrial Revolution land became more expensive relative to both labor and capital. Thus the price incentives to farmers in this period should have been pushing them to intensify use of land (increasing yields) and extend the use of labor and capital (reducing output per worker). We saw above that grain yield increases are the one well-attested feature of the 1770 to 1850 period.

Table 4.3 shows real rents, real wages, real capital costs, and the implied level of productivity in southern England in 1701-1730, 1761-1780, and 1846-1850, including the poor rate as a component of land rents. As can be seen there is little sign of any productivity gain in the south throughout this period. The table also shows the same data for the northern fifth of England, though here the prices used to create the real rents, wages, and capital costs are those of the south of the country and are hence probably too high in the eighteenth century. Productivity growth in the north is much greater (though still less than Crafts or Allen calculate for the entire country). If we combine the estimates for the north and the south, however, we find that productivity levels for England as a whole in both 1700 and 1770 were about 92 percent of their level in 1850. There was no agricultural revolution between the early eighteenth and mid-nineteenth centuries, merely modest productivity gains.

The objection may be raised that this method of calculating productivity growth will not capture gains in productivity from bringing waste land into cultivation. But in fact by design the rent series is constructed so that the addition of any newly cultivated land to an established plot gets counted as a rent increase on that plot. Thus the rent per acre measures the rent per acre of all land in the country.

The productivity growth calculation is also constructed in two ways that will exaggerate productivity gains. The first is by the inclusion of the poor rate in rents. Boyer (1990) argues that the poor rate was largely a system used by farmers to pay workers who were super-numerary in the winter, so that they would be available for harvest time. In that case, we would not include the poor rates as part of land rent, since they were merely a form of winter wages. The more exten-sive use of poor-rate support would allow the farmers to employ fewer people in the winter slack season. If the poor rate were abolished, land rents would not have risen and neither would wages have changed. Thus including it in land rents would be double counting.

If we believe that the poor rates were instead forced on farmers who were unable to rid themselves of excess labor, then we again might want to exclude them from the land rents. For although the efficiency

TABLE 4.3 Productivity Growth in England, 1701-1855

	1701-1730	1761-1780	1846-1855
South of England			
Rents (incl. taxes)	0.66	0.69	1.00
Wages	1.38	1.21	1.00
Capital costs	1.10	1.07	1.00
Productivity	0.98	0.94	1.00
North of England[a]			
Rents (incl. taxes)	0.47	0.53	1.00
Wages	0.65	0.92	1.00
Capital costs	1.10	1.07	1.00
Productivity	0.64	0.76	1.00
All of England and Wales			
Productivity	0.92	0.90	1.00

Notes: The rents, wages, and capital costs are all given relative to output prices.

a - Farm output prices for the north of England are estimated using those of the south. These prices are probably too high for meat and dairy products in the early years, exaggerating the apparent productivity growth.

Sources: South of England from Clark (1991c). North of England wage series from Bowley (1898) and Gilboy (1934), and rents from the *Charity Commission Reports, House of Commons*, Papers and Proceedings, 1819-1840.

of individual farms is measured by the rent, including the poor rate claims (the poor in effect becoming part owners of the land), the efficiency of the agricultural system is measured by excluding the poor rates. The existence of the poor rate represents a failure of the system in that it is unable to productively employ large numbers of workers. My preference is thus for the second method of excluding the poor rate, on either argument.

The second way in which the productivity growth calculation is biased upward is by the agricultural prices used to construct real wages and real rents. For the prices that are used are largely those paid for food products by institutions such as Eton College. But these prices include the costs of transporting food from the farm to the town, and we know that as a result of improvements in roads and the introduction of canals and railroads real transport costs fell from 1770 to 1850. The correct prices to use are the farmgate prices. The input price series in Table 4.3 thus exaggerates the increase in real prices of these inputs to farmers in 1850 compared with 1770.

It must be emphasized that this startling result is a preliminary one and that as more rent and wage evidence is collected it is possible that more productivity growth will appear. It does, however, seem very unlikely that there could have been productivity growth in agriculture that was as dramatic as both Crafts and Allen find.

What could be wrong with this conclusion? The method used to calculate productivity is appropriate, and indeed if we apply the same

FIGURE 4.3 Productivity in British Agriculture, 1700-1972

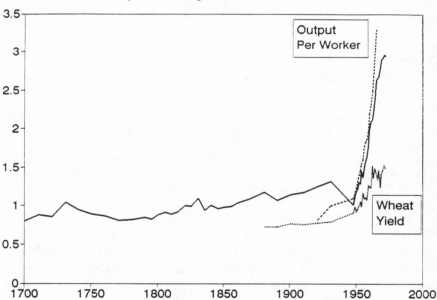

Note: This is only a very crude calculation for the period 1851-1972. Productivity in 1821-1825 is set equal to 1. The dotted lines show an index of output per worker from 1921 to 1965 and the yield per acre of wheat from 1884 to 1972. Productivity after 1921 is calculated including fertilizer as an input.

Source: Post-1851: Thompson (1907); Andrews, Mitchell, and Weber (1979); Mitchell (1988, pp. 214, 219, 678, 735).

method to data on wages, rents, prices, and capital costs for the years from 1851 to 1970, we get results that show a period of rapid productivity growth only after World War II. This accords well with the fact that output per acre and per worker both increased greatly just in this same period. Figure 4.3 shows the long productivity picture from 1701 to 1972. It also shows output per worker from 1921 to 1965 and wheat yields per acre from 1884 to 1975. The gains in output per worker and output per acre from 1948 to 1965 that correspond to rapid productivity growth measured through prices are of the order that Crafts (1985a) and Allen (1992a) posit for the period of the Industrial Revolution. They should leave their mark on the price series, but they do not. There was no agricultural revolution during the Industrial Revolution.

6. Agriculture Without an Agricultural Revolution?

Can we make sense of the Industrial Revolution period without an accompanying agricultural revolution? First we should be clear that the finding of little productivity growth in agriculture from 1700 to 1850 is consistent with all of the reliable information we have for agriculture in this period.

The major institutional change in agriculture in the years after 1700 was the enclosure of the open fields. The dominant medieval system of cultivation in the arable heartland of the country had been the open-field system. In the open fields, the land of each cultivator in the village would be held intermixed in a number of large fields -- the number varied greatly, but there were frequently three large arable fields, one for each year in the classical arable rotation. These common fields would have boundary fences, but the individual cultivators' plots, which were typically less than a half acre in size, would lie unfenced. A typical strip dimension would be 220 yards long and 5.5 or 11 yards wide. The plots in the common fields were individual property only when they were growing arable crops (or later when they were growing crops in the arable part of the rotation cycle). After harvest and in the fallow years set by the village custom, they were thrown open to the animals of all who had grazing rights in the fields.[24] Similarly, meadowland that was common would be private property only until

---

[24] These grazing rights were not open to all but were attached to ownership of land or cottages in the village.

the hay crop was cut, then it would be grazed in common. Typically, there would also be woods and pasture or waste ground in the village that would be common all year round. Often, too, the village would set rules about how and when the harvest had to be gathered and about the kinds and quantity of animals that could be grazed in the fields.[25]

The traditional rotation on open-field arable land was to take in turn a winter grain crop, such as wheat or rye (called winter grains because they were planted in the fall), then a spring grain crop, such as barley or oats, followed by a fallow year when the land was plowed to kill weeds but no crop was grown. But cultivation practices were much more flexible than this stereotype would suggest -- the rotations could be much more complex and involve other crops, such as beans, peas, and vetch. There is evidence that even as early as the fourteenth century the arable land was allowed to lie under grass crops for periods of years in order to restore the land's fertility.

The open-field system has fascinated historians and economists for many years. The collective nature of property and the communal regulation of cultivation practices led historians to believe that it was the institutional arrangements of the open fields that kept yields low in agriculture since they would make the introduction of new cropping practices difficult. In part, the weight given to the open fields as a retarding force in agriculture seems to have stemmed from a general ideological commitment on the part of many historians to pure private property as representing the improved state of society and communal property as representing the darkest forces of the tradition-bound past.

The enclosure of open-field land occurred over a long interval -- from before 1450 to 1900 -- and involved different mechanisms at different times. The earlier enclosures were achieved by one proprietor buying up all the land in the village and thus extinguishing the common rights, or by agreements between owners that required unanimity.[26] After 1740 a legal device called Parliamentary Enclosure, which required only that the owners of 75 to 80 percent of the land area agree to enclose, was widely employed. About 21 percent of the land area of Britain was enclosed by Parliamentary Enclosure from 1750 to 1830 (Chapman,

---

[25] Good descriptions of how the open-field system functioned can be found in Ault (1972); Orwin and Orwin (1938); and Slater (1907).

[26] Allen (1992b, pp. 27-28); Yelling (1977, pp. 1-93).

1987). At least as much land was enclosed by private means before 1750.

The large rent increases that were observed when open fields were enclosed in the late eighteenth century seem to be strong evidence for the inefficiency of the open-field system. Rents, it was said, often doubled or tripled upon enclosure.[27]

McCloskey (1975), however, points out that these very rent increases suggest that the enclosure of the open fields would actually have had modest impacts on the productivity of agriculture. If we look at an individual village, the total gain in income from enclosure will be approximated by the increase in rents, assuming that labor and capital are mobile.[28] But in order to measure the percentage gain in the efficiency of agriculture, we must divide the gain in income by the value of output per acre before enclosure. Suppose, for example, that the value of output per acre before enclosure was £3, and the rent was £0.5. If the rent doubled upon enclosure, the total value of output would increase to £3.5 (assuming the other inputs remained the same). Efficiency would increase by only 17 percent. Rents may have doubled upon enclosure, but before enclosure they were only on the order of one-sixth of the value of output, so the gain in efficiency from enclosure of a village would in general be only 17 percent. Also, no more than 30 percent of the total area of Britain was enclosed between 1700 and 1850. Thus the total efficiency gain in agriculture from enclosure would be no more than 5 percent. Small potatoes.

The rent increase may actually greatly overstate the benefits of enclosure for a variety of reasons. The period 1755 to 1810, when many enclosures took place, was one of rising nominal rents. Many tenants who held on leases at "rack" rents (market value rents) had reasonably long leases, with 21-year leases common. Their rent at the time of enclosure was thus frequently much less than the current market value of the land. In this case, the landlord would buy the tenant out of the lease on enclosure, and the land would be let at a new

---

[27] Chambers and Mingay conclude, for example, that "perhaps a doubling of rents, from about 7s to 15s per acre, was the common result of enclosure in the Midlands" (Chambers and Mingay, 1966, p. 85).
[28] See McCloskey (1975, pp. 155-160). None of the gains will appear in higher wages or higher returns to capital since both of these are mobile inputs the prices of which are determined by competition with other villages.

rent.   Other tenants held land "at will," so that the rent could be increased at any time.   But in practice such rents would be adjusted only occasionally, so that again in times of rising rents many of these tenants would pay less than the current market value.   Enclosure would be an occasion on which to make an adjustment of rents to market value.   In either case, the increase in rents upon enclosure would then be partially just the result of the land rent being updated.

A further complication with using rents to infer efficiency is that frequently under Parliamentary Enclosure the tithe holder would take land in lieu of the tithe right.   For arable they would receive up to one-fifth of the land as well as having their property fenced at the expense of the other owners.   Thus the increase in rent per acre in part represented the inclusion in the new rents of the tithe burden from which the owner had exonerated the land.[29]

There has also been some question about whether some of the gain in rents was just the expropriation by the landowners of informal communal rights that were exercised over at least some land before enclosure.   The "waste" areas of villages would provide fuel and fodder for landless villagers and sometimes also space for house building.   Some landless laborers may have been able to graze animals on the common fields through sufferance, as opposed to any legal claim.   In Parliamentary Enclosure these purely customary rights would be extinguished.   But since they were customary, we do not have any record of their significance before enclosure.   Chambers (1953) argues they were unimportant, Humphries (1990) argues they were significant. Neither has any real evidence.   Insofar as common rights were extinguished, some of the rent increase will be not an efficiency gain but just a transfer of ownership.

Enclosures typically required great capital expenditures, and this obscures the significance of the rent increase even more.   The new plots had to be fenced and new roads built.   Thus some of the gain in rent was not a costless efficiency gain but a return to capital expenditures.

The difficulties of assessing the impact of enclosure on efficiency from rent changes at the point of enclosure has led others to try to compare yields or efficiency in open-field as compared with enclosed villages at

---

[29] Arable tithe-free would rent for up to 25 percent more than that burdened with tithe; for pasture and meadow the premium was 14 to 17 percent (Evans, 1976, pp. 99-100).

a given time. Turner (1986) looks at grain yields in both types of village in about 1801 when national crop surveys were taken. He finds that on average grain yields were 19 percent higher in enclosed villages.[30] Allen and O Gráda similarly compare yields in open-field and enclosed villages from Arthur Young's tours in the late 1760s and find only a 7 to 12 percent increase in yields in enclosed villages.[31] But the interpretation of these figures is tricky. It is not clear whether this increase in yields was the result of greater efficiency (more output per unit of inputs) or of greater inputs. Also, the greater yields in enclosed villages may have had little to do with enclosure per se -- they could have stemmed partly from the fact that enclosure tended to occur first in the more fertile areas where it was more profitable, or it may be that the villages with the most energetic and progressive farmers were the ones that tended to enclose early.

Allen also reports rents on open-field and enclosed land in the South Midlands. From 1700 to 1849 rents on enclosed land were typically only 50 percent higher than rents on open-field land (Allen, 1992b, p. 172). This would imply that the total efficiency gain from the enclosure movement that occurred from 1700 to 1850 would be only on the order of 2.5 percent.

There is thus no contradiction between the wave of enclosures that occurred from 1750 to 1830 and the apparent lack of productivity growth in British agriculture during this period. When it came to productivity, enclosure was a sideshow.

We do know that grain yields increased by as much as 60 percent from 1700 to 1850. But this increase in grain yields, if it were not accompanied by any increase in grass yields or in output per worker, would itself only produce a productivity increase of about 11 percent, quite consistent with our finding of only a 15 percent overall productivity gain, which assumes there was little advance in productivity per worker.[32]

---

[30] Turner (1986, p. 686). Half the land would be in grass, and there is no indication of relative grass yields. Thus the overall yield gain from enclosure may be only half the 19 percent.

[31] Allen and O Gráda (1988, p. 98).

[32] This number is based on the fact that only about 50 percent of output was grain crops, so that the overall effect on yields per acre would be a 30 percent increase. This in turn would imply only an 11 percent increase in

There is no direct evidence of any major gains in output per worker. As was discussed previously, the direct evidence from agriculture on how long it took to perform particular tasks suggests that if overall yields increased little, then labor productivity changed by even less. This is demonstrated in Table 4.4, which gives calculations of output per worker on a notional farm on clay soils circa 1808 at various yield levels. The table shows the estimated output per worker on the arable and pasture sections of the farm under both a traditional arable rotation of wheat/barley/fallow and a new five-year rotation of wheat/beans/-fallow/barley/clover, as yield varies. As can be seen, output per worker on the arable does increase with increased yields, since many tasks such as plowing and sowing are invariant to yields. But a 20 percent increase in grain yields, such as we would expect from 1770 to 1850, produces only about a 10 percent increase in output per worker, since many tasks such as threshing and manuring depend one for one on yields and others such as harvesting are heavily yield dependent. On pasture land the output per worker is even less dependent on grass yields. The majority of the labor inputs here are for milking cows, making cheese and butter, and preparing feed for animals, none of which depends on yields per acre. When we combine these two sectors in such a way that the grain output of the farm is kept at half of total output (which roughly reflects the state of British agriculture in 1850), the overall output per worker increases by only one-third when yields increase by 120 percent, the increase from medieval to modern levels. And the effect of the switch to new rotations is to reduce output per worker slightly at any given yield. During the Industrial Revolution the implied overall gain in output per worker based on these figures is only on the order of 5 to 6 percent.

There was some mechanization of agriculture in this period, but this largely consisted of threshing grain by steam, and in the mid-nineteenth century hand threshing was still commonly used in much of the south of England. Thus the internal evidence from agriculture suggests that during the Industrial Revolution the gain in output per worker may well have been little more than 10 percent.

---

productivity if output per worker and per unit of capital did not change.

TABLE 4.4 Output per Worker and Yields on a Notional Farm

Arable yield level	Net yield, arable[a]	Net yield, pasture[a]	3-field system output per worker[b]			Rotation with clover output per worker[b]	
			Arable	Pasture	All	Arable	All
(a) Medieval							
12	48	43	2.1	4.7	3.0		
(b) 1770-1880							
21	94	76	3.0	5.2	3.8	3.1	3.6
(c) 1850							
25	114	90	3.4	5.3	4.1	3.3	3.8

Note: Pasture products are constrained to be one-half of output at all yield levels by adjusting the share of land in pasture and arable. Under the traditional rotation, arable is calculated to be 42 percent of the area, under the new rotations arable is 54 percent of the area since the arable now produces pasture products also.
a - shillings per acre
b - shillins of output per shillings of labor input
Sources: Batchelor (1808, pp. 70-162); Clark (1991b).

Thus there is nothing that we know about the agricultural sector itself that would preclude the productivity estimate above from being correct. The problems emerge when we consider the wider implications of slow productivity growth in agriculture.

7. Life Without the Agricultural Revolution

The main reason the absence of an agricultural revolution from 1700 to 1850 seems implausible is that it has a wide variety of implications for the development of the British economy that seem at variance with accepted wisdom.

Suppose, for example, that Scottish agriculture experienced productivity growth during the Industrial Revolution that was as great as in the north of England. Then the overall increase in productivity in British agriculture in this period would still be only 16 percent. If we assume that output per worker did not change, so that all the gains in productivity came from increases in yields, this would still imply only a 50 percent gain in total output over the period of the Industrial Revolution from gains in yield per acre and from bringing additional land into cultivation.

There has been a long debate about living standards in the Industrial Revolution, with some arguing that despite the productivity gains from industrialization, real living standards for many workers declined. To many observers it has seemed that the work of Lindert and Williamson had closed the debate -- living standards for even the poorest workers increased in the course of the Industrial Revolution. But with food imports at only one-fifth of estimated consumption by the mid-nineteenth century, an increase of only 50 percent in agricultural output would imply that consumption per capita fell by about 22 percent during the Industrial Revolution period, despite apparently rising real incomes. This is a decline in living standards that exceeds the dismal claims of even the worse pessimists!

There are three basic possibilities that would allow us to resolve this contradiction. The contradiction comes from equation (1) where,

$$c = (w/p)^\epsilon$$

since our direct estimates of c, consumption per capita, are much less than the indirect estimate from (w/p) and ϵ. Thus one or more of the following happened: (1) we missed a source of consumption in 1850, (2) the income elasticity of demand for food, ϵ, was much lower in the Industrial Revolution period than the cross-section studies imply, or (3) real wages, w/p, did not rise as much as recent studies suggest. I think that the resolution of the paradox may contain elements of all of the above possibilities.

One thing that can partially resolve this paradox is to widen the definition of the agricultural sector. The preindustrial agricultural sector provided not just food, it also provided the raw materials for clothing and bedding (wool, flax, dyestuffs, hides) and housing and furnishings (wood), and energy in the forms of wood and fodder for horses, as well as energy for human labor. If we look at imports circa 1850 we find that a lot of them supply raw materials that previously must have come from agriculture: cotton, wool, flax, hemp, hides, and wood. The coal industry in Britain greatly increased its output during the Industrial Revolution, supplying coal for fuel to households that would have previously relied on wood, turf, or furze for fuel and tallow candles for light, and supplying coal to such energy-intensive activities as brick making.

If we broaden our definition of "agriculture" to include these raw materials and energy-producing activities, then we get the picture of output and "imports," where imports now include the production of the coal-mining industry, as shown in Table 4.5. As can be seen using this broader definition, the share of "imports" in consumption in 1850 is 55 percent if we only count coal used for domestic heating or 81 percent if we count all coal. Such imports in 1770 are very much smaller. This implies that if the output of the agricultural sector increased by 50 percent from 1770 to 1850, consumption per capita of all the products of agriculture fell in the same interval by *only* 2 to 12 percent. Given that on the basis of an income elasticity of demand for food products of 0.7 we expect to see this rise by about 50 percent, we are still left with a huge unexplained gap between the anticipated demands for agricultural products in the mid-nineteenth century and the supplies of these products. The pessimists regarding the Industrial Revolution who claimed that real consumption standards stagnated or declined can take comfort in these figures.[33]

This story also implies that as a result of greater trade opportunities British agriculture in the period of the Industrial Revolution was becoming more specialized in food production and was getting out of producing such things as dyes, fuel, wood, and fibers.

But even with these generous corrections for "imports" of energy and raw materials, we are left with a "food gap" at the end of the Industrial Revolution period of at least 32 to 44 percent of expected consumption. Where is the missing food? The gap between the demands of the population for food and other agricultural products and the implied supplies from British agriculture can be reconciled in two remaining ways. Either real incomes rose less than is implied by the wage and cost-of-living series of such as Williamson and Lindert or the normal Engel's Law relationship between income and food expenditures did not hold for Britain during the Industrial Revolution period.

---

[33] An additional problem with this resolution is that by widening the definition of agriculture we also include products such as fibers and wood that have a higher income elasticity. This increases the expected rise in consumption per capita.

TABLE 4.5 "Food" Production and Imports, Britain, 1770 and 1850 (£ millions)

	Production 1846-1849	Imports 1846-1849	Production 1770	Imports 1770
Traditional Agriculture (grains, meat, dairy, eggs, sugar, wine, wool)	124	30	?	2
Including coffee, tea, tobacco, fibers, wood, hides, tallow, and domestic coal	127	69	?	9
All the above plus all other coal	127	102	(85)	13

Sources: John (1989); Mitchell (1988, pp. 221-234); Schumpeter (1960). Coal production from Flinn (1984, pp. 26, 303-305) and Church (1986, pp. 19, 53, 85-97).

There seems some room for maneuver in both directions. On the consumption side, one possible effect may have resulted from changes in residence and occupation during the Industrial Revolution, which could have reduced food expenditures at any given real income level. The Industrial Revolution saw a great change in occupations and in the location of the population. Agricultural work was energy intensive, so that workers had to consume large quantities of calories. This is borne out by a survey of the consumption of agricultural laborers conducted in 1862. The poorest of these workers, who were indeed the poorest workers in Britain in this period, consumed about 2,700 calories per day per adult male equivalent. But the more highly paid of these workers were consuming over 4,000 calories per day, far above modern consumption levels. Controlling for income, agricultural workers consumed perhaps 10 percent more food in value terms than urban workers in 1863.[34] Unfortunately, with only 17 to 30 percent of the population shifted from agriculture to other occupations in the Industrial Revolution, this implies that food demand in 1850 would

---

[34] See Clark, Huberman, and Lindert (1993).

have been 2 to 3 percent less than anticipated. This is a small effect, but if some of the higher consumption of agricultural workers came from their residence in the country, which imposed more energy demands in general for walking and entertainment, then the overall effect of industrialization might be greater, since a greater share of the population would be affected.

The other possibility we have to consider is that real income gains for the mass of workers are overstated by the standard series on wages and prices for the Industrial Revolution period. If there was little rise in living standards for the mass of people during the Industrial Revolution, then the failure of consumption of agricultural products per person to rise would be accounted for. The main issue here is whether the price indices we have for the cost of living understate the increase in the Industrial Revolution. Constructing accurate cost-of-living indices is difficult because of the lack of information on retail prices of some important elements of consumption -- particularly housing costs and clothing costs. The housing cost series Lindert and Williamson employ, by necessity, uses the rents on one set of rural cottages in Staffordshire as an index for housing costs in the entire country (Lindert and Williamson, 1983b, p. 9). Also, the clothing cost index in the years after 1800 is based on the cost of cloth and not on the cost of made-up clothing and shoes, which incorporates the technologically untransformed process of making the clothing from the raw cloth.

Mokyr has looked at the consumption of imported products such as tea, coffee, sugar, and tobacco as an index of living standards in Britain in the Industrial Revolution period. There was little increase in consumption per capita of most of these products from 1794 to 1850, even though the relative prices of these items did not increase.[35] This again is evidence for a failure of real incomes to increase during the period of the Industrial Revolution. The Smith Survey of 1862, alluded to previously, contains evidence that strengthens the pessimistic conclusions Mokyr draws from this data. For the survey shows that the income elasticity of demand for tea, coffee, and sugar was high, implying that there should have been robust increases in consumption

---

[35] Indeed, an extension of the sugar consumption per capita series back to 1770 shows that from 1770 to 1850 there was no clear upward trend in sugar consumption per capita once price changes are controlled for (Clark, Huberman, and Lindert, 1993).

per capita if there was strong real income growth. Even worse for the proponents of real income gains, at the same level of income per capita city dwellers consumed 17 percent more tea and coffee and about 13 percent more sugar than the rural population. This implies that consumption of tea, coffee, and sugar should have been increasing from 1790 to 1850, even if incomes per capita did not increase much just from the increasing urbanization of the population.

We can find other evidence in the movement of domestic agricultural output to support the idea that the problem lies in the real wage series. From the Smith Survey of 1862 we can calculate the income elasticity of demand for various food products. For grain and potato products this is only 0.23, so a 1 percent increase in real income increases consumption per capita by only 0.23 percent. But for meat and dairy products the elasticity is 1.12. This implies that if real incomes really doubled in the course of the Industrial Revolution, British agriculture should have undergone a very large structural transformation from producing grain products to producing animal products. Indeed, animal products output should have quadrupled from 1770 to 1850, while grain outputs would need only have doubled. The limited direct evidence from the agricultural sector suggests that no such transformation was taking place. The area under grains was not decreasing, and the animal stock was not increasing much.

Thus the pessimists, such as Mokyr, who believe that there was little increase in consumption per capita in the Industrial Revolution period, and perhaps even a decrease, can find plenty of evidence from British agriculture to support this conclusion. But the issue remains a puzzling and intriguing one, since if there was little growth in real incomes we confront various other problems. Feinstein estimates that output per person grew by 124 percent from 1770 to 1850; Crafts more modestly estimates that it grew by only 65 percent (Crafts, 1985a, p. 95; Feinstein, 1981, p. 141). Part of this is an assumed substantial contribution from agriculture, but even if we remove this there would be robust increases in output per capita. Where did that extra output go if not to the mass of food consumers? There is little sign of any surge in inequality in the Industrial Revolution period.[36] Thus we see

---

[36] Williamson (1985) reports that the period from 1770 to 1850 saw significant increases in income inequality, but Feinstein (1988b) shows that a constant level of inequality over this period is more plausible.

that our failure to observe an agricultural revolution anytime from 1700 to 1850 threatens to unravel the whole Industrial Revolution.

If output per acre rose by as much as 50 percent during the Industrial Revolution, then output per worker had to remain constant in this period. This implies that if the share of the labor force in agriculture in 1850 was 25 percent then the share in 1770 would be 42 percent. This is a surprisingly small share. As we saw above Crafts assumes that 48 to 56 percent of the population was in agriculture in 1760, and Allen's estimates imply that the share was even higher at 60 percent. This implies that prior to the Industrial Revolution the majority of the population of the country was not engaged in agriculture. Since there was little productivity change in the early eighteenth century, it further implies that if consumption per capita was constant over this interval the share of the labor force in agriculture in 1700 was still only 42 percent. Thus before the classic Industrial Revolution of the cotton mills, the steam engine, and the railway there must have been a "proto-industrial" revolution in the countryside, employing the surplus labor created by agricultural advance.

One way that total output in British agriculture could have risen by more than 50 percent that is consistent with the observed increase in productivity is if output per worker or per unit of capital had actually fallen. Suppose, for example, that more output was obtained by intensifying the application of labor to agriculture. Suppose by this means that output in agriculture was increased by 75 percent instead of 50 percent. Then output per worker must have correspondingly fallen by about 14 percent. But in this case the share of the labor force in agriculture in 1770 **falls** to 31 percent. There is thus almost no movement from agriculture to industry in the course of the Industrial Revolution! Thus it seems there is little room to generate gains in agricultural output through intensification without implying that a very small share of the labor force was in agriculture in 1770.

If agriculture already had such a high productivity level in England by the early eighteenth century, we are then faced with several other odd implications. In the literature on agricultural innovation in Britain it is widely reported that many of the innovations that are presumed to have eventually increased yields per acre -- most importantly sowing clover and turnips in the arable rotation -- were introduced from the advanced agriculture of the Low Countries in the seventeenth century (Fussell, 1959). But we see from Tables 4.1 and 4.3 that the estimated productivity of Low Countries agriculture in the mid-nineteenth century was only about 75 percent of that in Britain, so that British agriculture in the early eighteenth century seemingly had higher productivity than that of the Low Countries 150 years later. The British of the late seventeenth century seemingly would have little to learn from the Low Countries unless they adopted these innovations very quickly indeed.

The data in Table 4.1 also imply that if the agricultural revolution did not occur in the years 1700-1850, it must have occurred sometime between 1300 and 1700. For the implied productivity levels in the early eighteenth century are more than double those of medieval England using the most complete method of calculating productivity. Either that or medieval agriculture in Britain was much more productive than we have been led to believe.

8. The Causes of Increasing Grain Yields

The one well-attested improvement in agriculture that we do see in the period 1700 to 1850 is increases in grain yields. These, as we have already noted, seem to be the major source of measured productivity growth in British agriculture in this period. Why did grain yields increase?

There have been many theories explaining the rise of grain yields, including better cultivation of the land and the gradual evolution of better seed varieties. But the best candidate for explaining the increase in yields, the *nitrogen theory*, states that the nitrogen input for grain crops before the agricultural revolution was too small.

This is the argument of the Postan thesis on low medieval yields (Postan, 1966) and of Kerridge (1967), Chorley (1981), and Shiel (1991). When systematic experiments on plant nutrition began in England at Rothamsted in 1843, it was quickly established that at pre-1850 yields the key constraint on the growth of grain crops was the supply of nitrogen. The key to boosting the nitrogen input in preindustrial agriculture was to keep some of the land under nitrogen-fixing plants, such as clover.

Many writers have assumed that the only effective way to increase the supply of nitrogen was to introduce clover into the arable rotation.[37]

---

[37] See, for example, Chorley (1981).

Clover fixes much more nitrogen than other leguminous crops found in traditional rotations, such as beans and peas. Thus there has been a lot of research regarding the introduction and diffusion of clover in British agriculture. It is assumed that sown clover was a technical innovation that adventitiously appeared in the seventeenth century from the Low Countries. But other economic forces may have been at play, making clover a more attractive crop to use after 1700. For the period 1600 to 1750 saw a substantial decline in interest rates, to about half their level in 1600. Since the nitrogen fixed by clover would be released slowly to subsequent crops, the desirability of using clover in rotations would depend on the interest rate, which determines how valuable future benefits are compared to present ones. Thus there may have been price effects speeding the introduction of nitrogen-fixing crops just prior to the Industrial Revolution (Clark, 1992a).

9. Enclosure and the Labor Supply for Industrialization

Although we have already noted that enclosure had little effect on productivity in British agriculture, it has been argued that enclosure may have had significant effects on the rate at which labor moved out of agriculture and into industry. There is an argument of long standing, found in Marx for instance, that enclosure indirectly speeded industrialization and urbanization in Britain by creating an impoverished, landless rural proletariat that was rapidly displaced from the countryside (Marx, [1867] 1977, pp. 877-895, 908-913).[38] The claim is that enclosures would result in the loss of common rights for laborers and cottagers and would eliminate very small holders because of the costs of fencing their tiny holdings after enclosure. Parliamentary enclosure bills certainly frequently ran into opposition, implying that not everyone felt he or she would benefit from enclosure (Beckett, 1990, p. 42).

The argument has been nicely formalized by Cohen and Weitzman (1975). In their analysis they argue that enclosure was desired by owners purely because it eliminated the access of the village poor to various communal rights, such as fuel cutting, grazing, and squatting on the commons. This would imply that all the rent increase upon

---

[38] The most clear-cut enunciation of the view that enclosure served to deprive the landless and smallholders of their means of livelihood in the countryside is given by the Hammonds (Hammond and Hammond, 1911).

enclosure was represented by a loss to someone elsewhere. Enclosure was a redistribution of income from the landless laborers to the landowning class. But curiously in Cohen and Weitzman's analysis, this transfer of ownership rights would still represent an efficiency gain in the economy at large, which would show up as a more efficient distribution of labor between agriculture and industry. To see this, suppose that there was a minimum wage w_0 that a worker in agriculture had to receive to prevent him from leaving the agricultural sector and moving to the urban sector, which was determined by the wage in towns. Assume that the agricultural wage is kept at this minimum level by the rise of the rural population. The wage of workers in the countryside, w_0, will have two components -- the market wage, w_m, the agricultural worker receives and the common rights in the village that each worker enjoys, s: $w_0 = w_m + s$. When common rights were extinguished upon enclosure, the rural wage would drop below the wage needed to keep labor in the countryside. Thus workers would migrate to the cities until labor became scarce enough that $w_m = w_0$. The workers left in each individual village would be no worse off after enclosure, but there would be fewer of them. But the common rights that had previously been dissipated in keeping extraneous workers in the rural sector would now be a benefit to society.[39] Thus even an enclosure movement that sought purely to grab for the landowners the common rights of the laborers could result in gains to national income, in the sense that the income gained by the landlords would exceed that lost by the workers. As previously noted, the overall effects on the productivity of the economy would be small, since the transferred rents were small relative to GNP. But if the value of extra workers in the agricultural sector in producing extra output declined slowly as extra workers were added, then the redistribution could have had a big effect on the allocation of labor between agriculture and industry.

The actual effect of enclosure on pushing labor out of the agricultural sector has been a hotly debated topic. In the Cohen and Weitzman model, it depends on the assumption that there were significant common rights that were extinguished upon enclosure. As we have already seen, no one knows the significance of these rights. To test whether enclosure did result in an expulsion of labor from the

---

[39] Though a benefit that accrued to the landowners.

agricultural sector, historians have examined the movement of population over time in villages that were enclosed and unenclosed. The results show that in the post-1750s wave of Parliamentary Enclosures, there was no effect on population growth (Chambers, 1953; Gonner, 1966, p. 411-415). But Allen (1992b) finds that enclosures prior to 1675 did result in locales having significantly lower rates of population growth up until 1850. He conjectures that the reason is that earlier enclosures took place mainly when there was only one landowner or a small number of landowners in a village. The Poor Law in England required each parish to be responsible for all those who had acquired a "settlement" in the parish; normally a settlement was acquired by residing in the parish for more than a year. Since the poor were paid for by a tax on property, large landowners had an incentive to limit population to the available employment opportunities. They would do this by controlling house building and limiting households to one family. But in parishes with a large number of property owners, the incentive of each not to lease land for building would be much smaller. In confirmation of this reasoning, Allen shows that the rate of population growth in villages is predicted better by ownership concentration than by the date of enclosure. Thus Allen conjectures that those parishes that enclosed early would expel their surplus populations, and limit population growth, merely because they were parishes of concentrated ownership (Allen, 1992b, pp. 36-55).

Humphries has recently considered the effect of enclosure on the economic status of women and argues that the dispossessed under enclosure were largely women. The communal rights of the poor often took the form of access to grazing for cows, which provided women with income and employment in milking and butter and cheesemaking. The loss of common rights thus disproportionately hurt women, who lost most rural employment opportunities (Humphries, 1990).

10. Conclusion

We started by presenting the seemingly irrefutable evidence of a remarkable transformation of British agriculture, after centuries of stagnation, at exactly the time of the Industrial Revolution. But we then found apparently incontrovertible evidence, mainly from prices but with support from other considerations, that the agricultural sector was not transformed then but in some previous unheralded period of British history. This new evidence, if accepted, has wider ramifications for such issues as the movement of living standards in the Industrial Revolution, the rate of economic growth in the Industrial Revolution, and the extent of industrial development prior to the Industrial Revolution. This matter will not be resolved until we can somehow explain away one of these conflicting bodies of evidence. Thus the performance of agriculture in Britain has become central to most of the key debates on the Industrial Revolution. The good news is that there is certainly enough information available from prices, wages, and rents in the agricultural sector to eventually provide a definitive solution to the conundrum we have uncovered.

5

The Role of Human Capital
in the First Industrial Revolution[1]

David Mitch

It is a commonplace of modern economic policy discussions that a nation must have a well-educated work force to be competitive in the international marketplace (Chubb and Moes, 1990, pp. 8-9; M.I.T. Commission on Industrial Productivity, 1989, chap. 6; Reich, 1991). There are indications, however, that the first nation to undergo an industrial revolution had an only modestly educated work force. At the onset of England's Industrial Revolution in the late eighteenth century, barely half of its adult population could sign their names (at marriage), a rate that had not improved significantly by 1840, while England's first and most important stage of industrialization is commonly viewed as encompassing the period 1780-1830 (Schofield, 1973). As early as the 1850s, concern was being expressed about British loss of technological leadership resulting from, among other factors, the poor state of the nation's technical education (Pollard, 1989, pp. 116-117; Roderick and Stephens, 1981, pp. 221, 244). In the late eighteenth century, England's universities were generally viewed as corrupt and stagnant, especially in contrast with the intellectual vitality of Scottish and Dutch universities of the day (Lawson and Silver, 1973, pp. 209-218; O'Day, 1982, chaps. 11-12, 14).

There are three ways of resolving the contradiction between the claim that education is a prerequisite to economic growth and the apparent educational mediocrity of the first industrial nation. First, it can be argued that the level of formal education of England's work force

[1] Helpful comments received from the editor and Steven Nicholas are gratefully acknowledged.

during its Industrial Revolution has been understated or that the importance of informal methods of obtaining skills has been neglected. Alternatively, it can be argued that the importance of education to economic growth has been overstated and that economies can compensate (whether readily or with difficulty) for poorly educated work forces by other offsetting advantages. Finally, one can recognize that there are elements of truth in both positions and that it is necessary to accurately assess the extent of education in a work force and to avoid overstating the importance of education to economic growth. This chapter will consider the case for each of these positions. Whatever position prevails, the English Industrial Revolution clearly poses interesting questions for assessing the role of education in economic growth.

Education of the English Work Force
on the Eve of the Industrial Revolution

On the eve of its Industrial Revolution, England lacked a centralized organization for the propagation of education. Local endowments and charitable subscriptions, some existing for centuries, supported primary and secondary education. The Society for Promoting Christian Knowledge sponsored charity schools earlier in the eighteenth century, but it is a matter of dispute how far they spread (Jones, 1938; Simon, 1968). Myriad other types of schools, academies, and lecture series were also established in the eighteenth century; again it is unclear how extensive they were (Hans, 1951; Lawson and Silver, 1973, pp. 218-220; Simon, 1979). Surveys conducted at the behest of Parliament in 1818 and 1833 reveal that the majority of all elementary school students at the time were enrolled in private, for-profit schools (Mitch, 1982, p. 226). The proportion was probably no lower in the third quarter of the eighteenth century. It was also common for people to acquire basic literacy skills informally from relatives, acquaintances, or neighbors (Laqueur, 1976a; Spufford, 1979). As for higher education, Oxford dated back to the twelfth century and Cambridge to the thirteenth. Both universities had close ties to the church and also benefited from royal endowments.[2]

---

[2] Henry VIII, for example, established the Regius professorships of divinity, Greek, Hebrew, medicine, and civil law at each university, and in 1724 George I endowed them with a Regius chair of modern history.

The prevailing view of England's various educational institutions in the late eighteenth century is one of unrelenting mediocrity. Revisionists, however, have challenged this view, and Nicholas Hans has gone so far as to argue that the eighteenth century was an educational golden age for England, although his evidence has been criticized (Hans, 1951; Simon, 1979). Current scholarship generally continues to support the conclusion that education in the eighteenth century was mediocre, and this is commonly accounted for by the lack of government involvement. However, there is also a case for the revisionist interpretation that private education satisfied the demands of eighteenth-century English society. Support for this claim requires a more detailed review of the state of education at various levels in the mid-eighteenth century.

At the elementary level, a number of quantitative indicators point to educational mediocrity. Marriage register evidence indicates that large numbers of English adults in the third quarter of the eighteenth century were unable to sign their names. The national sample of 274 parishes constructed by Schofield (1973) indicates that about two-thirds of all grooms and two-fifths of all brides could sign their names at marriage in the 1770s. Although some of those who could not sign their names may still have been able to read, studies suggest that signature ability correlates with the ability to read well (Schofield, 1968). Moreover, the large number of adults who were unable to sign their names correlates with the lack of primary school education. Although the extent of elementary schooling is not known, there are indications that many parishes in England had no schools.[3]

The signature ability of England's adult population in the mid-eighteenth century was by no means worse than that of the rest of Europe on average.[4] But there were a number of areas of Europe, as

---

[3] The archbishop's visitation returns for the York diocese in 1743 indicate that 41 percent of the 645 parishes surveyed had no school, and the bishop's visitation articles for Oxford diocese in 1738 indicate that 70 percent of the 179 parishes surveyed had none (Lawson and Silver, 1973, pp. 191-192).

[4] A survey of the evidence for all of northwestern Europe concludes that, as of 1800, "more than half of adult males could sign their names and still more could read a simple text" (Houston, 1988, p. 150). For France as a whole, the signature rate at marriage during the period 1786 to 1790 has been estimated at only 47 percent for men and 27 percent for women (Graff, 1987,

well as New England, that are generally regarded as having a far more distinguished educational record.[5]

Scotland, in particular, has been commended for having a stronger educational system than England (Graff, 1987, pp. 246-48; Houston, 1985; Houston, 1988; O'Day, 1982, chap. 12). Its educational excellence has been attributed to (1) the emphasis of Scottish Reformation Protestantism and, in particular, John Knox's 1560 *Book of Discipline* on the role of education in moral and religious upbringing; (2) state provisions that evolved over the seventeenth century requiring each parish to establish a school; and (3) a tradition in which social mobility was seen to be acheivable through education (summarized by reference to "the lad of parts," the boy of humble origins who attained at least middle-class status through education). Registrar General's statistics indicate that by the mid-nineteenth century, signature rates in Scotland were higher than in England, and Stone has extrapolated from these figures that by 1750 as many as 75 percent of Scots getting married could sign their names (Stone, 1969, p. 127).

The claim that Scotland had higher literacy rates and superior provision of elementary schools than England has been challenged (Houston, 1985).[6] Houston and others have pointed out, for example, that well into the eighteenth century, many parishes in Scotland still did not support a single school despite the provisions of a law promulgated in 1696 (Houston, 1985, pp. 101, 113, 115, 146; Smout, 1969, p. 453). Many other Scottish parishes covered such large areas or had such large populations that a single school would fall far short of meeting their needs. Houston has also revised estimates of Scottish literacy for the mid-eighteenth century to challenge views that Scottish literacy

---

p. 193). In Spain and Russia, literacy rates had barely reached that level by the end of the nineteenth century (Cipolla, 1969, table 130).

[5] In the Catholic Mittalrhein region of Germany, in the late eighteenth century, over 80 percent of males and nearly two-thirds of females were able to sign their names at marriage (Graff, 1987, p. 188). In Iceland and Sweden, catechism surveys indicate near universal reading ability by the mid-nineteenth century (Graff, 1987, pp. 223-230).

[6] Much has also been made of high literacy levels in Sweden during the eighteenth century. But this claim has been challenged as well. See Sandin (1988).

rates before 1800 were substantially higher than English literacy rates.[7]

Defenders of England's provision of primary education in the eighteenth century have pointed to the networks of informal education noted previously. They have argued that the impact of these networks was enhanced by the incorporation of the printed word into popular culture through materials as diverse as religious tracts and melodramatic broadsides (Laqueur, 1976a; Spufford, 1979). They have also pointed to the numerous private, for-profit elementary schools aimed at the working classes (Higginson, 1974; Laqueur, 1976b). These schools have been commonly termed "dame schools" in light of the view that they were often run by elderly women, and whether they did more than provide a child-minding service has been hotly contested (Gardner, 1984; Hurt, 1971; Laqueur, 1976b; Leinster-Mackay, 1976; West, 1971).

Yet, notwithstanding the possibility that England's relative literacy standing and the accomplishments of informal education and private schools have been unjustly downgraded, one cannot ignore Schofield's (1973) clear evidence from marriage registers that just over half of the English adult population in the mid-eighteenth century had basic literacy skills.

The quality of education in the mid-eighteenth century has been viewed as worse at higher levels, which many accounts depict as stagnant and decadent. Revisionist historians have effectively argued that these depictions are exaggerated, but they do not give reason for thinking that accomplishments in secondary and higher education were any better than mediocre.

The backbone of English secondary education in the mid-eighteenth century was the grammar school, though it should be noted that the dividing line was often vague in grammar schools between secondary and primary education. There is little question that endowed

---

[7] Houston estimates adult male illiteracy rates in the Scottish Lowlands in the mid-eighteenth century at about 35 percent, only slightly better than Schofield's estimate for English males at this time of about 40 percent. In the Scottish Highlands, Houston estimates that adult male illiteracy rates in the mid-eighteenth century were 55 to 60 percent, substantially worse than in England (Houston, 1985, p. 56). Houston's estimates of female illiteracy are less precise but also suggest no marked advantage of Scotland over England for the mid-eighteenth century (Houston, 1985, pp. 57-70).

English grammar schools in the mid-eighteenth century had seen better days, especially during the expansion they experienced following the Reformation.[8] But how degenerate they had become has been disputed. Tompson argues that the extent of corruption has been exaggerated. Outright sinecures and cases of fraud, he found, were relatively infrequent (Tompson, 1971). In many instances, he argues, attempts to alter the arrangements of the original endowments reflected efforts to innovate and introduce new subjects or to adjust to changed circumstances.[9] Moreover, the rise in the eighteenth century of dissenting academies was by all accounts an important progressive aspect of secondary education. The development of dissenting academies encompassed three phases: (1) their foundation by individual clergy ejected from the Church of England; (2) their support, in the first half of the eighteenth century, by broader groups of dissenters, including individual churches and subscription funds; and (3) in the second half of the eighteenth century, their role in providing professional education, especially practical business education -- at this stage, they offered dissenting students with a viable alternative to university education (O'Day, 1982, pp. 213-215; Parker, [1914] 1969).

Overall, it is reasonably clear that conflicting forces were at work in secondary education during the eighteenth century. On the one hand, the endowments of many grammar schools had diminished in value in

---

[8] Lord Chief Justice Kenyon asserted in 1795 that many grammar school endowments had been corrupted to such an extent that they constituted "empty walls without scholars, and everything neglected but the receipt of salaries and emoluments. In some instances that have lately come within my own knowledge, there was not a single scholar in the schools though there were very large endowments to them" (Tompson, 1971, p. 100). This view was echoed by Arthur F. Leach, according to whom endowed grammar schools experienced a "late eighteenth century blight," the key components of which were "curricular 'degradation,' managerial corruption, and enrolment decline" (Tompson, 1971, p. 6).

[9] The apparent decline of grammar schools in England in the eighteenth century, according to O'Day (1982, pp. 197-204), reflected the declining availability of positions for clergy and, hence, demand for the classical education that grammar schools provided to prepare students for such positions. In support of this, she notes that some schools shifted from the traditional classical curriculum to one that included modern languages, accounting, and preparation for military and commercial vocations.

the late seventeenth and early eighteenth centuries. On the other hand, a new source of demand for secondary education was coming from students seeking commercial and other types of practical education, as reflected in the rise of the dissenting academies. The lack of aggregate figures on secondary enrollments or their trends during the eighteenth century makes it difficult to establish the net effect of these conflicting forces. There is not enough evidence to completely overturn traditional views of mediocrity, but clearly, secondary education was not universally stagnant.

Indications of decline at the university level are the most telling of all. Enrollments at Oxford and Cambridge were lower in the mid-eighteenth century than at any other point between 1650 and 1850 (Stone, 1974). In 1776, Adam Smith wrote of Oxford in the *Wealth of Nations* that "the greater part of the publick professors have, for these many years, given up altogether the pretence of teaching" (Smith, [1776] 1976, p. 761). And numerous other accounts have echoed Smith's contempt (Gibbon, [1796] 1961, chap. 3; Lawson and Silver, 1973, pp. 212, 214; Sutherland, 1973). According to one historian of Cambridge, "the professors of the eighteenth century have incurred the indignant scorn of posterity, and for the most part they deserve it" (Winstanley, 1935, p. 95). In contrast, the eighteenth century is viewed as a golden age for Scottish universities. While enrollments declined at Oxford and Cambridge, those at Scottish universities rose from 1,000 in 1700 to 2,700 in 1800 (O'Day, 1982, p. 277). While Cambridge and Oxford were still bound by the classical curricula set in place in 1570 and 1636, respectively, Scottish universities were actively introducing modern courses into their curricula (Lawson and Silver, 1973, p. 210).[10]

Although no one has argued that the eighteenth century was a golden age for Oxford or Cambridge, their defenders assert that the reports of

---

[10] The University of Edinburgh was especially notable for its advances, adding four chairs in law and four in science in the eighteenth century. Perhaps most significant of all was the faculty of medicine, which Edinburgh established in 1726 (O'Day, 1982, pp. 273-75; Smout, 1969, p. 476). Edinburgh and Glasgow were far more prominent centers for medical education in the eighteenth century than Oxford and Cambridge, and it is even likely that more *Englishmen* in the eighteenth century received medical training at Scottish universities than at the English universities (Inkster, 1991, pp. 75-76; O'Day, 1982, pp. 273-75; Smout, 1969, p. 478).

stagnation and slothfulness were exaggerated. According to Lucy Sutherland, serious teaching did occur at Oxford, and there is evidence of
rigorous assignments and examinations despite the testimony of Gibbon
and others to the contrary (Lawson and Silver, 1973, p. 212; O'Day,
1982, p. 275; Sutherland, 1973). And she argues that useful, if not
especially distinguished or original, scholarship and writing was
produced by Oxford fellows and professors (Sutherland, 1973). Despite
the traditional curricula and the emphasis on classics at Oxford and on
mathematics at Cambridge, capped off at both by examinations modeled
on scholastic disputations, opportunities to study more modern subjects
increased over the eighteenth century.[11]

In evaluating England's intellectual resources at the start of its
industrial revolution, it is important not to focus too heavily on the
shortcomings of Oxford and Cambridge. Higher intellectual pursuits
in the sciences and arts could flourish outside the universities. By the
early eighteenth century, it was common for free-lance lecturers in the

---

[11] New professorships were established at Cambridge and Oxford in the
eighteenth century in poetry, Anglo-Saxon, Arabic, chemistry, astronomy,
botany, and geology, in addition to the Regius chairs of modern history
previously mentioned (Lawson and Silver, 1973, p. 212). Musson and Robinson
note of Oxford and Cambridge in the eighteenth century, "science was being
studied there and increasing attention was being devoted to its industrial
applications" (Musson and Robinson, 1969, p. 167). One example of the
strengths and weaknesses of science at Oxford and Cambridge in the later
eighteenth century is provided by the case of Richard Watson, who became
Professor of Chemistry at Cambridge in 1764. Watson is often cited as an
example of the low state of science at Cambridge at this time. Watson himself
conceded that at the time of his appointment, he "knew nothing at all of
Chemistry, had never read a syllable on the subject; nor seen a single
experiment in it" (cited in Musson and Robinson, 1969, p. 167). However,
Watson worked energetically to remedy his ignorance of chemistry; his
lectures became quite popular; and among his published works on chemistry,
his *Chemical Essays* went through eleven editions and, according to Musson and
Robinson, "became one of the most widely read and appreciated books on
chemistry of the age" (Musson and Robinson, 1969, p. 168). What is of further
interest about Watson is his focus on applied chemistry. And interest in the
application of science to practical problems seems to have characterized other
teachers of science at Oxford and Cambridge in the late eighteenth and early
nineteenth centuries as well (Musson and Robinson, 1969, pp. 177-178).

sciences to offer lecture series for an admission fee in London and in the major provincial cities, such as Birmingham and Manchester (O'Day, 1982, p. 210).[12] Although such lecture courses may have fallen far short of universities as intellectual communities, they did offer flexibility and responsiveness to community interests (Inkster, 1991).

In sum, if England was not educationally distinguished in the mid-eighteenth century, it did have important educational resources available to its labor force. Although the expansion that occurred in the later nineteenth century can arguably be viewed as evidence of the importance of government support for education, the educational level of workers in the mid-eighteenth century is testimony that much was accomplished in the absence of extensive state activity.

What Happened to Educational Attainment During the Industrial Revolution?

On initial consideration, there would seem little question about general educational trends in England during its industrial revolution, 1780 to 1830. The national sample of 274 parishes constructed by Schofield reveals a modest improvement in signature rates at marriage during this period, about 60 percent for grooms and 40 percent for brides in 1780, rising to about 65 percent for grooms and 50 percent for brides in 1830 (Schofield, 1973). These trends, sluggish compared with the marked rise to almost universal literacy in the seventy years after 1830, seem consistent with the nation's limited efforts at providing subsidized day schooling compared with the later nineteenth century. At the secondary and university levels, the conditions for reform were being put in place, but direct improvement and expansion did not occur until after 1830.

However, the interpretation of these trends has been controversial. Despite an apparently uniform national trend in literacy and primary schooling, there was considerable variation in trends among individual regions. For example, in Bedfordshire between 1754 and 1844, literacy trends for the county as a whole were stagnant. After deteriorating,

---

[12] For example, John Desaguliers gave lectures in London on mathematics and natural philosophy between 1712 and 1744. He presented a course on mechanics, hydrostatics, pneumatics, and optics that met one evening a week during 1724 and 1725 at a cost of two and a half guineas (Lawson and Silver, 1973, pp. 218-219; O'Day, 1982, p. 210).

male illiteracy returned to its initial level of 55 percent; in contrast, in fourteen individual Bedford parishes male illiteracy fell by more than 10 percent and in twenty-four parishes it rose by more than 10 percent (Schofield 1973, pp. 447-448).

Furthermore, Nicholas and Nicholas (1992) recently found in a study of a sample of English convicts transported to Australia that for male convicts from urban areas, those who had reached the age of ten around 1807 actually had markedly higher literacy rates than those who had reached the age of ten between 1790 and 1795. They also report a less marked improvement in literacy for male convicts from rural areas for those who reached age ten around 1817 compared with those who reached age ten in the early 1790s. But for convicts reaching the age of ten after 1807 for urban males and after 1817 for rural males, Nicholas and Nicholas (1992) find that through 1835 literacy rates fell back toward their levels in the early 1790s.[13]

In Lancashire, where much of England's cotton textile industry was located, Sanderson (1972a) found that signature rates at marriage declined after 1750 and only clearly began to turn up after 1830. Three factors, according to Sanderson, explained these sluggish literacy trends. First, there was a lack of philanthropic funding for new school provision in the second half of the eighteenth century. Second, population growth in the industrializing areas of Lancashire rapidly outstripped school places, especially in subsidized schools. Third, the spread of the factory in cotton textile production increased the demand for child labor and, hence, the opportunity cost of schooling.[14]

---

[13] Nicholas and Nicholas (1992) measure literacy by the responses in convict records to questions as to whether convicts were able to read and write, could read only, or could neither read nor write. This could account for some of the difference between their findings and those of Schofield (1973), who measures literacy by signature ability. Nicholas and Nicholas do not report whether there were shifts in the regional composition of their sample over time. If such shifts were present, then this might make their sample less suitable for measuring national trends than Schofield's sample.

[14] Sanderson, in another article, details how the shift of cotton textile production to the factory increased the demand for children below the age of 10, and hence of prime school age, to tend spinning machinery, piecing broken yarn and scavenging for stray bits of cotton in the vicinity of the machinery (Sanderson, 1968).

The third explanation has provoked the most comment because it suggests that industrialization had an adverse impact on educational conditions, particularly for the working classes. This can be seen as part of the broader debate on the standard of living: Did industrialization improve the lot of the working classes? (Hobsbawm, 1975, p. 183; Nicholas and Nicholas, 1992, p.16).

Critics have questioned Sanderson's interpretation of the dip in literacy in Lancashire. Laqueur constructed an alternative literacy series based on a different sample of parishes (although there is some overlap) and found a downward trend in literacy between 1750 and about 1810 in contrast with the trough in the 1820s reported by Sanderson (Laqueur, 1974). Assuming that signature rates at marriage reflected educational circumstances about fifteen years earlier, Laqueur concluded that the sources of educational decline in Lancashire must have been at work between 1740 and the early 1800s. However, it is accepted that the factory method of production in cotton textiles was introduced into Lancashire in the mid-1770s and would not have influenced marriage register signature rates until the 1790s, well after decline set in and a period in which Laqueur locates an initial rise in these rates. Indeed, it has even been suggested that factory production did not become widespread until the 1790s and thus would have influenced marriage register signature rates only after about 1805, when, by Laqueur's evidence, signature rates were beginning to rise again (West, 1978).[15]

---

[15] In part, the discrepancy between Laqueur's and Sanderson's findings could be due to differences in their samples, neither of which is clearly representative of the population of all marriages in Lancashire cotton textile districts. Moreover, Sanderson focuses primarily on trends between 1813 and 1839, while Laqueur considers the entire period between 1750 and 1840. Perhaps most important of all, Laqueur's findings are based on ten-year averages, while Sanderson considers literacy rates for each year. Laqueur's sample of "industrial Lancashire" reaches a trough in both male and female literacy rates between 1810 and 1820. Although Sanderson's sample reaches a trough in 1814, he argues that literacy trends between 1813 and the late 1820s were so erratic that no clear upward trend can be established. Maintaining that another trough in literacy trends occurred between 1825 and 1830, he concludes that the forces depressing literacy rates were in effect about a decade longer than Laqueur allows for. Laqueur's use of ten-year averages would obscure the marked dip in literacy rates that Sanderson observed between 1826 and 1827 in his sample. Sanderson finds a clear upturn in

In response, Sanderson notes that child labor demand was only one of several influences on literacy trends and that it could have been offset by the rise of the Sunday school in the late eighteenth and early nineteenth centuries and by efforts of church groups to increase the provision of weekday schools (Sanderson, 1974).[16] The impact of child labor demand on literacy trends is still unclear; although, based on Laqueur's analysis, it seems that it was not a dominant one.

Laqueur focuses on the continuous rise in literacy rates in his samples starting in 1810, arguing that they reflect the influence of the factory system. He concludes that "the industrial revolution reversed, rather than initiated, the decline in working-class literacy" (Laqueur, 1974, pp. 100-101). Specifically, he attributes the education revival to the emergence of new educational institutions associated with industrialization (Sunday schools, church-supported day schools, and private schools). The trend seems to suggest that industrialization spurred a growing demand for educated labor. However, Laqueur's own estimates indicate that literacy rates at marriage were no higher for males and slightly higher for females at the end of the Industrial Revolution in the 1840s than they had been in 1750 (Laqueur, 1974, p. 99). One might conclude that negative influences on education offset the positive influence of a growing demand for educated labor; nevertheless, the estimates suggest that this demand did not rise by enough to markedly outweigh these negative influences. Although the in-migration of educated labor might not have been fully reflected in the marriage register evidence and the growth of demands for specific

---

signature rates only from the 1830s, which he attributes to schooling provided by the National Society and other philanthropic groups from the 1810s (Sanderson, 1974, p. 109). Since there is no obvious reason for preferring either Laqueur's or Sanderson's literacy estimates to the other's, the turning points for Lancashire literacy trends remain unclear. Nonetheless, Laqueur's estimates do imply that there were sizable areas of cotton-producing Lancashire where the introduction of the factory was not followed by marked, long-term declines in literacy rates, a result that contradicts the importance of the impact of the factory on opportunity costs and educational trends.

[16] A study by Sylvia Harrop of Cheshire parishes in which textile factories were established reinforces this argument. She finds that literacy trends varied depending on the extent of elite support for day school provision (Harrop, 1983).

types of educated labor might not be evident in aggregate evidence, one
is still struck by the fact that the demand for educated labor during the
Industrial Revolution in Lancashire did not grow by enough to pull
literacy rates significantly above preindustrial levels.[17]

The cotton textile industry has taken on symbolic significance in
accounts of the Industrial Revolution, but educational trends in areas
where cotton textiles figured less prominently also warrant examination. For example, literacy rates in the pottery district of Stoke, the
silk manufacturing district of Macclesfield, and the nail making area of
Dudley were affected in diverse ways by industrialization (Vincent,
1989, pp. 99-104). During industrialization, Stoke experienced an initial
shallow decline followed by erratic recovery, Macclesfield stagnation,
and Dudley a very pronounced decline; in the latter, however, there is
evidence that the decline could have begun before industrialization.
These cases support the hypothesis that industrialization affected
education trends adversely through demographic pressures on school

---

[17] According to E. G. West, "The view that literacy had no major
connexion with economic growth [in Industrial Revolution Lancashire] would
be even further weaker" if one considers the "depressant effect" of Irish
immigration into Lancashire (West, 1978). Irish immigrants, according to
West, would have received "the poorest of educations," so that the increase in
the numbers of Irish immigrants would have lowered literacy rates in
Lancashire between 1781 and 1800. West's main authority for establishing that
Irish immigration into Lancashire was sizable during the Industrial Revolution
is Redford ([1926] 1976, p. 134). However, Bythell argues that Redford
overstates the Irish presence in Lancashire before 1850, and other sources date
the main influx of Irish immigration from the 1820s and later (Bythell, 1969,
p. 63-66; Walton, 1987). West suggests that the Irish worked as unskilled
laborers, in construction for example, and thus released indigenous workers to
manufacturing jobs that had more occasion to use literacy. But if the
composition of labor demand would have been such as to attract sufficient
numbers of illiterate Irish immigrants so as to lower marriage register signature
rates, one must wonder how much the Industrial Revolution was increasing
the demand for literate labor in Lancashire. Finally, West's claim that Irish
immigrants had relatively low literacy rates may be incorrect. Nicholas and
Shergold, in an analysis of convicts transported to Australia between 1817 and
1839, find that Irish immigrants to Lancashire actually had slightly higher
literacy rates than other Lancashire convicts (Nicholas and Shergold, 1987b,
p.171)

facilities and by increasing the demand for child labor. They suggest, moreover, that there was considerable regional variation in the impact of industrialization on education.

Nicholas and Nicholas (1992) emphasize the decline in literacy rates in urban areas toward the end of the Industrial Revolution in their sample of English convicts transported to Australia. They note in particular the decline in male literacy in the north of England, the region they most closely associate with economic change (Nicholas and Nicholas, 1992, p.11). However, as previously noted, their data also show a marked improvement in male literacy in urban areas during the early Industrial Revolution, a result that suggests the presence of conflicting influences on educational trends for the industrial revolution as a whole.

Perhaps the most pervasive educational development of the Industrial Revolution was the rise of the Sunday school. In contrast, centralized provision of primary schooling appears to have been stagnant during the first part of the industrial revolution, up until about 1810; after this, the activities of the National Society and the British and Foreign School Society began to take hold. A common view is that Robert Raikes established the first Sunday schools in Gloucester in the early 1780s, although there is evidence that Sunday schools existed in England at a much earlier date (Laqueur, 1976c, pp. 23-24; O'Day, 1982, p. 255). By 1801, according to a recent estimate, enrollment had grown to over 200,000, by 1818 to 450,000, or 17.6 percent of the English population aged five to fifteen, and by 1833 to 1.36 million, or 45 percent (Laqueur, 1976c, p. 44). At this latter date, enrollment in Sunday schools was 1.2 times enrollment in day schools (Mitch, 1982, p. 230). Laqueur concludes that by the late 1820s virtually every working-class child in England outside of London must have attended a Sunday school at some point (Laqueur, 1976c, p. xi).[18]

---

[18] The parochial surveys of 1833 clearly indicate that the Sunday school was pervasive throughout England and Wales, with per capita enrollment rates in England ranging from a low of 3.7 percent in Middlesex to a high of 18.2 percent in Debyshire (Laqueur, 1976c, p. 49). As the low Middlesex enrollment figures would suggest, London was noted for the relatively low extent of its Sunday school activity (Laqueur, 1976c, pp. 54-58).

In the late eighteenth century, some Sunday schools drew their clientele from the lower middle classes (O'Day, 1982, p. 256), but in the first half of the

Throughout the Industrial Revolution, Sunday schools had a religious sponsorship and orientation from the Church of England and a variety of other denominations.[19] According to Hannah More, one of the early leaders of the Sunday school movement, the purpose of the schools was "to train up the lower classes in habits of industry and piety" (Lawson and Silver, 1973, p. 239). However, at least through the first half of nineteenth century, they also played a role in the secular instruction of the working classes.[20] Surveys of Sunday school

---

nineteenth century, they were attended predominantly by the working classes, including some adults (Laqueur, 1976c, pp. 87-89). About 10 percent of the pupils in the 1830s were over the age of fifteen, even in Sunday schools intended for children; and in the industrial areas of Bury, Salford, Manchester, and Birmingham, between 14 and 18 percent of the pupils were over the age of fifteen (Laqueur, 1976c, p. 90). Enrollments continued to grow after 1850, with rates peaking about 1880 and absolute numbers peaking just before World War I (Laqueur, 1976c, p. 246).

[19] In 1851, after over half a century of rapid expansion, only 3 percent of the Sunday school enrollments reported by the Census of Religion were in nondenominational schools (Laqueur, 1976c, p. 179). In the mid-nineteenth century, somewhat more Sunday schools were affiliated with dissenting denominations than with the Church of England. The tendency of denominational affiliations earlier in the century is less certain (Laqueur, 1976c, pp. 46-53).

[20] Alexander Field has challenged the view that Sunday schools offered secular instruction (Field, 1979). His challenge is based on his finding for Lancashire communities in 1841 that the ratio between Sunday school and weekday school enrollment was systematically related to occupational structure. Field finds that communities with a relatively high proportion of their work forces engaged in cotton textile production also had relatively high Sunday school enrollment rates. His explanation of this result is that communities with relatively large numbers of cotton textile workers were more likely to demand education for its socializing role than for cognitive training. He asserts that Sunday schools were more likely to emphasize the socializing aspects of education and day schools were more likely to emphasize cognitive training and that is why cotton textile communities put more emphasis on Sunday schools. Although Field's results are of interest, they encounter some difficulties. First, in his regression analysis he enters no controls for child labor demand and thus cannot rule out the possibility that cotton textile areas made more use of Sunday schools because of a relatively high weekday demand for child labor. Second, there is no reason why both

curricula conducted between 1834 and 1843 in eleven different cities or regions indicate that 99 percent of the pupils attended schools that taught reading and 21 percent were in schools that taught writing (Laqueur, 1976c, p. 103).[21]

Those who controlled Sunday schools were likely to have influenced what was taught. According to one view, religious and philanthropic groups, reflecting middle- and upper-class interests, used Sunday schools to impose values of piety and orderliness on the working classes. Laqueur has directly attacked that view, arguing that Sunday schools were "indigenous institutions of the working-class community rather than an imposition on it from the outside" (Laqueur, 1976c, p. 61). To support his claim, he puts forward examples of thirty-eight Sunday schools that were started at the initiative of working-class men and women; he asserts, moreover, that most teachers came from the working classes and that after 1810, 60 percent of all Sunday school teachers had once been Sunday school students themselves (Laqueur, 1976c, pp. 189, 252, 254). This evidence has been convincingly criticized, however, on the grounds that the thirty-eight examples

---

weekday and Sunday schools could not have offered both cognitive instruction and instruction focusing on morality and orderly behavior. There is abundant evidence that weekday schools did attempt to teach morality and orderliness as well as cognitive skills (Johnson, 1976; 1977). Admittedly, Sunday schools may have placed more emphasis on moral and religious training than weekday schools, but working-class children and adults attending Sunday schools could still have focused more on the cognitive training they offered than on their moral and religious agenda.

[21] The teaching of writing in Sunday schools was controversial. Some religious leaders argued that it should not be taught on the Sabbath because it would divert attention away from the central religious mission of the Sunday schools. But both in response to working-class demand and out of resentment over hierarchical control, many individual Sunday schools resisted prohibitions on teaching writing (Laqueur, 1976c, chap. 5). Further evidence of at least some secular content in what Sunday schools taught are the numerous spellers and readers designed specifically for Sunday school use (Laqueur, 1976c, pp. 113-119). That Sunday schools taught more than religious doctrine is also suggested by the length of time they were in session on a given Sunday. Surveys indicate that over 90 percent of the schools were in session for at least three hours and over 50 percent for at least four hours (Laqueur, 1976c, p. 106).

cannot accurately be depicted as exhibiting working-class initiative and because the social background of Sunday school teachers reveals little about the values they promoted in the classroom (Dick, 1980).

Sunday schools offered many working-class children their only exposure to formal schooling. The surveys referred to previously indicate that 10 to 55 percent of the children receiving any kind of formal schooling, depending on the region, were enrolled only in Sunday schools (Laqueur, 1976c, p. 99). Biographies of the working classes, which offer the advantage of a lifetime profile of educational experiences, indicate a similar range of individuals whose only education was acquired in Sunday schools.[22]

Based on surveys administered by the Sunday schools themselves and on autobiographical evidence, Laqueur concludes that the contribution of Sunday schools to working-class literacy was significant. However, quantitative analysis raises doubts about whether or not Sunday school attendance improved literacy. Regression analysis of the relationship between literacy rates and both day school and Sunday school enrollment rates at the county and the registration district levels indicates that while day school enrollment had a statistically significant positive association with literacy, Sunday school enrollment had a statistically significant negative association (Mitch, 1992a, 147).[23] And the modest improvement in signature rates at marriage that followed the severalfold increase in enrollment rates in Sunday schools is perhaps

---

[22] For example, in Michael Sanderson's collection of Lancashire biographies, eleven out of the fifty-eight subjects born before 1830 attended Sunday school only, and twenty-three subjects received at least some Sunday school instruction (Mitch, 1992a, pp. 136-137; Sanderson, 1966).

The role of Sunday schools probably changed over the nineteenth century. This is suggested by the changing correlation between weekday and Sunday school enrollment rates across counties. In 1818, the correlation was strongly positive, which could reflect the support that day schools provided for Sunday schools when the latter were first established. But in 1833 and 1851, the correlation was negative, suggesting the two types of schooling were substitutes. In 1858, the correlation was again positive, indicating the development of a more complementary role (Mitch, 1992a, p. 138).

[23] This finding probably reflects the fact that Sunday school enrollment was likely to be higher in an environment not conducive to the acquisition of literacy.

the most telling indication of their limited contribution to working-class literacy.[24]

During the Industrial Revolution, awareness of problems with existing institutions for secondary and higher education developed, and some initial steps were taken to reform and restructure them. But by the end of the Industrial Revolution, this reform process was only beginning. A major complaint against the grammar schools was that they violated the terms of their endowments requiring the provision of free education to students from poor families. However, according to Tompson, "the grammar schools' performance of their charitable function was satisfactory considering the educational and economic pressures acting on the schools" (Tompson, 1971, pp. 125-126). The significant changes that occurred in grammar schools throughout the eighteenth century, according to Tompson, were (1) the "introduction of non-classical subjects, chiefly the three R's; (2) a reduction in the number of pupils receiving classical instruction; (3) an increase in the number of schools charging fees (with over half the schools retaining some free

---

[24] The most optimistic interpretation of the signature rate series constructed by Schofield points to the fall in the proportion of brides unable to sign their names from about 65 percent in 1805 to just under 50 percent in 1840 and a decline for grooms from just over 40 percent to about 35 percent (Schofield, 1973; West, 1978). Schofield does attribute some of the improvement in female literacy to the rise of Sunday schools. However, over this same period, Laqueur's estimates indicate the Sunday school enrollment rates increased at least fivefold (Laqueur, 1976c, p. 44). In assessing the educational contribution of Sunday schools, one should allow both for the adverse influences on education they may have been offsetting and for their role in religious and moral instruction over and above any instruction in literacy skills. But their impact on literacy still appears modest relative to their spectacular increases in enrollments.

The very marked increase in literacy during the early Industrial Revolution that Nicholas and Nicholas (1992, p.9) report for their sample of English convicts could be interpreted as reflecting the contribution of the growth of Sunday schools. However, the problem then remains of accounting for the fall in literacy rates that Nicholas and Nicholas report for the later Industrial Revolution, a period when the growth of Sunday school enrollments continued to be robust.

instruction); and (4) a rising number of schools with boarders" (Tompson, 1971, p. 125).

In the first half of the nineteenth century, the Charity Commission's investigations into the alleged corruption of foundations and endowments for funding secondary schooling contributed to the reform of this level of education. These investigations were conducted between 1819 and 1836. Tompson concludes that the Commission accomplished a good deal in uncovering specific abuses but did little to spur more general reform (Tompson, 1979, pp. 34-36). In the mid-nineteenth century, many observers continued to perceive serious problems with secondary education. The Taunton Commission commented that, "The artizans, the small shopkeepers, the smaller farmers are in many places without any convenient means of educating their children at all, and still more often have no security that what education they do get is good" (Bryant, 1986, pp. 205-206).

By the end of the Industrial Revolution, reform at the university level was just beginning. In the early nineteenth century, examination reforms were implemented, and efforts were made to address the corruption of fellowships and professors who failed to lecture. But it was only in the 1850s, however, that a parliamentary commission was appointed to look into the full-scale reform of Oxford and Cambridge (Green, 1969; Lawson and Silver, 1973, pp. 297-299). And not until the last half of the century did the scholar-researcher come to prominence over the cleric at the two universities (Rothblatt, 1968). After accelerating in the very early nineteenth century, enrollments for the next fifty years at Oxford and Cambridge failed to keep up with population growth (Sanderson, 1972b, p. 3). Both the University of London, a secular institution, and King's College, an institution in London with Anglican affiliations, were founded in 1828 and both had a more professional, utilitarian orientation than Oxford and Cambridge. But any influence of these two institutions would have come only at the very end of the Industrial Revolution.

As noted in the previous section, dissenting academies were a more vibrant source of secondary and higher education than the grammar schools and Oxford and Cambridge. Although their graduates surely added to the quality of the labor force during the Industrial Revolution, this period does not appear to have been one of great expansion for these institutions.

The universities were relatively inactive in spreading scientific and technical knowledge during the Industrial Revolution; however, a variety of informal institutions emerged to perform this task. Scientific lecture series, such as those that occurred in London in the first half of the eighteenth century, flourished in the last half of the century not only in London but also in such major provincial centers such as Manchester, Birmingham, Sheffield, and Leeds, and even in smaller towns, such as Salisbury (Musson and Robinson, 1969, pp. 103-111, 120-121, 129-131, 144, 151, 164). Intellectual associations, with heterogeneous aims and membership, proliferated throughout the eighteenth century.[25] The early nineteenth century saw the establishment of the so-called mechanics institutes. Initially their aim was to provide instruction in science, especially its utilitarian applications, primarily for the more skilled segments of the working classes. There has been some debate about the success of mechanics institutes and whether their clientele increasingly became middle class or came from the working classes seeking education in the rudiments of literacy (Inkster, 1976;

---

[25] The Royal Society of London, which was founded in the seventeenth century and boasted such distinguished members as Newton, Boyle, and Hooke, began during the eighteenth century to cultivate an interest in the applied and utilitarian aspects of science (Jacob, 1988; Musson and Robinson, 1969). In the first half of the eighteenth century, literary and philosophical societies were established in Spalding, Stamford, Peterborough, Boston, and Doncaster (Musson and Robinson, 1969, p. 138), and they became more common in the second half of the century. Their focus also began to shift from literary and philosophical interests to more scientific and technological ones. Numerous offshoots of these as well as new entities with utilitarian interests in science were established. Their activities included organizing lecture series, paper presentations, and discussions on both scientific and more general cultural topics; establishing libraries for the use of members; and arranging for the demonstration and, sometimes, the purchase of scientific equipment. Some of these societies were relatively small and closely knit, such as the famous Lunar Society, which met in Birmingham and consisted of such distinguished members as Boulton, Watt, and Wedgwood (Schofield, 1963). The members of these organizations were commonly middle class with nonconformist religious affiliations, although their backgrounds could vary widely (Jacob, 1988). Agricultural societies constituted yet another type of intellectual society with utilitarian interests.

1983a; 1985).[26] Nevertheless, they provide yet another example of the diversity of educational resources available in England during the Industrial Revolution.

Despite the lack of centralized provision of education, a private market clearly developed to meet educational demands. The only obvious failure of this market was in communities with low population density that were unable to support a school, an obstacle for government provision as well (Mitch, 1992a, p. 149; 1992b). The other criticism of the market provision of education is the inability of parents to choose wisely. It has been argued that the schools supplied by a private market were often run by barely literate teachers, whose classes amounted to no more than child-minding services (Hurt, 1971). Other historians, however, argue that private schools were responsive to parental demands and were denigrated by middle-class observers who were more critical of the moral than of the literacy instruction offered by these private schools (Gardner, 1984; Laqueur, 1976a; West, 1971).[27] Therefore, although there still seems ample ground for characterizing England's educational performance as mediocre throughout the Industrial Revolution, the deficiency was not incontrovertibly on the supply side. And, according to some historians, if one takes into consideration England's informal intellectual resources, the educational level of its work force at the end of the Industrial Revolution was not at all undistinguished (Inkster, 1991; Jacob, 1988; Musson and Robinson, 1969).

---

[26] Some mechanics institutes seem to have evolved from earlier literary and philosphical societies (Inkster, 1985, pp. 4-6). By 1851, enrollments, as reported by the Census of Education, at evening schools (which would have included some mechanics institutes) amounted to only about 40,000; Inkster, however, conjectures that true participation in all forms of these organizations (which he has dubbed "Steam Intellect Societies") could have been almost 500,000 (Inkster, 1985, p. 16). In Liverpool alone around 1850, there were some thirty-nine mechanics institutes and similar self-improvement societies (Inkster, 1985, p. 48). Libraries and museums in conjunction with these societies emerged in the first half of the nineteenth century.

[27] Support for the revisionist view is provided by regressions across registration districts of literacy on school enrollments for the mid-nineteenth century, which indicate that whether a child was enrolled in a private or public school did not significantly influence the probability of being able to sign his or her name at marriage (Mitch, 1992a, pp. 147-148).

The Role of Education in the English Work Force
from 1780 to 1840

Just as in the 1990s, it is often presumed that raising the educational attainment of the work force will increase rates of economic growth, so some historians have asserted that education could have made an important contribution to England's Industrial Revolution (Hartwell, 1971a, p. 243; Stone, 1969, p. 130). However, skepticism has also been expressed about the economically productive value of education in recent times (Blaug, 1976; 1985), and David Landes expresses such skepticism in his now-classic study of the Industrial Revolution: "Although certain workers -- supervisory and office personnel in particular -- must be able to read and do the elementary arithmetical operations in order to perform their duties, a large share of the work of industry can be performed by illiterates; as indeed it was, especially in the early days of the industrial revolution" (Landes, 1969, p. 340). Two important studies were published in the early 1970s that challenged in more detail the contribution of primary education, in the form of literacy, to the English Industrial Revolution. The first, by Michael Sanderson, was based on Lancashire marriage registers from the 1830s. He finds that literacy rates in spinning and weaving occupations for factory cotton production were well under 50 percent and were far lower than literacy rates in more traditional craft occupations. Sanderson summarizes his findings as follows: "One thus finds the interesting situation of an emerging economy creating a whole range of *new* occupations which required even *less* literacy and education than the old ones (Sanderson, 1972a, p. 89 [Sanderson's emphasis]). He explains the low literacy rates of workers in cotton textile factories by citing a description of cotton manufacture in the twentieth century, which states that "the main difficulty in developing the cotton industry lies rather in the fact that it embodies in its 'know-how' a large element of manipulation or skill, i.e., that its processes cannot be described in such detail that a list of instructions can be given for every job" (Sanderson, 1972a, p. 91).

The second study, based on a national sample of marriages, reveals a relatively static level of literacy rates during the Industrial Revolution (Schofield, 1973). After noting high levels of female illiteracy in areas of high female industrial employment, 84 percent in Oldham in 1846, for example, Schofield argues, "Nor does the static nature of male illiteracy, both nationally until the decade 1805-1815, and in several occupational groups until the mid-nineteenth century, lend much support to the notion that an improvement in literacy necessarily precedes or accompanies economic growth."[28]

Recently, Nicholas and Nicholas (1992) have reported for their sample of English convicts declining literacy rates in the later Industrial Revolution for each of their three broad occupational skill classifications: skilled, semiskilled, and unskilled.

Of the two earlier studies, Sanderson's has received the most direct criticism. Laqueur accuses Sanderson of focusing too narrowly on factory work in examining the role of literacy in industrialization. Laqueur asserts of the cotton manufacturing regions of Lancashire, "Not only did the economy require supervisory personnel for whom literacy was necessary, or very nearly so, but it created a whole mass of ancillary jobs -- in engineering, transport, trade, retailing, finance and the older artisanal trades" (Laqueur, 1974, pp. 102-103).

To address the issue that divided Laqueur and Sanderson, one should consider the net tendency of the labor force in Lancashire textile regions to shift from occupations in which literacy is less likely to those in which it is more likely to be used. To address the question for the English Industrial Revolution generally, one should examine the English work force as a whole.

In the early eighteenth century, Mandeville made the case that the vast majority of the work force, whether, agricultural, manufacturing, or tertiary, had little occasion to make use of basic literacy, let alone higher-order skills that may have been acquired through formal education. Indeed, he went so far as to argue for the "Necessity there is for a certain Portion of Ignorance in a well-order'd Society."[29]

---

[28] Schofield continues, "Indeed, this long period of stability, and the marked contrast between the literacy of commercial classes and the illiteracy of much of the industrial labor force, suggest that for England, at least, the causal relationships between literacy and economic growth might profitably be reversed" (Schofield, 1973, pp. 453-454).

[29] Mandeville goes on to argue that Peter the Great was justified in promoting the spread of education only because "in proportion to the Extent of his Dominions and the Multitudes he commands, he had not that Number or Variety of Tradesmen and Artificers which the true Improvement of the Country required, and therefore was in the right in leaving no Stone unturn'd to procure them. But what is that to us who labour under a contrary disease?

There is little evidence during the hundred years after Mandeville made this statement that a marked redistribution occurred in the demands of the English labor market toward jobs in which formal education was strictly required.[30]

The limited extent of any increase in demand for educated labor is evident if one focuses on basic literacy, as commonly measured by

---

In short, Russia has too few Knowing Men, and Great Britain too many" (Mandeville, [1732] 1924, vol.1, p. 322).

[30] Addressing this issue is made difficult by the lack of reliable information on occupational distributions for the English labor force before 1841, when the census began collecting relevant data. However, it is reasonably certain that before 1841 only a small percentage of the labor force held occupations that required extensive formal education. Those categories that would require formal education were commerce and trade, large-scale farming -- which involved accounting and staying apace of new agricultural techniques -- and the professions. Lindert and Williamson's reworking of Massie's social tables for 1759 and Colquhoun's for 1802-1803 indicates a decline between those years in the percentage of the English labor force engaged in commerce and trade, agriculture -- excluding farm labor -- and the professions (Crafts, 1985a, p. 13). Deane and Cole's estimates of labor force distributions indicate that the percentage of the British labor force engaged in trade and transport between 1801 and 1841 rose by only 2 percentage points, the percentage engaged in public service and professional occupations declined, while the number of farmers changed very little over the nineteenth century (Deane and Cole, 1967, pp. 143-144). In fact, there has been some debate over trends in land ownership and numbers of farmers over the late eighteenth and early nineteenth centuries. Clapham (1930, pp. 98-105) suggests that the number of small farmers declined but warns against overstating this decline. Mingay (1963, pp. 94-99) suggests that the number of farmers dropped, which is consistent with Lindert's estimates for the later eighteenth century. Allen (1992b, pp.38-39, 44-45) argues that enclosure did result in destruction of the English peasantry and an increased concentration of landownership. But he argues that this occurred primarily before the late eighteenth century. Admittedly, Ashton and Clapham suggest that the number and role of middlemen expanded during the eighteenth century (Ashton, [1955] 1972, pp. 66-67; Clapham, 1930, chap. 6). But in sum, although there is much uncertainty surrounding changes in the occupational distribution, available evidence does not suggest that the overall demand for educated labor increased, and there may have been a shift away from sectors that required educated workers.

signature ability. Occupational information from the 1841 census together with information about the use of literacy in specific occupations allows one to estimate the proportion of the English labor force in occupations requiring literacy (Mitch, 1992a, pp. 14-15). In 1841 only 4.9 percent of male workers and only 2.2 percent of female workers were in occupations in which literacy was strictly required. Insofar as these percentages were no higher during the hundred years before 1841, and there is no reason to think that they were, then there was very little scope for a shift into occupations strictly requiring literacy during the industrial revolution. Moreover, for some occupations, there is evidence that literacy rates fell between the mid-eighteenth century and the early nineteenth century (Schofield, 1973, pp. 451-452).[31]

Because only a small proportion of the eighteenth-century English labor force was in occupations that required literacy, one cannot infer that literacy, or formal education more generally, was not useful for large segments of the labor force. Although expressing skepticism about the economic contribution of literacy, Schofield recognizes, in his samples of 1754-1844, a clear hierarchy of literacy rates by occupation. Indeed, he asserts that "this occupational hierarchy is one of the most consistent features of illiteracy in the past. It is to be found in all regions and at all times, regardless of the level of illiteracy" (Schofield, 1973, pp. 449-450).[32]

---

[31] Although these figures come from a limited number of parishes, they "at least suggest the possibility that for many males in a variety of occupations literacy did not become more essential as a cultural skill during this period." Based on the limited degree of school attendance documented for the late eighteenth century, according to Schofield, "practical economic skills were therefore learned within the context of the household and work-group, as part of a comprehensive process of socialization, of which apprenticeship is a well-known, but formalized example" (Schofield, 1973, p. 452).

[32] Such a hierarchy is also apparent in evidence for 1580-1700 (Cressy, 1980, chap. 6). Generally, gentlemen and professional men reported close to universal literacy by the seventeenth century, followed by merchants and larger farmers, with relatively high literacy rates. Next in the hierarchy were skilled craftsmen and then lesser-skilled craftsmen, with husbandmen, miners, and laborers at the bottom. In comparing various times and locations, one should make allowance for Schofield's observation that "naturally the differences between occupations vary, and sometimes categories, particularly

What is the significance of this occupational-literacy hierarchy? According to Schofield, "The common-sense interpretation . . . would seem to be that literacy had a different functional value in each of the occupational groups"(1973, p. 450). That is, literacy would be virtually required for the conduct of professional occupations; valuable for merchants in keeping records and accounts; and less useful for those involved in more manual occupations (Cressy, 1980, chap. 6). However, this hierarchy can reflect social origins as well as the functional uses of literacy. Indeed, one would expect this insofar as individuals acquired literacy primarily during childhood and their early teens when they were most influenced by their parents. Those in professional and commercial occupations were more likely to have had higher-status parents than those in lower-status occupations. And parents of relatively high occupational and social status were more likely to be literate themselves, thus enhancing their ability to convey literacy to their children. They were also more likely to have wanted for their children the benefits of culture and status associated with literacy in addition to its value in the workplace. In sum, the occupational-literacy hierarchy noted by Schofield could have been due to the influence of parental background on both occupation and literacy. In fact, a national sample of marriage registers for 1839-1843 indicates that controlling for father's occupation sizably weakens, but does not sever, the connection between son's occupation and literacy, thus supporting this argument (Mitch, 1992a, pp. 81-83).

There are, however, other indications that literacy could be a useful occupational skill during the Industrial Revolution. Job advertisements from the 1850s, just after the period of focus here, occasionally mention literacy as a desired characteristic for employment, even for occupations of modest status. For example, the Swan Brewers of Waltham Green advertised in the January 4, 1850, *London Times* for "a strong active, respectable looking man who can write plainly and who understands the management of a horse and cart." Those interested were to apply by letter in "the applicant's own handwriting."

Among the uses for literacy across occupations, three different functions can be distinguished. Some occupations directly called for workers to be able to read, write, and "cipher," to keep accounts and

---

some of the trades and crafts, exchange places" (Schofield, 1973, p. 450).

records, for example. Others, such as professional occupations, may have required literacy as a prerequisite for other more complex tasks, and some manual occupations may have required literate workers who could use designs, artists' plans, and models. Finally, some employers associated literacy with desired behaviors for their workers.

Occupations varied considerably in their literacy requirements (Mitch, 1992a, pp. 14-22). Those occupations that unequivocally required literacy included not only professional and clerical personnel but also railroad employees, who were expected to be able to use printed timetables and whose ability to read and write was thought to be a reflection of character. By the 1830s, policemen were commonly expected to be literate so that they could learn legal procedures and report arrests. In other occupations, literacy was likely to have been quite useful but not required. Those engaged in wholesale and retail trade, for example, may have found it helpful to keep accounts. On larger farms, especially, keeping accounts would seem to have been useful, although in practice farm accounts were commonly kept in a haphazard manner. In some manufacturing occupations, reading may have been important for reading labels or following designs.[33] In yet other occupations, the value of literacy was more marginal. In jobs where workers' compensation was based on piece work, a written record of a worker's output was frequently used to determine the appropriate payment. Although such records were most commonly kept by the employer, in some cases workers were expected to keep them; moreover, a literate worker would have been able to verify that they were correct. Literacy may also have been of value for domestic servants, both as an indication of good character and as a tool for keeping household accounts, issuing written instructions, and making household purchases.

If the English labor force in 1841 is classified by occupations according to the degree to which literacy was used, one finds that 4.9 percent of male workers were in occupations that required literacy; 22.5 percent were in occupations in which literacy was likely to have been useful; 25.7 percent, in occupations in which literacy was possibly useful; and 49.7 percent, in occupations in which literacy was unlikely to have been useful (Mitch, 1992a, pp. 14-15). Among female workers,

---

[33] This was true of textile dyers and makers of glass and artificial flowers.

2.2 percent in 1841 were in occupations in which literacy was required; 5.2 percent, in occupations in which literacy was likely to have been useful; 67.9 percent, in occupations in which literacy was possibly useful; and 24.7 percent, in occupations in which literacy was unlikely to have been useful.

Literacy did enhance opportunities for economic advancement. After 1837, marriage registers provided information on occupation of the father and the son, thereby allowing one to compare occupational distributions of literates and illiterates, controlling for father's occupation. By using wage rates by occupation, one estimate based on a national sample from 1869-1873 indicates that the mean difference in weekly wages between literate and illiterate sons of laborers was 13 percent of the weekly wage of an unskilled laborer for that time period (Mitch, 1982, p. 57). Studies grouping the occupations reported by grooms and their fathers into five broad categories according to status have found that for grooms whose fathers had a given occupational status, literate grooms tended to have a higher occupational status than illiterate grooms (Mitch, 1992a, pp. 22-25; Vincent, 1989, pp. 129-131).[34] Literacy also influenced the labor market prospects of women.

---

[34] For example, in a sample of marriages from 1839-1843, of grooms whose fathers were unskilled laborers, half of those who could sign their names reported occupations with a status higher than unskilled compared with only 20 percent of those who were unable to sign (Mitch, 1992a, p. 24). These comparisons suggest not only that those who could read and write had an advantage over those who could not in reaching higher-status occupations but also that literacy was neither essential for obtaining a high-status occupation nor an assurance of avoiding a low-status one. A plausible explanation is that literacy had to be combined with other skills, attitudes, and aptitudes to provide an advantage.

However, one indication that much of the advantage of literates over illiterates was due to literacy alone is that the types of occupations in which literates had the most advantage in entering were those in which literacy was most likely to be used. Of the higher probability of literate sons in reporting an occupation other than unskilled in the study of 1839-1843 marriages, over 80 percent is attributable to an advantage in movement into occupations where literacy was at least possibly useful (Mitch, 1992a, p. 26). Although literates did have an advantage over illiterates in entering textile manufacturing, where literacy was generally not very useful, they had no advantage in mining, another important industry in which ordinary operatives had no occasion to

Comparisons of the occupations reported by literate and illiterate brides for 1839-1843 indicate that literate brides were more likely to hold jobs in service and clothing manufacture, whereas illiterate brides were more likely to report occupations related to textile manufacture (Mitch, 1992a, pp. 33-35).[35]

Estimates of the social rate of return to literacy indicate that during 1839-1843 the return for men ranged from 9 percent to 42.5 percent and for women from 1 percent to 16.5 percent (Mitch, 1984). The rate of return on physical capital investments may have ranged from 5 to 20 percent. This suggests that if more resources would have been used to fund primary education, especially for males, English national income in the early 1840s could have been increased. The output gain from reallocating funds in this manner has been estimated at 2 percent to 7 percent of English national income in 1841 (Mitch, 1984). Although this gain is not negligible, it is modest relative to the total growth of output that occurred during the Industrial Revolution. This can be explained by the limited extent of the differential and by the relatively small amount of funds likely to have been reallocated.

Thus far, this assessment of the impact of education has focused on its influence on cognitive abilities. However, numerous scholars have argued that education's role has been primarily in shaping behaviors, attitudes, and values (Bowles and Gintis, 1976; Easterlin, 1981, p. 9) -- that is, in socialization -- and this aspect of education has been emphasized in the educational history of Britain over the last twenty years. Discussions of the socializing effects of education have considered three different types: (1) education as a means of instilling work discipline; (2) education as a means of preventing working-class crime, strikes, and rebellions; and (3) education as a tool for the middle and upper classes in imposing cultural hegemony and in counteracting working-class resistance in the struggle for power between social classes. Although historians have often lumped these three effects together, in

---

use literacy on the job (Mitch, 1992a, p. 28).

[35] Literate brides were also, not surprisingly, far more likely than illiterate brides to work as shopkeepers and school teachers, although only a small percentage of the female labor force held such occupations. But although literate and illiterate women tended to enter different occupations, evidence is lacking on whether the occupations entered by literates paid more than those entered by illiterates.

particular tending to subsume the first two under the third, it is instructive to consider each effect in turn.

The argument that the factory of the Industrial Revolution required more disciplined workers than in earlier times was given the following formulation by Andrew Ure (who was given notoriety by Marx as an apologist for the factory): "The main difficulty [with the factory] lay ... above all in training human beings to renounce their desultory habits of work, and to identify themselves with the unvarying regularity of the complex automaton" (Ure, 1835, p. 15). Complaints of factory proprietors and managers during the early Industrial Revolution centered on workers who kept irregular hours, took holidays when they pleased, failed to maintain constant vigilance over the machinery under their care, and embezzled raw materials (Pollard, 1963). And successful employers seem to have been able to find ways of instilling discipline in their workers.[36]

However, it is unlikely that formal schooling contributed to the development of a disciplined factory work force or that a growing demand for disciplined factory workers played a major role in the rise of mass education in England. Formal education receives only passing mention in accounts of how factories obtained disciplined workers in the early industrial revolution (McKendrick, 1961, p. 55; Pollard, 1963, pp. 268-269). Indeed, Sanderson's findings, cited earlier, point to the relatively low levels of formal education, as evidenced by literacy skills, among Lancashire textile workers; and investigators for the Newcastle

---

[36] According to Ure, one of the first cotton textile factory owners "had to train his work people to a precision and assiduity altogether unknown before, against which their listless and restive habits rose in continued rebellion" (Ure, 1835-1836, p. 259). The pioneer of factory organization in pottery production, Josiah Wedgwood, developed discipline among his work force by introducing printed rules and a primitive clocking-in system, along with encouragement of training (McKendrick, 1961). A classic account of the Industrial Revolution states, "The second generation of employers -- such as the younger Boulton, Watt, Wedgwood, or Crawshay -- was perhaps more alive than the first to the losses that might arise from irregularity or carelessness on the part of labour. Men trained in the concern were appointed as managers and foremen; piece-rates and bonus schemes were introduced to stimulate effort; and fines were imposed for drunkenness, sloth, and gaming. The new methods of administration, the new incentives, and the 'new discipline' were as much a part of the revolution as the technical inventions themselves" (Ashton, 1948, p. 85).

Commission in the late 1850s also noted the low levels of formal education among textile workers, miners, and metalworkers in the midlands (Great Britain, 1861, p. 249). It is significant that both weekday school enrollment rates and local funding for subsidizing weekday elementary schools were relatively low in industrial districts through the first half of the nineteenth century (Marsden, 1987; Mitch, 1992a, pp. 118, 121-122).[37]

Some middle-class reformers clearly did perceive that by educating the working classes the incidence of crime, strikes, and riots would decline. Investigators for local statistical societies, such as Joseph Fletcher, seemed almost obsessed with establishing that ignorance was a major cause of working-class crime (Cullen, 1975, pp. 142-144). A serious riot in Wales precipitated a major parliamentary investigation into educational conditions in Wales in 1847 (Great Britain, 1847). Following a miners' strike in 1844, according to Colls, mine owners in Northumberland and Durham established schools in their miners' villages (Colls, 1976). Johnson (1976), among others, has noted that the government began to provide elementary education in the 1830s and 1840s, just as working-class revolutionary movements, such as Chartism, were reaching their peak. The notion that working-class education could serve as a form of "moral police" recurred among its advocates (Field, 1979; Johnson, 1970; Johnson, 1976; Quick, 1974). However, not only is the effectiveness of mass schooling as a form of moral police open to doubt, but one must also explain why working-class parents began to send, and pay to send, their children to schools designed primarily for this purpose (Quick, 1974, p. 192).

---

[37] Field (1979) and Quick (1974) have suggested that Sunday schools may have been the main agencies for conveying moral training in industrial areas while providing little in the way of literacy instruction. But neither they nor anyone else has demonstrated that Sunday school training alone had a significant impact on the work habits of the industrial work force or that the desire to influence those work habits was a major force behind the Sunday school movement.

The willingness of textile factory owners to provide schooling for their child employees in the first third of the nineteenth century appears to have varied considerably, with owners of larger factories being more likely to provide schools. See Sanderson (1967).

At a more general level, it has been argued that mass education was used by the middle and upper classes as a way of coping with class conflict and counteracting working-class efforts to overthrow the existing order (Bowles and Gintis, 1976; Johnson, 1976; Quick, 1974). According to this point of view, educated workers would be more likely to accept the existing social and economic hierarcy and to accept their lot as wage earners (Johnson, 1970; 1976). Important subthemes are that existing working-class values and behaviors were depraved and degenerate (Johnson, 1970; 1977) and that there were grounds for fearing educational movements initiated by the working-classes themselves (Colls, 1976; Quick, 1974).

The central issues involved in the view that education could preserve the existing social order and was an instrument in the class struggle are beyond the scope of this survey, which focuses on the contribution of education to economic performance. It is plausible that the Industrial Revolution led to social tensions, which, in turn, provided incentives for the middle and upper classes to support mass education. However, a number of historians have argued that the notion of education as "social control" oversimplifies the reasons for upper- and middle-class support for education, neglects the possibility of working-class resistance to education provided for this purpose, and oversimplifies the nature of class conflict (Duffy, 1981; Heesom, 1981; Marcham, 1978; Silver, 1977; Stedman Jones, 1977).

Despite England's resources at the university level, it has been argued that technological advance during the British Industrial Revolution was primarily due to the practical experience of men of little or no formal scientific training. For example, George Atwood, a lecturer in natural philosophy at Cambridge in the late eighteenth century, was skeptical that the theory of motion could be useful to a mechanic assembling power-driven machinery: "Machines of this sort owe their origin and improvement to other sources: it is from long experience of repeated trials, errors, deliberations, [and] corrections, continued through the lives of individuals, and by successive generations of them, that sciences, strictly called practical, derive their gradual advancement" (cited in Musson and Robinson, 1969, p. 84).

But this perspective has been questioned by Musson and Robinson, who have described in considerable detail connections between the pursuit of scientific inquiry and the development of new technologies. They describe how industrialists in Manchester, London, and a number of other towns and cities attended itinerant lectures on scientific subjects and maintained an active interest in scientific issues and developments. They argue that, in general, those who ran manufacturing and commercial enterprises were frequently in contact with scientific societies in England. The development of the chlorine bleaching process is cited by Musson and Robinson as an example, which they claim was an important late eighteenth-century technological advance in England that stemmed from extensive communications with the French chemist Berthollet (Musson and Robinson, 1969, chap. 8). Although Musson and Robinson concede that the link between science and technology during this period is not well defined, they argue that it should not be ignored.[38]

Morris Berman (1972) acknowledges that Musson and Robinson demonstrated an association between scientific activity and industrial innovation but failed to show that knowledge of science was directly responsible for any important technical advance during the Industrial Revolution. A. Rupert Hall (1974), equally skeptical about the contribution of science to the development of new technology during the Industrial Revolution, argues that the state of eighteenth-century science was so primitive that scientific knowledge was of little value to the inventor. Even in the development of chlorine bleach, which Musson and Robinson describe as a clear example of the contribution of scientific knowledge to technical development, Hall argues that despite Watt's "acute interest" in the invention and his communications with Berthollet, this did not lead to "commercial success" (Hall, 1974, p. 137). Hall allows that technological developments may have benefited from a scientific procedure centered on "empirical technical research,"

---

[38] In the following statement, Landes also acknowledges this link: "It is often stated that the Newcomen machine and its forerunners would have been unthinkable without the theoretical ideas of Boyle, Torricelli, and others; and that Watt derived much of his technical competence and imagination from his work with scientists and scientific instruments at Glasgow." But he maintains that "once the principle of the separate condenser was established, subsequent advances owed little or nothing to theory" (Landes, 1969, p. 104).

which he suggests falls into a category between "inspired tinkering" and "applied science."[39]

Education could also conceivably have helped to foster migration, entrepreneurship, social mobility, arbitrage, and movement from inferior to superior working and living conditions. Because education can affect an economy in so many ways, its full impact is difficult to evaluate. What is notable about the English Industrial Revolution is that, apparently, education did not have to be universally present for the factors just listed to make significant contributions to economic growth. For example, for the mid-nineteenth century, there is evidence that literacy helped promote social and geographic mobility (see, for example, Nicholas and Shergold, 1987a, pp. 36-38). Yet mobility was possible even among the illiterate. Thus, illiterate sons of laborers had as good a chance of entering the mining sector as literate sons of laborers, and geographic mobility was likely to have been involved here (Mitch, 1992a, p. 28).

Factors other than formal schooling influenced the development of economically productive skills and ability. Alfred Marshall alluded to these in *Industry and Trade*, written in the early twentieth century:

The mere accumulation of knowledge stunts rather than educates the mind . . . . [England] still holds a leadership, almost unchallenged except by other English speaking countries, in that education of character which is obtained from individual activities, rather than from instruction whether verbal or in print. The playground had a notable share in the "real" education of her youth: and the paths of the ocean have been the Universities of an exceptional number of her men (Marshall, 1923, p. 96).

During the Industrial Revolution, workers developed skills primarily through on-the-job training, of which three significant forms have been identified (More, 1980): apprenticeship, migration, and "following-up." The nature and influence of each will be considered in turn. Apprenticeship, the oldest form, traditionally involved a written contract, known as an indenture, which bound apprentice to master. The contract stipulated that the master would instruct the apprentice

---

[39] Hall suggests that the contribution of applied science was "as the rational and experimental study of techniques. without presupposing the injection of important elements of abstract theory, or of pure scientific discoveries" (Hall, 1974, p.145). He proposes the term "great technical designer" to refer to someone making a contribution of this nature (Hall, 1974, pp. 146-148).

in his craft and provide the apprentice with board and lodging; in exchange, the apprentice would work for a set period of time, commonly five to seven years, at lower wages than the apprentice might otherwise earn. The Statute of Apprentices, enacted in 1562-1563, stated that no person could practice any "trade, craft, or mystery" unless he had first served an apprenticeship of seven years. Although this statute was not repealed until 1814, it was generally ignored by the mid-eighteenth century (Dunlop, 1912).

Apprenticeship agreements, both oral and written, were certainly common throughout the eighteenth and nineteenth centuries (Elbaum, 1989; More, 1980; Thompson, 1963), even if they were not legally enforced. However, it is difficult to say with any precision how widespread they were. Apprenticeship was most commonly associated with such artisanal crafts as hatting, flint glassmaking, cabinetmaking, carriage building, and wheelwrighting, as well as with many construction occupations and with the metalworking trades of Sheffield and the West Midlands (More, 1980, chap. 3). There is no evidence that apprenticeship rose markedly during the Industrial Revolution, whereas there is general agreement that it was on the decline by the last half of the nineteenth century. However, Elbaum (1989) claims that apprenticeship persisted in many skilled occupations well into the twentieth century. He estimates that the internal rate of return to apprenticeship in the early twentieth century was quite high, between 21 percent and 27 percent, which suggests how effective it could be as a means of training skilled workers.

Migration involved rotating trainees from task to task within a given firm and by moving them among firms. This method most commonly occurred in occupations that involved tending machinery, in the metalwork trades of Birmingham, and in coal hewing and railway work (More, 1980, chap. 6).

Following-up was when a trainee was assigned to a gang or as an assistant to a more skilled worker. While working full time, the trainee would also learn the task of the more skilled workers in his unit. This method of training was used in a number of the occupations often associated with the leading industries of the Industrial Revolution, for example cotton spinning. Boys would enter the industry in their teens and would be assigned the task of piecing together broken cotton threads; by their mid-twenties, if openings were available, they would work their way up to be minders of the cotton spinning machinery

(Lazonick, 1990, chap. 3; More, 1980, chap. 6). Following-up was also used to train iron and steel workers (More, 1980, chap.6).

The division of labor could also have influenced the development of skills in the work force. Adam Smith, in Book 1 of the *Wealth of Nations*, emphasizes that division of labor enhanced skills by improving dexterity and raising the probability of inventiveness. But in Book 5, he also argues that the division of labor produced classes of workers who focused on a few repetitive tasks, leading to intellectual torpor and atrophy among such groups (Rosenberg, 1965; West, 1964). Babbage suggests the possibility "that the master manufacturer, by dividing the work to be executed into different processes, each requiring different degrees of skill or force, can purchase exactly that precise quantity of both which is necessary for each process" (Braverman, 1974, p. 79). And Andrew Ure emphasizes that the division of labor, when accomplished with the use of power-driven machinery, reduces the level of skill required at each stage of production and thus permits the substitution of unskilled and semiskilled labor for more "self-willed and intractable" skilled labor (Ure, 1835, pp. 20-23).

Accounts of the sweated trades in the clothing and shoemaking industries in the nineteenth century reflect similar themes, though by emphasizing division into tasks without the key role of mechanization (Schmiechen, 1984, pp. 27-28, 30). In contrast, Berg (1985, p. 195) has suggested that the division of labor was behind the development of skill in the building trades. And Lazonick emphasizes that the influence of the division of labor on skill levels is ambiguous, suggesting that it can lead to worker or managerial control over production processes (Lazonick, 1990, pp. 60-62, 102).

To assess whether or not these methods of skill development, whether on-the-job training or the division of labor, contributed to England's rapid economic growth during the Industrial Revolution despite the indifferent quality of formal education, it is necessary to consider trends in labor force skill levels in the late eighteenth and early nineteenth centuries. Accounts are conflicting as to whether skill levels were rising or falling over this period. Marx ([1887] 1967, vol. 1, pp. 422-424) and Thompson (1963, pp. 257-262) argue that, overall, skill levels fell; Marx points to the substitution of machinery for skilled labor, Thompson to the repeal in 1814 of the Statute of Apprentices. Nicholas and Nicholas (1992) interpret the rising illiteracy rates they find among skilled workers in the later Industrial Revolution in their sample of English convicts as evidence of deskilling. In contrast, a number of accounts indicate that the British labor force in the mid-nineteenth century was reputed to have been highly skilled (Crafts and Thomas, 1986; Harley, 1974). And Samuel argues that skilled handicraft occupations grew apace with industrialization and that "nineteenth century capitalism created many more skills than it destroyed" (Samuel, 1977, p. 59), while Harris maintains that the growing number of technologies using coal as an energy source created occupations that comprised "a precarious combination of manipulative skill embodying a physical training and a judgement requiring both experience and intelligence" (Harris, 1976, p. 182). Berg, referring specifically to the Birmingham metalworking industry, states that "industrialization brought a form of dualism whereby both large-scale and extremely small-scale firms probably grew at the expense of substantial artisans and medium-size manufacturers" (Berg, 1985, p. 282). The small-scale firms, which she terms "garret masters," used low-paid workers, often women, in very specialized tasks, a process known as "sweating." In the absence of more complete evidence, it seems reasonable to concur with Pollard's agnosticism as to trends in skill in the first half of the nineteenth century: "It is not even possible to say with any certainty whether the proportion of skilled and semi-skilled workers as a whole rose or fell in this period; all one can say is that the nature of skill and the sources of privilege were different in the new conditions, both within the factory and without" (Pollard, 1978, p. 123).[40]

In sum, there is little evidence to suggest that education played a central role in England's Industrial Revolution, suggesting in turn that it has been possible for economies to compensate for poorly educated work forces with other offsetting advantages. This is not to say that education made no contribution whatever. Literacy and, more importantly, on-the-job training do seem to have raised economic productivity in at least some circumstances. Employers and policymakers did value education for its influence on working-class behavior and socialization. But there is little support for the view that the contribution of educa-

---

[40] Another relevant question, raised by a number of authors, is whether skilled workers were more productive than unskilled workers or whether skills were "socially created," for example, through unions restricting entry into skilled occupations and thus increasing their wages (see More, 1980, chap. 1, for a survey; Lazonick, 1990).

tion was central. Perhaps the most telling point is the minimal extent of the shift of the labor force toward occupations likely to make use of formal education and the uncertainty concerning the extent of a shift toward relatively skilled occupations more generally during the Industrial Revolution.

Was There an Educational Threshold
for England's Industrial Revolution?

Despite the apparent modesty of the direct contribution of education to England's Industrial Revolution, some writers have argued that the educational level of the English labor force was critical during the Industrial Revolution because it exceeded a "threshold" level necessary for further economic growth. The notion of an educational threshold can be attributed to the influential article of Bowman and Anderson (1963) in which they use mid-twentieth-century data in cross-country comparisons to show that all countries with a moderate per capita income ($300 in 1955 dollars) had literacy rates of at least 30 percent. Because their findings are solely "stylized facts," based on cross-country comparisons, they emphasize the tentative nature of their findings, the uncertainty as to direction of causation (that is, the possibility that rising incomes led to higher levels of education), and the importance of further examination of what they term "how and process questions of socioeconomic change" (Bowman and Anderson, 1963, p. 279). Despite these caveats, their result has acquired almost the status of a law of nature among some writers and has frequently been referred to in the case of the English Industrial Revolution (Laqueur, 1974; Nicholas and Nicholas, 1992; Tranter, 1981; West, 1978).

To assess the relevance of Bowman and Anderson's findings, it is necessary to consider explanations of why an educational threshold should exist and whether there is reason to think that these explanations applied to England in the late eighteenth and early nineteenth centuries.

As for the first issue, it is notable that Bowman and Anderson offer no definite explanation for the existence of an educational threshold, referring instead only to "problems of scale and structural breakthrough."[41] One possible explanation is based on occupations in which literacy, not to mention other types of knowledge, are either required or considered very valuable. These would include professional occupations and those in large-scale commerce. As mentioned previously, in 1841, 4.9 percent of the male work force and 2.2 percent of the female work force were in occupations in which literacy was strictly required (Mitch, 1992a, p. 15). These groups compare with those with a secondary education in twentieth-century developing countries, such as secondary graduates in Africa who fill positions as agricultural assistants, medical technicians, secretaries, bookkeepers, nurses, teachers, and business leaders (Lewis, 1965, p. 6). They make up 5 percent to 10 percent of the work force (Lewis, 1965, p. 5). One should probably allow for a margin above the 10 percent upper bound just cited to provide for a talent pool for replenishment of workers with the natural ability and intelligence that would most effectively use the training and schooling associated with occupations where formal education was of high priority. In this respect, a literacy threshold probably applied to England in the eighteenth and early nineteenth centuries (Stone, 1969, p. 130). By the mid-eighteenth century, however, virtually all of northwestern Europe was well above the literacy threshold suggested here; and this does not explain England's early industrial success.[42]

One may accept that Bowman and Anderson's findings establish a literacy threshold for the twentieth century without necessarily concluding that the same threshold applied in the late eighteenth and early nineteenth centuries. The difficulty of extrapolating an empirical relationship between literacy and economic growth from one time period to one a century or more distant has been expressed as follows:

---

[41] Indeed, the last sentence of their study emphasizes the importance, as noted in the text, of further examination of "the 'how' and the 'process' questions of socioeconomic change" in interpreting their findings (Bowman and Anderson, 1963, p. 279).

[42] In contrast, Russia in the nineteenth century had an adult literacy rate of less than 30 percent, which probably constituted a serious impediment to its industrialization (Cipolla, 1969). For example, the fact that newly established steel companies in late-nineteenth-century Russia had to use expensive foreign metallurgists and foremen can in part be attributed to the country's low literacy rate (McKay, 1970, pp. 255, 257)

The present literacy threshold in poor countries may be lower than 40 percent [a level that Blaug suggests *may* have characterizedBritain during the Industrial Revolution] due to the better technical facilities for oral communication that are available in the modern world. On the other hand, it may be higher owing to the demands of the more complex technology of the twentieth century. It is difficult to sustain the view that these two opposite considerations cancel out, leaving us where we were before we invoked the muse of history (Blaug, 1970, pp. 64-65).

In sum, it is not at all evident that any literacy threshold that applied to the mid-twentieth century was also relevant for the later eighteenth century. And England would have been joined in surpassing any literacy threshold relevant to the later eighteenth century by a number of other countries with far less remarkable records of economic growth.

Was the First Industrial Revolution Different?

To return to the initial theme of this survey, how can the educational mediocrity and limited economic role of education during England's Industrial Revolution be reconciled with the economic importance commonly assigned to education in the later twentieth century? By the mid-twentieth century, literacy does seem to be expected for even low-level operative manufacturing occupations in England and the United States (Hogan, 1982, p. 161; Levine, 1986, pp. 135-149). In late nineteenth-century England, however, most manufacturing employers exhibited little concern as to whether the workers that they hired could read or write (Mitch, 1992a, p. 251 n. 76; Vincent, 1989, p. 120).

One explanation for the importance of education to economic growth in the twentieth century is that technological change has increasingly become based on mastery of scientific principles, thereby increasing the demand for formal scientific training. Crafts and Thomas provide a concise statement of this perspective when they suggest that "the source of Britain's industrial leadership in the nineteenth century was a favourable endowment of natural resources, combined with a stock of labour sufficient to exploit these advantages; Britain's handicap in the later part of the century was a scarcity of the human capital which was an essential input to the technologically progressive product-cycle industries that dominated the Second Industrial Revolution" (Crafts and Thomas, 1986, p. 643; see also Nicholas and Nicholas, 1992). To support their characterization, they present evidence that between 1870 and 1935 Britain had a comparative advantage in exporting unskilled-labor-intensive commodities and a comparative disadvantage in exporting human-capital-intensive commodities. This evidence is consistent with the findings of this survey that education was not a major contributing factor to England's economic growth during the Industrial Revolution.

The English economy's reliance on informal instruction and on-the-job training during the Industrial Revolution became an obstacle, according to some authors, as the nature of technogical advance began to demand a mastery of formal scientific principles. Alfred Marshall asserted that "the present age calls for a new class of improvements of method, and -- in a less degree -- for improvements of appliances, which cannot be created by a single alert individual. Many of those, by which man's command over nature has been enlarged during the last few decades, have been the product of sustained researches by large groups of specially qualified students extending over long periods of time" (Marshall, 1923, p. 96).

Some historians disagree with this account. Inkster (1983a, p. 45) argues that insofar as the British economy after 1870 shifted toward trade and services, technology and science were "decreasingly important as an effective constraint on the progress of the economy." Nicholas (1985) argues that on-the-job training and part-time instruction *were* effective substitutes for formal technical education, which was evident in the apparent absence of shortages of technical personnel in such key industries as engineering, shipbuilding, and marine architecture and in the rate of British productivity growth, which did not lag behind that of other countries.

Resolving this controversy would take us beyond the focus of this study. But one theme that seems to underlie all of these perspectives is that substitution is always possible and that there are a variety of feasible strategies for increasing the rate of economic growth. This, in turn, harks back to two key themes of this survey. First, education was not indispensable to economic growth during England's Industrial Revolution, although it surely did make a positive contribution. Second, numerous forms of informal instruction served as alternatives to formal education. Thus, the First Industrial Revolution provides evidence that, at least under some circumstances, other factors of production can substitute for an educated labor force.

Bibliography

Akerlof, George A., and Janet L. Yellen, eds. 1986. *Efficiency Wage Models of the Labor Market.* Cambridge: Cambridge University Press.

Allen, Robert C. 1979. "International Competitiveness in Iron and Steel, 1850-1913." *Journal of Economic History* 39:911-937.

———. 1988. "Inferring Yields from Probate Inventories." *Journal of Economic History* 47:117-126.

———. 1992a. "Agriculture During the Industrial Revolution, 1700-1850." In Roderick Floud and Donald N. McCloskey, eds., *The Economic History of Britain Since 1700.* 2d ed. Cambridge: Cambridge University Press.

———. 1992b. *Enclosure and the Yeoman: The Agricultural Development of the South Midlands, 1450-1850.* Oxford: Clarendon Press.

Allen, Robert C., and Cormac O Gráda. 1988. "On the Road Again with Arthur Young: English, Irish, and French Agriculture During the Industrial Revolution." *Journal of Economic History* 38:93-116.

Andrews, David, Mark Mitchell, and Adolf Weber. 1979. *The Development of Agriculture in Germany and the U.K.: 3. Comparative Time Series, 1870-1975.* Ashford, Kent: Wye College. Miscellaneous Study, no. 4.

Arthur, W. Brian. 1988. "Self-Reinforcing Mechanisms in Economics." In P. W. Anderson, K. J. Arrow, and D. Pines, eds., *The Economy as an Evolving Complex System.* New York: Addison Wesley.

———. 1989. "Competing Technologies, Increasing Returns, and Lock in by Historical Events." *Economic Journal* 99:116-131.

Artz, Frederic. 1966. *The Development of Technical Education in France, 1500-1850.* Cambridge, Mass.: MIT Press.

Ashton, T. S. 1924. *Iron and Steel in the Industrial Revolution.* Manchester: Manchester University Press.

———. 1948. *The Industrial Revolution, 1760-1830.* Oxford: Oxford University Press.

———. [1955] 1972. *An Economic History of England: The 18th Century.* London: Methuen.

Ault, Warren O. 1972. *Open-Field Farming in Medieval England.* London: Allen and Unwin.

Bairoch, Paul. 1979. "*Ecarts internationaux des niveaux de vie avant la Revolution industrielle.*" *Annales: economies, societes, civilisations* 34:145-171.

———. 1981. "The Main Trends in National Economic Disparities Since the Industrial Revolution." In Paul Bairoch and Maurice Lévy-Leboyer, eds., *Disparities in Economic Development Since the Industrial Revolution.* New York: St. Martin's Press.

_____. 1982. "International Industrialization Levels from 1750 to 1980." *Journal of European Economic History* 11:269-334.

_____. 1989. "European Trade Policy, 1815-1914." In P. Mathias and S. Pollard, eds., *The Cambridge Economic History of Europe.* Vol. 8, *Industrial Economies: the Development of Economic and Social Policies.* Cambridge: Cambridge University Press.

Batchelor, Thomas. 1808. *General View of the Agriculture of the County of Bedford.* London: Sherwood, Neely, and Jones.

Baumol, William, Sue Anne Batey Blackman, and Edward N. Wolff. 1989. *Productivity and American Leadership: The Long View.* Cambridge, Mass.: MIT Press.

Beckett, J. V. 1990. *The Agricultural Revolution.* Oxford: Basil Blackwell.

Berg, Maxine. 1980. *The Machinery Question and the Making of Political Economy, 1815-1848.* Cambridge: Cambridge University Press.

_____. 1985. *The Age of Manufactures.* London: Fontana Press.

Berg, Maxine, and Pat Hudson. 1992. "Rehabilitating the Industrial Revolution." *Economic History Review* 45:24-50.

Berman, Morris. 1972. "An Essay Review of A. E. Musson and Eric Robinson, *Science and Technology in the Industrial Revolution.*" *Journal of Social History* 5:521-526.

Bessemer, Henry. [1905] 1989. *Sir Henry Bessemer, F.R.S.: An Autobiography.* London: Institute of Metals.

Bienefeld, M. A. 1972. *Working Hours in British Industry.* London: London School of Economics and Political Science, Weidenfeld and Nicolson.

Birse, Ronald M. 1983. *Engineering at Edinburgh University: A Short History, 1673-1983.* Edinburgh: School of Engineering, University of Edinburgh.

Black, Robert, and Claire Gilmore. 1990. "Crowding Out During Britain's Industrial Revolution." *Journal of Economic History* 50:109-131.

Blanqui, Jerome-Adolphe. 1837. *Histoire de l'Economie Politique.* Paris: Guillaumin.

Blaug, Mark. 1968. *Economic Theory in Retrospect.* Rev. ed. Homewood, Ill.: R. D. Irwin.

_____. 1970. *An Introduction to the Economics of Education.* Harmondsworth, England: Penguin Books.

_____. 1976. "The Empirical Status of Human Capital Theory: A Slightly Jaundiced Survey." *Journal of Economic Literature* 14:827-855.

_____. 1985. "Where Are We Now in the Economics of Education?" *Economics of Education Review* 4:17-28.

Bordo, Michael D., and Eugene N. White. 1991. "A Tale of Two Currencies: British and French Finance During the Napoleonic Wars." *Journal of Economic History* 51:303-316.

Bowles, Samuel, and Herbert Gintis. 1976. *Schooling in Capitalist America: Educational Reform and the Contradictions of Economic Life.* New York: Basic Books.

Bowley, A. L. 1898. "The Statistics of Wages in the United Kingdom During the Last Hundred Years (Part I), Agricultural Wages." *Journal of the Royal Statistical Society* 61:702-722.

Bowman, Mary Jean, and C. Arnold Anderson. 1963. "Concerning the Role of Education in Development." In Clifford Geertz, ed., *Old Societies and New States: The Quest for Modernity in Africa and Asia.* Glencoe, Ill.: Free Press.

Boyer, George R. 1990. *An Economic History of the English Poor Law, 1750-1850.* Cambridge: Cambridge University Press.

Braudel, Fernand. 1984. *The Perspective of the World: Civilization and Capitalism, 15th-18th Century.* New York: Harper and Row.

Braverman, Harry. 1974. *Labor and Monopoly Capital: The Degradation of Work in the Twentieth Century.* New York: Monthly Review Press.

Brenner, Reuven. 1987. *Rivalry.* New York: Cambridge University Press.

Brenner, Robert. 1976. "Agrarian Class Structure and Economic Development in Pre-Industrial Europe." *Past and Present* 70:30-74.

Briavoinne, Natalis de. 1839. *De l'Industrie en Belgique, Causes de Décadence et de Prosperité.* Brussels: Societé Typographique Belge.

_____. 1840. *Memoire sur l'etat de la population, des fabriques, des manufactures et du commerce dans les Pays-Bas, depuis Albert et Isabelle jusqu'a la fin du siecle dernier.* Brussels: Academie Royale des Sciences et des Lettres de Bruxelles.

Brown, John C. 1990. "The Condition of England and the Standard of Living: Cotton Textiles in the Northwest, 1806-1850." *Journal of Economic History* 50:591-615.

Brown, Michael K. 1989. "Piecing Together the Past: Recent Research on the American China Manufactory, 1769-1772." *Proceedings of the American Philosophical Society* 133:555-579.

Bruland, Tine. 1982. "Industrial Conflict as a Source of Technical Innovation: Three Cases." *Economy and Society* 11:91-121.

Bryant, Margaret. 1986. *The London Experience of Secondary Education.* London: Athlone Press.

Buchinsky, Moshe, and Ben Polak. 1993. "The Emergence of a National Capital Market in England, 1710-1880," *Journal of Economic History* 53:1-24.

Burt, Roger. 1991. "The International Diffusion of Technology in the Early Modern Period: The Case of the British Non-ferrous Mining Industry." *Economic History Review* 44:249-271.

Bythell, Duncan. 1969. *The Handloom Weavers.* London: Cambridge University Press.

_____. 1978. *The Sweated Trades.* New York: St. Martin's Press.

Cain, P. J. and A. G. Hopkins. 1980. "The Political Economy of British Expansion Overseas, 1750-1914." *Economic History Review* 33:463-490.

Calhoun, Craig. 1982. *The Question of Class Struggle: Social Foundations of Popular Radicalism During the Industrial Revolution.* Chicago: University of Chicago Press.

Calomiris, Charles, and Glenn Hubbard. 1991. "Tax Policy, Internal Finance, and Investment: Evidence from the Undistributed Profits Tax of 1936-1937." Unpublished manuscript.

Cameron, Rondo. 1967. *Banking in the Early Stages of Industrialization.* New York: Oxford University Press.

_____. 1982. "The Industrial Revolution: A Misnomer." *The History Teacher* 15:377-384.

_____. 1985. "A New View of European Industrialization." *Economic History Review* 38:1-23.

_____. 1990. "La Révolution Industrielle Manquée." *Social Science History* 14:559-565.

_____. 1991. Review of *The Lever of Riches* by Joel Mokyr. *American Historical Review* 96:1164-1165.

Cannadine, David. 1984. "The Present and the Past in the English Industrial Revolution, 1880-1980." *Past and Present* 103:131-172.

Cardwell, D.S.L. 1972. *Turning Points in Western Technology.* New York: Neale Watson Science History Publication.

Catling, Harold. 1970. *The Spinning Mule.* Newton Abbot, England: David & Charles.

Central Statistical Organization. 1987. *Statistical Abstract, 1985.* New Delhi, India.

Chambers, J. D. 1953. "Enclosure and Labour Supply in the Industrial Revolution." *Economic History Review* 5:319-343.

Chambers, J. D., and Mingay, G. E. 1966. *The Agricultural Revolution, 1750-1880.* London: Batsford.

Chapman, J. 1987. "The Extent and Nature of Parliamentary Enclosure." *Agricultural History Review* 35:25-35.

Chapman, Stanley D. 1971. "The Cost of Power in the Industrial Revolution in Britain: The Case of the Textile Industry." *Midland History* 1(Autumn): 1-24.

_____. 1987. *The Cotton Industry in the Industrial Revolution.* 2d ed. Basingstoke: Macmillan Education, Ltd.

Chapman, Stanley D., and John Butt. 1988. "The Cotton Industry." In Charles Feinstein and Sidney Pollard, eds., *Studies in the Capital Formation in the United Kingdom, 1750-1920.* Cambridge: Cambridge University Press.

Chaptal, J. A. 1819. *De l'industrie francaise.* 2 vols. Paris: A. A. Renouard.

Chartres, J. A. 1985. "The Marketing of Agricultural Produce." In Joan Thirsk, ed., *The Agrarian History of England and Wales*. Vol. 5, *1640-1750. II. Agrarian Change*. Cambridge: Cambridge University Press.

Chorley, G.P.H. 1981. "The Agricultural Revolution in Northern Europe, 1750-1880: Nitrogen, Legumes, and Crop Productivity." *Economic History Review*. 34:71-93.

Chubb, John, and Terry Moes. 1990. *Politics, Markets and America's Schools*. Washington, D.C.: Brookings.

Church, Roy. 1986. *The History of the British Coal Industry*. Vol 3, *1830-1913*. Oxford: Clarendon Press.

Cipolla, Carlo. 1965. *The Economic History of World Population*. Harmondsworth, England: Pelican Books.

_____. 1969. *Literacy and Development in the West*. Harmondsworth, England: Penguin Books.

_____. 1980. *Before the Industrial Revolution*. New York: Norton.

Clapham, John H. 1923. *The Economic Development of France and Germany 1815-1914*. 2d ed. Cambridge: Cambridge University Press.

_____. 1930. *An Economic History of Modern Britain*. Vol 1, *The Early Railway Age 1820-1850*. 2d ed. Cambridge: Cambridge University Press.

_____. 1952. *An Economic History of Modern Britain*. Vol. 2, *Free Trade and Steel, 1850-1886*. Cambridge: Cambridge University Press.

Clark, Gregory. 1987a. "Why Isn't the Whole World Developed? Lessons from the Cotton Mills." *Journal of Economic History* 47:134-167.

_____. 1987b. "Productivity Growth Without Technical Change in European Agriculture Before 1850." *Journal of Economic History* 47:419-432.

_____. 1988. "The Cost of Capital and Medieval Agricultural Technique." *Explorations in Economic History* 25:265-294.

_____. 1991a. "Labour Productivity in English Agriculture, 1300-1860." In Bruce Campbell and Mark Overton, eds., *Land, Labour, and Livestock: Historical Studies in European Agricultural Productivity*. Manchester: Manchester University Press, 211-235.

_____. 1991b. "Yields per Acre in English Agriculture, 1300-1860: Evidence from Labor Inputs." *Economic History Review* 46:445-460.

_____. 1991c. "In Search of the Agricultural Revolution: Southern England, 1611-1850." Paper presented at the All-University of California Conference in Economic History, Davis.

_____. 1991d. "Labor Productivity and Farm Size in English Agriculture before Mechanization: A Note." *Explorations in Economic History* 28:248-257.

_____. 1992a. "The Economics of Exhaustion, the Postan Thesis, and the Agricultural Revolution." *Journal of Economic History* 52:61-84.

_____. 1992b. "Factory Discipline." Unpublished manuscript, University of California, Davis.

Clark, Gregory, Michael Huberman, and Peter Lindert. 1993. "The British Food Puzzle, 1770-1860." Agricultural History Center, University of California, Davis, Working paper No. 70.

Clark, Jonathan C. D. 1986. *Revolution and Rebellion*. Cambridge: Cambridge University Press.

Clark, William. 1991. "The Scientific Revolution in the German Nations." In Roy Porter and Mikulas Teich, eds., *The Scientific Revolution in National Context*. Cambridge: Cambridge University Press.

Clarkson, Leslie A. 1985. *Proto-Industrialization: The First Phase of Industrialization?* London: Macmillan.

Coats, A. W. 1958. "Changing Attitudes to Labour in the Mid-Eighteenth Century." *Economic History Review* 11:35-51. Reprinted in M. W. Flinn and T. C. Smout, eds. 1974. *Essays in Social History*. Oxford: Clarendon Press.

Cohen, Jon S. 1981. "Managers and Machinery: An Analysis of the Rise of Factory Production." *Australian Economic Papers* 20:24-41.

Cohen, Jon S., and Martin Weitzman. 1975. "A Marxian Model of Enclosure." In W. N. Parker and E. L. Jones, eds., *European Peasants and Their Markets: Essays in Agrarian Economic History*. Princeton: Princeton University Press.

Cole, Harold L., George J. Mailath, and Andrew Postlewaite. 1991. "Social Norms, Savings Behavior, and Growth." Unpublished manuscript, CARESS Working Paper no. 91-14.

Cole, W. A. 1981. "Factors in Demand, 1700-1780." In R. C. Floud and D. N. McCloskey, eds., *The Economic History of Britain Since 1700*. Vol. 1. Cambridge: Cambridge University Press.

Cole, W. A. 1981. "Factors in Demand, 1700-1780." In R. C. Floud and D. N. McCloskey, eds., *The Economic History of Britain Since 1700*. Vol. 1. Cambridge: Cambridge University Press.

_____. 1989. Review of *Studies in Capital Formation in the United Kingdom*, ed. Charles H. Feinstein and Sidney Pollard. *Economic History Review* 42:601-602.

Coleman, D. C. 1983. "Proto-Industrialization: A Concept Too Many." *Economic History Review* 36:435-448.

Collier, Frances. 1964. *The Family Economy of the Working Classes in the Cotton Industry, 1784-1833*. Manchester: Manchester University Press.

Collins, B. 1981. "Irish Emigration to Dundee and Paisley During the First Half of the Nineteenth Century." In J. M. Goldstrom and L. A. Clarkson, eds., *Irish Population, Economy, and Society: Essays in Honour of K. H. Connell*. Oxford: Clarendon Press.

Collins, Michael. 1983. "Long-Term Growth of the English Banking Sector and Money Stock, 1844-80." *Economic History Review*. 36:379-395.

Colls, Robert. 1976 "'Oh Happy English Children!': Coal, Class and Education in the North-East." *Past and Present* 73:75-99.

_____. 1981. "A Rejoinder: Debate -- Coal, Class and Education in the North-East." *Past and Present* 90:152-165.

Cottrell, P. L. 1980. *Industrial Finance, 1830-1914.* London: Methuen.

Crafts, N.F.R. 1976. "English Economic Growth in the Eighteenth Century: A Re-examination of Deane and Cole's Estimates." *Economic History Review* 29:226-235.

_____. 1977. "Industrial Revolution in Britain and France: Some Thoughts on the Question 'Why Was England First?'" *Economic History Review* 30:429-441.

_____. 1981. "The Eighteenth Century: A Survey." In R. C. Floud and D. N. McCloskey, eds., *The Economic History of Britain Since 1700.* Vol. 1, Cambridge: Cambridge University Press.

_____. 1982. "Regional Price Variations in England in 1843: An Aspect of the Standard of Living Debate." *Explorations in Economic History* 19:51-70.

_____. 1983a. "British Economic Growth, 1700-1831: A Review of the Evidence." *Economic History Review* 36:177-199.

_____. 1983b. "Gross National Product in Europe, 1870-1910: Some New Estimates." *Explorations in Economic History* 20:387-401.

_____. 1985a. *British Economic Growth During the Industrial Revolution.* New York: Oxford University Press.

_____. 1985b. "Industrial Revolution in England and France: Some Thoughts on the Question 'Why was England First?'" In Joel Mokyr, ed., *The Economics of the Industrial Revolution.* Totowa, N.J.: Rowman and Allanheld.

_____. 1985c. "Income Elasticities of Demand and the Release of Labour by Agriculture During the British Industrial Revolution: A Further Appraisal." In Joel Mokyr, ed., *The Economics of the Industrial Revolution.* Totowa, N.J.: Rowman and Allanheld.

_____. 1985d. "English Workers' Real Wages During the Industrial Revolution: Some Remaining Problems." *Journal of Economic History* 45:139-144.

_____. 1987. "British Economic Growth, 1700-1850: Some Difficulties of Interpretation." *Explorations in Economic History* 24:245-268.

_____. 1989a. "Real Wages, Inequality and Economic Growth in Britain, 1750-1850: A Review of Recent Research." In P. Scholliers, ed., *Real Wages in Nineteenth and Twentieth Century Europe.* Oxford: Berg.

_____. 1989b. "The Industrial Revolution: Economic Growth in Britain, 1700-1860." In Anne Digby and Charles Feinstein, eds., *New Directions in Economic and Social History.* Chicago: Lyceum Books.

_____. 1989c. "British Industrialization in an International Context." *Journal of Interdisciplinary History* 19:415-428.

Crafts, N.F.R., and C. K. Harley. 1992. "Output Growth and the Industrial Revolution: A Restatement of the Crafts-Harley View." *Economic History Review* 45:703-730.

Crafts, N.F.R., S. J. Leybourne, and T. C. Mills. 1989. "Trends and Cycles in British Industrial Production, 1700-1913." *Journal of the Royal Statistical Society* 152:43-60.

_____. 1991. "Britain." In Richard Sylla and Gianni Toniolo, eds., *Patterns of European Industrialization: The Nineteenth Century*. London: Routledge.

Crafts, N.F.R., and Mark Thomas. 1986. "Comparative Advantage in UK Manufacturing Trade, 1910-1935." *The Economic Journal* 96:629-645.

Craig, Gordon. 1980. *Germany, 1866-1945*. New York: Oxford University Press.

Cressy, David. 1980. *Literacy and the Social Order: Reading and Writing in Tudor and Stuart England* Cambridge: Cambridge University Press.

Crouzet, François. 1965. "Capital Formation in Great Britain During the Industrial Revolution." In *The Proceedings of the Second International Conference of Economic History*. The Hague, 1965. Reprinted in F. Crouzet, ed. 1972. *Capital Formation in the Industrial Revolution*. London: Methuen.

_____. 1966. "*Angleterre et France au XVIIIe siècle: essai d'analyse comparée de deux croissances économiques.*" *Annales: économies, sociétés, civilisations* 21:254-291.

_____, ed. 1972. *Capital Formation in the Industrial Revolution*. London: Methuen.

_____. 1985a. *The First Industrialists: The Problems of Origins*. Cambridge: Cambridge University Press.

_____. 1985b. *De la Superiorité de l'Angleterre sur la France*. Paris: Perrin.

_____. 1987. *L'Economie Britannique et le Blocus Continental* 2d ed. Paris: Economica.

_____. 1991. "The Huguenots and the English Financial Revolution." In Patrice Higonnet, David S. Landes, and Henry Rosovsky, eds., *Favorites of Fortune: Technology, Growth, and Economic Development Since the Industrial Revolution*. Cambridge: Harvard University Press.

Cullen, Michael. 1975. *The Statistical Movement in Early Victorian Britain*. Hassocks, Sussex: Harvester Press.

Cunningham, William. 1885. *The Growth of English Industry and Commerce in Modern Times*. Cambridge: Cambridge University Press.

_____. [1907] 1922. *The Industrial Revolution*. Cambridge: Cambridge University Press. These are sections reprinted from the 1907 edition of *The Growth of English Industry and Commerce*, 403-886.

Daumas, Maurice. 1979. "Introduction." In Maurice Daumas, ed., *A History of Technology and Invention, Vol. III: The Expansion of Mechanization, 1725-1860*. New York: Crown.

David, Paul A. 1975. *Technical Choice, Innovation and Economic Growth.* New York: Cambridge University Press.

Davis, Ralph. 1979. *The Industrial Revolution and British Overseas Trade.* Leicester: Leicester University Press.

Deane, Phyllis. 1955. "The Implications of Early National Income Estimates for the Measurement of Long-Term Economic Growth in the United Kingdom." *Economic Development and Cultural Change* 4:3-38.

_____. 1957. "The Output of the British Woolen Industry." *Journal of Economic History* 17:207-223.

_____. 1961. "Capital Formation in Britain Before the Railway Age." *Economic Development and Cultural Change* 9:352-368.

_____. 1965. *The First Industrial Revolution.* Cambridge: Cambridge University Press.

Deane, Phyllis, and W. A. Cole. 1962. *British Economic Growth, 1688-1959.* Cambridge: Cambridge University Press.

_____. 1967 and 1969. *British Economic Growth, 1688-1959.* 2d ed. Cambridge: Cambridge University Press.

Deane, Phyllis, and H. J. Habakkuk. 1963. "The Take-off in Britain." In W. W. Rostow, ed., *The Take-off into Sustained Growth.* London: Macmillan.

De Vries, Jan. 1992. "Between Purchasing Power and the World of Goods: Understanding the Household Economy in Early Modern Europe." In John Brewer and Roy Porter, eds., *Consumption and the World of Goods.* London: Routledge. Forthcoming.

Dick, Malcolm. 1980. "The Myth of the Working-class Sunday School." *History of Education* 9:27-41.

Dosi, Giovanni. 1988. "Sources, Procedures, and Microeconomic Effects of Innovation." *Journal of Economic Literature* 26:1120-1171.

Duffy, Brendan. 1981. "Debate--Coal, Class and Education in the North-East." *Past and Present* 90:142-151.

Dunlop, O. Jocelyn. 1912. *English Apprenticeship and Child Labour: A History.* London: T. Fisher Unwin.

Dutton, H. I. 1984. *The Patent System and Inventive Activity During the Industrial Revolution.* Manchester: Manchester University Press.

Earl, Donald C. 1980. *On the Absence of the Railway Engine.* Hull: University of Hull. (Inaugural lecture for the chair of professor of classics, delivered 14 February 1980.)

Easterlin, Richard. 1981. "Why Isn't the Whole World Developed?" *Journal of Economic History* 41:1-19.

Elbaum, Bernard. 1989. "Why Apprenticeship Persisted in Britain but Not in the United States." *Journal of Economic History* 49:337-350.

Ellison, Thomas. [1886] 1968. *The Cotton Trade of Great Britain.* London: Frank Case.

Engels, Friedrich. [1845] 1887, 1958. *Die Lage der arbeitenden Klasse in England.* Leipzig. English trans. by F. K. Wischnewetzky. 1887. *The Condition of the Working Class in England in 1844.* New York: J. W. Lovell. New translation by W.O. Henderson and W.H. Chaloner. 1958. Stanford: Stanford University Press.

Engerman, Stanley L. 1972. "The Slave Trade and British Capital Formation in the Eighteenth Century: A Comment on the Williams Thesis." *Business History Review* 46:430-443.

Evans, E. J. 1976. *The Contentious Tithe: The Tithe Problem and English Agriculture, 1750-1850.* London: Routledge and Kegan Paul.

Evans, Francis T. 1981. "Roads, Railroads, and Canals: Technical Choices in Nineteenth-Century Britain." *Technology and Culture* 22:1-34.

_____. 1982. "Wood Since the Industrial Revolution: A Strategic Retreat?" *History of Technology* 7:37-56.

Eversley, D.E.C. 1967. "The Home Market and Economic Growth in England, 1750-1780." In E. L. Jones and G. E. Mingay, eds., *Land, Labour and Population in the Industrial Revolution.* London: E. Arnold.

Fairchilds, Cissie. 1992. "A Comparison of the 'Consumer Revolutions' in Eighteenth-Century England and France." Unpublished paper, submitted to the Economic History Association Annual Meeting, Boston.

Falkus, M. E. 1982. "The Early Development of the British Gas Industry, 1790-1815." *Economic History Review* 35:217-234.

Farley, Susan. 1965/1966. "The Nineteenth Century Corn Laws Reconsidered." *Economic History Review* 18:562-573.

Feinstein, Charles. 1978. "Capital Formation in Great Britain." In P. Mathias and M. M. Postan, eds., *The Cambridge Economic History of Europe.* Vol. 7. Cambridge: Cambridge University Press.

_____. 1981. "Capital Accumulation and the Industrial Revolution." In Roderick Floud and Donald N. McCloskey, eds., *The Economic History of Britain Since 1700.* Vol. 1. Cambridge: Cambridge University Press.

_____. 1988a. "National Statistics." In Charles Feinstein and Sidney Pollard, eds., *Studies in the Capital Formation in the United Kingdom, 1750-1920.* Cambridge: Cambridge University Press.

_____. 1988b. "The Rise and Fall of the Williamson Curve." *Journal of Economic History* 48:699-729.

Feinstein, Charles, and Sidney Pollard, eds. 1988. *Studies in Capital Formation in the United Kingdom, 1750-1920.* Oxford: Clarendon Press.

Field, Alexander James. 1979. "Occupational Structure, Dissent, and Educational Commitment: Lancashire, 1841." *Research in Economic History* 4:235-287.

Findlay, Ronald. 1982. "Trade and Growth in the Industrial Revolution." In Charles P. Kindleberger and Guido di Tella, eds., *Economics in the Long*

View: Essays in Honor of W. W. Rostow. Vol. I. New York: New York University Press.

———. 1990. *The "Triangular Trade" and the Atlantic Economy of the Eighteenth Century: A Simple General Equilibrium Model.* Essays in International Finance. Princeton: Princeton University Press.

Fine, Ben, and Ellen Leopold. 1990. "Consumerism and the Industrial Revolution." *Social History* 15:151-179.

Flinn, Michael W. 1959. "Timber and the Advance of Technology: A Reconsideration." *Annals of Science* 15:109-120.

———. 1966. *Origins of the Industrial Revolution.* London: Longmans.

———. 1978. "Technical Change as an Escape from Resource Scarcity: England in the Seventeenth and Eighteenth Centuries." In William N. Parker and Antoni Maczak, eds., *Natural Resources in European History.* Washington, D.C.: Resources for the Future.

———. 1984. *The History of the British Coal Industry.* Vol. 2, *1700-1830.* Oxford: Clarendon Press.

Floud, Roderick, and Donald McCloskey, eds. 1981. *The Economic History of Britain Since 1700.* Cambridge: Cambridge University Press.

Floud, Roderick, Kenneth Wachter, and Annabel Gregory. 1990. *Height, Health, and History: Nutritional Status in the United Kingdom, 1750-1980.* Cambridge: Cambridge University Press.

Fogel, Robert W. 1964. *Railroads and American Economic Growth: Essays in Econometric History.* Baltimore: Johns Hopkins.

———. 1983. "Scientific History and Traditional History." In Robert W. Fogel and G. R. Elton, eds., *Which Road to the Past?* New Haven and London: Yale University Press.

———. 1989. "Second Thoughts on the European Escape from Hunger: Famine, Price Elasticities, Entitlements, Chronic Malnutrition, and Mortality Rates." NBER Working Paper.

———. 1991. "The Conquest of High Mortality and Hunger in Europe and America: Timing and Mechanisms." In Patrice Higonnet, David S. Landes, and Henry Rosovsky, eds., *Favorites of Fortune: Technology, Growth, and Economic Development Since the Industrial Revolution.* Cambridge: Harvard University Press.

Freudenberger, Herman. 1974. "Das Arbeitjahr." In Ingomar Bog et al., eds., *Wirtschaftliche und Soziale Strukturen im saekularen Wandel.* Hanover: Schaper.

Freudenberger, Herman, and Gaylord Cummins. 1976. "Health, Work, and Leisure Before the Industrial Revolution." *Explorations in Economic History.* 13:1-12.

Fussell, G. E. 1959. "The Low Countries' Influence on English Farming." *English Historical Review* 74:611-622.

Gardner, Phil. 1984. *The Lost Elementary Schools of Victorian England*. London: Croom Helm.

Gaski, John F. 1982. "The Cause of the Industrial Revolution: A Brief, 'Single-Factor' Argument." *Journal of European Economic History* 11(Spring):227-233.

Geary, Frank. 1984. "The Cause of the Industrial Revolution and 'Single-Factor' Arguments: An Assessment." *Journal of European Economic History* 13(Spring):167-173.

Gerschenkron, Alexander. 1962. *Economic Backwardness in Historical Perspective: A Book of Essays*. Cambridge, Mass.: Harvard University Press, Belknap Press.

_____. 1968. *Continuity in History and Other Essays*. Cambridge, Mass.: Harvard University Press.

Gibbins, Henry De Beltgens. 1895. *The Industrial History of England*. London: Methuen.

Gibbon, Edward. [1796] 1961. *The Autobiography of Edward Gibbon*. New York: Meridian Press.

Gilboy, E. W. 1932. "Demand as a Factor in the Industrial Revolution." In A. H. Cole, ed., *Facts and Factors in Economic History*. Reprinted in R. M. Hartwell, ed. 1967. *The Causes of the Industrial Revolution in England*. London: Methuen.

_____. 1934. *Wages in Eighteenth Century England*. Cambridge: Harvard University Press.

Gilfillan, S. C. 1935. *The Sociology of Invention*. Cambridge, Mass.: MIT Press.

Gille, Bertrand. 1978. *Histoires des Techniques: Technique et Civilisations, Technique et Sciences*. Paris: Editions Gallimard.

Gillispie, Charles C. 1957. "The Natural History of Industry." *Isis* 48:398-407.

_____. 1980. *Science and Polity in France at the End of the Old Regime*. Princeton: Princeton University Press.

Glennie, Paul. 1993. "Measuring Crop Yields in Early Modern England." In B.M.S. Campbell and M. Overton, eds., *Land, Labour, and Livestock: Historical Studies in European Agricultural Productivity*. Manchester: Manchester University Press. Forthcoming.

Gonner, E.C.K. 1966. *Common Land and Enclosure*. New York: Kelley Reprint.

Good, D. F. 1973. "Backwardness and the Role of Banking in Nineteenth-Century European Industrialization." *Journal of Economic History* 33:845-850.

Graff, Harvey. 1987. *The Legacies of Literacy: Continuities and Contradictions in Western Culture and Society*. Bloomington: Indiana University Press.

Grantham, George. 1989. "Agricultural Supply During the Industrial Revolution: French Evidence and European Implications." *Journal of Economic History* 49:43-72.

Great Britain. 1818. Vol. 6. "Report from the Select Committee Appointed to Consider the Effect of the Laws Which Regulate or Restrain the Interest of Money."

———. 1847. Vol. 27. "Reports of the Commissioners of Inquiry into the State of Education in Wales."

———. 1861. Vol. 21, pt. 2. "Reports of Assistant Commissioners to the Commission Appointed to Inquire into the State of Popular Education in England."

Green, Vivian Hubert Howard. 1969. *The Universities.* Harmondsworth: Penguin.

Greenberg, Dolores. 1982. "Reassessing the Power Patterns of the Industrial Revolution: An Anglo-American Comparison." *American Historical Review* 87:1237-1261.

Griffiths, Richard. 1979. *Industrial Retardation in the Netherlands, 1830-1850.* The Hague: M. Nijhoff.

Griffiths, Trevor, Philip A. Hunt, and Patrick O'Brien. 1992. "Patenting and Inventive Activity in the British Textile Industry, 1700-1800." *Journal of Economic History* 52:881-906.

Griliches, Zvi. 1990. "Patent Statistics as Economic Indicators." *Journal of Economic Literature* 28:1645-1660.

Guillerme, André. 1988. "Wood vs. Iron: The Strength of Materials in Early 19th Century France." *History and Technology* 6:239-252.

Guinnane, Timothy. 1991. "Economics, History, and the Path of Demographic Adjustment: Ireland after the Famine." *Research in Economic History* 13:147-198.

Habakkuk, H. J. 1962. *American and British Technology in the Nineteenth Century: The Search for Labor-saving Inventions.* Cambridge: Cambridge University Press.

———. 1963. "Population Problems and European Economic Development in the Late Eighteenth and Nineteenth Centuries." *American Economic Review* 53:607-618.

Habakkuk, H. J. and P. M. Deane. 1962. "The Take-off in Britain." In W. W. Rostow, ed., *The Economics of Take-off into Sustained Growth.* London: Macmillan.

Hagen, Everett E. 1967. "British Personality and the Industrial Revolution: The Historical Evidence." In T. Burns and S. B. Saul, eds., *Social Theory and Economic Change.* London: Tavistock Publications.

Hall, A. Rupert. 1974. "What Did the Industrial Revolution in Britain Owe to Science?" In Neil McKendrick, ed., *Historical Perspectives: Studies in English Thought and Society.* London: Europa Publications.

Hall, A. Rupert, and Marie Boas Hall. [1964] 1988. *A Brief History of Science.* Ames: Iowa State University Press.

Hammond, J. L. and B. Hammond. 1911. *The Village Labourer, 1760-1832.* London: Longmans, Green and Co.

Hans, Nicholas. 1951. *New Trends in Education in the Eighteenth Century.* London: Routledge & Kegan Paul.

Harley, C. Knick. 1974. "Skilled Labour and the Choice of Technique in Edwardian Industry." *Explorations in Economic History* 11:391-414.

_____. 1980. "Transportation, the World Wheat Trade and the Kuznets Cycle, 1850-1913." *Explorations in Economic History* 18:218-250.

_____. 1982. "British Industrialization Before 1841: Evidence of Slower Growth During the Industrial Revolution." *Journal of Economic History* 42:267-289.

_____. 1988. "Ocean Freight Rates and Productivity, 1740-1913: The Primacy of Mechanical Invention Reaffirmed." *Journal of Economic History* 48:851-876.

_____. 1990. "The State of the British Industrial Revolution: A Survey of Recent Macroeconomic Assessment." Research Report 9012. Department of Economics, University of Western Ontario.

Harris, J. R. 1976. "Skills, Coal and British Industry in the Eighteenth Century." *History* 61:167-182.

Harris, John. 1992. "The First British Measures Against Industrial Espionage." In Ian Blanchard, A. Goodman, and J. Newman, eds., *Industry and Finance in Early Modern History.* Stuttgart: Steineer.

Harrop, Sylvia. 1983. "Literacy and Educational Attitudes as Factors in the Industrialization of North-East Cheshire, 1760-1830." In W. B. Stephens, ed., *Studies in the History of Literacy: England and North America.* Leeds: Museum of the History of Education, University of Leeds.

Hartwell, R. M. 1971a. *The Industrial Revolution and Economic Growth.* London: Methuen.

_____. 1971b. "Historical Analogism, Public Policy, and Social Science in Eleventh and Twelfth Century China." *American Historical Review* 76:690-727.

_____. 1990. "Was There an Industrial Revolution?" *Social Science History* 14:567-576.

Hartwell, R. M., and S. L. Engerman. 1975. "Models of Immiseration: The Theoretical Basis of Pessimism." In Arthur J. Taylor, ed., *The Standard of Living in Britain During the Industrial Revolution.* London: Methuen.

Hauser, Henri. 1931. *Les debuts du capitalisme.* New ed. Paris: Felix Alcan.

Hawke, G. R. 1970. *Railways and Economic Growth in England and Wales, 1840-1870.* Oxford: Oxford University Press.

Heaton, H. 1937. "Financing the Industrial Revolution." *Bulletin of the Business Historical Society* 11. Reprinted in F. Crouzet, ed. 1972. *Capital Formation in the Industrial Revolution.* London: Methuen.

Hawke, G. R. 1970. *Railways and Economic Growth in England and Wales, 1840-1870*. Oxford: Oxford University Press.

Heaton, H. 1937. "Financing the Industrial Revolution." *Bulletin of the Business Historical Society* 11. Reprinted in F. Crouzet, ed. 1972. *Capital Formation in the Industrial Revolution*. London: Methuen.

Heesom, A. J. 1981. "Debate -- Coal, Class and Education in the North-East." *Past and Present* 90:136-142.

Heim, Carol, and Philip Mirowski. 1987. "Interest Rates and Crowding-Out During Britain's Industrial Revolution." *Journal of Economic History* 47:117-139.

_____. 1991. "Crowding Out: A Response to Black and Gilmore." *Journal of Economic History* 51:701-706.

Helling, Gertrud. 1977. *Nahrungsmittel-Produktion und Weltaussenhandel seit Anfang des 19. Jahrhunderts*. Berlin: Akademie-Verlag.

Hernes, Gudmund. 1989. "The Logic of the Protestant Ethic." *Rationality and Society* 1:123-162.

Hicks, J. R. 1946. *Value and Capital*. Oxford: Clarendon Press.

_____. 1969. *A Theory of Economic History*. Oxford: Oxford University Press.

Higginson, J. H. 1974. "Dame Schools." *British Journal of Educational Studies* 22:166-181.

Hikino, Takashi, and Alice H. Amsden. 1993. "Staying Behind, Stumbling Back, Sneaking Up, Soaring Ahead: Late Industrialization in Historical Perspective." In William James Baumol, Richard R. Nelson, and Edward N. Wolff, eds., *International Convergence of Productivity, with Some Evidence of History*. Oxford: Oxford University Press. Forthcoming.

Hills, Richard L. 1979. "Hargreaves, Arkwright, and Crompton: Why Three Separate Inventors?" *Textile History* 10:114-126.

Hirsch, Fred. 1976. *Social Limits to Growth*. Cambridge, Mass.: Harvard University Press.

Hobsbawm, Eric J. 1962. *The Age of Revolution, 1789-1848*. New York: New American Library.

_____. 1975. "The Standard of Living Debate." In Arthur J.Taylor, ed., *The Standard of Living in Britain in the Industrial Revolution*. London: Methuen.

Hoffmann, Walther G. 1955. *British Industry, 1700-1950*. Oxford: Basil Blackwell. Reprinted 1965.

Hogan, David. 1982. "Making It in America: Work, Education, and Social Structure." In Hervey Kantor and David Tyack, eds., *Work, Youth, and Schooling*. Stanford: Stanford University Press.

Holderness, B. A. 1988. "Agriculture, 1770-1860." In C. H. Feinstein and Sidney Pollard, eds., *Studies in Capital Formation in the United Kingdom, 1750-1920*. Oxford: Clarendon Press.

Honeyman, Katrina, and Jordan Goodman. 1991. "Women's Work, Gender Conflict, and Labour Markets in Europe, 1500-1900." *Economic History Review* 44:608-628.

Hopkins, Eric. 1982. "Working Hours and Conditions During the Industrial Revolution: A Reappraisal." *Economic History Review* 35:52-66.

Hoppit, Julian. 1986. "Financial Crises in Eighteenth Century England." *Economic History Review* 39:39-58.

———. 1987. "Understanding the Industrial Revolution." *Historical Journal* 30:211-224.

———. 1990. "Counting the Industrial Revolution." *Economic History Review* 43:173-193.

Horrell, Sara and Jane Humphries. 1992a. "Neither Welcome nor Understood: the Transition to Male Breadwinner Family in British Industrialization." Unpublished Manuscript, Cambridge University.

———. 1992b. "Old Questions, New Data, and Alternative Perspectives: Families' Living Standards in the Industrial Revolution." *Journal of Economic History* 52:849-880.

Houston, R. A. 1985. *Scottish Literacy and the Scottish Identity: Illiteracy and Society in Scotland and Northern England, 1600-1800.* Cambridge: Cambridge University Press.

———. 1988. *Literacy in Early Modern Europe: Culture and Education, 1500-1800.* London: Longman.

Huberman, Michael. 1986. "Invisible Handshakes in Lancashire: Cotton Spinning in the First Half of the Nineteenth Century." *Journal of Economic History* 46: 987-998.

———. 1991. "How Did Labor Markets Work in Lancashire? More Evidence on Prices and Quantities in Cotton Spinning, 1822-1852." *Explorations in Economic History* 28: 87-120.

———. 1992. "Escape From the Market: Fair Wages in Lancashire, 1800-1850." Unpublished manuscript, Trent University.

Huck, Paul F. 1992. "Infant Mortality and the Standard of Living During the Industrial Revolution." Unpublished Ph.D. diss., Northwestern University.

Hudson, Pat. 1983. "From Manor to Mill: the West Riding in Transition." In Maxine Berg, Pat Hudson and Michael Sonenscher, eds., *Manufacture in Town and Country Before the Factory.* Cambridge: Cambridge University Press.

———. ed. 1989. *Regions and Industries: A Perspective on the Industrial Revolution in Britain.* Cambridge: Cambridge University Press.

———. 1992. *The Industrial Revolution.* London: Edward Arnold.

Hueckel, Glenn. 1981. "Agriculture During Industrialization." In R. C. Floud and D. N. McCloskey, eds., *The Economic History of Britain Since 1700.* Vol. 1. Cambridge: Cambridge University Press.

Hughes, J.R.T. 1970. *Industrialization and Economic History.* New York: McGraw-Hill.

Humphries, Jane. 1990. "Enclosures, Common Rights, and Women: The Proletarianization of Families in the Late Eighteenth and Early Nineteenth Centuries." *Journal of Economic History* 50:17-42.

Hunt, E. H. 1986. "Industrialization and Regional Inequality: Wages in Britain, 1760-1914." *Journal of Economic History* 46:935-966.

Hunt, E. H., and F. W. Botham. 1987. "Wages in Britain During the Industrial Revolution." *Economic History Review* 40:380-399.

Hurt, John S. 1971. "Professor West on Early Nineteenth-Century Education." *Economic History Review* 24:624-632.

Huzel, James P. 1969. "Malthus, the Poor Law, and Population in Early Nineteenth Century England." *Economic History Review* 22:430-452.

_____. 1980. "The Demographic Impact of the Old Poor Law: More Reflections on Malthus." *Economic History Review* 33:367-381.

Hyde, Charles. 1977. *Technological Change and the British Iron Industry.* Princeton, N.J.: Princeton University Press.

Inikori, Joseph. 1987. "Slavery and the Development of Industrial Capitalism in England." *Journal of Interdisciplinary History* 17:771-793.

_____. 1989. "Slavery and the Revolution in Cotton Textile Production in England." *Social Science History* 13:343-379.

Inkster, Ian. 1976. "The Social Context of an Educational Movement: A Revisionist Approach to the English Mechanics Institutes, 1820-1850." *Oxford Review of Education* 2:277-307.

_____. 1983a. "Introduction: Aspects of the History of Science and Science Culture in Britain, 1780-1850 and Beyond." In Ian Inkster and Jack Morrell, eds., *Metropolis and Province.* Philadelphia: University of Pennsylvania Press.

_____. 1983b. "Technology as the Cause of the Industrial Revolution: Some Comments." *Journal of European Economic History* 12:651-657.

_____. 1985. "Introduction: The Context of Steam Intellect in Britain (to 1851)." In Ian Inkster, ed., *The Steam Intellect Societies: Essays on Culture, Education and Industry Circa 1820-1914.* Nottingham: Department of Adult Education, University of Nottingham.

_____. 1991. *Science and Technology in History: An Approach to Industrial Development.* New Brunswick: Rutgers University Press.

Jackson, R. V. 1987. "The Structure of Pay in Nineteenth-Century Britain." *Economic History Review* 40:561-570.

_____. 1990. "Government Expenditure and British Economic Growth in the Eighteenth Century: Some Problems of Measurement." *Economic History Review* 43:217-235.

_____. 1992. "Rates of Industrial Growth During the Industrial Revolution." *Economic History Review* 45:1-23.

Jacob, Margaret C. 1988. *The Cultural Meaning of the Scientific Revolution.* New York: Alfred A. Knopf.

Jeremy, David. 1977. "Damming the Flood: British Government Efforts to Check the Outflow of Technicians and Machinery, 1780-1843." *Business History Review* 51:1-34.

_____. 1981. *Transatlantic Industrial Revolution:The Diffusion of Textile Technologies Between Britain and America, 1790-1830s.* Cambridge, Mass.: MIT Press.

John, A. H. 1989. "Statistical Appendix." In G. E. Mingay, ed., *The Agrarian History of England and Wales.* Vol 6, *1750-1850.* Cambridge: Cambridge University Press.

Johnson, Richard. 1970. "Educational Policy and Social Control in Early Victorian England." *Past and Present* 49:96-119.

_____. 1976. "Notes on the Schooling of the English Working Class, 1780-1850." In Roger Dale, Geoff Esland, and Madeleine MacDonald, eds., *Schooling and Capitalism: A Sociological Reader.* London: Routledge & Kegan Paul in association with the Open University Press.

_____. 1977. "Educating the Educators: 'Experts' and the State 1833-9." In A. P. Donajgrodzki, ed., *Social Control in Nineteenth Century Britain.* London: Croom Helm.

Jones, Eric L. 1965. "Agriculture and Economic Growth in England, 1660-1750: Agricultural Change." *Journal of Economic History* 25:1-18.

_____. 1968. "Agricultural Origins of Industry." *Past and Present* 40:58-71.

_____. 1974. *Agriculture and the Industrial Revolution.* Oxford: Blackwell.

_____. 1981a. "Agriculture, 1700-1800." In R. C. Floud and D. N. McCloskey, eds., *The Economic History of Britain Since 1700.* Vol 1. Cambridge: Cambridge University Press.

_____. 1981b. *The European Miracle: Environments, Economies and Geopolitics in the History of Europe and Asia.* Cambridge: Cambridge University Press. 2d ed. 1987.

_____. 1988. *Growth Recurring: Economic Change in World History.* Oxford: Clarendon Press.

Jones, M. G. 1938. *The Charity School Movement: A Study of Eighteenth-Century Puritanism in Action.* Cambridge: Cambridge University Press.

Jones, S.R.H. 1982. "The Organization of Work: A Historical Dimension." *Journal of Economic Behavior and Organization* 3:117-137.

Kerridge, Eric. 1967. *The Agricultural Revolution.* London: Allen and Unwin.

Keynes, John Maynard. 1936. *General Theory of Employment, Interest, and Money.* New York: Harcourt, Brace.

Kiesewetter, H. 1991. "Competition for Wealth and Power: The Growing Rivalry Between Industrial Britain and Industrial Germany, 1815-1914." *Journal of European Economic History* 20:271-299.

Kindleberger, Charles P. 1964. *Economic Growth in France and Britain, 1851-1950*. Cambridge, Mass.: Harvard University Press.

Klemm, Friedrich. 1964. *A History of Western Technology*. Cambridge, Mass.: MIT Press.

Komlos, John. 1989a. "Thinking About the Industrial Revolution." *Journal of European Economic History* 18:191-206.

———. 1989b. *Nutrition and Economic Development in the Eighteenth-Century Hapsburg Monarchy: An Anthropometric History*. Princeton: Princeton University Press.

Kriedte, P. 1981. "Proto-Industrialization Between Industrialization and De-Industrialization." In P. Kriedte, H. Medick, and J. Schlumbohm, eds., *Industrialization Before Industrialization*. Cambridge: Cambridge University Press.

Krikkiat, Phipatseritham, and Kunio Yoshihara. 1989. "Thailand: Industrialization Without Development." *East Asian Cultural Studies* 28:91-100.

Kronick, David A. 1962. *A History of Scientific and Technical Periodicals*. New York: Scarecrow Press.

Kuhn, Thomas S. 1977. *The Essential Tension: Selected Studies in Scientific Tradition and Change*. Chicago: University of Chicago Press.

Kussmaul, Ann. 1990. *A General View of the Rural Economy of England, 1538-1840*. Cambridge: Cambridge University Press.

Kuznets, Simon. 1955. "Economic Growth and Income Inequality." *American Economic Review* 45:1-28.

Kuznets, Simon. 1966. *Modern Economic Growth: Rate, Structure and Spread*. New Haven: Yale University Press.

Landes, David S. 1965a. "Factor Costs and Demand: Determinants of Economic Growth." *Business History* 7:15-33.

———. 1965b. "Technological Change and Development in Western Europe, 1750-1914." In H.J. Habakkuk and M. Postan, eds., *The Cambridge Economic History of Europe*, Vol VI part 1. Cambridge: Cambridge University Press.

———. 1969. *The Unbound Prometheus: Technological Change and Industrial Development in Western Europe from 1750 to the Present*. Cambridge: Cambridge University Press.

———. 1972. "Statistics as a Source for the History of Economic Development in Western Europe: The Protostatistical Era." In Val R. Lorwin and Jacob M. Price eds., *The Dimensions of the Past: Materials, Problems, and Opportunities for Quantitative Work in History*. New Haven, Yale University Press.

———. 1976. "The Standard of Living in the Industrial Revolution Reconsidered." In Otto Busch, ed., *Industrialisierung und "Europaische Wirtschaft" im 19. Jahrhundert: Eine Tagungsbericht*. Berlin: Walter de Gruyter.

_____. 1983. *Revolution in Time: Clocks and the Making of the Modern World.* Cambridge, Mass.: Harvard University Press.

_____. 1986. "What Do Bosses Really Do?" *Journal of Economic History* 46:585-623.

_____. 1987. "Debate: The Ordering of the Urban Environment: Time, Work and the Occurrence of Crowds, 1790-1835." *Past & Present* 116:192-205.

_____. 1990. "Why Are We So Rich and They So Poor?" *American Economic Review* 80:1-13.

_____. 1991. "Does It Pay to Be Late?" In Jean Batou, ed., *Between Development and Underdevelopment: The Precocious Attempts at Industrialization of the Periphery, 1800-1870.* Geneva: Droz.

_____. 1992. "*Homo Faber, Homo Sapiens*: Knowledge, Technology, Growth, and Development." *Contention* 1:81-107.

Laqueur, Thomas. 1974. "Debate: Literacy and Social Mobility in the Industrial Revolution in England." *Past and Present* 64:96-107.

_____. 1976a. "The Cultural Origins of Popular Literacy in England, 1500-1800." *Oxford Review of Education* 2:255-275.

_____. 1976b. "Working Class Demand and the Growth of English Elementary Education." In Lawrence Stone, ed., *Schooling and Society.* Baltimore: Johns Hopkins University Press.

_____. 1976c. *Religion and Respectability: Sunday Schools and Working Class Culture, 1780-1850.* New Haven: Yale University Press.

Lawson, John, and Harold Silver. 1973. *A Social History of Education in England.* London: Methuen.

Lazonick, William. 1990. *Competitive Advantage on the Shop Floor.* Cambridge: Harvard University Press.

Lee, Clive. 1986. *The British Economy Since 1700.* Cambridge: Cambridge University Press.

Lee, Ronald D. 1973. "Population in Pre-Industrial England: An Econometric Analysis." *Quarterly Journal of Economics* 87:581-607.

_____. 1988. "Population Homeostasis and English Demographic History." In R. I. Rotberg and T. K. Rabb, eds., *Population and Economy.* Cambridge: Cambridge University Press.

Lees, Lynn H. 1979. *Exiles of Erin: Irish Migrants in Victorian London.* Manchester: Manchester University Press.

Leinster-Mackay. 1976. "Dame Schools: A Need for Review." *British Journal of Educational Studies* 24:33-48.

Levasseur, Emile. 1911. *Histoire du Commerce de la France,* 2 Vols. Paris: A. Rousseau.

Levine, David. 1987. *Reproducing Families: The Political Economy of English Population History.* Cambridge: Cambridge University Press.

Levine, Kenneth. 1986. *The Social Context of Literacy*. London: Routledge and Kegan Paul.

Lewis, W. A. 1965. *Education and Economic Development*. University of Saskatchewan, University Lectures no. 6. Saskatoon: University of Saskatchewan.

Lindert, Peter H. 1980. "English Occupations, 1670-1811." *Journal of Economic History* 40:685-712.

———. 1986. "Unequal English Wealth Since 1670." *Journal of Political Economy* 94:1127-1162.

———. 1992. "Unequal Living Standards." In Roderick Floud and Donald N. McCloskey, eds., *The Economic History of Britain since 1700*. 2d ed. Cambridge: Cambridge University Press. Forthcoming.

Lindert, Peter H., and Jeffrey G. Williamson. 1982. "Revising England's Social Tables, 1688-1812." *Explorations in Economic History* 19:385-408.

———. 1983a. "Reinterpreting England's Social Tables, 1688-1913." *Explorations in Economic History* 20:94-109.

———. 1983b. "English Workers' Living Standards During the Industrial Revolution: A New Look." *Economic History Review* 36:1-25.

———. 1985a. "English Workers' Living Standards during the Industrial Revolution: A New Look." In Joel Mokyr, ed., *The Economics of the Industrial Revolution*. Totowa, N.J.: Rowman and Littlefield.

———. 1985b. "English Workers' Real Wages: Reply to Crafts." *Journal of Economic History* 45:145-153.

Lines, Clifford. 1990. *Companion to the Industrial Revolution*. New York: Facts on File.

Lloyd-Jones, Roger. 1990. "The First Kondratieff: The Long Wave and the British Industrial Revolution." *Journal of Interdisciplinary History* 20:581-605.

Lyons, John S. 1989. "Family Response to Economic Decline: Handloom Weavers in Early Nineteenth-Century Lancashire." *Research in Economic History* 12:45-91.

McCloskey, Donald. 1973. "New Perspectives on the Old Poor Law." *Explorations in Economic History* 10:419-436.

———. 1975. "The Economics of Enclosure: A Market Analysis." In W. N. Parker and E. L. Jones, eds., *European Peasants and Their Markets: Essays in Agrarian Economic History*. Princeton: Princeton University Press.

———. 1981. "The Industrial Revolution: A Survey." In R. C. Floud and D. N. McCloskey, eds., *The Economic History of Britain Since 1700*. Vol 1. Cambridge: Cambridge University Press.

———. 1985. "The Industrial Revolution, 1780-1860: A Survey." In Joel Mokyr, ed., *The Economics of the Industrial Revolution*. Totowa, N. J.: Rowman and Allanheld.

_____. 1987. "Continuity in Economic History." In J. Eatwell, M. Milgate, and P. Newman, eds., *The New Palgrave*. New York: Stockton Press.

_____. 1988. "The Storied Character of Economics." *Tijdschrift voor Geschiedenis* 101:643-654.

_____. 1990a. *If You're So Smart: The Narrative of Economic Expertise*. Chicago: University of Chicago Press.

_____. 1990b. "Ancients and Moderns." *Social Science History* 14:289-303.

_____. 1991. "Kinks, Tools, Spurts and Substitutes: Gerschenkron's Rhetoric of Relative Backwardness." In Richard Sylla and Gianni Toniolo, eds., *Patterns of European Industrialization: The Nineteenth Century*. London: Routledge.

_____. 1992. "Introductory Chapter for the Period 1780-1860." In Roderick Floud and D. N. McCloskey, eds., *The Economic History of Britain, 1700-1980*. 2d ed. Cambridge: Cambridge University Press. Forthcoming.

MacFarlane, Alan. 1978. *The Origins of English Individualism*. Oxford: Blackwell.

McKay, John. 1970. *Pioneers for Profit: Foreign Entrepreneurship and Russian Industrialization, 1885-1913*. Chicago: University of Chicago Press.

McKendrick, Neil. 1961. "Josiah Wedgwood and Factory Discipline." *The Historical Journal* 4:30-55.

_____. 1974. "Home Demand and Economic Growth: A New View of the Role of Women and Children in the Industrial Revolution." In N. McKendrick, ed., *Historical Perspectives: Studies in English Thought and Society in Honour of J. H. Plumb*. London: Europa Publications.

_____. 1982. "Commercialization and the Economy." In Neil McKendrick, John Brewer, and J. H. Plumb, eds., *The Birth of a Consumer Society*. Bloomington: Indiana University Press.

MacKie-Mason, Jeffrey K. 1990. "Do Firms Care Who Provides Their Financing?" In R. Glenn Hubbard, ed., *Asymmetric Information, Corporate Finance, and Investment*. Chicago: University of Chicago Press.

MacLeod, Christine. 1988. *Inventing the Industrial Revolution: The English Patent System, 1660-1880*. Cambridge: Cambridge University Press.

_____. 1991. "The Paradoxes of Patenting: Invention and Its Diffusion in 18th and 19th Century Britain, France, and North America." *Technology and Culture* 32:885-910.

McNeill, William H. 1982. *The Pursuit of Power*. Chicago: University of Chicago Press.

Maddison, Angus. 1982. *Phases of Capitalist Development*. Oxford: Oxford University Press.

Malthus, Thomas R. 1820. *Principles of Political Economy*. London: J. Murray.

Mandeville, Bernard. [1732] 1924. *The Fable of the Bees*. Oxford: Oxford University Press.

Mankiw, N. Gregory, David Romer, and David N. Weil. 1992. "A Contribution to the Empirics of Economic Growth." *Quarterly Journal of Economics* 107:407-437.

Mantoux, Paul. 1928. *The Industrial Revolution in the Eighteenth Century*. New York: Harper Torchbooks. Rev. ed. 1961.

Marcham, A. J. 1978. Review of *Popular Education and Socialization in the Nineteenth Century*, ed. Phillip McCann. *History of Education* 7:69-73.

Marglin, S. A. 1974-1975. "What Do Bosses Do?" *Review of Radical Political Economy* 6(1974) and 7(1975). Reprinted in A. Gorz, ed. 1976. *The Division of Labour: the Labour Process and Class Struggle in Modern Capitalism*. Hassocks: Harvester Press.

Marsden, W. E. 1987. *Unequal Educational Provision in England and Wales: The Nineteenth-Century Roots*. London: Woburn.

Marshall, Alfred. 1923. *Industry and Trade*. 4th ed. London: Macmillan.

Marx, Karl. [1867] 1887, 1967, 1977. *Das Kapital*. English translation, *Capital*, by Samuel Moore and Edward Aveling with preface by Friedrich Engels. 2 vols. London: S. Sonnenschein, Lowrey, and Co., 1887. Reprint. New York: International Publishers, 1967. Reprint. New York: Vintage Books, 1977.

Mathias, Peter. 1969. *The First Industrial Nation: An Economic History of Britain, 1700-1914*. London: Methuen.

_____. 1979. *The Transformation of England*. New York: Columbia University Press.

Mathias, Peter and John Davis (eds.). 1989. *The First Industrial Revolution*. Oxford: Basil Blackwell.

Matsuyama, Kiminori. 1991. "Increasing Returns, Industrialization, and Indeterminacy of Equilibrium." *Quarterly Journal of Economics* 106:617-634.

_____. 1992. "Agricultural Productivity, Comparative Advantage, and Economic Growth." *Journal of Economic Theory* 58:317-334.

Mayshar, Joram. 1983a. "On Divergence of Opinion and Imperfections in Capital Markets." *American Economic Review* 73:114-128.

_____. 1983b. "Financial Constraints on Investment by the Firm." Unpublished manuscript, Department of Finance, KGSM, Northwestern University.

Medick, H. 1981. "The Proto-Industrial Family Economy." In P. Kriedte, H. Medick, and J. Schlumbohm, eds., *Industrialization Before Industrialization*. Cambridge: Cambridge University Press.

Millward, Robert. 1981. "The Emergence of Wage Labor in Early Modern England." *Explorations in Economic History* 18:21-39.

Mingay, Gordon. 1963. *English Landed Society in the Eighteenth Century*. London: Routledge and Kegan Paul.

_____. 1969. "Dr Kerridge's 'Agricultural Revolution': A Comment." *Agricultural History* 43:477-481.

_____, ed. 1977. *The Agricultural Revolution: Changes in Agriculture, 1650-1880.* London: Adam and Charles Black.

MIT Commission on Industrial Productivity. 1989. *Made in America: Regaining the Productive Edge.* Cambridge: MIT Press.

Mitch, David. 1982. "The Spread of Literacy in Nineteenth-Century England." Ph.D diss., University of Chicago.

_____. 1984. "Underinvestment in Literacy? The Potential Contribution of Government Involvement in Elementary Education to Economic Growth in Nineteenth-Century England." *Journal of Economic History* 44:557-566.

_____. 1992a. *The Rise of Popular Literacy in Victorian England: The Influence of Private Choice and Public Policy.* Philadelphia: University of Pennsylvania Press.

_____. 1992b. "The Rise of Popular Literacy in Europe." In Bruce Fuller and Richard Rubinson, eds., *The Political Construction of Education.* New York: Praeger.

Mitchell, B. R. 1975. *Abstract of European Historical Statistics.* London: Methuen.

_____. 1988. *British Historical Statistics.* 2d ed. Cambridge: Cambridge University Press.

Mitchell, B. R., and P. Deane. 1962. *Abstract of British Historical Statistics.* Cambridge: Cambridge University Press.

Modigliani, F. 1961. "Long-Run Implications of Alternative Fiscal Policies and the Burden of the National Debt." *Economic Journal* 71:730-755.

Mokyr, Joel. 1975. "Capital, Labour and the Delay of the Industrial Revolution in the Netherlands." *Economic History Yearbook* (Amsterdam) 38:280-299.

_____. 1976a. *Industrialization in the Low Countries, 1795-1850.* New Haven: Yale University Press.

_____. 1976b. "Growing-Up and the Industrial Revolution in Europe." *Explorations in Economic History* 13:371-396.

_____. 1983. *Why Ireland Starved.* London: Allen and Unwin.

_____. 1985a. "The Industrial Revolution and the New Economic History." In Joel Mokyr, ed., *The Economics of the Industrial Revolution.* Totowa, N.J.: Rowman and Allanheld.

_____. 1985b. "Demand vs. Supply in the Industrial Revolution." In Joel Mokyr, ed., *The Economics of the Industrial Revolution.* Totowa, N.J.: Rowman and Allanheld.

_____. ed. 1985c. *The Economics of the Industrial Revolution.* Totowa, N.J.: Rowman and Allanheld.

_____. 1987. "Has the Industrial Revolution Been Crowded Out? Some Reflections on Crafts and Williamson." *Explorations in Economic History* 24:293-319.

_____. 1988. "Is There Still Life in the Pessimist Case? Consumption During the Industrial Revolution, 1790-1850." *Journal of Economic History* 48:69-92.

_____. 1990a. *The Lever of Riches: Technological Creativity and Economic Progress.* New York: Oxford University Press.

_____. 1990b. "Punctuated Equilibria and Technological Progress." *American Economic Review.* 80:350-54.

_____. 1991a. "Was There a British Industrial Evolution?" In Joel Mokyr, ed., *The Vital One: Essays Presented to Jonathan R. T. Hughes.* Greenwich, Conn.: JAI Press. *Research in Economic History.* Suppl. 6. Greenwich, Conn.: JAI Press, 1991.

_____. 1991b. "Dear Labor, Cheap Labor, and the Industrial Revolution." In Patrice Higonnet, David S. Landes, and Henry Rosovsky, eds., *Favorites of Fortune: Technology, Growth, and Economic Development Since the Industrial Revolution.* Cambridge: Harvard University Press.

_____. 1992a. "Technological Change, 1700-1830." In Roderick Floud and D. N. McCloskey, eds., *The Economic History of Britain, 1700-1980.* 2d ed. Cambridge: Cambridge University Press. Forthcoming.

_____. 1992b. "Progress and Inertia in Technological Change." In John James and Mark Thomas, eds., *Capitalism in Context: Essays in Honor of R. M. Hartwell.* Forthcoming.

Mokyr, Joel, and N. E. Savin. 1976. "Stagflation in Historical Perspective: The Napoleonic Wars Revisited." In P. Uselding, ed., *Research in Economic History.* Vol. 1. Greenwich, Conn.: JAI Press.

Mokyr, Joel, and Cormac O Gráda. 1988. "Poor and Getting Poorer? Living Standards in Ireland Before the Famine." *Economic History Review* 41:209-235.

More, Charles. 1980. *Skill and the English Working Class, 1870-1914.* New York: St. Martin's.

Muller, Jerry Z. 1990. "Justus Moser and the Conservative Critique of Early Modern Capitalism." *Central European History* 23:153-178.

Musson, Albert E. 1975. "Continental Influences on the Industrial Revolution in Great Britain." In Barrie M. Ratcliffe, ed., *Great Britain and Her World: Essays in Honor of W. O. Henderson.* Manchester: Manchester University Press.

_____. 1976. "Industrial Motive Power in the United Kingdom, 1800-1870." *Economic History Review* 29:415-439.

_____. 1978. *The Growth of British Industry.* London: Batsford.

Musson, A. E., and Eric Robinson. 1969. *Science and Technology in the Industrial Revolution.* Manchester: Manchester University Press.

Nardinelli, Clark. 1980. "Child Labor and the Factory Acts." *Journal of Economic History* 40:739-755.

_____. 1990. *Child Labor and the Industrial Revolution.* Bloomington: Indiana University Press.

Neal, Larry. 1990. *The Rise of Financial Capitalism: International Capital Markets in the Age of Reason.* Cambridge: Cambridge University Press.

_____. 1992. "The Finance of Business During the Industrial Revolution." In Roderick Floud and Donald N. McCloskey, eds., *The Economic History of Britain Since 1700.* 2d ed. Cambridge: Cambridge University Press. Forthcoming.

Nef, John U. 1933. *The Rise of the British Coal Industry.* 2 vols. London: G. Routledge and Sons.

_____. 1934. "The Progress of Technology and the Growth of Large-Scale Industry in Great Britain, 1540-1640." *Economic History Review* 5:3-24.

_____. 1957. *Industry and Government in France and England, 1540-1640.* Ithaca: Cornell University Press.

Nicholas, Stephen J. 1985. "Technical Education and the Decline of Britain." In Ian Inkster, ed., *The Steam Intellect Societies.* Nottingham: Department of Adult Education, University of Nottingham.

Nicholas, Stephen J., and Jacqueline M. Nicholas. 1992. "Male Literacy, 'Deskilling' and the Industrial Revolution." *Journal of Interdisciplinary History* 23:1-18.

Nicholas, Stephen J. and Deborah Oxley. 1992. "The Living Standards of Women during the Industrial Revolution," Unpublished paper.

Nicholas, Stephen J., and Peter Shergold. 1987a. "Intercounty Labour Mobility During the Industrial Revolution: Evidence from the Australian Transportation Records." *Oxford Economic Papers* 39:624-640.

_____. 1987b. "Human Capital and the Pre-Famine Irish Emigration to England." *Explorations in Economic History* 24:158-177.

North, Douglass C. 1968. "Sources of Productivity Change in Ocean Shipping, 1600-1850." *Journal of Political Economy* 76:953-970.

_____. 1981. *Structure and Change in Economic History.* New York: Norton.

_____. 1990. *Institutions, Institutional Change, and Economic Performance.* Cambridge: Cambridge University Press.

North, Douglass C., and Barry Weingast. 1989. "Constitutions and Commitment: Evolution of Institutions Governing Public Choice in Seventeenth Century England." *Journal of Economic History* 49:803-832.

Nye, John V. 1991a. "The Myth of Free-Trade Britain and Fortress France." *Journal of Economic History* 51:23-46.

_____. 1991b. "Lucky Fools and Cautious Businessmen: Entrepreneurship and the Measurement of Entrepreneurial Failure." In Joel Mokyr, ed., *The Vital One: Essays Presented to Jonathan R. T. Hughes.* Greenwich, Conn.: JAI Press.

O'Brien, Patrick. 1983. *Railways and the Economic Development of Western Europe, 1830-1914.* London: Macmillan.

_____. 1985. "Agriculture and the Home Market for English Industry, 1660-1820." *English Historical Review* 38:773-800.

_____. 1986. "Do We Have a Typology for the Study of European Industrialization in the XIXth Century?" *Journal of European Economic History* 15:291-333.

_____. 1991. "The State and the Economy, 1688-1815." Institute of Historical Research mimeo. Draft chapter for R. Floud and D. N. McCloskey, eds., *The Economic History of Britain Since 1700.* 2d ed. Cambridge: Cambridge University Press. Forthcoming.

O'Brien, Patrick, and Stanley L. Engerman. 1981. "Changes in Income and its Distribution During the Industrial Revolution." In Roderick Floud and Donald N. McCloskey, eds., *The Economic History of Britain Since 1700.* 1st ed. Vol. 1. Cambridge: Cambridge University Press.

_____. 1991. "Exports and the Growth of the British Economy from the Glorious Revolution to the Peace of Amiens." In Barbara Solow, ed., *Slavery and the Rise of the Atlantic System.* Cambridge: Cambridge University Press.

O'Brien, Patrick, Trevor Griffiths, and Philip Hunt. 1991. "Political Components of the Industrial Revolution: Parliament and the English Cotton Textile Industry, 1660-1774." *Economic History Review* 44:395-423.

O'Brien, Patrick, and Caglar Keyder. 1978. *Economic Growth in Britain and France, 1780-1914: Two Paths to the 20th Century.* London: Allen and Unwin.

O'Day, Rosemary. 1982. *Education and Society, 1500-1800.* London: Longmans.

O Gráda, Cormac. 1992. *Ireland, 1780-1939: A New Economic History.* Oxford: Oxford University Press.

Olson, Mancur. 1982. *The Rise and Decline of Nations.* New Haven: Yale University Press.

Orwin, Charles Stewart, and Christabel Susan Orwin. 1938. *The Open Fields.* Oxford: Oxford University Press.

Overton, Mark. 1979. "Estimating Grain Yields from Probate Inventories: An Example from East Anglia, 1585-1735." *Journal of Economic History* 39:363-378.

_____. 1991. "The Determinants of Crop Yields in Early Modern England." In B.M.S. Campbell and M. Overton, eds., *Land, Labour, and Livestock: Historical Studies in European Agricultural Productivity.* Manchester: Manchester University Press.

Pacey, Arnold. 1975. *The Maze of Ingenuity: Ideas and Idealism in the Development of Technology.* New York: Holmes and Meier.

_____. 1990. *Technology in World Civilization.* Cambridge, Mass.: MIT Press.

Parker, Irene. [1914] 1969. *Dissenting Academies in England.* Cambridge: Cambridge University Press.

Parker, William N. 1979. "Industry." In Peter Burke, ed., *The New Cambridge Modern History.* Vol. 13. Companion Volume. Cambridge University Press.

_____. 1984. *Europe, America, and the Wider World.* Cambridge: Cambridge University Press.

Paulinyi, Akos. 1986. "Revolution and Technology." In Roy Porter and Mikulas Teich, eds., *Revolution in History.* Cambridge: Cambridge University Press.

Perkin, Harold J. 1969. *The Origins of Modern English Society, 1780-1880.* London: Routledge and Kegan Paul.

Persson, Karl Gunnar. 1991. "The Never Ending Controversy: Agrarian and Industrial Productivity Growth in Britain, 1750-1860." Discussion paper 91-04, Institute of Economics, University of Copenhagen.

Phelps Brown, E. H. 1988. *Egalitarianism and the Generation of Inequality.* Oxford: Oxford University Press.

Phelps Brown, E. H., and Sheila V. Hopkins. 1956. "Seven Centuries of the Prices of Consumables, Compared with Builders' Wage Rates." *Economica* 23:296-314.

Polanyi, Karl. [1944] 1985. *The Great Transformation.* Boston: Beacon Press.

Pollard, Sidney. 1963. "Factory Discipline in the Industrial Revolution." *Economic History Review* 16:254-271.

_____. 1964. "Fixed Capital in the Industrial Revolution." *Journal of Economic History* 24:299-314. Reprinted in F. Crouzet, ed. 1972. *Capital Formation in the Industrial Revolution.* London: Methuen.

_____. [1965] 1968. *The Genesis of Modern Management.* London: Penguin.

_____. 1978. "Labour in Great Britain." In Mathias and Postan, eds., *The Cambridge Economic History of Europe.* Vol. 6. Cambridge: Cambridge University Press.

_____. 1980. "A New Estimate of British Coal Production, 1750-1850." *Economic History Review* 33:212-235.

_____. 1981. *Peaceful Conquest: The Industrialization of Europe, 1760-1970.* Oxford: Oxford University Press.

_____. 1985. "Industrialization and the European Economy." In Joel Mokyr, ed., *The Economics of the Industrial Revolution.* Totowa, N.J.: Rowman and Allanheld.

_____. 1988. "Coal Mining." In Charles Feinstein and Sidney Pollard, eds., *Studies in the Capital Formation in the United Kingdom, 1750-1920.* Cambridge: Cambridge University Press.

_____. 1989. *Britain's Prime and Britain's Decline: The British Economy, 1870-1914.* London: Edward Arnold.

Porter, Roy. 1992. "The Heart of the Country." *The New Republic,* (May 4):35-38.

Postan, M. M. 1935. "Recent Trends in the Accumulation of Capital." *Economic History Review* 6:1-12. Reprinted in F. Crouzet, ed. 1972. *Capital Formation in the Industrial Revolution.* London: Methuen.

_____. 1966. "Agrarian Society in Its Prime: Part 7, England." In M. M. Postan, ed., *Cambridge Economic History of Europe. Vol. 1, The Agrarian Life of the Middle Ages.* Cambridge: Cambridge University Press.

Pressnell, L. S. 1956. *Country Banking in the Industrial Revolution.* Oxford: Clarendon Press.

Prince, Hugh C. 1989. "The Changing Rural Landscape, 1750-1850." In G. E. Mingay, ed., *The Agrarian History of England and Wales.* Vol. 6, *1750-1850.* Cambridge: Cambridge University Press.

Quick, Patricia. 1974. "Education and Industrialization: Elementary Education in Nineteenth Century England and Wales." Ph.D diss., Department of Economics, Harvard University.

Randall, Adrian. 1991. *Before the Luddites.* Cambridge: Cambridge University Press.

Ranis, G., and J.C.H. Fei. 1969. "Economic Development in Historical Perspective." *American Economic Review* 59:386-400.

Redford, Arthur. [1926] 1964, 1976. *Labour Migration in England, 1800-1850.* Manchester: Manchester University Press, 1964. Reprint. Manchester: Manchester University Press, 1976.

Reich, Robert. 1991. *The Work of Nations.* New York: Alfred A. Knopf.

Reid, D. A. 1976. "The Decline of St. Monday, 1766-1876." *Past and Present* 71:76-101.

Reynolds, Terry S. 1983. *Stronger than a Hundred Men: A History of the Vertical Water Wheel.* Baltimore: Johns Hopkins University Press.

Richardson, David. 1987. "The Slave Trade, Sugar, and British Economic Growth, 1748-1776." *Journal of Interdisciplinary History* 17:739-769.

Richardson, Philip. 1989. "The Structure of Capital During the Industrial Revolution Revisited: Two Case Studies from the Cotton Textile Industry." *Economic History Review* 42:484-503.

Riley, James C. 1991. "Nutrition in Western Europe, 1750-1985: Melioration and Deterioration." Presented at the meeting of the Social Science History Association.

Robinson, Sherman. 1989. "Multisectoral Models." In H. Chenery and T. N. Srinivasan, eds., *Handbook of Development Economics.* Vol. 2. Amsterdam: Elsevier Science Publishers B.V.

Roderick, Gordon, and Michael Stephens. 1981. "The Role of Government." In Gordon Roderick and Michael Stephens, eds., *Where Did We Go Wrong?: Industry, Education and the Economy of Victorian Britain.* Barcombe, Lewes, Sussex: The Falmer Press.

Roehl, Richard. 1976. "French Industrialization: A Reconsideration." *Explorations in Economic History* 13:233-281.

Rosenberg, Nathan. 1963. "Technological Change in the Machine Tool Industry, 1840-1910." *Journal of Economic History* 33:414-443.

_____. 1965. "Adam Smith on the Division of Labour: Two Views or One?" *Economica* 32:127-139.

_____. 1967. "Anglo-American Wage Differences in the 1820s." *Journal of Economic History* 27:221-229.

_____. 1976. *Perspectives in Technology.* Cambridge: Cambridge University Press.

Rostow, W. W. 1960. *The Stages of Economic Growth.* Cambridge: Cambridge University Press. Reprinted 1963.

_____, ed. 1963. *The Take-off into Sustained Growth.* London: Macmillan.

_____. 1985. "No Random Walk: A Comment." In Joel Mokyr, ed., *The Economics of the Industrial Revolution.* Totowa, N.J.: Rowman and Allanheld.

Rothblatt, Sheldon. 1968. *The Revolution of the Dons: Cambridge and Society in Victorian England.* New York: Basic Books.

Rowlands, Marie B. 1989. "Continuity and Change in an Industrializing Society: The Case of the West Midlands Industries." In Pat Hudson, ed., *Regions and Industries: A Perspective on the Industrial Revolution in Britain.* Cambridge: Cambridge University Press.

Rule, John. 1983. *The Experience of Labour in Eighteenth-Century English Industry.* New York: St. Martin's Press.

Rutherford, T. 1988. "General Equilibrium Modelling with MPS/GE." Unpublished manuscript, Department of Economics, University of Western Ontario.

Sabel, Charles, and Jonathan Zeitlin. 1985. "Historical Alternatives to Mass Production: Politics, Markets, and Technology in Nineteenth-Century Industrialization." *Past and Present* 108:133-176.

Samuel, Raphael. 1977. "Workshop of the World: Steam Power and Hand Technology in Mid-Victorian Britain." *History Workshop* 3:6-72.

Sanderson, Michael. 1966. "The Basic Education of Labour in Lancashire, 1780-1839." Ph.D. diss., Cambridge University.

_____. 1967. "Education and the Factory in Industrial Lancashire, 1780-1840." *Economic History Review* 20:266-279.

_____. 1968. "Social Change and Elementary Education in Industrial Lancashire, 1780-1840." *Northern History* 3:131-154.

_____. 1972a. "Literacy and Social Mobility in the Industrial Revolution in England." *Past and Present* 56:75-104.

_____. 1972b. *The Universities and British Industry, 1850-1970.* London: Routledge and Kegan Paul.

_____. 1974. "A Rejoinder--Debate: Literacy and Social Mobility in the Industrial Revolution in England." *Past and Present* 64:108-112.

Sandin, Bengt. 1988. "Education, Popular Culture, and the Surveillance of the Population in Stockholm Between 1600 and the 1840s." *Continuity and Change* 3:357-390.

Saul, S. B. 1970. *Technological Change: The United States and Britain in the Nineteenth Century.* London: Methuen.

Scherer, F. Michael. 1984. *Innovation and Growth.* Cambridge, Mass.: MIT Press.

Schmiechen, James. 1984. *Sweated Industries and Sweated Labour: The London Clothing Trades, 1860-1914.* Urbana, Ill.: University of Illinois Press.

Schmookler, Jacob. 1966. *Invention and Economic Growth.* Cambridge, Mass.: Harvard University Press.

Schofield, Robert. 1963. *The Lunar Society of Birmingham.* Oxford: Clarendon Press.

Schofield, Roger. 1968. "The Measurement of Literacy in Pre-Industrial England." In J. Goody, ed., *Literacy in Traditional Societies.* Cambridge: Cambridge University Press.

_____. 1973. "Dimensions of Illiteracy, 1750-1850." *Explorations in Economic History* 10:437-454.

Schumpeter, Elizabeth B. 1960. *English Overseas Trade Statistics, 1697-1808.* Oxford: Clarendon Press.

Schwarz, L. D. 1990. "Trends in Real Wage Rates, 1750-1790: A Reply to Hunt and Botham." *Economic History Review* 43:90-98.

Scitovsky, Tibor. 1971. *Welfare and Competition.* Rev. ed. Homewood, Ill.: R. D. Irwin.

Scrimshaw, N. S. 1983. "Functional Consequences of Malnutrition for Human Populations." In R. I. Rotberg and T. K. Rabb, eds., *Hunger and History.* Cambridge: Cambridge University Press.

Sée, Henri. 1925. "A propos du mot 'industrie,'" *Revue Historique,* Vol. 149, pp. 58-61.

Sen, Amartya. 1987. *The Standard of Living.* Cambridge: Cambridge University Press.

Shammas, Carole. 1990. *The Pre-Industrial Consumer in England and America.* Oxford: Clarendon Press.

Shiel, Robert S. 1991. "Improving Soil Productivity in the Pre-Fertilizer Era." In B.M.S. Campbell and M. Overton, eds., *Land, Labour, and Livestock: Historical Studies in European Agricultural Productivity.* Manchester: Manchester University Press.

Shoven, J. B., and J. Whalley. 1984. "Applied General Equilibrium Models of Taxation and International Trade." *Journal of Economic Literature* 22:1007-1051.

Silver, Harold. 1977. "Aspects of Neglect: The Strange Case of Victorian Popular Education." *Oxford Review of Education* 3:57-69.

Simon, Joan. 1968. "Was There a Charity School Movement?" In Brian Simon, ed., *Education in Leicestershire, 1540-1940.* Leicester: Leicester University Press.

_____. 1979. "Private Classical Schools in Eighteenth-Century England: A Critique of Hans." *History of Education* 8:179-191.

Slater, Gilbert. 1907. *The English Peasantry and the Enclosure of the Common Fields*. London: A. Constable.

Smelser, Neil J. 1959. *Social Change in the Industrial Revolution*. Chicago: University of Chicago Press.

Smith, Adam. 1759. *Theory of Moral Sentiments*. London: A. Millar.

_____. [1776] 1976. *An Inquiry into the Nature and Causes of the Wealth of Nations*. Cannan ed. Chicago: University of Chicago Press. Reprint. Oxford: Oxford University Press, 1976.

_____. 1978. *Lectures on Jurisprudence*. Oxford: Clarendon Press.

Smout, T. C. 1969. *A History of the Scottish People, 1560-1830*. New York: Charles Scribner's and Sons.

Snell, K.D.M. 1985. *Annals of the Labouring Poor: Social Change and Agrarian England, 1660-1900*. Cambridge: Cambridge University Press.

Snooks, Graeme D. 1990. "Economic Growth during the Last Millennium: A Quantitative Perspective for the British Industrial Revolution." Working Paper no. 140. Department of Economic History, Australian National University.

Sokoloff, Kenneth. 1988. "Inventive Activity in Early Industrial America: Evidence from Patent Records, 1790-1846." *Journal of Economic History* 48:813850.

Sokoloff, Kenneth L., and David Dollar. 1991. "Agricultural Seasonality and the Organization of Manufacturing During early Industrialization: The Contrast Between Britain and the United States." NBER Research Report, no. 33. Cambridge, Mass.

Solar, Peter. 1983. "Poor Relief and Economic Development in Britain and Ireland until the mid-Nineteenth Century." Unpublished manuscript.

_____. 1992. "The Contribution of Poor Relief to English Economic Development before the Industrial Revolution." Unpublished manuscript.

Solow, Barbara L. 1987. "Capitalism and Slavery in the Exceedingly Long Run." *Journal of Interdisciplinary History* 17:711-737.

Solow, Robert. 1957. "Technological Change and the Aggregate Production Function." *Review of Economics and Statistics* 39:312-320.

Soltow, Lee. 1968. "Long-Run Changes in British Income Inequality." *Economic History Review* 21:17-29.

Spufford, Margaret. 1979. "First Steps in Literacy: The Reading and Writing Experiences of the Humblest Seventeenth-Century Spiritual Autobiographers." *Social History* 4:407-435.

Stedman Jones, Gareth. 1977. "Class Expression Versus Social Control?: A Critique of Recent Trends in the Social History of 'Leisure.'" *History Workshop* 4:162-170.

Stiglitz, Joseph E., and Andrew Weiss. 1981. "Credit Rationing in Markets with Imperfect Information." *American Economic Review* 71:393-410.

Stone, Lawrence. 1969. "Literacy and Education in England, 1640-1900." *Past and Present* 42:69-139.

———. 1974. "Size and Composition of Oxford Student Body." In Lawrence Stone, ed., *University in Society*. Vol. 1. Princeton: Princeton University Press.

Styles, John. 1983. "Embezzlement, Industry, and the Law in England, 1500-1800." In Maxine Berg, Pat Hudson and Michael Sonenscher, eds., *Manufacture in Town and Country Before the Factory*. Cambridge: Cambridge University Press, pp. 173-208.

———. 1992. "Manufacturing, Consumption and Design in Eighteenth Century England." In John Brewer and Roy Porter, eds., *Consumption and the World of Goods*. London: Routledge. Forthcoming.

Styles, P. 1963. "The Evolution of the Law of Settlement." *University of Birmingham Historical Journal* 9:33-63.

Sullivan, Richard J. 1984. "Measurement of English Farming Technological Change, 1523-1900." *Explorations in Economic History* 21:270-289.

———. 1989. "England's 'Age of Invention': The Acceleration of Patents and Patentable Invention During the Industrial Revolution." *Explorations in Economic History* 26:424-452.

———. 1990. "The Revolution of Ideas: Widespread Patenting and Invention During the English Industrial Revolution." *Journal of Economic History* 50:349-363.

Sutherland, Lucy. 1973. *The University of Oxford in the Eighteenth Century: A Reconsideration*. Oxford: Blackwell.

Swain, John. 1986. *Industry Before the Industrial Revolution: North-East Lancashire, 1500-1640*. Manchester: Manchester University Press for the Chetham Society.

Sylla, Richard, and Gianni Toniolo. 1991. *Patterns of European Industrialization: The Nineteenth Century*. London: Routledge.

Szostak, Rick. 1989. "The Organization of Work: The Emergence of the Factory Revisited." *Journal of Economic Behavior and Organization* 11:343-358.

———. 1991. *The Role of Transportation in the Industrial Revolution*. Montreal: McGill's-Queen's University Press.

Taylor, Arthur J., ed. 1975. *The Standard of Living in Britain in the Industrial Revolution*. London: Methuen.

Taylor, J. S. 1969. "The Mythology of the Old Poor Law." *Journal of Economic History* 29:292-297.

Temin, Peter. 1973. "Labor Scarcity and the Problem of American Industrial Efficiency in the 1850s." In Peter Temin, ed., *New Economic History*. Harmondsworth: Penguin Books.

Thirsk, Joan. 1987. *Agricultural Regions and Agrarian History in England, 1500-1750*. Basingstoke: Macmillan.

Thomas, Brinley. 1985. "Food Supply in the United Kingdom during the Industrial Revolution." In Joel Mokyr, ed., *The Economics of the Industrial Revolution*. Totowa, N.J.: Rowman and Allanheld.

Thomas, Keith. 1987. "Numeracy in Early Modern England." *Transactions of the Royal Historical Society*, 5th ser., 37:103-132.

Thomas, R. P., and D. N. McCloskey. 1981. "Overseas Trade and Empire, 1700-1860." In R. C. Floud and D. N. McCloskey, eds. *The Economic History of Britain Since 1700*. Vol. 1. Cambridge: Cambridge University Press.

Thompson, E. P. 1963. *The Making of the English Working Class*. New York: Vintage Books.

———. 1967. "Time, Work-Discipline and Industrial Capitalism." *Past and Present* 38:56-97. Reprinted in M. W. Flinn and T. C. Smout, eds. 1979. *Essays in Social History*. Oxford: Clarendon Press.

———. 1991. *Customs in Common: Studies in Traditional Popular Culture*. New York: New Press.

Thompson, F.M.L. 1968. "The Second Agricultural Revolution, 1815-1880." *Economic History Review* 21:62-77.

Thompson, R. J. 1907. "An Inquiry into the Rent of Agricultural Land in England and Wales in the Nineteenth Century." *Journal of the Royal Statistical Society* 70:587-625.

Tompson, Richard. 1971. *Classics or Charity?: The Dilemma of the 18th Century Grammar School*. Manchester: Manchester University Press.

———. 1979. *The Charity Commission and the Age of Reform*. London: Routledge and Kegan Paul.

Toynbee, Arnold. [1884] 1969. *Toynbee's Industrial Revolution: A reprint of Lectures on the Industrial Revolution*. New York and Newton Abbot: David and Charles.

Tranter, N. L. 1981. "The Labour Supply, 1780-1860." In Roderick Floud and Donald McCloskey, eds., *The Economic History of Britain Since 1700*. Vol. 1. Cambridge: Cambridge University Press.

Trebilcock, C. 1969. "'Spin-off' in British Economic History: Armaments and Industry, 1760-1914." *Economic History Review* 22:474-490.

Turnbull, Gerard. 1987. "Canals, Coal, and Regional Growth During the Industrial Revolution." *Economic History Review* 40:537-560.

Turner, Michael. 1982. "Agricultural Productivity in England in the Eighteenth Century: Evidence from Crop Yields." *Economic History Review* 35:489-510.

_____. 1986. "English Open Fields and Enclosures: Retardation or Productivity Improvements." *Journal of Economic History*.41:669-692.

Tuttle, Carolyn. 1983. "The Industrial Revolution and the Effect on the Market for Child Labor." Unpublished manuscript, Northwestern University.

_____. 1986. "Children at Work in the British Industrial Revolution." Ph.D. diss., Northwestern University.

Unwin, George. 1924. *Samuel Oldknow and the Arkwrights*. Reprint ed. New York: Augustus Kelley, 1968.

Urdank, Albion. 1990. *Religion and Society in a Cotswold Vale*. Berkeley: University of California Press.

Ure, Andrew. 1835. *The Philosophy of Manufactures*. London: Knight.

_____. 1835-1836. *The Cotton Manufacture of Great Britain*. London: Knight.

Usher, Abbott Payson. 1920. *An Introduction to the Industrial History of England*. Boston: Houghton Mifflin.

Van Zanden, J. L. 1991. "The First Green Revolution: The Growth of Production and Productivity in European Agriculture, 1870-1914." *Economic History Review* 44:215-239.

Veliz, Claudio. 1980. *The Centralist Tradition of Latin America*. Princeton: Princeton University Press.

Viennet, Odette. 1947. *Napoleon et l'industrie francaise: La crise de 1810-1811*. Paris: Plon.

Ville, Simon. 1987. *English Shipowning During the Industrial Revolution: Michael Henly and Son, London Shipowners, 1770-1830*. Manchester, Manchester University Press.

Vincent, David. 1989. *Literacy and Popular Culture: England, 1750-1914*. Cambridge: Cambridge University Press.

Von Tunzelmann, G. Nicholas. 1978. *Steam Power and British Industrialization to 1860*. Oxford: Oxford University Press.

_____. 1981. "Technical Progress During the Industrial Revolution." In R. Floud and D. McCloskey, eds., *The Economic History of Britain Since 1700*. Vol. 1. Cambridge: Cambridge University Press.

_____. 1985. "The Standard of Living Debate and Optimal Economic Growth." In Joel Mokyr, ed., *The Economics of the Industrial Revolution*. Totowa, N.J.: Rowman and Allanheld.

Wadsworth, A. P. and J. De Lacy Mann. 1931. *The Cotton Trade and Industrial Lancashire*. Manchester: Manchester University Press.

Wallerstein, Immanuel. 1989. *The Modern World-System III: the Second Era of Great Expansion of the Capitalist World Economy, 1730-1840s*. San Diego: Academic Press.

Walton, John K. 1987. *Lancashire: A Social History, 1558-1939*. Manchester: Manchester University Press.

_____. 1989. "Protoindustrialization and the First Industrial Revolution: The Case of Lancashire." In Pat Hudson, ed., *Regions and Industries: A Perspective on the Industrial Revolution in Britain*. Cambridge: Cambridge University Press.

Weatherill, Lorna. 1988. *Consumer Behaviour and Material Culture in Britain, 1660-1760*. New York: Routledge.

Weible, Robert, ed. 1986. *The World of the Industrial Revolution: Comparative and International Aspects of Industrialization*. North Andover, Mass.: Museum of American Textile History.

Weir, David. 1989. "Tontines, Public Finance, and Revolution in France and England, 1688-1789." *Journal of Economic History* 49:95-124.

Weiss, Andrew. 1990. *Efficiency Wages: Models of Unemployment, Layoffs, and Wage Dispersion*. Princeton: Princeton University Press.

West, E. G. 1964. "Adam Smith's Two Views in the Division of Labour." *Economica* 31:23-32.

_____. 1971. "The Interpretation of Early Nineteenth-Century Educational Statistics." *Economic History Review* 24:633-652.

_____. 1978. "Literacy and the Industrial Revolution." *Economic History Review* 31:369-383.

Wiener, Martin J. 1981. *English Culture and the Decline of the Industrial Spirit, 1850-1890*. Cambridge: Cambridge University Press.

Wijnberg, Nachoem M. 1992. "The Industrial Revolution and Industrial Economics," *Journal of European Economic History* 21: 153-167.

Williams, Eric. 1944. *Capitalism and Slavery*. Chapel Hill: University of North Carolina Press.

Williamson, Jeffrey G. 1984. "Why Was British Growth So Slow During the Industrial Revolution?" *Journal of Economic History* 44:687-712.

_____. 1985. *Did British Capitalism Breed Inequality?* London: Allen and Unwin.

_____. 1986. "The Impact of the Irish on British Labor Markets during the Industrial Revolution." *Journal of Economic History* 46:693-720.

_____. 1987a. "Debating the British Industrial Revolution." *Explorations in Economic History* 24:269-292.

_____. 1987b. "Did English Factor Markets Fail During the Industrial Revolution?" *Oxford Economic Papers* 39:641-678.

_____. 1990a. *Coping with City Growth During the British Industrial Revolution*. Cambridge: Cambridge University Press.

_____. 1990b. "New Views on the Impact of the French Wars on Accumulation in Britain." Discussion Paper, no. 1480. Cambridge, Mass.: Harvard Institute of Economic Research.

_____. 1991. "Productivity and American Leadership: A Review Article." *Journal of Economic Literature* 29:51-68.

———. 1992. "The Evolution of Global Labor Markets in the First and Second World Since 1830: Background Evidence and Hypotheses." NBER Working Paper, no. 36. Cambridge, Mass.: NBER.

Williamson, Oliver. 1980. "The Organization of Work: A Comparative Institutional Assessment." *Journal of Economic Behavior and Organization* 1:5-38.

Wilmot, Sarah. 1990. *'The Business of Improvement': Agriculture and Scientific Culture in Britain, c.1700-c.1870.* Historical Geography Research Series, no. 24. Cheltenham.

Winstanley, D. A. 1935. *Unreformed Cambridge.* Cambridge: Cambridge University Press.

Woronoff, Denis. 1984. *L'industrie Siderurgique en France Pendant la Revolution et l'Empire.* Paris: Ecole de Hautes Etudes en Sciences Sociales.

Wright, Gavin. 1987. *Old South, New South: Revolutions in the Southern Economy Since the Civil War.* New York: Basic Books.

Wrigley, E. A. 1967. "A Simple Model of London's Importance in Changing English Society and Economy, 1650-1750." *Past and Present* 37:44-70.

———. 1972. "The Process of Modernization and the Industrial Revolution in England." *Journal of Interdisciplinary History* 3:225-259.

———. 1985. "Urban Growth and Agricultural Change: England and the Continent in the Early Modern Period." *Journal of Interdisciplinary History* 15:683-728.

———. 1986. "Urban Growth and Agricultural Change: England and the Continent in the Early Modern Period." In R. I. Rotberg and T. K. Rabb, eds., *Population and Economy.* Cambridge: Cambridge University Press.

———. 1987. *People, Cities, and Wealth.* Oxford: Basil Blackwell.

———. 1988. *Continuity, Chance and Change: The Character of the Industrial Revolution in England.* New York: Cambridge University Press.

Wrigley, E. A., and R. S. Schofield. 1981. *The Population History of England, 1541-1871: A Reconstruction.* Cambridge: Cambridge University Press.

Yelling, J. A. 1977. *Common Field and Enclosure in England, 1450-1850.* London: Macmillan.

Young, Arthur. [1790] 1929. *Travels in France During the Years 1787, 1788, and 1789.* Edited by Constantia Maxwell. Cambridge: Cambridge University Press.

About the Book

The Industrial Revolution remains a defining moment in the economic history of the modern world. But what kind and how much of a revolution was it? And what kind of "moment" could it have been? These are just some of the larger questions among the many that economic historians continue to debate. In this volume a distinguished set of scholars present and defend their latest views on essential aspects of the Industrial Revolution. The editor's extensive introduction is a major survey and evaluation of contemporary research in this field.

This is an essential book for economic historians and, indeed, for any historian of Great Britain in the eighteenth and nineteenth centuries.

About the Contributors

Gregory Clark is Associate Professor of Economics at the University of California, Davis, and specializes in industrial and agricultural history with special emphasis on productivity growth.

C. Knick Harley is Professor of Economics at the University of Western Ontario, London, Canada, and specializes in macroeconomic aspects of the Industrial Revolution and the Atlantic economy in the nineteenth century.

David S. Landes is Coolidge Professor of History and Professor of Economics at Harvard University, Cambridge, Massachusetts. He is the author of *The Unbound Prometheus* and, more recently, *Revolution in Time: Clocks and the Making of the Modern World.*

David Mitch is Associate Professor of Economics at the University of Maryland Baltimore County, Catonsville, Maryland. He is the author of *The Rise of Popular Literacy in Victorian England.*

Joel Mokyr is Professor of Economics and History at Northwestern University, Evanston, Illinois. His most recent books are *Why Ireland Starved* and *The Lever of Riches: Technological Creativity and Economic Progress.*

Index